THE ROUGH GUIDE TO
AMSTERDAM

**ROUGH
GUIDES**

Contents

HANDSOME AMSTERDAM HOUSE

Introduction to
Amsterdam

With its olive-green canals and handsome gabled houses, waterfront bars, bustling markets and exquisite art, Amsterdam never fails to charm. But there are plenty of surprises here too: long seen as an anything-goes place for stoners and Red Light District prowlers, Amsterdam is shrugging off its old image, smartening up and looking to the future. Over a billion euros has been invested in cultural projects, with the revamping of showpiece sights in the Museum Quarter and the regeneration of the long-neglected docklands with some cutting-edge architecture. That said, for all its focus on reinvention, Amsterdam's streets and canals retain a laidback, small-city feel that you just don't get in any other European capital. It's a city that's proud of its character, and the perfect balance it strikes between business and bohemia.

Amsterdam is still far from being as diverse a city as, say, London or Paris; huge numbers of people have migrated from the former colonies in Suriname and Indonesia, as well as from Morocco and Turkey, but almost all live and work outside the centre and can seem almost invisible to the casual visitor. Indeed, there is an ethnic and social homogeneity in the city centre that seems to counter everything you may have heard about Dutch integration. It's a contradiction that is typical of Amsterdam. The city is world-famous as a place where the possession and sale of cannabis are tolerated – and yet for the most part Amsterdammers themselves don't really partake in the stuff. And while Amsterdam is renowned for its tolerance towards all styles of behaviour – the locals are more than happy for you to cycle through town in a silver bikini if the mood strikes you – a more conventional big city would be hard to find. In recent years a string of hardline city mayors have had some success in diminishing Amsterdam's image as a counterculture icon: visitors are welcomed as warmly as ever, and letting your hair down is positively encouraged, but locals are now upfront about wanting tourists to behave as good guests – rowdy, drunken behaviour is frowned upon – and due to new legislation, numbers of the city's famous coffeeshops are dwindling.

AMSTERDAM

N

0 — 500
metres

River IJ

Ulhaven
PIET HEINKADE

AMSTERDAM OOST

Muiderpoort Station

ZEEBURG

LINNAEUSSTRAAT

Muziekgebouw aan't IJ

NOORD

OOSTERDOK

NEMO

Oosterpark

Artis Royal Zoo

SARPHATISTRAAT

NUIDTSKADE

PLANTAGE

PLANTAGE MIDDENLAAN

EVE

IJ TUNNEL

Oosterdok

DE RUIJTERKADE

WEESPERSTRAAT

WIBAUTSTRAAT

River IJ

PRINS HENDRIKKADE

OLD JEWISH QUARTER

VALKENBURGERSTRAAT

WESTERDOK

Centraal Station

RED LIGHT DISTRICT

NIEUW-MARKT

WATERLOO-PLEIN

River Amstel

AMSTELDIJK

DAMRAK

OLD CENTRE

THE DAM

VAN WOUSTRAAT

NIEUWEZIJDSVOORBURGWAL

Koninklijk Paleis

ROKIN

MUNT-PLEIN

REMBRANDT-PLEIN

UTRECHTSESTRAAT

Herengracht

RAADHUISSTRAAT

VIJZELSTRAAT

GRACHTENGORDEL SOUTH

DE PIJP

Keizersgracht

GRACHTENGORDEL WEST

F. BOLSTRAAT

Prinsengracht

ROZENGRACHT

LEIDSESTRAAT

WETERINGSCHANS

JORDAAN

Singelgracht

ROZENGRACHT

LEIDSE-PLEIN

STADHOUDERSKADE

HOBBEMAKADE

Rijksmuseum

MUSEUM QUARTER

NASSAUKADE

Van Gogh Museum

MUSEUM PLEIN

Kostverloren-vaart

VAN BAERLESTRAAT

Da Costagracht

CONST HUYGENSSTRAAT

DE LAIRESSESTRAAT

Westelijk Marktkanaal

Bilderdijkgracht

STAATSLIEDENBUURT

AMSTERDAM WEST

KINKERSTRAAT

Jacob Van Lennepkanaal

OVERTOOM

Vondelpark

JAN VAN GALENSTRAAT

DA COSTASTRAAT

DE CLERCQSTRAAT

Kostverloren-vaart

JAN EVERTSENSTRAAT

Admiralengracht

AMSTERDAM ON THE WATER

Amsterdam is defined by **water**, and its buildings complement their surroundings everywhere you look, whether it's in the classic canal views of the seventeenth-century city or the contemporary developments in the former docklands. If you want to make the most of the city's unique watery environment, start with a **canalboat tour** (see page 24) or rent a **canal bike** (see page 23). Then explore the artificial islands of the **Oosterdok** district (see page 95), east of Centraal Station, which offers one of the most authentic insights into Amsterdam's seafaring past, whether you're inspecting the replica of an eighteenth-century East Indiaman or strolling past the quays and warehouses of the Entrepotdok.

You could also take a ferry from behind Centraal Station to the **NDSM shipyard** – one of the city's coolest cultural hangouts – to have breakfast in a converted shipping container at *Pllek* (see page 169) and explore artists' studios. Other watery wonders include the **EYE Filmmuseum** (see page 103), with its splendid riverside location, bar-restaurant and film-focused library, the **Woonbootmuseum**, or Houseboat Museum (see page 61) – which provides a glimpse of what it's really like to live on Amsterdam's waterways – and **Marken** (see page 135), a timewarp ex-island that's just a bus ride away.

However, some things haven't changed, and it's hard not to be drawn in by Amsterdam's fun summer festivals, the cheery intimacy of its cafés, its first-rate art galleries and its air of upbeat positivity. Amsterdammers themselves make much of their city and its attractions being *gezellig*, a rather overused Dutch word roughly corresponding to a combination of "cosy", "lived-in" and "warmly convivial". Nowhere is this more applicable than in the city's unparalleled variety of watering holes – whether it's a timeworn "brown café" or one of a raft of newer, more stylish bars. An increasingly creative restaurant scene and lively nightlife are further draws, and the city's compactness means that it's an easy hop from a candlelit canalside dinner in the centre to the cool bars of the regenerated NDSM shipyard over the River IJ, for example. In fact, thanks to its manageable size and its prevailing atmosphere of friendly inclusiveness, you can really get under the skin of Amsterdam in a stay of just a few days; there can be few capital cities that have such immediate, accessible appeal.

What to see

The city's layout is determined by a web of canals radiating out from a historical core to loop right round Amsterdam's compact centre; it takes about forty minutes to walk from one end of the centre to the other. Butting up to the River IJ, the **Old Centre** spreads south from Centraal Station, bisected by Damrak and its continuation, Rokin, the city's main drag; en route is the **Dam**, the main square. The Old Centre remains Amsterdam's commercial heart, as well as the hub of its bustling street life, holding myriad shops, bars and restaurants. The area is also home to the **Red Light District**, which contains dozens of fine old buildings, most memorably the **Oude Kerk** and the **Koninklijk Paleis**.

The Old Centre is bordered by the first of the major canals, the Singel, whose curve is mirrored by those of the Herengracht, Keizersgracht and Prinsengracht – collectively known as the **Grachtengordel**, or "Girdle of Canals". This is Amsterdam's most delightful area, full of handsome seventeenth- and eighteenth-century canal houses with decorative gables, and narrow, dreamy canals. Here you'll also find perhaps the city's most celebrated attraction, the **Anne Frank Huis**, the house in which the young Jewish diarist hid away during the German occupation of World War II, now a poignant reminder of the Holocaust.

Immediately to the west of the Grachtengordel lies the **Jordaan**, one-time industrial slum and now almost entirely gentrified. The same applies to the adjacent **western docklands**, dredged out of the river to create extra wharves and shipbuilding space during the seventeenth century; only in the past few decades has the shipping industry moved out.

On the other side of the centre is the **old Jewish quarter**, home to a thriving Jewish community until the German occupation of World War II, with a number of absorbing sights, including the **Esnoga** (Portuguese Synagogue) and the **Joods Historisch Museum** (Jewish Historical Museum). The adjacent **Plantage** is greener and

more suburban, holding the excellent **Verzetsmuseum** (Dutch Resistance Museum) and **Artis Royal Zoo**. Just north, the **eastern docklands** is another formerly industrial area that has undergone rapid renewal; attractions here include **NEMO**, a science and technology museum, and the **Scheepvaartmuseum** (Maritime Museum). The regeneration continues across the River IJ in **Amsterdam Noord**, with the futuristic **EYE Filmmuseum** and, further north still, the **NDSM shipyard**, a hub of cutting-edge culture. Amsterdam's **Museum Quarter**, southwest of the centre, contains the city's premier art museums, principally the **Rijksmuseum** with its wonderful collection of Dutch paintings, including several of Rembrandt's finest works; the excellent **Van Gogh Museum**, which holds the world's largest collection of the artist's paintings; and the **Stedelijk Museum**, dedicated to contemporary art. All lie just a stone's throw from the city's finest park, the **Vondelpark**, while east of the museums is cosmopolitan **De Pijp**, the city's first real suburb.

Beyond the centre, the **outer districts** are relatively short of attractions – notable exceptions being the wooded parkland of the **Amsterdamse Bos** and the fascinating ethnographic exhibits of the **Tropenmuseum**, south and east of the centre respectively.

Talk to Amsterdammers about visiting other parts of their country and you may well be met with looks of amazement, but don't be put off. The Netherlands is a small nation with an outstanding public transport system that makes a large slice of the country easily reachable. The choice of possible **day-trips** is extensive: the town of **Haarlem**, the old Zuider Zee ports of **Marken**, **Volendam** and **Enkhuizen**, and the pretty town of **Edam** are all worth a visit – not to mention the much-touted **Keukenhof Gardens**, which are at their best during the spring and early summer.

When to go

Amsterdam enjoys a fairly temperate **climate**, with warm summers and moderately cold and wet winters. The weather is certainly not severe enough to make much difference to the city's routines. That said, high summer – roughly late June to August – sees the city packed to the gunnels, with parts of the centre almost overwhelmed by the tourist throng, whereas spring and autumn are not too crowded and can be especially beautiful, with mist hanging over the canals and low sunlight beaming through the cloud cover. At any time of the year, but particularly in summer, try to book your accommodation in advance.

AVERAGE DAILY TEMPERATURES AND MONTHLY RAINFALL

	Jan	Feb	Mar	Apr	May	Jun	Jul	Aug	Sep	Oct	Nov	Dec
Max/min (°C)	5/1	6/0	9/4	13/5	17/8	19/12	21/14	21/14	18/11	14/8	9/5	7/4
Max/min (°F)	41/34	43/32	48/39	55/41	63/46	66/54	70/57	70/57	64/52	57/46	48/41	45/39
Rainfall (mm)	78	43.6	89	39	51	60	63	60	80	105	76	72

Author picks

Our writers have explored every corner of Amsterdam while researching this guide; their favourite ways to spend their time are below. For the definitive list of the highlights you really shouldn't miss, see page 10.

Get around on two wheels Explore the city as Amsterdammers do: on two wheels. Rent a bike to cycle along the canals (see page 22) or join a bike tour that includes visits to the homes of local artists (see page 24).

Eat, drink and be merry Take a food tour (see page 167); head to Foodhallen, a converted 1902 tram depot filled with stalls selling gourmet street food and craft cocktails (see page 170); or take a boozy tasting tour at the Heineken Experience (see page 117).

Discover the NDSM shipyard Hop on the ferry to this trendy district, home to a hotel in a crane (see page 150), a café inside a shipping container (see page 160) and old warehouses brimming with antiques.

Cruise the canals Granted, most of the canal cruises are pretty cheesy, but there are a couple of gems, such as a pirate-themed boat ride for kids (see page 210), and a fine-dining cruise for grown-ups (see page 24) aboard a nineteenth-century boat.

Eye-popping architecture See a film, browse the exhibitions or just marvel at the sleek white lines of the EYE (see page 188); check out the Stedelijk Museum's striking design (see page 115); or catch a concert at the state-of-the-art Muziekgebouw (see page 185).

Say cheese Edam has a celebrated summer cheese market (see page 140); if you don't make it there, don't worry, as you'll find plenty of choice at the city's specialist cheese shops (see page 196) and at the Noordermarkt's organic market (see page 54).

Top terraces Amsterdam in the sunshine is a sight to behold. Bask on NEMO's sun-trap rooftop (see page 211), sample home-made beers in the shade of a windmill at *Brouwerij 't IJ* (see page 178), take in the views at *SkyLounge Amsterdam* (see page 178) or soak up the sun with a cocktail in hand at *Hanneke's Boom* (see page 178).

> Our author recommendations don't end here. We've flagged up our favourite places – a perfectly sited hotel, an atmospheric café, a special restaurant – throughout the Guide, highlighted with the ★ symbol.

CYCLING IN AMSTERDAM
DINNER CRUISE

15

things not to miss

It isn't possible to see everything Amsterdam has to offer on a short trip, and we don't suggest you try. What follows, in no particular order, is a selective taste of the city's highlights, from elegant canalside architecture and vibrant markets to outstanding art collections and traditional bars. All entries have a page reference to take you straight into the Guide, where you can find out more. Coloured numbers refer to chapters in the Guide section.

1 KONINKLIJK PALEIS
See page 37
Co-opted by the Dutch royals but originally Amsterdam's town hall, this building speaks volumes about the city during the Golden Age.

2 VAN GOGH MUSEUM
See page 113
The world's most comprehensive collection of the artist's work – simply unmissable.

3 ANNE FRANK HUIS
See page 57
The museum created in the Secret Annex – home to Anne Frank and her family for two years during World War II – is Amsterdam's most moving sight.

4 THE VONDELPARK
See page 116
The leafy Vondelpark, with its ponds, footpaths and colony of parakeets, is the city's most attractive park.

5 BROWN CAFÉS
See page 174
Amsterdam is famous for its brown cafés – dark, cosy and very traditional.

6 THE BEGIJNHOF
See page 40
The fourteenth-century Begijnhof is one of the quietest and prettiest corners of the city centre.

7 THE EYE
See page 103
This striking, avant-garde building houses a top-notch film museum.

8 BROUWERSGRACHT
See page 54
In a city full of pretty canals, the Brouwersgracht might just be the prettiest.

9 OUDE KERK
See page 46
The city's oldest and most venerable church, slap-bang in the middle of the Red Light District.

10 KING'S DAY
See page 219
Amsterdammers let their hair down on King's Day, the city's biggest and wildest annual knees-up.

11 RIJKSMUSEUM
See page 106
Amsterdam's greatest museum, home to the world's largest collection of Dutch paintings.

12 CYCLING
See page 22
Get around the city like a local by renting a bike for the day.

13 MUZIEKGEBOUW
See page 185
A world-class performance venue in a stunningly contemporary building.

14 INDONESIAN FOOD
See page 163
Fill up on Amsterdam's ethnic food speciality.

15 PROEFLOKALEN
See page 77
Served ice-cold, *jenever*, the Dutch version of gin, is the nation's favourite spirit, and these "tasting houses" are the traditional places to sample it.

11

12

AMSTERDAM CYCLISTS

Basics

Getting there

Most visitors to Amsterdam arrive by air to Schiphol International Airport, or by train to Centraal Station. From the UK, there are plenty of flights, though taking the train is just as easy and almost as quick. From North America and Canada the main decision is whether to fly direct – easy enough as Schiphol is a major international hub, served by dozens of short- and long-haul airlines – or to route via London, picking up a budget flight onwards from there. From Australia and New Zealand, all flights to Amsterdam require one or two stops on the way; from South Africa, direct flights are available.

Prices rise during high season (June–Aug) and dip in low season (mid-Nov to Easter). Fares also increase if travelling on weekends.

Flights from the UK and Ireland

Amsterdam is one of the **UK**'s most popular short-haul destinations, and you'll find loads of choice – in carriers, flight times and departure airports. Aside from the major full-service carriers – KLM (W klm.com) and British Airways (W ba.com) – there are plenty of no-frills airlines operating flights to Amsterdam, including easyJet (W easyjet.com), Transavia (W transavia.com) and Jet2 (W jet2.com), as well as business-oriented CityJet (W cityjet.com).

Flights to Amsterdam's **Schiphol International Airport** (pronounced "skip-oll") take roughly an hour from London, or ninety minutes from Scotland and the north of England. Between them, KLM and easyJet have a good number of daily flights out of London – Heathrow, Gatwick, Stansted, Luton and London City – plus direct flights from many of the UK's **regional airports**, including Birmingham, East Midlands, Cardiff, Southampton, Norwich, Liverpool, Manchester, Leeds-Bradford, Humberside, Newcastle, Teesside, Edinburgh, Glasgow and Aberdeen.

Whichever route you choose, it's hard to say precisely what you'll **pay** at any given time: the price depends hugely on when you book and when you fly, what offers are available – and how lucky you are. However, flying from London to Amsterdam with one of the low-cost airlines between April and September, you'll pay around £70 return, including taxes, travelling at convenient times at the weekend, as opposed to £120 with one of the full-service carriers. Weekday travel will cost £30–60 with a budget carrier, £100 or so with a full-service airline. If you want more flexibility with your ticket you'll pay more, as you will if you book at the last minute – economy return tickets from London to Amsterdam can cost anything up to £1000.

From the **Republic of Ireland**, Aer Lingus (W aerlingus.com) operates several daily flights from Dublin and Cork, for around €100 return, depending on the season, with fares rising at peak times. You might get a slightly cheaper offer (around €90) from Ryanair for a non-stop flight from Dublin. From **Northern Ireland**, the most economical option is with easyJet out of Belfast International (fares are around £60–80).

Flights from the US and Canada

Amsterdam's Schiphol Airport is among the most popular and least expensive gateways to Europe from **the US**, and finding a convenient and good-value flight is rarely a problem. KLM (W klm.com) and Delta (W delta.com), which operate a joint service, offer the widest range of flights, with **direct** or one-stop flights to Amsterdam from twenty US cities, and connections from dozens more. United (W united.com) also flies direct to Amsterdam from Chicago and Houston, while Delta operates from Atlanta and New York. Other airlines fly **via London** and other European capitals – indirect flights are nearly always cheaper.

Booking far enough in advance, you should be able to find a **fare** between April and September for US$700–900 return from New York (flight time 8hr 10min) or Chicago (8hr), US$900–1000 from Atlanta (10hr), and around US$1300 from LA (10hr 30min),

---

A BETTER KIND OF TRAVEL

At Rough Guides we are passionately committed to travel. We believe it helps us understand the world we live in and the people we share it with – and of course tourism is vital to many developing economies. But the scale of modern tourism has also damaged some places irreparably, and climate change is accelerated by most forms of transport, especially flying. All Rough Guides' flights are carbon-offset, and every year we donate money to a variety of environmental charities.

though booking less than a couple of weeks in advance can push these prices up considerably.

From **Canada**, KLM/Delta flies direct to Amsterdam year-round from Vancouver (9hr 30min) and from Toronto (7hr 10min). There are also plenty of one-stop options via Frankfurt, London and Paris. **Fares** from Toronto start from around Can\$750, from Vancouver around Can\$1200.

Flights from Australia, New Zealand and South Africa

There are **no direct flights** to the Netherlands from **Australia and New Zealand**: all involve at least one stop. Singapore Airlines (W singaporeair.com), Etihad (W etihad.com), Emirates (W emirates.com), Malaysia Airlines (W malaysiaairlines.com) and Qatar Airways (W qatarairways.com) offer the most direct routes out of Sydney (stopping in Singapore, Abu Dhabi, Dubai, Kuala Lumpur and Doha, respectively). Flights from Christchurch go via Sydney and London and from Wellington via Melbourne or Sydney and London. One further option is to pick up a cheap ticket to London, and then continue your journey to Amsterdam with one of the no-frills budget airlines (see page 17).

From **South Africa**, KLM (W klm.com) offers **direct flights** to Amsterdam, with services from Cape Town and Johannesburg. South African Airways (W flysaa. com) and Lufthansa (W lufthansa.com) offer one-stop flights via Frankfurt or Munich.

Fares from Sydney or Melbourne start from around Aus\$1300, and from Auckland NZ\$1500. Direct flights with KLM from Cape Town and Johannesburg cost around R10500.

By train

The simplest and quickest way to travel from the UK to Amsterdam by **train** is to take the **Eurostar** from London nonstop to Amsterdam (3hr 41min), in operation since 2018. Trains depart from King's Cross St Pancras International station in central London and go via Brussels and Rotterdam.

A standard return **fare** to Amsterdam costs around £140, but special deals are commonplace, especially in the low season. Book through Voyages-SNCF (Rail Europe in the US and Canada; W raileurope-world. com) or directly at W eurostar.com.

The Dutch Railways website (W ns.nl) has full **timetable** details (in English) of trains from stations in the UK to any station in the Netherlands.

A much longer – but cheaper – **rail-and-ferry route**, the **Dutchflyer**, is also available, through Stena Line (W stenaline.co.uk) in conjunction with Abellio

Greater Anglia trains. The journey operates twice daily, with trains departing London's Liverpool Street station bound for Harwich, where they connect with the ferry over to the Hook of Holland – the Hoek van Holland. The whole journey takes between nine and eleven hours. From the Hook, there are frequent trains to Rotterdam (every 30min–1hr; 30min), where you change for Amsterdam (1hr). As for **fares**, a standard return costs from £166 on an overnight sailing, cabin included (cabins are compulsory on overnight sailings). Tickets are available from Abellio Greater Anglia, or you can book with Stena.

By bus

Travelling by **long-distance bus** is generally the cheapest way of reaching Amsterdam from the UK, but it is very time-consuming: the journey from London to Amsterdam takes twelve hours or more. **Eurolines** (see opposite) operates numerous services daily from London Victoria Coach Station to Amsterdam. A standard fare is €69 return, though promotional return fares can be snapped up for much less (€39). A cheap German operator Flixbus (W flixbus.com) also offers daily services to Amsterdam at around €30.

By car

To reach Amsterdam **by car or motorbike**, you can either take a ferry, or – preferable for its hassle-free crossing – go via the **Channel Tunnel**. Note that Eurotunnel only carries cars and motorbikes, not cyclists or foot passengers. Amsterdam is roughly 370km from the exit in Calais.

There are up to four shuttle trains per hour (only three in total from midnight–6am), taking 35minutes (45min for some night departure times); you must check in at Folkestone at least thirty minutes before departure. It's possible to turn up and buy your **ticket** at the tollbooths (exit the M20 at junction 11a), though it's a good idea to book in advance through W eurotunnel.com in high season.

Fares depend on the time of year, time of day and length of stay (the cheapest ticket is for a day-trip, followed by a five-day return); it costs less to travel between 10pm and 6am, while the highest fares are reserved for weekend departures and returns in July and August. Prices are charged per vehicle; short-stay savers between April and October for a car start at around £80. If you wish to stay more than five days, a standard return costs from around £130, while a "Flexiplus" fare, which entitles you to change your plans at the last minute, costs more still. Some special offers are usually also available.

By ferry

Three operators run **ferries** from the UK direct to **ports in the Netherlands**, and all offer year-round services. The fastest route – also available as a rail-and-ferry option from London (see opposite) – is with Stena Line (ⓦstenaline.com), which sails from Harwich in Essex to the Hook of Holland. The journey time is 6 hours 15 minutes; travelling at night always takes longer and you have to book a cabin. P&O Ferries (ⓦpoferries.com) operates from Hull to Rotterdam (11hr), while DFDS Seaways (ⓦdfdsseaways.co.uk) sails once daily from Newcastle (North Shields) to IJmuiden (14hr), half an hour's drive from Amsterdam.

Aside from the options direct to Dutch ports, you might want to consider the ferry routes to **Belgium and France**. P&O sails once a day (overnight) from Hull to Zeebrugge in Belgium (14hr 30min), while DFDS Seaways operates a year-round service from Dover to the French border town of Dunkerque (2hr).

Fares vary hugely, depending on when you leave, how long you stay, if you have a car, and the number of passengers. Discounts for students and under-26s are available.

Agents and operators

TRAVEL AGENTS

ebookers ☎ 020 3788 4832, ⓦebookers.com. Low fares on an extensive selection of scheduled flights and package deals.
North South Travel ☎ 01245 608 291, ⓦnorthsouthtravel. co.uk. Friendly, competitive travel agency, offering discounted fares worldwide. Profits are used to support projects in the developing world, especially the promotion of sustainable tourism.
STA Travel UK ☎ 0333 321 0099, US ☎ 1 800 781 4040, Australia ☎ 134 782, New Zealand ☎ 0800 474 400; ⓦstatravel.com. Worldwide specialists in independent travel; also student IDs, travel insurance, car rental, rail passes and more. Good discounts for students and under-26s.
Trailfinders Worldwide ☎ 020 7084 6500; ⓦtrailfinders.com. Efficient agents for independent travellers.

RAIL CONTACTS

Abellio Greater Anglia UK ☎ 0345 600 7245, ⓦgreateranglia. co.uk.
Eurostar UK ☎ 03432 186 186, outside UK ☎ 01233 617 575; ⓦeurostar.com.
EuroTunnel UK ☎ 0844 335 35, ⓦeurotunnel.com.
International Rail UK ☎ 0871 231 0790, ⓦinternationalrail.com.
Rail Europe US ☎ 1 800 622 8600, Canada ☎ 1 800 361 7245; ⓦraileurope.com.
Voyages-SNCF UK ☎ 0844 848 5848, ⓦen.oui.sncf.

BUS CONTACTS

Eurolines UK ☎ 0871 781 8178, ⓦeurolines.eu.
Flixbus ☎ 178 829 8784; ⓦflixbus.co.uk.

FERRY CONTACTS

DFDS Seaways UK ☎ 0871 522 9995, outside the UK ☎ +44 (0)330 333 0245; ⓦdfdsseaways.co.uk.
P&O Ferries UK ☎ 353 1 686 9467; ⓦpoferries.com.
Stena Line UK ☎ 08447 70 70 70, Ireland ☎ 1 907 5555; ⓦstenaline.co.uk.

Arrival

Arriving in Amsterdam by train and plane could hardly be easier. Schiphol, Amsterdam's international airport, is a quick and convenient train ride away from Centraal Station, the city's international train station, which is itself just a ten-minute metro ride from Amstel Station, the terminus for long-distance and international buses. Centraal Station is also the hub of Amsterdam's excellent public transport network, whose trams, buses and metro combine to reach every corner of the city and its suburbs.

By plane

Amsterdam's international airport, **Schiphol** (☎020 794 0800, ⓦschiphol.nl), is located about 15km southwest of the city centre. It's one of the busiest airports in Europe, and one of the best organized, with an efficient **transfer** system to the city and the rest of the country. Arriving passengers are channelled through to a large and well-signposted plaza, which has all the **facilities** you would expect – car rental desks, banks, exchange offices, left-luggage facilities, ATMs and a **VVV** tourist office with accommodation booking service, as well as a rail ticket office.

Trains run from the airport's train station to Amsterdam's Centraal Station every six minutes during the day and less frequently at night (midnight–6am); the journey takes 15 minutes and costs €4.30 one way with OV-chipkaart. Alternatively, you could buy the Amsterdam Travel Ticket (see box, page 22), which includes a return train ticket from the airport to city centre.

Hotel shuttles are another option; the Connexxion service (☎088 339 4741, ⓦschiphol-hotelshuttle.nl) arranges shuttles that depart from platform A7 at Schiphol Plaza outside the Arrivals/Departure halls every thirty minutes (on the

AMSTERDAM ADDRESSES

For the uninitiated, Amsterdam **addresses** can be a little confusing. Addresses are written as, for example, "Kerkstr. 79 II", which means the second-floor apartment at Kerkstraat 79. The ground floor is indicated by **hs** (*huis*, house) after the number; the basement is **sous** (*sousterrain*). In some cases, especially in the **Jordaan**, streets with the same name have **1e**, **2e**, **3e** and even occasionally **4e** in front of the name, to differentiate between them; these are abbreviations for *Eerste* (first), *Tweede* (second), *Derde* (third) and *Vierde* (fourth). Many **side streets** take the name of the main street they run off, with the addition of the word *dwars*, meaning "crossing"; for instance, Palmdwarsstraat is a side street off Palmstraat. Furthermore, and for no apparent reason, some dead-straight cross streets change their name – so that, for example, in the space of about 300m, 1e Bloemdwarsstraat becomes 2e Leliedwarsstraat and then 3e Egelantiersdwarsstraat.

T/O (*tegenover*, or "opposite") in an address shows that the address is a boat: hence "Prinsengracht T/O 26" would indicate a boat to be found opposite Prinsengracht 26.

The main **Grachtengordel canals** begin their numbering at Brouwersgracht and increase as they progress anticlockwise. By the time they reach the Amstel, Herengracht's house numbers are in the 600s, Keizersgracht's in the 800s and Prinsengracht's in the 900s.

---

half-hour) from 6am to 9pm at a cost of €17 one way, €28 return; it's best to book online in advance. The route varies with the needs of the passengers it picks up at the airport, but buses take about thirty minutes to get from the airport to the city centre. The Amsterdam Airport Express bus #397 (Ⓦ connexxion.nl) departs every 5–7 minutes for the city centre, from platform B11 at Schiphol Plaza to Museumplein, the Rijksmuseum or Leidseplein, and tickets cost €6 single, €10 return; the journey takes half an hour. There are also plenty of **taxis**; the fare from Schiphol to most parts of the city centre is €40–60, and the journey takes around twenty minutes, longer if there's traffic.

By train

Amsterdam's **Centraal Station** (CS) has regular connections with key cities in **Germany**, **Belgium** and **France**, as well as all the larger towns and cities of **the Netherlands** and, as of 2018, also a direct link with London. Amsterdam also has several suburban train stations, but these are principally for commuters. Centraal Station has lots of **facilities**, including left-luggage lockers (see page 28), plenty of ATMs and a GVB office, as well as lots of shops and places to eat. For all rail enquiries contact **NS** (Netherlands Railways; international enquiries ☎030 230 0023, domestic enquiries ☎30 751 5155, Ⓦ ns.nl).

By bus

Eurolines' long-distance international **buses** arrive at **Duivendrecht Station**, about 5km to the southeast of Centraal Station. The metro journey to Centraal Station takes about fifteen minutes.

City transport

Almost all of Amsterdam's leading attractions are clustered in or near the city centre, within easy walking – and even easier cycling – distance of each other. For longer jaunts, the city has a first-rate public transport system run by GVB, comprising trams, buses, a smallish four-line metro system and four passenger ferries across the River IJ to the northern suburbs. Centraal Station is the hub of the system, with a multitude of trams and buses departing from outside on Stationsplein, which is also the location of a metro station and a GVB information office.

By tram, bus and metro

The city centre is crisscrossed by **trams**. The most useful are trams #1, #2 and #5, which link Centraal Station with Leidsestraat and the Rijksmuseum every ten minutes or so during the day. You can get on at the front door or at the back, remembering to swipe your transport pass at the box posted beside the doors. Please note that, as of March 2018, cash payment on public transport (including buses and trams) has been completely eliminated. **Buses** are mainly useful for going to the outskirts, and the same applies to the **metro**, which has city-centre stations at Centraal Station, Nieuwmarkt and Waterlooplein. Trams, buses and the metro operate daily between 6am and midnight, supplemented by a limited number of **nightbuses** (*nachtbussen*), which run roughly every thirty minutes from half-past midnight until 7am (there is a separate fare of €4.50

AMSTERDAM TRAMS, BUSES AND THE METRO

River IJ

River Amstel

River Amstel

STOPS AT CENTRAAL STATION

Metro	51 52 53 54
Tram	2 4 11 12 13 14 17 24 26
Bus	18 21 22 48

20   Tram with stop

15   Bus line with stop

(M)   Metro/station

Centraal Station

GVB

Beurs

Waag

Nieuwmarkt

MR. VISSERSPLEIN

Stadhuis

Waterlooplein

Artis Zoo

Muiderpoort

Oosterpark

Wibautstraat

ZEEBURGERDIJK

MAURITSKADE

AMSTELDIJK

Weesperplein

51-53-54

Oosterdok

Rokin

DAM

Singel

Herengracht

Keizersgracht

Prinsengracht

Herengracht

Keizersgracht

Prinsengracht

Singel

Wijzelgracht

Singelgracht

Sarphatipark

De Pijp

STADHOUDERSKADE

Van Gogh Museum

Rijksmuseum

Museumplein

NASSAUKADE

Singelgracht

Erasmuspark

Vondelpark

N

TRAVEL TICKETS AND PASSES

To travel on Amsterdam's GVB network, you will need an electronic **OV-chipkaart** (Ⓦ ov-chipkaart.nl), a smart card which needs to be checked against an electronic reader when you enter and leave the public transport system – and also when you change trains, metros, trams or buses on the same journey; if you forget, the card soon stops working. The OV-chipkaart comes in two formats – paper and plastic. **Paper (disposable) OV-chipkaarts** are designed for occasional users of the transport system – whether it be for single journeys or one- or two-day bus or rail passes. Single-journey tickets cost €3 (valid 1hr), or €7.50 for 24hr, €12.50 for 48hr or €17.50 for 72hr, with children aged 4–11 eligible for a Children's Day Card (€3.75/24hr). You can buy the paper OV-chipkaart from bus and tram drivers, from the GVB office on Stationsplein (see below), at metro stations and at many hotels.

For extended stays, you might consider purchasing a rechargeable **plastic OV-chipkaart**, which costs €7.50 and is sold at train and bus stations, including automatic ticketing machines – but not by bus and tram drivers. Before your journey, you load up the card with the required credit – a minimum of €4 for urban transport and €20 for rail (there is also the possibility of automatic reload; check the website for details). At the end of your visit, any unspent credit can be reclaimed at any public transport ticket office.

Another option for travellers flying into Schiphol Airport is the **Amsterdam Travel Ticket**, which is available for one, two or three days (€16/€21/€26, respectively) including a return train ticket to/from the airport and unlimited travel on all GVB trams, buses, metros and ferries.

If you'd like to explore further afield just for the day – for example, with a trip to Haarlem – consider the **GVB Amsterdam & Region** day ticket, which costs €18.50 (nightbuses included). There are also two- and three-day tickets, which cost €26 and €33.50, respectively.

Finally, for visitors only exploring Amsterdam and planning to do a fair bit of sightseeing, the VVV's **I amsterdam card** (see page 30) includes unlimited travel on all GVB trams, buses and the metro for a period of 24, 48, 72 or 96 hours (€59/€74/€84/€94). Finally, note that the GVB tries hard to keep **fare-dodging** to a minimum, and wherever you're travelling, and at whatever time of day, there's a reasonable chance you'll have your ticket checked. If you are caught without a valid ticket, you risk an on-the-spot fine of €50 (plus the unpaid fare).

for the nightbus). All tram and bus stops display a detailed **map** of the network. For further details on all services, head for the main **GVB information office** on Stationsplein (Mon–Fri 7am–9pm, Sat & Sun 8am–9pm; ☎ 0900 8011, Ⓦ en.gvb.nl), or check the journey planner on the website. The GVB's free, English-language *Tourist Guide to Public Transport* is very helpful, and they also provide a **free transport map**. The 9292 public-transport app (Ⓦ 9292.nl/en) is another good tool for planning your journey, and it also features a tram network map.

By bike

Bikes are to Amsterdammers what cabs are to New Yorkers: essential. Cycling is also one of the most agreeable ways to explore the city, and there's an excellent network of designated **cycle lanes** (*fietspaden*). Much to the chagrin of the city's taxi drivers, the needs of the cyclist often take precedence over those of the motorist, and by law, if there's a collision it's always the driver's fault.

Bike rental is straightforward, with lots of rental outlets (*fietsenverhuur*) in central Amsterdam, some of

which also organize **bike tours** (see page 24). Most places charge around €7 for three hours, €9–13 per day or 24 hours, €25 for three days and around €50 for a week, for a standard bicycle with no gears and backpedal brake; cycles with gears and handbrakes cost about a third more. All rental outlets ask for some type of security, usually in the form of a cash deposit (€20–50), a credit card (debit cards not accepted) and/ or your passport.

Finally, if you want to **buy a bike**, always go to a reputable bike shop; never buy from the street or in a bar as the bike will almost certainly have been stolen. **Bike theft** is a real problem, so make sure you have a good lock – they can be bought cheaply at the city's flea market, among other places. We've included some useful **cycling terms** in the Language section (see page 258).

BIKE RENTAL OUTLETS

Bike City Bloemgracht 68–70 ☎ 020 626 3721, Ⓦ bikecity.nl; daily 9am–5.30pm. A basic selection of city bikes.

MacBike Central Station ☎ 020 620 0985, Oosterdokskade 149 ☎ 020 811 5100, Waterlooplein 199 ☎ 020 428 7005, Weteringschans 2 ☎ 020 528 7688; Ⓦ macbike.nl; daily

9am–6pm. Outlets across the city, some of which offer repairs and organize guided cycling tours (daily at 2pm; €20/person, bike rental included).

Orange Bike Buiksloterweg 5C ☎064 684 2083, ⓦorange-bike. nl; daily 9am–6pm. This place rents out delightfully painted "Art Bikes" and offers a wide variety of themed 3–4hr bike tours (€22.50/person).

Rent a Bike Damstraat 20–22 ☎ 020 625 5029, ⓦ rentabike.nl; daily 9am–6pm. Has a large range of bikes, including tandems, kids' bikes and scooters, plus cargo bikes for carrying babies.

Yellow Bike Nieuwezijds Kolk 29 ☎ 020 620 6940, ⓦ yellowbike. nl; daily 9.30am–5pm. Based near Centraal Station, this is one of the most distinctive rental companies thanks to their bright yellow bikes. They also offer daily bike tours (see page 24).

By car

The centre of Amsterdam is geared up for trams and bikes rather than **cars** as a matter of municipal policy. Pedestrianized zones as such are not extensive, but motorists still have to negotiate a convoluted one-way system, avoid getting boxed onto tramlines and steer around herds of cyclists.

Driving into the city is strongly discouraged by the authorities; parking your car in the outer suburbs and entering the city by tram or metro is a better idea. If you do take your car into the centre, you'll find that **on-street parking** is very limited – with far too many cars chasing too few spaces – and can be quite expensive. Every street where parking is permitted is metered between 9am and at least 7pm every day, until midnight in the city centre. The **standard rate** is €5/hr within the Grachtengordel and city centre, around €30–45 for the day (9am–7pm) and €20 or so for the evening (7pm–midnight). An entire day's parking (9am–midnight) costs around €45, and you can buy a ticket for the whole week for a whopping €180. Tickets are available from meters if you are paying by the hour. If you overrun your ticket, you can expect to be clamped by eager traffic wardens, who can free your car for €190 (daily 9am–9pm; ☎020 251 3787), plus the outstanding fine(s). The charges are even higher if your car is towed away.

Signs on all the main approach roads to Amsterdam indicate which of the city's **car parks** have spaces; those in the centre charge comparable rates to the metered street spaces. Some of the most central 24hr car parks are: P1 Amsterdam Centre (Prins Hendrikkade 20a; €5/hr, up to a maximum of €55/day; ⓦp1.nl); De Bijenkorf (Beursplein 15; €3/29min, maximum €55/day; ⓦq-park.nl); De Kolk (Nieuwezijds Kolk 18; €3/29min, maximum €55/day; ⓦq-park.nl); Muziektheater (Waterlooplein, under City Hall; €0.50/minute, maximum €47.50/day; ⓦparkeren-amsterdam.com). Much cheaper and easier is the **Park and Ride** scheme: large car parks on the outskirts of town serviced regularly by metro trains, buses and trams that ferry you into the city centre; parking costs €1–8/24hr. Look for the blue P+R logo on the A10 or A2 motorways (check ⓦiamsterdam.com for more details).

WATER TRANSPORT

Cruising along Amsterdam's canals might not be the fastest way of getting from A to B – but it's certainly picturesque. In addition to the following options there are also a number of guided tours and dinner cruises to choose from (see page 24).

Stromma Canal Bikes ☎ 020 217 0501, ⓦ stromma.nl. These four-seater pedalos take a lifetime to get anywhere but are nevertheless good fun. You can rent them – assuming the weather is good – at various piers (daily 9am–5.30pm, later in July and Aug): on the Singelgracht, opposite the Rijksmuseum; at the Westerkerk near the Anne Frank Huis; and behind Leidseplein. They can be picked up at one location and left at any of the others. The cost is from €10/hr or €15/90 minutes per person, plus a refundable deposit of €20, and there's a 25 percent discount with the I amsterdam card (see page 30).

Stromma Canal Bus ☎ 020 217 0501, ⓦ stromma.nl. Operates dinner cruises and hop on-hop off boat cruises covering Amsterdam's main sights and museums. Circular routes meet at various points: at the jetty opposite Centraal Station beside Prins Hendrikkade; on the Singelgracht opposite the Rijksmuseum; and by the Stadhuis on Waterlooplein. In high season boats leave every 25min or so between 9.25am and 6.20pm. A day ticket, allowing you to hop on and off as many times as you like, costs from €20.50, or from €23 for 48hr; children aged 4–12 are half price and there are online discounts.

GVB Ferries ⓦ https://en.gvb.nl. Four ferry routes shuttle across the River IJ to allow access to the NDSM and Noord districts. You can catch one of the blue-hulled boats that ply each route for free (check the GVB website for timetables).

Lovers Canal Cruises ☎ 020 530 1090, ⓦ lovers.nl. Operates a hop on-hop off route, with seven stops located at or near many of the city's major attractions. In summer, boats depart from opposite Centraal Station every 15min (daily 9.15am–6.15pm; in winter 10am–5.15pm) and a day ticket costs €25 (children aged 4–12 €12.50).

GUIDED TOURS

No one could say the Amsterdam tourist industry doesn't make the most of its **canals**, with a veritable armada of glass-topped **cruise boats** shuttling along the city's waterways, offering everything from quick hour-long excursions to fully fledged dinner cruises. There are also numerous tours **by bike** and **on foot**. A selection is given below, but if you have a specific interest – Dutch art, for example – it's well worth asking at the **VVV** (see page 30) to see what's on offer.

BY BOAT

There are several major operators that occupy the prime pitches – the jetties near Centraal Station on Stationsplein, beside the Damrak and on Prins Hendrikkade. Boat trips – and especially the shorter and less expensive ones – are extremely popular, and long queues are common throughout the summer. **Prices** are fairly uniform, with a one-hour tour costing around €20 per adult, €10 per child (4–12 years old), and around €25 for a ninety-minute cruise at night. The big companies also offer more **specialized boat trips** – such as Amsterdam Jewel Cruises' luxury dinner trips (see below) or a pirate-themed kids' cruise (see page 210). Bear in mind that I amsterdam card and Holland Pass holders are entitled to a free cruise (see page 30).

Amsterdam Jewel Cruises Singel 235 ☎ 020 422 1385, ⓦ amsterdamjewelcruises.com. Dinner cruises can be pretty tacky, but Jewel Cruises are a cut above, offering a three-course à la carte dinner aboard a plush wood-panelled 1898 riverboat. Depart daily at 7.30pm; from €110/person.

Rederij P. Kooij Opposite Rokin 125 ☎ 020 623 3810, ⓦ rederijkooij.nl. In business for over a century, Rederij P.

Kooij offers a standard range of day and night cruises at competitive prices. Also has a (more crowded) jetty opposite Centraal Station on Stationsplein, and by Leidseplein. The 1hr canal cruises depart every 30min and cost €11 (kids aged 4–12 €7); 2hr Candlelight Cruises run from April to Oct and depart daily at 9pm (adults €29.50, kids aged 4–12 €14.75).

ON FOOT AND BY BIKE

Guided **cycle rides** are offered by many of the bike rental outlets (see page 22) as well as tour companies, and there are numerous **walking tours** on offer, including food tours (see page 167). You can also download a free walking or cycling tour onto your smartphone and explore at your own pace – ask at the tourist office.

AllTourNative Admiraal de Ruijterweg ☎ 063 874 1645, ⓦ alltournative-amsterdam.com. This company takes you around the city on two wheels (but also on foot or by boat), revealing off-the-beaten-track places hiding graffiti, street art, squats, artist communities and lesser-trodden Amsterdam attractions. Tours run by locals, start from around €15/person.

Mee in Mokum Keizersgracht 346 ☎ 020 625 1390, ⓦ gildeamsterdam.nl. Guided 2hr 30min–3hr walking tours of the Old Centre and the Jordaan provided by long-time Amsterdam residents. Tours run Tues–Sun at 11am and 2pm, departing from Museumcafe Mokum (Kalverstraat 92) and cost €10/person. Advance reservations required.

Sandemans New Europe ⓦ neweuropetours.eu. An excellent introduction to the city's history – and it's free.

These popular 2.5hr tours depart from in front of the national monument on the Dam daily, every hour between 10am and 2pm. They also offer tours of the Red Light District (€16) and bike tours (€20).

Urban Home & Garden Tours R Hogerbeetsstraat 2 ☎ 062 168 1918, ⓦ uhgt.nl. These daily 3hr tours explore a number of the city's canal houses and gardens, and are guided by landscape gardeners and art historians. Prices vary; cash only.

Yellow Bike Tours Nieuwezijds Kolk 29 ☎ 020 620 6940, ⓦ yellowbike.nl. Yellow Bike organizes "Small" (2hr; Mar–Oct daily 10.30am; Nov–Feb 1.30pm) and "Big" (3hr; Mar–Oct daily 1.30pm) guided cycling tours around the city, costing €29.50/person, including bike rental. Advance reservations required.

Finally, note that some of the larger **hotels** either have their own parking spaces or offer special deals with nearby car parks.

CAR RENTAL AGENCIES

Avis ⓦ avis.com.
Budget ⓦ budget.com.
Diks Autoverhuur ⓦ diks.net.

Europcar ⓦ europcar.com.
Hertz ⓦ hertz.com.
Sixt ⓦ sixt.nl.

Taxis

Due to the various obstacles that Amsterdam motorists face, **taxis** are not as much use as they are in many other cities. They are, however, plentiful: there's a taxi rank on Stationsplein to the right-hand side of Centraal Station, and other ranks are liberally distributed across the city centre. You can't just hail a taxi on the street because they're not allowed to stop. Registered city cabs bear the initials "TCA". If all else fails, call Taxicentrale on ☎ 020 777 7777.

Fares are metered and are reasonably high, but distances are small; the trip from Centraal Station to the Leidseplein, for example, will cost around €12 (€2.98 is the maximum start price, €2.19/km after that). Be warned that there are taxi drivers who will try to set a fixed price for a ride, especially late at night – usually to their own advantage. Don't argue, but ask them to turn on the meter instead. For something a bit different you could take an Amsterdam Bike Taxi (☎ 065 348 1860) or book DiscoTaxi (☎ 065 469 8187), a cab that's decorated with disco lights.

The media

English-speakers will find themselves quite at home in Amsterdam, as Dutch TV broadcasts a wide range of British programmes, and English-language newspapers from around the world are readily available.

Newspapers and magazines

British newspapers are on sale at most newsagents on the day of publication, for around €4. Current issues of UK and US **magazines** are widely available too, as is the *International Herald Tribune*.

Of the **Dutch newspapers**, *NRC Handelsblad* is a right-of-centre paper that has perhaps the best news coverage and a liberal stance on the arts; *De Volkskrant* is a progressive, leftish daily; the far right-wing *De Telegraaf* boasts the highest circulation figures in the country and has a well-regarded financial section; *Algemeen Dagblad* is a right-wing broadsheet; and the Amsterdam-centric *Het Parool* ("The Password") and the news magazine *Vrij Nederland* ("Free Netherlands") are the successors of underground Resistance newspapers printed during the World War II occupation. The Protestant *Trouw* ("Trust"), another former underground paper, is centre-left in orientation with a focus on religion.

Bundled in with the weekend edition of the *International Herald Tribune* is **The Netherlander**, a small but useful business-oriented review of Dutch affairs in English.

TV and radio

Dutch **TV** isn't the best, but English-language programmes and films fill up a fair amount of the schedule – and they are always subtitled, never dubbed. Many bars and most hotels have at least two of the big pan-European **cable and satellite** channels – including MTV, CNN and Eurosport – and most cable companies also give access to a raft of foreign television channels, including Britain's BBC1 and BBC2. Other channels regularly run English-language movies with Dutch subtitles.

Dutch **radio** has numerous stations catering for every niche, though there's next to no **English-language programming**, apart from the overseas-targeted Radio Netherlands Worldwide (🌐 rnw.org), which broadcasts Dutch news in English, with articles on current affairs, lifestyle issues, science, health and so on, and the BBC World Service (🌐 bbc.co.uk/worldservice), which broadcasts pretty much all day in English on 648kHz (AM) around Amsterdam. The Voice of America (🌐 bbc.co.uk/worldserviceradio) and Radio Canada International (🌐 rcinet.ca/en) have their frequencies listed on their respective websites.

Travel essentials

Crime and personal safety

Though Amsterdam is relatively untroubled by **crime** in comparison with other European cities, there is nevertheless more street crime than there used to be, and it's advisable to be on your guard against **petty theft**. Take the usual precautions, and beware of distraction ploys on the street, such as someone asking for directions while an accomplice puts their hand in your bag. If you're on a **bike**, make sure it is properly locked; bike theft and resale is a major industry here.

As for **personal safety**, it's generally possible to walk around most parts of the city without fear of harassment or assault, but wherever you go at night it's always better to err on the side of caution. In particular, Amsterdam's **Red Light District** can have an unpleasant, threatening undertow (although the crowds of people act as a deterrent), as can the area around **Centraal Station** and certain quiet parts of **De Pijp**. In general, try not to wander around looking lost. Using public transport, even late at night, isn't usually a problem, but if in doubt take a taxi.

If you are robbed, you'll need to go to a **police station** to report it, not least because your insurance company will require a police report; remember to

DRUGS

While **cannabis** isn't actually legal in the Netherlands, it is widely tolerated (see page 171). As far as **other drugs** go, ecstasy, LSD, speed and cocaine are as illegal in the Netherlands as they are anywhere else, and possession could mean a stay in jail. Buying off the street is extremely risky: in recent years a number of tourists have been hospitalized, and three have died, after buying "white heroin" from street dealers, which they believed to be cocaine. Magic mushrooms are just as illegal as hard drugs, though you can still buy "grow-your-own" kits or truffles, which are claimed to have a similar effect.

make a note of the report number – or, better still, ask for a copy of the statement itself. If your credit card is stolen, report the theft immediately to your card company (see page 28).

If you're **detained by the police**, you don't automatically have the right to a phone call, although in practice they'll probably phone your consulate for you – not that consular officials have a reputation for excessive helpfulness, particularly in **drug** cases (see below). If your alleged offence is a minor matter, you can be held for up to six hours without questioning; if it is more serious, you can be detained for up to 24 hours.

There are police stations at the following locations: Nieuwezijds Voorburgwal 104–108; Beursstraat 33; Elandsgracht 117; Marnixstraat 148; Lijnbaansgracht 219; Prinsengracht 1109; and Ferdinand Bolstraat 190.

Discounts and concessions

Concessionary rates are available at all tourist sights, as well as on the public transport system. Rates vary, but usually over-65s and under-18s get a discounted price, while children aged 4 and under get in for free; family tickets are common too.

Electricity

The Dutch electricity supply runs at 220v AC. British equipment needs only a plug adaptor; American items require a transformer and an adaptor.

Entry requirements

Citizens of EU countries, plus citizens of Australia, New Zealand, Canada and the US, do not need a visa to enter the Netherlands if staying for **three months or less**, but

they do need a current **passport**. Travellers from South Africa need a passport and a tourist visa before leaving for the Netherlands for a visit of less than three months.

EU residents planning on staying **longer than three months** do not need a residence permit, but they do need to register with **IND**, the Immigration and Naturalization Service (W ind.nl). In Amsterdam, go to the Vreemdelingenpolitie (Foreign Police) at Johan Huizingalaan 757 (T 020 559 6300), armed with your birth certificate and proof that you have the funds to finance your stay, a fixed address and health insurance. Other nationalities wishing to stay in the Netherlands for more than three months need an **entry visa** and a **residence permit**. The rules are complicated, so consult your Dutch embassy at home before departure. EU citizens no longer need a permit to be able to **work** in the Netherlands, but pretty much everyone else does – again, enquire at the nearest Dutch embassy before you depart for the latest regulations.

Wherever you're from, a good source of **information** if you're planning a long-term stay is a nonprofit organization called Access (T 0900 222 2377, W access-nl. org). They operate a very useful English-language information line on everything from domestic services to legal matters, as well as running courses on various aspects of Dutch administration and culture.

FOREIGN EMBASSIES AND CONSULATES IN THE NETHERLANDS

Australia Carnegielaan 4, 2517 KH The Hague T 070 310 8200, W netherlands.embassy.gov.au.

Canada Sophialaan 7, 2514 JP The Hague T 070 311 1600, W canadainternational.gc.ca.

Ireland Scheveningseweg 112, 2584 AE The Hague T 070 363 0993, W dfa.ie.

New Zealand Eisenhowerlaan 77, 2517 KK The Hague T 070 346 9324, W mfat.govt.nz.

South Africa Wassenaarseweg 40, 2596 CJ The Hague T 070 392 4501, W zuidafrika.nl.

UK Lange Voorhout 10, 2514 ED The Hague T 070 427 0427, W gov.uk/government/world/organisations/british-embassy-the-hague; Consulate General: Koningslaan 44, PO Box 75488, 1075 AE Amsterdam T 070 4270 427.

US John Adams Park 1, 2244 BZ Wassenaar, Hague T 070 310 2209, W nl.usembassy.gov; Consulate General: Museumplein 19, 1071 DJ Amsterdam T 020 575 5309, W nl.usembassy.gov/embassy-consulate/amsterdam.

EMERGENCIES

In an **emergency** – police, fire or ambulance – call T 112.

Health

As a member of the European Union, the Netherlands has free reciprocal health agreements with other member states. **EU citizens** are entitled to free treatment within the Netherlands' public healthcare system on production of a European Health Insurance Card (**EHIC**), which you can order over the phone (☏0300 330 1350) or online at ⓦehic.org.uk; allow up to 21 days for delivery. The EHIC is free of charge and valid for up to five years. **Australians** are able to receive treatment through a reciprocal arrangement with Medicare (check with your local office for details).

In an **emergency** phone ☏112. If you're reliant on **free treatment** within the EU health scheme, try to make this clear to the ambulance staff, and, if you're taken to hospital (*ziekenhuis*), to the medic you subsequently encounter. If possible, it's a good idea to hand over a photocopy of your EHIC on arrival at the hospital to ensure your status is clearly understood. As for describing symptoms, you can be pretty sure that someone will speak English. Without an EHIC you won't be turned away from a hospital, but you will have to pay for any treatment you receive and should therefore get an official receipt, a necessary preamble to the long-winded process of trying to get at least some of the money back through insurance.

You can get the address of an **English-speaking doctor** from your local pharmacy, tourist office or hotel. If you're entitled to free treatment under the EU health agreement, double-check that the doctor is both working within, and regarding you as a patient of, the public health care system. Bear in mind, though, that even within the EU agreement you may still have to pay a significant portion of the prescription charges (although senior citizens and children are exempt). Most private health insurance policies don't cover prescription charges either, and although the "excesses" are usually greater than the cost of the medicines, it's worth keeping receipts just in case.

Drugstores (*drogist*) sell non-prescription drugs as well as toiletries, tampons, condoms and the like. **Pharmacies** (*apotheek*; generally open Mon–Fri 9am–5.30pm, but often closed Mon mornings) handle prescriptions.

Dental treatment is not within the scope of the EU health agreement; enquire at the local tourist office or your hotel reception for an English-speaking dentist.

HOSPITALS

Academic Medical Centre (AMC) Meibergdreef 9 ☏020 566 9111, ⓦamc.nl.
Onze Lieve Vrouwe Gasthuis Oosterpark 9 ☏020 599 9111, ⓦolvg.nl.

Sint Lucas Ziekenhuis Jan Tooropstraat 164 ☏020 510 8911, ⓦolvg.nl.
VU Medical Centre De Boelelaan 1117 ☏020 444 4444, ⓦvumc.nl.

PHARMACIES

Apotheek Koek, Schaeffer & Van Tijen Vijzelgracht 19, Grachtengordel south ☏020 623 5949, ⓦalphega-apotheek.nl; Mon–Fri 8.30am–5.30pm, Sat 10am–3pm.
Benu Pharmacy Dam Beursstraat 39 ☏020 624 4331, ⓦbenuapotheek.nl; Mon–Fri 8.30am–5.30pm, Sat 9am–5pm, Sun noon–5pm.
Lairesse Apotheek De Lairessestraat 40, Museum Quarter ☏020 662 1022, ⓦdelairesseapotheek.nl; Mon–Fri 8.30am–6pm, Sat 10am–5pm.

Insurance

Even though EU health care privileges apply in the Netherlands, you'd do well to take out an **insurance policy** before travelling to cover against theft, loss, illness or injury. A typical policy usually provides cover for the loss of baggage, tickets and – up to a certain limit – cash or cheques, as well as cancellation or curtailment of your journey. Many policies can be chopped and changed to exclude coverage you don't need: sickness and accident benefits can often be excluded or included at will. If you need to make a **claim**, you should keep all receipts, and in the event that you have anything stolen, you must obtain an official statement from the police.

Visitors planning **longer stays** (at least three months) are required by Dutch law to take out private health insurance, which means that the cost of items not within the scope of the EU scheme, such as dental treatment and repatriation on medical grounds, will be covered.

Internet

Internet connections in the Netherlands are among the fastest in the world and now most hotels, hostels and cafés provide free **wi-fi** for their guests. A map of free wi-fi hotspots in Amsterdam is available at ⓦwifi-amsterdam.nl/free_wifi_internet.html. There's also free internet access at the main library, Bibliotheek (see page 98).

Laundry

Larger hotels generally provide a **laundry** service, though this tends to be expensive. **Self-service** laundries charge around €6–8 for a wash and dry. The best option is Clean Brothers at Westerstraat 26, Jordaan (daily 8am–8pm), which also does service

ROUGH GUIDES TRAVEL INSURANCE

Rough Guides has teamed up with WorldNomads.com to offer great travel insurance deals. Policies are available to residents of over 150 countries, with cover for a wide range of adventure sports, 24hr emergency assistance, high levels of medical and evacuation cover and a stream of travel safety information. Roughguides.com users can take advantage of their policies online 24/7, from anywhere in the world – even if you're already travelling. And since plans often change when you're on the road, you can extend your policy and even claim online. Roughguides.com users who buy travel insurance with WorldNomads.com can also leave a positive footprint and donate to a community development project. For more information, go to ⓦroughguides.com/travel-insurance.

washes, dry-cleaning and ironing. In the Old Centre try the Happy Inn Laundromat at Warmoesstraat 30 (daily 8am–10pm); in Grachtengordel south there's Powders at Kerkstraat 367 (daily 8am–10pm).

Left luggage

There's a staffed **left-luggage** desk on Level -1 of the **airport**, between Arrivals halls 1 and 2 (open 24hrs a day); items can be stored for up to a month, at a cost of €6–9 per piece (depending on their size) per day. There are also left-luggage lockers dotted throughout the airport at Departures lounges 1, 2 and 3 and Arrivals Hall 3. Small items cost roughly €6/day, medium €7/day, large €8/day and very bulky items €11.50/day; the maximum storage time is seven ays, and payment is by credit card only. At **Centraal Station** – near platform 2b (follow the suitcase signs) – you'll find bankcard-operated left-luggage lockers, which cost €7 for a small one, or €10 for a larger one, for 24 hours.

Lost property

Schiphol airport's **lost property** desk is in the Arrivals Hall (daily 7am–6pm; ⓣ0900 0141). For items lost on trams, buses or the metro, contact GVB's lost property office, Kromme Mijdrechtstraat 25 (Mon–Wed & Fri 9am–5pm, Thurs 9am–7pm; ⓣ0900 8011). For property lost on a train, go to the 24hr service office at Centraal Station (Stationsplein 15) or call customer service on ⓣ030 751 5155). After five days all unclaimed property goes to the Central Lost Property Office in Utrecht (Mon–Fri 8am–5pm; ⓣ0900 321 2100, ⓦns.nl), where they're stored for three months; fill in the tracing form on the website. If you lose something in the street or park, try the police lost property office at Korte Leidsedwarsstraat 52 (Mon–Fri 9am–4pm; ⓣ020 251 0222).

Mail

Ninety percent of post offices in the Netherlands closed in 2012 as a result of cost-cutting in the newly privatized system. Amsterdam still has a main office at Singel 250 (Mon–Fri 8am–6pm, Sat 9am–5pm; ⓦpostnl.nl); otherwise postal transactions can be carried out at **PostNL** service points, inside stores marked with the PostNL/TNT logo, including the Albert Hejn supermarket at Jodenbreestraat 21, old Jewish quarter (Mon–Sat 8am–8pm, Sat noon–5pm). **Stamps** are sold at a wide range of outlets, including many supermarkets, shops and hotels. **Postboxes** are everywhere; the slot labelled *overige* is for post going outside Amsterdam or abroad.

Maps

The **maps** in this guide should be adequate for most purposes, but if you need one on a larger scale, or with a street index, then pick up the Freytag-Berndt und Artaria 1:10,000 *Amsterdam City Pocket Map* (€4.99), which marks the key sights and has the added advantage of being waterproof and rip-proof. If you want a map covering the outer suburbs as well, your best bet is the Falk map of Amsterdam (1:15,000). Other options include the city maps sold by the VVV, which come complete with a street index, and the handily compact, spiral-bound street atlases produced by Falk (suburbs: 1:12,500; centre 1:7500).

Money

The **currency** of the Netherlands is the **euro** (€), divided into 100 cents. At the time of writing the exchange rate was €1.43 to £1 and €0.92 to $1. There are **notes** of €500, €200, €100, €50, €20, €10 and €5, and **coins** of €2, €1, 50c, 20c, 10c, 5c and 2c. For up-to-date exchange rates, consult the currency converter website ⓦxe.com.

The Netherlands is a **cash** society; as a general rule, people prefer to pay for most things with notes and coins. However, **debit and credit cards** are widely accepted at most shops and restaurants. The easiest way to access funds when abroad is from an **ATM**, though your bank will levy a charge for foreign withdrawals.

To cancel **lost or stolen** cards, call the following 24hr numbers: American Express (☎020 504 8666); MasterCard (☎0800 022 5821); Visa (☎0800 022 3110).

Changing money

Banks usually offer the best deals on changing money. **Banking hours** are Monday to Friday 9am to 4pm; all are closed on public holidays (see below). Outside these times, changing money is rarely a problem; there's a nationwide network of **GWK exchange offices**, which are open late every day, and at Amsterdam Centraal Station and Schiphol airport, 24 hours a day. GWK offers competitive rates and charges reasonable commissions, but some other agencies don't, so be cautious. VVV tourist offices (see page 30) also exchange money, as do most hotels and campsites and some hostels, but their rates are generally poor.

Opening hours and public holidays

The Dutch weekend fades painlessly into the working week, with many smaller shops and businesses staying closed on Monday mornings until noon. However, normal shop **opening hours** are Monday to Saturday 9am to 6pm and Sunday noon to 5pm, with many places remaining open till late on Thursday evenings.

Most **restaurants** are open for dinner from about 5.30 or 6pm, and though many close as early as 9.30pm, a few stay open past 11pm. **Bars**, **cafés** and most **coffeeshops** are open all day from around 10am; most close at 1am during the week and 2am at weekends. **Clubs** generally open their doors from 11pm to 4am during the week, and some stay open until 5am at the weekend.

Most **shops** and banks are closed on **public holidays** (*nationale feestdagen*), which provide the perfect excuse to take to the streets. The most famous is **King's Day** on April 27 (see page 219), which is celebrated throughout the Netherlands but with particular gusto in Amsterdam. Note that **Good Friday** is not a public holiday, but many locals take this day off.

Museums are usually open daily from 9 or 10am to 5pm (some smaller museums are closed on Monday), with a few staying open until 7 or even 10pm (Eye Filmmuseum, Anne Frank Huis). Though closed for Christmas and New Year, state-run museums adopt Sunday hours on the remaining public holidays. **Galleries** tend to be open from Tuesday to Sunday from noon to 5pm. Precise opening hours are quoted throughout this guide.

PUBLIC HOLIDAYS

January 1 (New Year's Day) Nieuwjaarsdag
Easter Sunday Eerste Paasdag
Easter Monday Tweede Paasdag
April 27 (King's Day) Koningsdag
May 5 (Liberation Day; a public holiday every five years, next in 2020) Bevrijdingsdag
Ascension Day (40 days after Easter: mid-May to early June) Hemelvaartsdag
Whitsun (7th Sun after Easter: mid-May to early June) Pinksteren
Whit Monday (7th Mon after Easter: mid-May to early June) Pinksterenmaandag
December 25 (Christmas Day) Eerste Kerstdag
December 26 (Boxing Day) Tweede Kerstdag

Phones

The **country code** for the Netherlands is ☎31, and the area code for Amsterdam is ☎020; mobile numbers start with ☎06. Numbers prefixed ☎0800 are free; those prefixed ☎0900 are premium-rate – a (Dutch) message before you're connected tells you how much you will be paying for the call, and you can only call them from within the Netherlands.

There is good coverage for **mobile phones/ cellphones** all over the Netherlands. UK mobile phones generally work without any problems, but some US and Canadian cellphones can't access the European GSM network; check with your service provider. Prepaid SIM cards are available in telephone shops (try the Rokin and around Kalverstraat) and in some supermarkets. **Phone booths** are rare, but there are a few at major locations, such as Centraal Station. **Phonecards** can be bought at outlets like tobacconists and VVV offices, and in several denom-

CALLING HOME FROM ABROAD

To make an international call, dial the international access code (in the Netherlands it's 00), then the destination's country code, before the rest of the number. Note that the initial zero is omitted from the area code when.dialling the UK, Ireland, Australia and New Zealand from abroad.
Australia international access code + 61
New Zealand international access code + 64
UK international access code + 44
US and Canada international access code + 1
Ireland international access code + 353
South Africa international access code + 27

TOURIST PASSES

Various **tourist passes** are available. The VVV's much-touted **I amsterdam card** provides numerous savings and costs €59 for one day, €74 for two consecutive days, €87 for three consecutive days and €98 for four consecutive days. You can buy one online (ⓦiamsterdam.com), or from the tourist office on arrival (see opposite). The card includes a city map, a free canal cruise, unlimited use of the GVB public transport system, including trams, buses (not Connexxion airport buses) and metros, plus free entrance to Amsterdam's best museums (but not the Anne Frank Huis, and there's only a €2.50 saving on Rijksmuseum tickets). There's also a 25 percent discount on bike rental, tours, concert performances and some restaurants.

An alternative if you're staying for more than a couple of days is the **Museumkaart**, which gives free entry to most museums in the whole of the Netherlands for 31 days, including the Rijksmuseum and the Anne Frank Huis, but it doesn't include public transport; it costs €59.90 (less if you're 24 or under). For details or to order online, see ⓦmuseumkaart.nl, or you can buy one at any participating museum.

Finally, the Amsterdam **Holland Pass** (ⓦhollandpass.com) is a one-month all-in-one pass that you can buy online. It includes a free one-way train ride from Schiphol airport to Centraal Station; a free hop on-hop off sightseeing bus tour or one-hour canal cruise; and fast-track free entry to one or more of the major museums and attractions (depending which pass you buy). Options range from the Small (€40), which gets you free entry into one major museum and one other attraction, to Large (€71), with free entry to three major sights plus three other attractions.

inations, beginning at €5. The **cheapest time** to make international calls is between 8pm and 8am during the week, and all day at weekends.

To speak to the **operator** (domestic and inter-national), call ☎0800 0410; for **directory enquiries**, dial ☎0900 8008 (domestic) or ☎0900 8418 (international). The **Dutch phone directory** is available (in Dutch) at ⓦdetelefoongids.nl.

Time

Amsterdam is on **Central European Time** (CET) – one hour ahead of London, six hours ahead of New York, nine hours ahead of Los Angeles and eight hours behind Sydney. **Daylight saving** operates from the end of March to the end of October.

Tipping

Tipping isn't quite as routine a matter as it is in the US or even in the UK. However, you are expected to leave something if you have enjoyed good service – up to around ten percent of the bill should suffice in most restaurants, while hotel porters and taxi drivers may expect a euro or two on top of the fare.

Tourist information

Information on Amsterdam is easy to get hold of, either before you leave, from the **Netherlands Board of Tourism** (ⓦholland.com), which highlights upcoming events and is strong on practical information, or on the ground from the city's excellent tourist offices, known as the **VVV** (pronounced "fay-fay-fay"). The VVV has a useful **website** (ⓦiamsterdam.com).

Tourist offices provide **advice and information** and sell **maps**, as well as public transport **tickets** and tourist passes (see box). They also take bookings for canal cruises and other organized **excursions** (see page 24), and operate an efficient **accommodation reservation service** – useful in high season when finding accommodation isn't always easy. Tourist offices are also a good source of advice on anything remotely cultural, and you can buy tickets and pick up copies of **listings magazines**: the monthly *Uitkrant* magazine, which is comprehensive and free but in Dutch, or the superior *A-mag* (€4.95), produced in English by the VVV. Finally, there are also a few tourist information touch screens around town: at the Stadsschouwburg box office (Leidseplein 26) and at all the Park and Ride locations (see page 23).

TOURIST OFFICES

I amsterdam Store In the northern hall of the IJ-hal above Centraal Station; Mon–Wed 8am–7pm, Thurs–Sat 8am–8pm, Sun 8am–6pm. As well as offering information, this office sells tickets, regional products and gifts.

VVV Schiphol Airport Arrivals 2 at Schiphol Plaza; daily 7am–10pm.

VVV Stationsplein Directly across from the main station entrance; Mon–Sun 9am–6pm.

Travellers with disabilities

Despite its general social progressiveness, the Netherlands is only just getting to grips with the requirements of people with **mobility problems**. In Amsterdam, the most obvious difficulty you'll face is in negotiating the cobbled streets and narrow, often broken pavements of the older districts, where the key sights are often located. Similarly, provision for people with disabilities on **public transport** is only average, although the situation is improving – many new buses are now wheelchair accessible. On the plus side, practically all public buildings, including museums, theatres, cinemas, concert halls and hotels, are obliged to provide access, and do.

Bear in mind that a lot of the older, narrower hotels are not allowed to install lifts, so check first. Places that have been certified **wheelchair accessible** now bear an International Accessibility Symbol (IAS).

If you're planning to use the **Dutch train network** during your stay and would appreciate assistance on the platform, phone the Bureau Assistentieverlening Gehandicapten (Disabled Assistance Office; daily 7am–11pm; ☎030 235 7822) at least three hours before your train departs, and there will be someone to meet and help you at the station. NS, the Netherlands Railways association, publishes information about train travel for people with disabilities at Ⓦns.nl and in leaflets stocked at main stations.

Accessible Travel Netherlands (Ⓦ accessibletravelnl.com) is an Amsterdam-based tour operator specializing in holidays for those with special-access needs. They offer tours and can arrange transport, accommodation, personal assistants and equipment rental.

AMSTERDAM MUSEUM

The Old Centre

The Old Centre is Amsterdam's most vivacious district, an oval-shaped tangle of picturesque canals and narrow streets, confined in the north by the River IJ and to the west and south by the Singel. Most people arrive at Centraal Station, with the Old Centre spreading out before them: Damrak, the main drag, arrows south to the heart of the Old Centre, the Dam, overseen by the magnificent Koninklijk Paleis. East of Damrak is the Red Light District, whose prevailing seediness is offset by dozens of fine canal houses and two prime attractions, the Gothic Oude Kerk and the attic church, Ons' Lieve Heer Op Solder. But perhaps more than anything else, it's the buzz of the Old Centre that is its main appeal, and if the rain comes, as it often does, you can just hunker down in one of the district's beguiling brown cafés.

1

The **Old Centre** is where Amsterdam began, developing in stages, each of which was marked by the digging of new canals to either side of Damrak – now without a canal, but originally the location of the main waterway linking the River IJ and the Dam. The city was booming by the fourteenth century, yet, time and again, the wooden buildings of medieval Amsterdam went up in smoke, until finally, after a particularly severe fire in 1452, timber was banned in favour of brick and stone – and it's the handsome canal houses built after the ban that now provide the Old Centre with most of its architectural high points.

Damrak

Running from Centraal Station to the Dam, **Damrak** – a broad, rather unenticing avenue still lined with tacky restaurants and souvenir shops despite long-running regeneration Project 1012 – slices south into the heart of the city, first passing an inner harbour crammed with the bobbing canal cruise boats of Amsterdam's vast tourist industry. Damrak was a canal until 1672, when it was filled in, but up until then it was the city's nautical lifeline, with boats sailing up it to discharge their goods right in the centre of town on the main square. Thereafter, with the docks moved elsewhere, Damrak became a busy commercial drag, as it remains today, with the Dam, at its end, becoming the centre of municipal power.

Centraal Station

Trams #1, #2, #5, #9, #13, #16, #17, #24 and buses #18, #21, #22, #32, #33, #34, #35 and #48 run from the station

With its high gables and cheerful brickwork, the neo-Renaissance **Centraal Station** is an imposing prelude to the city. At the time of its construction on an artificial island in the 1880s, it aroused much controversy because it effectively separated the centre from the River IJ, source of the city's wealth, for the first time in Amsterdam's long history. There was controversy about the choice of architect too: the man chosen, **Petrus J.H. Cuypers**, was Catholic, and in powerful Protestant circles there were mutterings about the vanity of his designs (he had recently completed the Rijksmuseum) and their unsuitability for Amsterdam. In the event, the station was built to Cuypers' design, but it was to be his last major commission; thereafter he spent most of his time building parish churches. Whatever you think about the building it's certainly a nice place to arrive. Its grand arches and cavernous main hall have a suitable sense of occasion, and from here all of the city lies before you.

The Dutch seem to have been redesigning **Stationsplein**, the long and wide square in front of Centraal Station, forever. It awaits yet another makeover, set for 2018–2023, with plans for new natural-stone tiling and parking for 7000 bicycles; in the meantime it remains a mishmash, packed with trams, taxis and bikes, edged by ovals of water, and dotted with barrel organs, chip stands and street performers in summer.

St Nicolaaskerk

Prins Hendrikkade 73 • Mon & Sat noon–3pm, Tues–Fri 11am–4pm • Free • Ⓦ nicolaas-parochie.nl • A 3min walk from Centraal Station

Across the water from Stationsplein rise the twin towers and dome of **St Nicolaaskerk**, the city's foremost Catholic church, dedicated to the patron saint of sailors – and of Amsterdam. Like the station, it dates back to the 1880s, but here the cavernous interior holds some pretty dire religious murals, mawkish concoctions only partly relieved by swathes of coloured brickwork. Above the high altar is the crown of the Habsburg **Emperor Maximilian**, very much a symbol of the city and one you'll see again and again. Amsterdam had close ties with Maximilian – in the late fifteenth century he came here as a pilgrim and stayed on to recover from an illness. The burghers funded many of his military

THE OLD CENTRE

● EATING

RESTAURANTS

Bird	12
Blauw aan de Wal	18
Brakke Grond	24
Catala	32
De Compagnon	31
Golden Chopsticks	1
Hemelse Modder	22
Kantjil en de Tiger	16
Kobe House	29
Lastage	7
Lucius	25
Mappa	34
Me Naam Naan	14
Nam Kee	21
New King	15
Oriental City	21
Pannenkoekenhuis Upstairs	28
Restaurant Vermeer	3
Sampurna	37
De Silveren Spiegel	4
Skek	20
Supperclub	19
Van Beeren	23
Van Kerwijk	30
Vasso	27
D'Vijff Vlieghen	

CAFES

De Bakkerswinkel	10
Bistro Berlage	11
Café Esprit	33
Cafe de Jaren	36
Gartine	31
Gebr. Niemeijer	1
Greenwoods	6
Hofje van Wijs	8
Koffieschenkerij de Oude Kerk	13
Puccini	34
Staalmeesters	35

■ DRINKING AND NIGHTLIFE

BARS

BeerTemple	26
De Bekeerde Suster	25
Bubbles & Wines	27
De Buurvrouw	28
Café Belgique	17
Café de Dokter	35
Café de Gaeper	20
Café het Paleis	1
Dante	23
De Engelbewaarder	39
Gollem	18
Hoppe	37
In 't Aepjen	4
In de Wildeman	8
Lokaal 't Loosje	22
Mata Hari	13
De Ooievaar	5
Poco Loco	19
Schuim	24
Tales & Spirits	6
The Tara	31
Wynand Fockink	21

CLUBS

Bitterzoet	38
Club NL	36
Disco Dolly	32
Winston Kingdom	29

LIVE MUSIC VENUES

Akhnaton	7
De Buurvrouw	28
Casablanca	10
De Engelbewaarder	32
Kapitein Zeppos	34
'Skek	9
Winston International	18

LGBTQ BARS & CLUBS

Cuckoo's Nest	3
Dirty Dicks	15
The Eagle	14
Getto	12
Prik	16
The Web	2

COFFEESHOPS

Dampkring	40
Grasshopper	11
Kadinsky	30
Rusland	33

Passenger Ferries to EYE, NDSM Shipyard & Waterland

Centraal Station

Stationsplein

Open Havenfront

Prins Hendrikkade

GVB

Chet Baker Memorial

Nieuwe Brugsteeg

St Nicolaaskerk

Schreierstoren

Oosterdok

Scheepvaarthuis

Marionetten Theater

Fo Guang Shan He Hua

Waag

Zeedijk

RED LIGHT DISTRICT

Ons' Lieve Heer Op Solder

Oude Kerk

Prostitution Info Centre

Sex Museum

Tony's Chocolonely Super Store

Vondel Plaque

The Beurs van Berlage

Drake's

Beurspassage

De Bijenkorf

War Memorial

THE DAM

Nieuwe Kerk

Koninklijk Paleis

Magna Plaza

Torensluis

Lutherse Kerk

Damrak

Rokin

Singel

Herengracht

Brouwersgracht

Raadhuisstraat

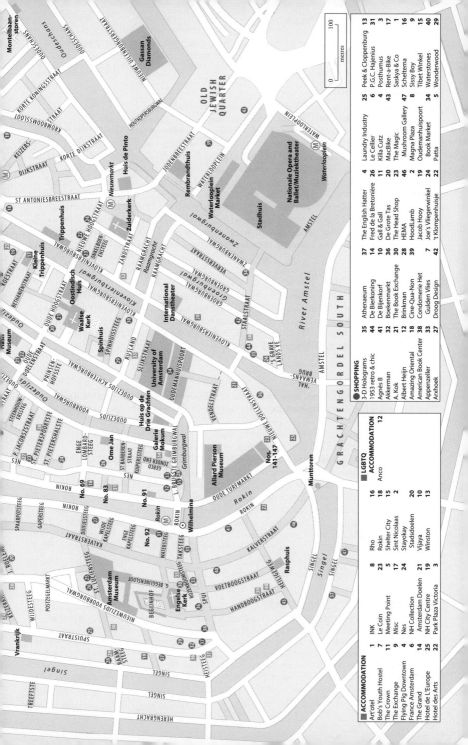

1

expeditions, and in return he let the city use his crown in its coat of arms, a practice which – rather surprisingly – survived the seventeenth-century revolt against Spain.

The Schreierstoren

Prins Hendrikkade 94, at the top of the Geldersekade canal • A 4min walk from Centraal Station

The squat **Schreierstoren** (Weepers' Tower), just around the corner from St Nicolaaskerk, is a rare surviving chunk of the city's **medieval wall**. Originally, the tower overlooked the River IJ and it was here, it's said, that women gathered to watch their menfolk sail away, though, like many good stories, this is apparently apocryphal: "Schreierstoren" refers to the sharp angle – the "schreye" – at which it was built, rather than the weeping women. Nonetheless, an old and weathered stone plaque inserted in the wall is a reminder of all those supposed sad farewells, and another much more recent plaque recalls the departure of Henry Hudson from here in 1609. On this particular voyage Hudson stumbled across the "Hudson" river and an island the locals called Manhattan. The colony that grew up there became known as New Amsterdam, a colonial possession that was only renamed New York after the English seized it in 1664.

The Sex Museum

Damrak 18 • Daily 9.30am–11.30pm • €4 • ☎ 020 622 8376, ⓦ sexmuseumamsterdam.nl • A 4min walk from Centraal Station

The first real sight – if you can call it that – along Damrak is Amsterdam's **Sex Museum**, whose tawdry exhibits are, to many minds, either laughable or offensive – or both. As an attempt to cash in on the city's reputation for sex, however, its assorted erotica, from porn photos to statues, have proved very popular.

The Beurs

Damrak 213–247 • Opening hours depend on exhibitions • Regular, hour-long guided tours €14.50/person • Book tours in advance on ☎ 020 530 4141 or ⓔ info@beursvanberlage.nl, ⓦ beursvanberlage.nl • Tram #4, #9, #16 or #24 to the Dam, or an 8min walk from Centraal Station

Hogging the east side of Damrak, just beyond the mini-harbour, is the imposing bulk of the **Beurs**, the old Stock Exchange – known as the "Beurs van Berlage" – a seminal work designed at the turn of the twentieth century by the leading light of the Dutch Modern movement, **Hendrik Petrus Berlage** (1856–1934). Berlage rerouted Dutch architecture with this building, forsaking the historicism that had dominated the nineteenth century, whose prime practitioner had been Cuypers (see page 33). Instead Berlage opted for a style with cleaner, heavier lines, inspired by the Romanesque and the Renaissance, but with the minimum of ornamentation. In so doing, he anticipated the Expressionism that swept across northern Europe from 1905 to 1925. The Beurs has long since lost its commercial function and nowadays hosts concerts and conferences, as well as exhibitions on modern art and design. Nonetheless, the building is still the main event, notably the handsome shallow-arched arcades and

---

CHET BAKER'S LAST BLAST

Born in Oklahoma, **Chet Baker** (1929–88) was arguably one of the finest jazz trumpeters of all time, his reputation established by a string of superlative performances in the 1950s. However, Baker was also addicted to heroin, which brought him regular periods in jail, a chaotic lifestyle – and a couple of bad beatings. In his later years, Baker spent most of his time in Europe and it was in Amsterdam that he came to an untimely end: on May 13, 1988, he either fell or threw himself out of the window of Room 210 of the *Prins Hendrik Hotel*, at **Prins Hendrikkade 52** – just south of St Nicolaaskerk. An evocative plaque of the man in full blow is now pinned to the hotel facade.

elaborate brickwork of the main hall. If you don't want to stump up for a guided tour, you can still see some of Berlage's work – plus three tiled scenes of the past, present and future by the Dutch artist Jan Toorop – in the convivial *Bistro Berlage* (see page 158) at the south end of the building abutting Beursplein, or in Tony's Chocolonely Super Store (Oudebrugsteeg 15).

De Bijenkorf

Dam 1 • Mon & Sun 11am–9pm, Tues–Sat 10am–9pm • ☎ 088 245 4488, ⓦ debijenkorf.nl • Tram #4, #9, #16 or #24 to the Dam, or a 10min walk from Centraal Station

Something of a city institution, **De Bijenkorf** – literally "beehive" – is a sprawling department store that extends south along Damrak to the Dam. De Bijenkorf posed all sorts of problems for the Germans when they first occupied the city in World War II. The store was a Jewish concern, so the Nazis didn't really want their troops shopping here, but it was just too popular to implement a total ban. The bizarre solution was to prohibit German soldiers from shopping on the ground floor, where the store's Jewish employees were concentrated, as they always had been, in the luxury goods section. These days it's a good all-round department store, with the usual floors of designer goods, cosmetics and homeware.

The Dam

Tram #4, #9, #16 or #24 to the Dam, or a 10min walk from Centraal Station

Situated at the very heart of the city, **Dam square**, usually known simply as the **Dam,** gave Amsterdam its name – it was here, in the thirteenth century, that the River Amstel was dammed and the fishing village that grew around it became known as "Amstelredam". Boats could sail down Damrak into the square, and unload in the middle of the village, which soon prospered by trading herring for Baltic grain. Later, the building of Amsterdam's principal church, the **Nieuwe Kerk**, followed by the town hall (now the **Koninklijk Paleis**), formally marked the Dam as Amsterdam's centre. Today it's an open and airy, but somehow rather desultory space, despite – or perhaps partly because of – the presence of the main municipal **war memorial**, a prominent stone tusk adorned by bleak, suffering figures and decorated with the coats of arms of each of the Netherlands' provinces (plus the ex-colony of Indonesia). The memorial was designed by **Jacobus Johannes Pieter Oud** (1890–1963), a De Stijl stalwart (see page 249) who thought the Expressionism of Berlage much too flippant.

The Koninklijk Paleis

The Dam • Daily 10am–5pm, but closed on state occasions – check the website • €10 • ☎ 020 522 6161, ⓦ paleisamsterdam.nl • Tram #4, #9, #16 or #24 to the Dam, or a 10min walk from Centraal Station

The city's most impressive building, the **Koninklijk Paleis** – the Royal Palace – dominates its surroundings, an imposing sandstone structure that was built as an exercise in municipal tub-thumping when Amsterdam was at the peak of its power. The building's title is deceptive: the building started out as the **Stadhuis** (Town Hall), and only had its first royal occupant when Louis Bonaparte moved in during the French occupation (see page 38).

The exterior

The **exterior** of the palace is very much to the allegorical point: twin tympani depict Amsterdam as a port and trading centre, the one at the front presided over by Neptune and a veritable herd of unicorns. Above these panels are representations of the values the city council espoused – at the front, Prudence, Justice and Peace, to the rear

1

THE KONINKLIJK PALEIS: TOWN HALL TO ROYAL PALACE

At the time of the **Koninklijk Paleis**' construction, in the middle of the seventeenth century, Amsterdam was pre-eminent among Dutch towns, and had just resisted William of Orange's attempts to bring it to heel. Predictably, the city council craved a **residence** that was a declaration of Amsterdam's municipal power and pride, and they opted for a startlingly progressive design by **Jacob van Campen**, who proposed a Dutch rendering of the classical principles revived in Renaissance Italy. Initially, there was opposition to the plan from the council's Calvinist minority, who pointed out that the proposed **Stadhuis** would dwarf the neighbouring Nieuwe Kerk, an entirely inappropriate ordering, they suggested, of earthly and spiritual values. However, when the Calvinists were promised a new church spire (which was never built) they promptly fell into line, and in 1648 work started on what was then the largest town hall in Europe, supported by no fewer than 13,659 wooden piles driven into the Dam's sandy soil – a number every Dutch schoolchild remembers by adding a "1" and a "9" to the number of days in the year. The poet Constantijn Huygens called the new building "The world's Eighth Wonder / With so much stone raised high and so much timber under".

The Stadhuis received its **royal designation** in 1808, when Napoleon's brother Louis, recently installed as king, commandeered it as his residence. Lonely and isolated, Louis abdicated in 1810 and hightailed it out of the country. Afterwards, possession of the palace became something of a sore point between the royal family and the city; the initial compromise kept the building as royal property on condition that the royals stayed here for part of the year, but the Oranges almost universally failed to make much of an appearance. This irritated many Amsterdammers, and in the 1930s the Oranges offered the city fifteen million guilders to build a new city hall in return for a new agreement, which allowed them to use the palace whenever they wanted, with ownership passing to the state (as distinct from the city); the new town hall, on Waterlooplein (see page 85), was finally completed in the 1980s. Nowadays the Dutch royals live down in the Huis ten Bosch, near the Hague, and use the Royal Palace for state occasions (of which there are many).

Temperance and Vigilance – on either side of a muscular, globe-bearing Atlas. One deliberate precaution, however, was the omission of a central doorway – just in case the mob turned nasty (as they were wont to do) and stormed the place.

The Citizens' Hall

The **interior** also proclaims the pride and confidence of the Golden Age, principally in the lavish **Citizens' Hall**, an extraordinarily handsome, arcaded marble chamber where the enthroned figure of Amsterdam looks down on the earth and the heavens, which are laid out at her feet in three circular, inlaid marble maps, one each of the eastern and western hemispheres, the other of the northern sky. Other allegorical figures ram home the municipal point: flanking "Amsterdam" to left and right are Wisdom and Strength, and the reliefs to either side of the central group represent good governance; on the left is the god Amphion, who plays his lyre to persuade the stones to pile themselves up into a wall; and to the right Mercury attempts to lull Argos to sleep – stressing the need to be vigilant.

Council rooms and chambers

Beyond the Citizens' Hall, the good-natured and witty symbolism that pervades almost all of the building continues: cocks fight above the entrance to the Commissioner of Petty Affairs; **Ferdinand Bol's** painting in the **Burgomasters' Council** room depicts an unsuccessful attempt to bribe and then frighten (with the elephant trumpeting behind the curtain) a Roman consul; and a medallion above the door of the Bankruptcy Chamber shows the fall of Icarus, surrounded by marble carvings depicting hungry rats scurrying around an empty money chest and nibbling at unpaid bills. In the **Magistrates' Court** is a second Bol painting, *Moses the Lawgiver*, depicting Moses descending from Mount Sinai with the Ten Commandments, but most of the paintings displayed in the palace are of little distinction.

The High Court of Justice

The decorative whimsy fizzles out in the **High Court of Justice** at the front of the building, close to the entrance. Inside the consciously intimidating chamber, the judges sat on the marble benches flanked by heavyweight representations of Righteousness, Wisdom, Mercy and so forth as they passed judgement on the hapless criminal in front of them; even worse, the crowd on the Dam could view the proceedings through the barred windows, almost always baying for blood. They usually went home contented; as soon as the judges had passed the death sentence, the condemned were whisked up to the wooden scaffold attached to the front of the building and promptly dispatched.

The Nieuwe Kerk

The Dam • Hours vary with the exhibition, but usually daily 10am–6pm • €8–11 • ☎ 020 626 8168, Ⓦ nieuwekerk.nl • Tram #4, #9, #16 or #24 to the Dam, or a 10min walk from Centraal Station

Vying for importance with the Royal Palace is the adjacent **Nieuwe Kerk**, which – despite its name (literally "new church") – is an early-fifteenth-century structure built in a late flourish of the Gothic style, with a forest of pinnacles and high, slender gables. Badly damaged by fire on several occasions, and unceremoniously stripped of most of its fittings by the Calvinists, the **interior** is a hangar-like affair of sombre demeanour, whose sturdy compound pillars soar up to support the wooden vaulting of the ceiling. Among a scattering of decorative highlights, look out for an extravagant, finely carved mahogany **pulpit** that was fifteen years in the making, a cleverly worked copper **chancel screen** and a flashy, Baroque **organ case**.

Behind the chancel screen, there's also the spectacularly vulgar **tomb** of **Admiral Michiel de Ruyter** (1607–76), complete with trumpeting angels, conch-blowing Neptunes and cherubs. In a long and illustrious naval career, de Ruyter trounced, in succession, the Spaniards, the Swedes, the English and the French, and his rise from deck hand to Admiral-in-Chief is the stuff of national legend. His most famous exploit was a raid up the River Thames to Medway in 1667 and the seizure of the Royal Navy's flagship, *The Royal Charles*; the subsequent Dutch crowing almost drove Charles II to distraction. De Ruyter was buried here with full military honours and much national mourning. The Nieuwe Kerk is still used for state occasions and coronations, as well as temporary art exhibitions.

Magna Plaza

Nieuwezijds Voorburgwal 182 • Mon 11am–7pm, Tues, Wed, Fri & Sat 10am–7pm, Thurs 10am–9pm, Sun noon–7pm • Ⓦ magnaplaza.nl • Tram #4, #9, #16 or #24 to the Dam, or a 10min walk from Centraal Station

Behind the Koninklijk Paleis, you can't miss the old Neogothic post office of 1899, a grand affair whose red-brick interior has been converted into the **Magna Plaza shopping mall** with its numerous clothing chains. The whimsical embellishments adorning the building did much to continue the city's tradition of plonking towers on every major building, partly out of civic pride and partly to contribute to the city's spiky skyline. Nevertheless, the architect responsible, a certain C.G. Peters, took a surprising amount of flack for his creation, which was widely mocked as "postal Gothic".

The Nieuwe Zijde

To the west of Damrak lies the Old Centre's **Nieuwe Zijde**, whose outer boundary was marked in the 1500s by a defensive wall, hence the name of its principal avenue, **Nieuwezijds Voorburgwal** ("In Front of the Town Wall on the New Side"). The wall disappeared as the city grew, and in the nineteenth century the canal that ran through the middle of Nieuwezijds Voorburgwal was earthed in, leaving the unusually

1

wide thoroughfare that you see today. This area was, however, badly mauled by the developers in the 1970s and – give or take a scattering of old canal houses – there's no great reason to linger.

The Lutherse Kerk

Kattengat 1 • No public access • A 7min walk from Centraal Station

The Nieuwe Zijde's most distinctive structure is the **Lutherse Kerk** (Lutheran Church), a round, seventeenth-century edifice whose copper dome gives this area its nickname, **Koepelkwartier** (Copper quarter). Church domes are a rarity in Amsterdam, but this one was no stylistic peccadillo: until the late eighteenth century, only Dutch Reformed churches were permitted the (much more fashionable) bell towers, so the Lutherans got stuck with a dome. It's a grand building, seen to best advantage from the Singel canal, but it has been dogged by bad luck; in 1882 the interior was gutted by fire and, although it was repaired, the cost of maintenance proved too high for the congregation, who decamped in 1935. After many years of neglect, the adjacent *Renaissance Hotel* bought the church, turning it into a conference centre.

Spuistraat

Tram #1, #2, or #5 to the Dam/Paleisstraat

Spuistraat, running parallel with Nieuwezijds Voorburgwal, is a fashionable street, liberally sprinkled with bars and restaurants, especially as it approaches the Spui (see below) at its southern end. Spuistraat is also the location of one of central Amsterdam's last remaining (legal) **squats**, *Vrankrijk*, at no. 216, a labyrinthine affair putting on club nights and special events – see ⓦvrankrijk.org.

South of the Dam

The southern part of the Old Centre, between the Rokin and the Singel, is one of Amsterdam's busiest districts, mostly on account of pedestrianized **Kalverstraat**, a hectic shopping street. Taken as a whole, it's not a particularly engaging area, but it does have its moments, most enjoyably in the cloistered tranquillity of the **Begijnhof** and among the bars and cafés of the **Spui**. A brace of museums add interest: the sprawling **Amsterdam Museum** and the enjoyable archeological collection of the **Allard Pierson Museum**.

The Spui

Tram #1, #2 or #5 to Spui

At its top and buzziest end Spuistraat opens out onto the **Spui**, a wide, tram-clanking square flanked by the Athenaeum bookshop (see page 193) and a number of appealing café-bars. In the middle is a cloying statue of a young boy, known as **'t Lieverdje** ("Little Darling" or "Loveable Scamp"), a gift to the city from a cigarette company in 1960. It was here in the mid-1960s, with the statue seen as a symbol of the addicted consumer, that the playful Sixties anarchist group, the **Provos** (see page 235), organized some of their most successful *ludiek* (pranks) – much to the irritation of the police.

The Begijnhof

Access either from Gedempte Begijnensloot or from the wooden doorway on the Spui • Daily 9am–5pm • Free • ☎ 020 622 1918, ⓦ begijnhofamsterdam.nl • Tram #1, #2 or #5 to Spui

A huddle of immaculately maintained old houses looking onto a central green, their backs to the outside world, Amsterdam's delightful **Begijnhof** was founded in the

THE BEGIJNHOF – A WOMAN'S REFUGE

One corollary of the urbanization of the Low Countries from the twelfth century onwards was the establishment of **begijnhoven** (*béguinages* in French) in almost every city and town. These were semi-secluded communities, where widows and unmarried women – the **begijns** (*béguines*) – lived together, the better to do pious acts, especially caring for the sick. The origins of the *begijn* movement are obscure, but it would seem that the initial impetus came from a Liège priest, a certain Lambert le Bègue ("the Stammerer"), a religious reformer who died in 1177. The main period of growth came a little later when *begijnhoven* were established in Bruges, Ghent and Amsterdam. In **construction**, *begijnhoven* followed the same general plan, with several streets of whitewashed, terraced, brick cottages hidden away behind walls and gates and surrounding a central garden and chapel.

Begijn **communities** were different from convents in so far as the inhabitants did not have to take vows and had the right to return to the secular world if they wished. At a time when hundreds of women were forcibly shut away in convents for all sorts of reasons (primarily financial), this element of choice was crucial. In the Netherlands, the *begijn* movement faded away after the Reformation.

fourteenth century as a home for the *begijns* (*béguines*) – members of a Catholic sisterhood living as nuns, but without vows and with the right to return to the secular world (see box). The original medieval complex comprised a series of humble brick cottages, but these were mostly replaced by the larger, grander houses of today shortly after the Reformation, though the secretive, enclosed design survived. A couple of pre-Reformation buildings also remain, including the **Houten Huys**, at no. 34, whose wooden facade dates from 1477, the oldest in Amsterdam and erected before the city forbade the construction of timber houses as an essential precaution against fire.

The Engelse Kerk

No admission except during church services (Sun at 10.30am) • Free • ⓦ ercadam.nl

The **Engelse Kerk** (English Reformed Church), beside the central green, is also of medieval construction, but it was taken from the *begijns* and given to Amsterdam's English community during the Reformation. Plain and unadorned, the church is of interest for its carefully worked pulpit panels, several of which were designed by a youthful **Piet Mondriaan** (1872–1944), the leading De Stijl artist – although to see them you'll have to attend a church service.

The Begijnhofkapel

Mon 1–6.30pm, Tues–Fri 9am–6.30pm, Sat & Sun 9am–6pm • Free

Amsterdam's *begijns* may have lost their original church (see above) but in keeping with the terms of the *Alteratie* (see page 227), they were allowed to celebrate Mass inconspicuously in the clandestine Catholic **Begijnhofkapel**, which they established in the house just opposite. It's still used today, a homely little place with some terribly sentimental religious paintings.

The Amsterdam Museum

Kalverstraat 92 & Sint Luciënsteeg 27 • Daily 10am–5pm • €13.50 • ☎ 020 5231 822, ⓦ amsterdammuseum.nl • Tram #1, #2 or #5 to Spui or #4, #9, #14, #16 or #24 to Rokin

One of the city's most popular attractions, the **Amsterdam Museum** occupies the smartly restored but rambling seventeenth-century buildings of what was once the municipal orphanage. A visit begins with the **Amsterdam DNA** section, which provides an overview – perhaps an overly laudatory overview – of the city's historical

1

development by means of seven short films and a selection of prime artefacts; some interactive, others not, and including a number of fine paintings. Thereafter, the museum spreads over three main floors, and gets rather more confusing as you negotiate its many levels and corridors – be sure to collect a museum map at the ticket office.

Broadly, the ground floor concentrates on the Golden Age; the first floor focuses on the eighteenth and nineteenth centuries; and the second floor deals with the modern era, from 1940 onwards. The last is perhaps the most intriguing section, covering a wide range of topics, notably the German occupation of World War II; the demise of the Amsterdam shipbuilding industry; Johan Cruyff and his fellow footballers; the squatters' movement; the Provos (see page 235); and immigration. Here also is a so-called "White Car" – *De Witkar* – which looks something like a golf buggy and was part of an early environmental move to do something about the city's traffic congestion: the idea was that these simple, publicly owned vehicles would be the only ones allowed in the city centre. By 1979, there were 35 on the road, but the more reactionary climate of the 1980s put paid to the whole idea.

Two other parts of the museum merit a visit: the external **courtyard**, where the orphans had their own little cubby holes – not for toys, but for their tools and few possessions; and the **Schuttersgalerij**.

Amsterdam Gallery

Gedempte Begijnensloot • Daily 10am–5pm • Free • ☎ 020 5231 822, ⓦ amsterdammuseum.nl

Part glassed-in passageway, part art gallery, the **Amsterdam Gallery** – the Civic Guard Gallery – is an adjunct to the Amsterdam Museum. Traditionally, it was hung with huge group portraits of the **Amsterdam militia**, but nowadays the paintings are regularly rotated and feature more modern groups – ballet choreographers and Ajax football stars for example. That said, look out for Bartholomew van der Helst's *Governors and Governesses of the Spinhuis*, which is often on display and captures both the sternness of the institution (see page 49) and its daily routine.

Kalverstraat

Tram #4, #9, #14, #16 or #24 to the Dam

Pedestrianized **Kalverstraat**, curving south from the Dam, is one of Amsterdam's main shopping streets, heaving at weekends and lined with mainstream shops. The street has been a commercial centre since medieval times, when it started out as a calf market, but today it's pretty much indistinguishable from any major shopping street in any European capital.

Heiligeweg

Tram #1, #2 or #5 to Koningsplein

Workaday **Heiligeweg**, or "Holy Way", which links Kalverstraat with the Singel, was once part of a much longer route used by pilgrims heading into Amsterdam, and is still used for part of the Stille Omgang, or Silent Procession (see page 218). Every other religious reference disappeared centuries ago, but there is one interesting edifice here: the fanciful gateway of the old **Rasphuis** (House of Correction) that now fronts a shopping mall at the foot of Voetboogstraat. The gateway is surmounted by a sculpture of a woman punishing two criminals chained at her sides above the single word "Castigatio" ("Punishment"). Beneath is a carving by **Hendrick de Keyser** (see page 62), showing wolves and lions cringing before the whip; the inscription reads: "It is a virtue to subdue those before whom all go in dread."

The Rokin

Tram #4, #9, #14, #16 or #24 to Spui/Rokin

Picking up where Damrak left off, the **Rokin** cuts south in a wide sweep that follows the former course of the River Amstel. The Rokin was the business centre of the nineteenth-century city, and although it has lost much of its prestige it is still flanked by an attractive medley of architectural styles, incorporating everything from grandiose nineteenth-century mansions to more utilitarian modern buildings. One initial highlight as you stroll south is the handsome Art Nouveau-meets-Art Deco building at **no. 69**, the former offices of Marine Insurance. Others include the much earlier canal house at **no. 81**; the attractive stone mansion at **no. 91** with its unusual pediment eagles; and, across the street at **no. 92**, the Hajenius cigar shop (see page 202) with its flashy gilt interior.

Statue of Queen Wilhelmina

A prominent equestrian **statue** of **Queen Wilhelmina** (1880–1962) marks the spot where the Rokin hits the canal system. Born in The Hague, Wilhelmina came to the throne in 1890 and abdicated in favour of her daughter, Juliana, 58 years later – a mammoth royal stint by any standard. After her retirement she wrote a memoir, *Lonely but not Alone*, which explored her strong religious beliefs, but her popularity was based on her determined resistance to the Germans in World War II, when she was the figurehead of the government-in-exile in London.

The Allard Pierson Museum

Oude Turfmarkt 127 • Tues–Fri 10am–5pm, Sat & Sun 1–5pm • €10 • ☎ 020 525 2556, ⊛ allardpiersonmuseum.nl • Tram #4, #9, #14, #16 or #24 to Spui/Rokin

The **Allard Pierson Museum**, housed in the sturdy Neoclassical building that used to be the headquarters of the Dutch central bank, is a good old-fashioned archeological museum spread over two floors. It's not large, but it has a wide-ranging collection of finds mainly retrieved from Egypt, Greece and Italy, and most of the labelling is in both English and Dutch. The ground floor is used for temporary exhibitions and the Egyptian artefacts, among which is a fascinating section on the **Coptic Christians**, who still account for around ten percent (eight million) of the Egyptian population. The Copts modified the traditional Egyptian mummy by replacing the stereotyped face with a real likeness of the dead person – the museum has several fine examples. Also of note is a delightful model of a ship and its crew from the Middle Kingdom: a funerary object designed to transport the soul of the dead to the afterlife.

Upstairs, the highlight is the museum's Greek **pottery**, with superb examples of both the black- and red-figured wares produced in the sixth and fifth centuries BC. Look out also for several ornate Roman **sarcophagi** – especially the whopper made of marble and decorated with Dionysian scenes – as well as Etruscan funerary urns and carvings, including an amazingly precise statue of a baby in swaddling clothes. The museum is undergoing a full refurbishment, with an extension making space for the Van Nijl tot Amstel collection (From the Nile to the Amstel). Most of the galleries are already open to the public, except for the early Greek (due to open in August 2018) and Egyptian (spring 2019) sections.

Oude Turfmarkt 141–147

Tram #4, #9, #14, #16 or #24 to Muntplein

Now part of the university, a striking set of seventeenth-century **canal houses** has survived just beyond the Allard Pierson Museum at **Oude Turfmarkt 141–147**. Each is graced by a bottle- or spout-shaped gable, elegant reminders of the area's commercial heyday before the 1930s, when most of the Rokin canal was filled in.

1 The Red Light District and around

The whole area to the east of Damrak, between Warmoesstraat, Nieuwmarkt and Damstraat, is the **Red Light District**, known locally as "**De Wallen**" ("The Walls") on account of the series of low brick walls that contain its canals. By and large, the area is pretty seedy, though the legalized prostitution here has long been one of the city's most distinctive and popular draws. It wasn't always so: the handsome facades of **Oudezijds Voorburgwal** in particular recall ritzier days, when this was one of the wealthiest parts of the city, richly earning its nickname the "Velvet Canal". Nowadays, both Oudezijds Voorburgwal and its twin **Oudezijds Achterburgwal** – plus their narrow connecting passages – are thronged with "**window brothels**" and at busy times the on-street haggling over the price of various sex acts is drowned out by a surprisingly festive atmosphere, with entire families grinning more or less amiably at the women in the windows or discussing the specifications (and feasibility) of the sex toys in the shops. In recent years, the city council has made determined efforts to clean the district up, so the drug addicts, dealers and hawkers that once infested the area are far less prominent, but there's still an uneasy undertow that might put you off dawdling. And don't even think about taking a picture of a "window brothel" unless you're prepared for some major grief from the prostitutes or their pimps.

Window brothels and sex shops aside, the district does contain two prime attractions: the medieval **Oude Kerk** and the clandestine Catholic church of **Ons' Lieve Heer Op Solder**. Further south, the Red Light District fizzles out by the time you reach **Damstraat**, beyond which both Oudezijds Voorburgwal and Oudezijds Achterburgwal become positively respectable.

Warmoesstraat

Tram #4, #9, #16 or #24 to the Dam, or a 10min walk from Centraal Station

Soliciting hasn't always been the principal activity on sleazy **Warmoesstraat**. It was once one of the city's most fashionable streets, home to Holland's foremost poet, **Joost van den Vondel** (1587–1679), who ran his hosiery business from no. 110 in between writing and hobnobbing with the Amsterdam elite – a plaque on the Art Nouveau building that now stands here marks the spot. Vondel was a kind of Dutch Shakespeare; his *Gijsbrecht van Amstel*, a celebration of Amsterdam during its Golden Age, is one of the classics of Dutch literature, and he wrote regular, if ponderous, official verses, including well over a thousand lines on the inauguration of the town hall. Vondel had more than his share of hard luck too: his son frittered away the modest family fortune and Joost lived out his last few years as doorkeeper of the pawnshop on Oudezijds Voorburgwal known as "Ome Jan" (see page 49), dying of hypothermia at what was then the remarkable age of 92. Witty to the end, he suggested his own epitaph: "Here lies Vondel, your grief withhold, for he hath suffered death from cold". His name lives on most prominently in the city's largest park, the Vondelpark (see page 116).

The Prostitution Information Centre (PIC)

Enge Kerksteeg 3, just off Oudekerksplein • Wed–Fri 10am–5pm, Sat 10am–7pm; prebooked tours Wed, Fri & Sat at 5pm; 1hr 30min • Tours €17.50 (self-guided tour €3) • ☎ 020 420 7328, ⍟ www.pic-amsterdam.com • Tram #4, #9, #16 or #24 to the Dam, or a 10min walk from Centraal Station

A legally recognized *stichting* or charitable foundation, the **Prostitution Information Centre**, right by the Oude Kerk and flanked by window brothels, was founded in 1994 by Mariska Majoor, a former sex worker. Her main aim was to provide prostitutes, their clients and visitors with clear, dispassionate information about the industry – and

1

COMMERCIAL SEX IN AMSTERDAM

Developed in the 1960s, the Netherlands'– and especially Amsterdam's – liberal approach to social policy has had several unforeseen consequences, the most dramatic being its international reputation as a centre for both drugs and **prostitution**. However, the tackiness of the **Red Light District** is just the surface sheen on what has been a serious attempt to address the reality of sex for sale, and to integrate this within a normal, ordered society. In Dutch law, prostitution has long been legal, but the state had always drawn the line at brothels and soliciting in public. The difficulties this created for the police were legion, so finally, in 1996, a special **soliciting zone** was established and four years later brothels **brothels** were legalized in the hope that together these changes would bring a degree of stability to the sex industry: in particular, it was thought that the regulation of "**window brothels**" would reduce the number of sex workers who plied their trade illicitly in bars and hotels. These changes were partly the result of a long and determined campaign by **De Rode Draad** (The Red Thread), a sex workers' advocacy group-cum-trade union, which did much to improve the lot of its members by fighting for regular employment rights before it went bankrupt in 2009.

In the event, the new legislation created new problems: almost at a stroke, full-on legalization turned the city's sex trade into a much bigger business, one that was attractive to – and increasingly run by – **organized crime**, gangsters who were adept at pimping and human trafficking. Mindful of these issues, the mayor of Amsterdam **Job Cohen** took action, refusing licenses for many of the larger brothels and closing about a third of the window brothels (dropping from almost 500 in 2007 to just under 300 now). Moreover, the peep shows, strip clubs and window brothels sit alongside indie art galleries, boutiques and thrift shops. Since 2007 the national government has also been tightening regulations, raising the legal age of sex-for-sale from 18 to 21 in 2013 and looking at compulsory registration schemes for sex workers, which has provoked a lot of controversy, especially among the brothel owners. In May 2017, a window brothel run by sex workers – My Red Light – was set up with the help of a progressive mayor to empower workers and help create a safe working environment. Whatever the outcome, it seems likely that the number of prostitutes in Amsterdam will diminish further over the next few years, and the district may begin to take on a very different complexion.

thereby encourage mutual respect or at least greater understanding. The centre holds a small café and shop, the **Wallenwinkel**, which sells books, pamphlets and souvenirs of the Red Light District – postcards, fridge magnets, T-shirts and the like; the PIC also runs ninety-minute **tours** of the Red Light District.

The Oude Kerk

Oudekerksplein 23 • Mon–Sat 10am–6pm, Sun 1–5.30pm • €10 • ☎ 020 625 8284, ⊛ oudekerk.nl • Tram #4, #9, #16, #24 or #25 to the Dam, or a 10min walk from Centraal Station

Bang in the middle of the Red Light District is Amsterdam's most appealing church, the **Oude Kerk**, an attractive Gothic structure with high-pitched gables and finely worked lancet windows. There's been a church on this site since the middle of the thirteenth century, but most of the present building dates from a century later, funded by the pilgrims who came here in their hundreds following a widely publicized **miracle**. The story goes that, in 1345, a dying man regurgitated the Host he had received here at Communion, and when it was thrown on the fire afterwards, it did not burn. The unburnable Host was placed in a chest and installed in a long-lost chapel somewhere off Nieuwezijds Voorburgwal, before finally being transferred to the Oude Kerk a few years later. It disappeared during the Reformation, but to this day thousands of the faithful still come to take part in the annual **Stille Omgang**, a silent nocturnal procession held in mid-March and terminating at the Oude Kerk. The church is also regularly used for art displays and concerts.

The interior
The Protestants cleared the church of almost all of its ecclesiastical paraphernalia during the Reformation, but its largely bare, three-aisled **interior** does hold several interesting features. These include some folksy misericords, an exquisite wooden vaulted ceiling and the unadorned memorial tablet of **Rembrandt**'s first wife, Saskia van Uylenburgh, beneath (and just to the left of) the smaller of the two organs. Much more diverting, however, are the three beautifully coloured **stained-glass windows** beside the ambulatory in what was once the Chapel of Our Lady. Dating from the 1550s, all three depict religious scenes – from left to right: the Annunciation, the Adoration of the Shepherds and the Assumption of the Virgin – and each is set above its respective donors. The characters are shown in Classical gear with togas and sandals and the buildings in the background are firmly Classical too, reflecting both artistic fashion and a belief that Greco-Roman detail was historically accurate. A fourth, rather different stained-glass window is located on the other side of the ambulatory.

A secular piece from 1655, it features the Spanish king Philip IV ceding independence to a representative of the United Provinces (the Netherlands) under the terms of the Treaty of Munster of 1648, part of the Peace of Westphalia which wrapped up the Thirty Years' War. Like the earlier windows, the architectural backdrop is Classical, but here it's to emphasize the dignity of the proceedings – and the king and the Dutch emissaries wear contemporary clothes.

The Oudekerkstoren
Oudekerksplein • Tours: April–Oct Mon–Sat 1–7pm, every 30min • €8 • ☎ 020 625 8284, ⓦ oudekerk.nl

The tower of the Oude Kerk – the **Oudekerkstoren** – is the oldest in the city. From the top there are grand views over the centre, with the Red Light District in the foreground – though whether the view justifies the hefty admission charge is a matter of debate.

Ons' Lieve Heer Op Solder
Oudezijds Voorburgwal 38 • Mon–Sat 10am–6pm, Sun 1–6pm • €11 • ☎ 020 624 6604, ⓦ opsolder.nl • Tram #4, #9, #16 or #24 to the Dam, or a 10min walk from Centraal Station

The northern reaches of Oudezijds Voorburgwal are flanked by a series of handsome, seventeenth-century canal houses, among which is the delightful **Ons' Lieve Heer Op Solder** (Our Dear Lord in the Attic), which was momentarily the city's principal Catholic place of worship and is now one of Amsterdam's most enjoyable museums.

Despite the *Alteratie* of 1578 (see page 227), the new Protestant regime treated its Catholics relatively well – commercial pragmatism has always outweighed religious zeal here – but there was a degree of discrimination; Catholic churches were recycled for Protestant use and their members no longer allowed to practise openly. The result was an eccentric compromise: Catholics were allowed to hold services in any private building providing that the exterior revealed no sign of their activities – hence the development of the city's **clandestine churches** (*schuilkerken*), of which the Ons' Lieve Heer op Solder is the only one to have survived intact. Incidentally, the museum was formerly known as – and is still sometimes called – the **Amstelkring**, meaning "Amstel Circle", after the group of nineteenth-century historians who saved the building from demolition. There's a bright and airy café and a gift shop, too.

The interior
Visitors begin by threading their way up through the old merchant's house, which has been restored to something like its seventeenth-century appearance with furnishings and fittings reminiscent of interiors by Vermeer or de Hooch, and complete with a confessional box and priest's room. Eventually you reach the loft, where the narrow **nave** of Ons' Lieve Heer op Solder has been skilfully shoehorned into the available space. Overlooked by elegant balconies, the nave has an ornately carved organ at one

1

end and a mock-marble high altar, decorated with Jacob de Wit's mawkish *Baptism of Christ*, at the other. Even the patron of the church, one Jan Hartman, clearly had doubts about de Wit's efforts – the two spares he procured just in case are now displayed behind the altar.

Zeedijk

A 5min walk from Centraal Station

Curving round the northern edge of the Red Light District is **Zeedijk**, which was originally just that – a dyke to hold back the sea – but it's now a busy thoroughfare linking Stationsplein with Nieuwmarkt. Until fairly recently, this narrow street was the haunt of drug addicts, and a no-go area at night, but it's been cleaned up and is currently flourishing as the main hub of Amsterdam's small but vibrant **Chinatown**. There are numerous Chinese, Thai and Vietnamese restaurants here as well as a Buddhist temple, the garish **Fo Guang Shan He Hua**, near the south end of the street at Zeedijk 106. At its north end, Zeedijk abuts the *Prins Hendrik Hotel*, where Chet Baker breathed his last (see page 36).

Nieuwmarkt

Metro Nieuwmarkt or a 15min walk from Centraal Station

The eastern reaches of the Red Light District peter out at cobbled **Nieuwmarkt**, a wide-open, airy square that was long one of the city's most important marketplaces, and the place where Gentiles and Jews from the nearby Jewish quarter (see Chapter 4) – just southeast along St Antoniesbreestraat – traded. All that came to a traumatic end during World War II, when the Germans cordoned off the Nieuwmarkt with barbed wire and turned it into a holding pen. After the war, the square's old exuberance never returned, though it does host a few fruit and veg stalls from Monday to Friday, a small organic food market on Saturday, and an antiques and book market on summer Sundays (see page 200).

The Waag

The focus of Nieuwmarkt is the multi-turreted **Waag**, which was built as one of the city's fortified gates – Sint Antoniespoort – in the 1480s. It was no sooner built than Amsterdam's expansion made it obsolete and the ground floor was turned into a municipal weighing-house, with the rooms upstairs taken over by the surgeons' guild. It was here that the surgeons held lectures on anatomy and public dissections, the inspiration for Rembrandt's *Anatomy Lesson of Dr Tulp*, displayed in the Mauritshuis collection in The Hague. Abandoned by the surgeons and the weigh-masters in the nineteenth century, the building served as a furniture store and a fire station before falling into disuse, though it is now a café-bar and restaurant (ⓦindewaag.nl).

The Hash Marihuana Hemp Museum

Oudezijds Achterburgwal 148 • Daily 10am–10pm • €9 • ☏ 020 624 8926, ⓦ hashmuseum.com • Metro Nieuwmarkt or tram #4, #9, #16 or #24 to the Dam

The long-established **Hash Marihuana Hemp Museum**, on the southern edge of the Red Light District, features displays on various types of dope and the numerous ways there are to consume it. The museum also exhibits all manner of cannabis-related artefacts, samples of textiles and paper made with hemp and pamphlets explaining the medicinal properties of cannabis. There's a gift shop too, selling pipes, books, videos and souvenirs. Amsterdam's reliance on imported dope ended in the late 1980s with the emergence of hydroponic growing techniques, whereby marijuana – and in particular a variety bred in America, called skunk – was able to flourish under artificial lights and without soil. Nowadays well over half the dope sold in the city's coffeeshops is grown in the Netherlands, and this museum is positively evangelical about how to join in.

The Spinhuis

Spinhuissteeg 1, adjacent to Oudezijds Achterburgwal 187 • No public access • Tram #4, #9, #16 or #24 to Spui

Once a house of correction for "fallen women", the **Spinhuis** has been turned into offices, but the old front door has survived intact, with an inscription by the seventeenth-century Dutch poet Pieter Cornelisz Hooft: "Cry not, for I exact no vengeance for wrong but to force you to be good. My hand is stern but my heart is kind." Such moralizing is unlikely to have impressed the inmates, who endured long hours and harsh discipline working on the Spinhuis's looms and spinning wheels. Curiously, workhouses like this used to figure on tourist itineraries; for a small fee the public was allowed to watch the women at work, and at carnival times admission was free and large crowds came to jeer and mock. The justification for this was that shame was supposed to be part of the reforming process, but in fact the municipality unofficially tolerated brothels and the incarcerated women had simply been singled out for exemplary punishment.

Ome Jan

Oudezijds Voorburgwal 300 • No public access • Tram #4, #9, #16 or #24 to Spui

The large brick and stone-trimmed building at Oudezijds Voorburgwal 300 has been known as **Ome Jan** ("Uncle John's") ever since the days when it was central Amsterdam's pawnshop. The poet **Vondel** (see page 44) ended his days working here, and a short verse above the fancy stone entranceway, which comes complete with the city's coat of arms, extols the virtues of the pawnshop – and the evils of usury.

Huis op de Drie Grachten and around

Tram #4, #9, #16 or #24 to Spui

At the southern end of **Oudezijds Voorburgwal**, the appealing **Galerie Mokum** art shop (see page 192), at no. 334, uses the old Jewish nickname for the city, but the prettiest building hereabouts is the early seventeenth-century step-gabled **Huis op de Drie Grachten** (House on the Three Canals), at Oudezijds Voorburgwal 249, whose red shutters and mullion windows sit on the corner with Oudezijds Achterburgwal. The character of the city changes just across the canal to the south, where a narrow nub of land is packed with **university** buildings, mostly modern or nineteenth-century structures built in the Dutch vernacular style.

Kloveniersburgwal and around

Dug in the fifteenth century, long and dead-straight **Kloveniersburgwal** was once part of the city's defences, forming a watery ring round medieval Amsterdam together with Geldersekade and the Singel. As the city expanded, it lost its original function, its walls demolished to make way for the mansions of the well-heeled, the most extravagant of which was the **Trippenhuis**, which survives today. The canal takes its name from a division of the Civic Guard, the *kloveniers* (literally "arquebusiers"), who were themselves named after the heavy, muzzle-loaded firearm they carried; Rembrandt painted the *kloveniers* in his famed group portrait *The Night Watch*, which now hangs in the Rijksmuseum (see page 106).

From Kloveniersburgwal, it's a short hop over to one of the city's prettiest canals, **Groenburgwal**, and one of Amsterdam's principal churches, the **Zuiderkerk**.

KLEINE TRIPPENHUIS

On the west bank of the Kloveniersburgwal canal, at no. 26, the **Kleine Trippenhuis**, now a lingerie shop, is one of the narrowest houses in Amsterdam, albeit with an attractively carved facade and a balustrade featuring a brace of centaurs. Legend has it that the coachman of the Trip family (see below) was so taken aback by the size of the new family mansion that he exclaimed he would be happy with a home no wider than the Trips' front door – which is exactly what he got. His reaction to his new lodgings is not recorded.

The Trippenhuis

Kloveniersburgwal 29 • No public access • Metro Nieuwmarkt or a 15min walk from Centraal Station

Built for the Trip family in 1662, the **Trippenhuis**, on the east side of Kloveniersburgwal, is a grand, if somewhat overblown, mansion which comes complete with Corinthian pilasters and a grand frieze. The Trips, who made their money as arms dealers and manufacturers, were one of the richest families in Amsterdam and a powerful force among the **Magnificat**, the clique of families (Six, Trip, Hooft and Pauw) who shared power during the Golden Age. One part of the Trip family dealt with the Baltic trade, another with the manufacture of munitions (in which they had the municipal monopoly), but in addition they also had trade interests in Russia and the Middle East, much like the multinationals of today. In the nineteenth century the Rijksmuseum collection was displayed here, but the house now contains the Dutch Academy of Sciences (◍knaw.nl).

The Oostindisch Huis

Kloveniersburgwal 48 • No public access • Tram #4, #9, #16 or #24 to the Dam

The **Oostindisch Huis**, the former headquarters of the Dutch East India Company, occupies a monumental red-brick structure with high-pitched gables and perky dormer windows at the corner of Oude Hoogstraat. Built in 1605 shortly after the founding of the Company, it was from here that the directors organized and regulated their immensely lucrative trading interests in the Far East, importing shiploads of spices, perfumes and exotic woods. This trade underpinned Amsterdam's Golden Age; predictably, the people of what is now Indonesia, the source of most of the raw materials, received little in return. Nevertheless, despite the building's historic significance, the interior is of little interest today, being occupied by university classrooms and offices.

The Oudemanhuispoort

Book stalls Mon–Sat 9am–5pm • Tram #4, #9, #14, #16 or #24 to Spui

Once part of an almshouse complex for elderly men – hence the unusual name – the **Oudemanhuispoort** is now no more than the covered passageway linking Kloveniersburgwal and Oudezijds Achterburgwal. It accommodates a string of **secondhand book stalls**, which make for an excellent browse.

Staalstraat

Tram #4, #9, #14, #16 or #24 to Spui

A dinky little bridge spans the southern end of Kloveniersburgwal to reach pedestrianized **Staalstraat**, which cuts across one of the most picturesque corners of the city on its way to Waterlooplein (see page 85). Staalstraat offers an especially lovely view down **Groenburgwal**, a narrow and almost impossibly pretty waterway framed by dignified old canal houses with the Zuiderkerk looming beyond.

The Zuiderkerk

Zuiderkerkhof • Open for special events and concerts only • ☎ 020 308 0399, ⓦ zuiderkerkamsterdam.nl • Metro Nieuwmarkt

Dating from 1611, the **Zuiderkerk** was the first church in Amsterdam to be built specifically for the Protestants. It was designed by the prolific architect and sculptor, **Hendrick de Keyser** (see page 61), whose distinctive – and very popular – style extrapolated elements of traditional Flemish design with fanciful detail and frilly towers added wherever possible. De Keyser stuck to a Gothic design for the main body of the church, but the soaring **Zuidertoren** (tower) is a fine illustration of his work, with balconies and balustrades, arches, urns and columns.

The church was deconsecrated in the 1930s, but it was here that the bodies of the dead were temporarily stored and piled up during the terrible winter – the "Hunger Winter" – of 1944–45. Nowadays it's used for events, concerts and conferences.

St Antoniesbreestraat

Metro Nieuwmarkt

Once an important thoroughfare linking Nieuwmarkt and the city centre with the Jewish quarter, **St Antoniesbreestraat** lost its huddle of old shops and houses in the 1980s when they were demolished to make way for a main road, which – as it turned out – was never built. The buildings that flank much of the street today hardly fire the soul, even if the modern symmetries – and Cubist coloured panels – of the apartment blocks that sprawl along part of it are visually arresting.

Huis de Pinto

St Antoniesbreestraat 69 • Mon–Fri 10.30am–5.30pm, Sat 1–5pm • Free • ☎ 020 370 0210, ⓦ huisdepinto.nl

St Antoniesbreestraat may have been assaulted by the developers, but the **Huis** de **Pinto** has somehow managed to survive, and has been turned into a community cultural centre. Easily spotted by its off-white Italianate **facade**, the house is named after Isaac de Pinto, a Jew who fled Portugal to escape the Inquisition and subsequently became a founder of the Dutch East India Company (see page 95). Pinto bought this property in 1651 and had it remodelled in grand style, with a facade interrupted by six lofty pilasters that lead the eye up to the blind balustrade. The mansion was the talk of the town, even more so when de Pinto had the **interior** painted in a similar style – pop in to admire the birds and cherubs of the original painted ceiling.

GRACHTENGORDEL GABLES

The Grachtengordel

The western reaches of medieval Amsterdam were once enclosed by the Singel, part of the city's protective moat, but this is now just the first of five canals that stretch right around the city centre, extending anticlockwise from Brouwersgracht to the River Amstel in a "girdle of canals", or Grachtengordel. This is without doubt the most charming part of Amsterdam, a lattice of olive-green waterways and little humpback bridges overlooked by street upon street of handsome seventeenth-century canal houses, almost undisturbed by later development. It's the district's laidback, easy-going atmosphere that appeals, rather than any specific sight, with one remarkable exception: the Anne Frank Huis, where the young Jewish diarist hid from the Germans in World War II.

The Grachtengordel is a subtle cityscape – full of surprises, with a bizarre carving here, an unusual facade stone (used to denote name and occupation) there – and one in which the **gables** overlooking the canals gradually evolved (see page 54). The grandest Grachtengordel houses are concentrated along the so-called **De Gouden Bocht** – the Golden Bend – on Herengracht between Leidsestraat and the Amstel. Here, the architectural decorum – and arguably the aesthetic vigour – of the seventeenth century are left behind for the overblown, French-influenced mansions that became popular with the city's richest merchants in the 1700s. In addition to the unmissable **Anne Frank Huis**, the area's highlights include the **Tassenmuseum Hendrikje** of bags and purses, and a pair of restored merchants' mansions, the **Museum Willet-Holthuysen** and the **Museum Van Loon**.

Brief history

The three main **Grachtengordel canals** – **Herengracht** (Gentlemen's Canal), **Keizersgracht** (Emperor's Canal, named after the Holy Roman Emperor and fifteenth-century patron of the city, Maximilian) and **Prinsengracht** (Princes' Canal, named in honour of the princes of the House of Orange) – were dug in the seventeenth century as part of a comprehensive plan to extend the boundaries of a city no longer able to accommodate its burgeoning population. The idea was that the council would buy up the land around the city, dig the canals, and lease plots back to developers, thus increasing the size of the city from two to seven square kilometres. The plan was passed by the city council in 1607 and work began six years later, against a backdrop of corruption, with Amsterdammers in the know buying up the land they knew the city would soon have to purchase.

It was a monumental task, and the conditions imposed by the council were strict. The three **main waterways** were set aside for the residences and businesses of the richer and more influential Amsterdam merchants, while the **radial cross streets** were reserved for more modest artisans' homes. Meanwhile, newly arrived immigrants set to cash in on Amsterdam's booming economy were assigned, albeit informally, to the Jodenhoek – "Jews' Corner" – (see Chapter 4) and the Jordaan (see Chapter 3).

In the Grachtengordel, everyone – even the wealthiest merchant – had to comply with a set of strict and detailed **planning regulations**. In particular, the council prescribed the size of each building plot – the frontage was set at 30ft, the depth 200 – and although there was a degree of tinkering, the end result was the loose conformity you can see today: tall, **narrow residences**, whose individualism is mainly restricted to the stylistic permutations among the gables (see page 54). Even the colour of the front doors was once regulated, with choice restricted to a shade that has since become known as "Amsterdam Green" – still something of a rarity outside the Netherlands. It took decades to complete the project, but by the 1690s it was all pretty much finished off – at a time, ironically, when Amsterdam was in economic decline.

In essence, the Grachtengordel is a tribute to the architectural tastes of the city's middle class, an amalgam of personal wealth and aesthetic uniformity – individuality and order – that epitomized Amsterdam's Protestant bourgeoisie in its pomp.

GRACHTENGORDEL ORIENTATION

This chapter covers the first four canals of the Grachtengordel – the Singel, Herengracht, Keizersgracht and Prinsengracht – as they sweep down from Brouwersgracht to the Amstel. For the purposes of this guide, the district has been split into two: **Grachtengordel west** and **Grachtengordel south** – divided at roughly the halfway point, **Leidsegracht**. There's no obvious walking route around the area – indeed you may well prefer to wander around as the mood takes you – but the description given here goes from north to south, taking in all the highlights on the way. On all three of the main canals, **street numbers** begin at Brouwersgracht and increase as you go south.

2

THE GRACHTENGORDEL'S GABLES

More than any other architectural feature it's the **gable** that distinguishes Amsterdam's old houses. The earliest, dating from the early seventeenth century, are **crow-stepped gables**, but these were largely superseded from the 1650s onwards by **neck gables** and **bell gables**, both named for the shape of the gable top. Some are embellished, many have decorative cornices, and the fanciest – which mostly date from the eighteenth century – sport full-scale **balustrades**. The plainest gables are those of former **warehouses**, where the deep-arched and shuttered windows line up on either side of loft doors that were once used for loading and unloading goods, winched by pulley from the street down below. Indeed, outside **pulleys** remain a common feature of houses and warehouses alike, and are often still in use as the easiest way of moving furniture into the city's myriad apartments.

Grachtengordel west

Stretching south from Brouwersgracht to the Leidsegracht, **Grachtengordel west** boasts a fine selection of seventeenth-century canal houses. These are perhaps at their prettiest along **Herengracht** between Wolvenstraat and Leidsegracht, and this is where you'll also find the **Bijbels Museum** (Bible Museum), home to an idiosyncratic assortment of models of ancient Jewish temples. Nevertheless, easily the most popular attraction hereabouts is the **Anne Frank Huis**, on Prinsengracht, which is itself just a short stroll from the soaring architecture of the **Westerkerk**. In recent years, the area has become one of the city's top spots for **shopping**: north of Leidsegracht, the main canals, Herengracht, Keizersgracht and Prinsengracht, are intersected by cross streets lined with shops. The focus is the **Negen Straatjes** (see page 191), where you can buy everything from handmade chocolates to designer toothbrushes – Amsterdam at its creative, imaginative best.

Brouwersgracht

A 5min walk from Centraal Station

Running east to west along the northern edge of the three main canals is **Brouwersgracht**, one of the most picturesque waterways in the city. Look down any of the major canals from here and you'll see the gentle interplay of water, barge, brick and stone that gives the city its distinctive allure. In the seventeenth century, Brouwersgracht lay at the edge of Amsterdam's great harbour and was one of the major arteries linking the open sea with the city centre. Thronged by vessels returning from – or heading off to – every corner of the globe, it was lined with storage depots and warehouses. **Breweries** flourished here too – hence its name – capitalizing on their ready access to shipments of fresh water. Today, the harbour bustle has moved way out of the centre to the northwest, and the **warehouses**, with their distinctive spout-neck gables and shuttered windows, have been converted into some of the most expensive apartments in the city. There's an especially fine uninterrupted row of these warehouses at **Brouwersgracht 172–212**, on the north side of the canal just beyond Prinsengracht. You'll also find some handsome merchants' houses on Brouwersgracht, as well as moored houseboats and a string of quaint little swing bridges, making it altogether one of the prettiest canals in the whole of the city and a pleasant area for a stroll.

The Noordermarkt

ⓦ jordaanmarkten.nl • A 7min walk from Centraal Station

In the shadow of the Noorderkerk (see page 56), the **Noordermarkt** is a large, if somewhat unimpressive, square located just south of Brouwersgracht, along the west side of Prinsengracht. The square comes to life on market days: there's a popular

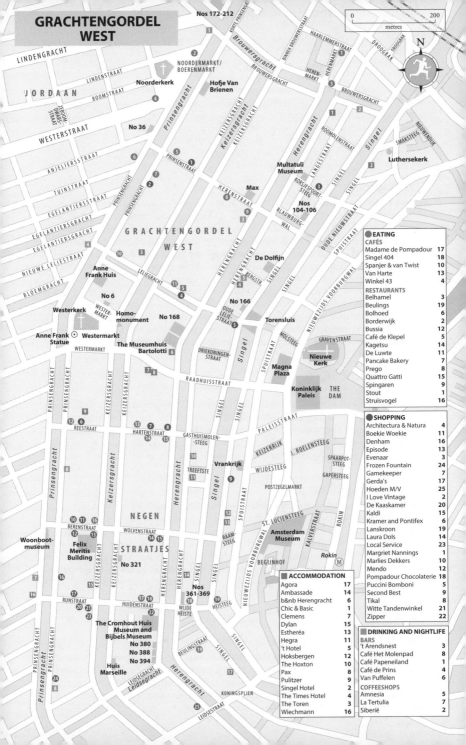

GRACHTENGORDEL WEST

Nos 172–212

LINDENGRACHT

JORDAAN

WESTERSTRAAT

LINDENSTRAAT
BOOMSTRAAT

Noorderkerk
No 36

STRAAT
ANJELIERS
2DE-ANJ
1STE-AN

ANJELIERSSTRAAT

TUINSTRAAT

EGELANTIERSSTRAAT

EGELANTIERSGRACHT

EGELANTIERSGRACHT

NIEUWE LELIESTRAAT

BLOEMGRACHT

Anne
Frank Huis

No 6

Westerkerk   WESTER-   Homo-
MARKT   monument   No 168

Anne Frank   Westermarkt
Statue

WESTERMARKT   The Museumhuis
Bartolotti

DRIEKONINGEN-
STRAAT

RAADHUISSTRAAT

PRINSENGRACHT
PRINSENGRACHT
KEIZERSGRACHT
KEIZERSGRACHT

REESTRAAT

HARTENSTRAAT

GASTHUISMOLEN-
STEEG

Vrankrijk

TREEFTSTE

NEGEN

Woonboot-
museum

BERENSTRAAT

Felix
Meritis
Building

WOLVENSTRAAT

STRAATJES   No 321

Nos
361–369

RUNSTRAAT

HUIDENSTRAAT

The Cromhout Huis
Museum and
Bijbels Museum   No 380

No 388

No 394

Huis
Marseille

LEIDSEGRACHT
Leidsegracht

BEULINGSTRAAT

KONINGSPLEIN

LEIDSESTRAAT

NOORDERMARKT/
BOERENMARKT

Hofje Van
Brienen

KEIZERSGRACHT
KEIZERSGRACHT
KEIZERSGRACHT

PRINSENSTRAAT

HERENSTRAAT   Max

Nos
104–106

BLAUWBURG-
WAL

De Dolfijn

No 166

OUDE
LELIE-
STRAAT

Torensluis

BROUWERSGRACHT
Brouwersgracht

BROUWERSGRACHT

HERENGRACHT

ROOMOLENSTRAAT

LANGESTRAAT

KORSJESPOORT-
STEEG

NIEUWEZIJDS VOORBURGWAL

GRAVENSTRAAT

Nieuwe
Kerk

Magna
Plaza

Koninklijk   THE
Paleis   DAM

KONTE PRINSENGR

BROUWERSGRACHT

BINNEN BROUWERSSTRAAT

HAARLEMMERSTRAAT

HAARLEMMERDIJK

HEREN-
MARKT

Singel

SMAKSTEEG
NIEUWENDIJK

Luthersekerk

SPUISTRAAT

OUDE NIEUWSTRAAT

MOLSTEEG

SPUISTRAAT

PALEISSTRAAT

KEIZERRIJK   J. ROELENSTEEG

WIJDESTEEG

POSTZEGELMARKT

SPAARPOT-
STEEG

GAPERSTEEG

ST. LUCIENSTEEG

KALVERSTRAAT   ROKIN

Amsterdam
Museum

Rokin   M

BEGIJNHOF

NIEUWEZIJDS VOORBURGWAL

HEISTEEG

WIJDE HEISTE

DROOGBAK

N

Multatuli
Museum

GRACHTENGORDEL
WEST

0   200
metres

EATING

CAFÉS
Madame de Pompadour	17
Singel 404	18
Spanjer & van Twist	10
Van Harte	13
Winkel 43	4

RESTAURANTS
Belhamel	3
Beulings	19
Bolhoed	6
Borderwijk	2
Bussia	12
Café de Klepel	5
Kagetsu	14
De Luwte	11
Pancake Bakery	7
Prego	8
Quattro Gatti	15
Spingaren	9
Stout	1
Struisvogel	16

SHOPPING
Architectura & Natura	4
Boekie Woekie	11
Denham	16
Episode	13
Evenaar	3
Frozen Fountain	24
Gamekeeper	7
Gerda's	17
Hoeden M/V	25
I Love Vintage	2
De Kaaskamer	20
Kaldi	15
Kramer and Pontifex	6
Lanskroon	19
Laura Dols	14
Local Service	23
Margriet Nannings	1
Marlies Dekkers	10
Mendo	12
Pompadour Chocolaterie	18
Puccini Bomboni	5
Second Best	9
Tikal	8
Witte Tandenwinkel	21
Zipper	22

ACCOMMODATION
Agora	17
Ambassade	14
b&nb Herengracht	6
Chic & Basic	1
Clemens	7
Dylan	15
Estheréa	13
Hegra	11
't Hotel	5
Hoksbergen	12
The Hoxton	10
Pax	8
Pulitzer	9
Singel Hotel	4
The Times Hotel	2
The Toren	3
Wiechmann	16

DRINKING AND NIGHTLIFE

BARS
't Arendsnest	3
Café Het Molenpad	8
Café Papeneiland	1
Café de Prins	4
Van Puffelen	6

COFFEESHOPS
Amnesia	5
La Tertulia	7
Siberië	2

farmers' market, the Boerenmarkt, on Saturdays (see page 200), a lively affair with organic fruit and vegetables, freshly baked bread and a plethora of oils and spices for sale. Alongside is the Noordermarkt flea market, selling antiques, curios, jewellery, records and much more besides (see page 200).

Look out also for a **statue** of three figures bound to each other, a poignant tribute to the bloody Jordaanoproer riot of 1934, part of a successful campaign to stop the government cutting unemployment benefits during the Depression; you'll find the statue just in front of the church's west door. The inscription reads "The strongest chains are those of unity". Pinned to the outside of the church, there's also a **plaque** remembering the Communists and Jews who were rounded up here by the Germans in February 1941.

The Noorderkerk

Noordermarkt • Mon 10.30am–12.30pm, Sat 11am–1pm • Free • ☎ 020 626 6436, ⊛ noorderkerk.org • A 7min walk from Centraal Station

Louring over the Noordermarkt is Hendrick de Keyser's **Noorderkerk**, the architect's last creation and probably his least successful, finished two years after his death in 1623. A bulky, overbearing brick building, it represented a radical departure from the conventional church designs of the time, having a symmetrical Greek cross floor plan, with four equally proportioned arms radiating out from a steepled centre. Uncompromisingly dour, it proclaimed the serious intent of the Calvinists who worshiped here in so far as the pulpit – and therefore the preacher – was at the centre and not at the front of the church, a symbolic break with the Catholic past. Nevertheless, it's still hard to understand quite how de Keyser, who designed such elegant structures as the Westerkerk, could have ended up creating this. Weekly concerts are held here every Saturday at 2pm from June to September – see ⊛ noorderkerkconcerten.nl.

Prinsengracht 36

A 7min walk from Centraal Station

Just along the canal from the Noordermarkt stands **Prinsengracht 36**, whose especially well-proportioned – if attenuated – facade dates from 1650. The fancily decorated neck gable is the feature that catches the eye, but the pilasters are much more architecturally unusual. Look out also for the pulley for winching things up the outside of the building – and the little door beneath it providing access to what was once a storage area.

The Hofje Van Brienen

Prinsengracht 85–133 • Mon–Fri 9am–6pm, Sat 9am–2pm • Free • A 7min walk from Centraal Station

A trim, brown-brick courtyard complex on the site of what was once a brewery, the **Hofje Van Brienen** was built as an almshouse in 1804 to the order of a certain Arnout van Brienen, who added a matching brick church (no entry) for good measure. A well-to-do merchant, van Brienen had locked himself in his own strongroom by accident and, in a panic, he vowed that if he was rescued he would build a *hofje* (see page 74) – he was and he did.

Herenstraat

Tram #1, #2, #5, #13 or #17 to Nieuwezijds Kolk

Near the Hofje Van Brienen is the most northerly of the Grachtengordel's cross streets, **Prinsenstraat** and its continuation **Herenstraat**, where the old tradesmen's houses, with their high gables and ground-floor commercial premises, now accommodate a string of knick-knack and clothes shops. This is Amsterdam shopping at its most enjoyable – and there's an architectural surprise here too: the *Restaurant Max*, at Herenstraat 14, possesses a delightful Art Deco facade.

Blauwburgwal

Tram #1, #2, #5, #13 or #17 to Nieuwezijds Kolk

Herenstraat opens out into the **Blauwburgwal**, a short and inordinately pretty slip of a canal, which had the misfortune to be hit by a bomb during the German invasion of 1940. The bomber in question had been damaged by anti-aircraft fire and dropped its load at random. This was very much a one-off: the speed of the German occupation meant that central Amsterdam was hardly damaged at all, though this incident alone cost 44 lives.

2

The Multatuli Museum

Korsjespoortsteeg 20, just off Herengracht • Tues 10am–5pm, Wed–Sun noon–5pm • Free, but donation appreciated • ☎ 020 638 1938, ⓦ multatuli-museum.nl • Tram #1, #2, #5, #13 or #17 to Nieuwezijds Kolk

Amsterdam's tiniest museum, the **Multatuli Museum**, occupies the birthplace and family home of **Eduard Douwes Dekker** (1820–87), Holland's most celebrated nineteenth-century writer and a champion of free thinking, who wrote under the pen name Multatuli. Dekker worked as a colonial official in the Dutch East Indies for eighteen years, becoming increasingly disgusted by the graft and corruption. He returned to Amsterdam in 1856 and spent the next four years encapsulating his East Indies experiences in the elegantly written satirical novel *Max Havelaar*, which enraged the Dutch merchant class, but is now something of a Dutch literary classic (see page 256). The museum's one room is filled with letters, first editions and a small selection of his furnishings, including the chaise longue on which he breathed his last.

Singel 104–166

Tram #1, #2, #5, #13 or #17 to Nieuwezijds Kolk

Equipped with the largest bell gables in the city, **Singel 104–106** are twin mansions dating to the 1740s, though what they boast in size they lack in elegance. Further south is the red-brick and stone-trimmed **De Dolfijn** (The Dolphin), at nos. 140–142. This was once home of Captain Banningh Cocq, one of the militiamen depicted in Rembrandt's *The Night Watch* (see page 109), but it takes its name from a late sixteenth-century Dutch grammar book written by the first owner, one Hendrick Spieghel. Nearby, **Singel 166** has the narrowest facade in the city – just 1.8m wide. It overlooks the **Torensluis**, easily the widest bridge in the Grachtengordel and decorated with a whopping bust of Multatuli (see above).

Leliegracht

Tram #13, #14 or #17 to Westermarkt

One of the tiny radial canals that cut across the Grachtengordel, **Leliegracht** is a charming street, very pretty and home to a number of bookshops and bars. Leliegracht also holds one of the city's finest examples of **Art Nouveau architecture** – the tall and striking building at the Leliegracht-Keizersgracht junction. Designed by Gerrit van Arkel in 1905, it was originally the headquarters of a life insurance company, hence the two mosaics with angels recommending policies to bemused earthlings.

The Anne Frank Huis

Prinsengracht 263–267 • April–May & Sept–Oct daily 9am–10pm; June–Aug daily 8.30am–10pm; Nov–April Sun–Fri 9am–7pm, Sat 9am–9pm; closed Yom Kippur• €10 online only (€15.50, including programme), book up to two months in advance • ☎ 020 556 7105, ⓦ annefrank.org • Tram #13, #14 or #17 or bus #752 or #754, #758 to Westermarkt

In 1957, the Anne Frank Foundation set up the **Anne Frank Huis** in the premises on Prinsengracht where the young diarist and her family hid from the Germans during

2

World War II. Since the posthumous publication of her diaries, Anne Frank has become extraordinarily famous, in the first instance for recording the iniquities of the Holocaust, and latterly as a symbol of the fight against oppression in general and racism in particular.

A **visit** typically takes in the main body of the building – the premises of what was then the Frank business, including the ground-floor warehouse and old offices. This part offers several well-chosen displays setting the historical scene: exhibits providing brief biographies of those who sought refuge here, information on the Franks' Dutch helpers and video interviews with some of the leading characters, including Anne's father Otto Frank, and her friend Hanneli Goslar. There are also displays on the persecution of the Jews – from gradual exclusion and forced segregation (the Frank sisters attended the Jewish Lyceum created in 1941), through to arrest and deportation to the concentration camps. Further sections include the Diary Room, devoted to Anne as a writer/diarist and the importance of Anne's diary to other prisoners, most notably Nelson Mandela.

Ultimately, you arrive at the entrance to the **Secret Annex**, or *achterhuis*, which was separated from the rest of the house by a **false bookcase**. The Secret Annex was stripped of furniture long ago, but it still bears traces of its former occupants – such as the movie-star pin-ups in Anne's bedroom and the marks on the wall recording the children's heights. Anne Frank was only one of about 100,000 Dutch Jews who died during World War II, but this, her final home, provides one of the most enduring testaments to its horrors and, despite the crowds, most people find a visit very moving. Since 2017 the museum has been undergoing vast renovations, which include a new visitors' route and an extension (among other additions such as cloakrooms, a café and gift shop). Despite the ongoing works, the museum remains open. Additionally, June 2018 saw the launch of Anne Frank House VR, a virtual-reality tour in several languages that can be downloaded free of charge from the Oculus website (Ⓦoculus.com).

The Westerkerk

Prinsengracht 281 • **Church** Mon–Fri 10am–3pm, plus April–Oct Sat 10am–3pm • Free • ☎ 020 624 7766, Ⓦ westerkerk.nl • **Westertoren**: Daily: April–Oct 10am–8pm • €8 • ☎ 020 689 2565, Ⓦ westertorenamsterdam.nl • Tram #13, #14 or #17, or bus #752 or #754, #758 to Westermarkt

Trapped in the *achterhuis*, Anne Frank liked to listen to the bells of the **Westerkerk**, until they were taken away to be melted down for the German war effort. The church still dominates the district, its 85m tower, the **Westertoren** – without question Amsterdam's finest – soaring graciously above its surroundings and offering panoramic views of the city centre from its balconies. On its top perches the crown of the Emperor Maximilian, a constantly recurring symbol of Amsterdam (see page 33) and the finishing touch to what was then only the second city church to be built expressly for the Protestants. The church was designed by **Hendrick de Keyser** (see page 61) and completed ten years after his death in 1631. Its construction was part of the general enlargement of the city, but whereas the exterior is all studied elegance, the interior – as required by the Calvinist congregation – is bare and frugal. Apart from the long, plain-glass **windows**, which allow the light to pour in, the main features of note are the huge Baroque **organ** and the fancy wooden **pulpit** with its overlarge sounding board, where Protestant ministers once thundered away for hours on end. The merchant elite may have set their minds against "idolatrous" adornment, but they certainly were not averse to asserting status: the boxed-in benches at the base of several of the nave's stone columns were **gentlemen's pews**, reserved for – and rented by – the wealthy.

The Westermarkt

Tram #13, #14 or #17, or bus #752 or #754, #758 to Westermarkt

The **Westermarkt**, an open and breezy square edging the Westerkerk, contains two evocative **statues**. Just to the south of the church entrance, by Prinsengracht, is a small, poignant

2

THE STORY OF ANNE FRANK

The story of **Anne**, author of *The Diary of a Young Girl*, her sister, parents and their friends, is well known. Anne's father, **Otto Frank**, was a well-to-do Jewish businessman who fled Germany in December 1933 after Hitler came to power, moving to Amsterdam, where he established a spice-trading business on Prinsengracht. After the German occupation of the Netherlands, Otto – along with many other Jews – felt he could avoid trouble by keeping his head down. However, by 1942 it was clear that this would not be possible; Amsterdam's Jews were isolated and conspicuous, confined to certain parts of the city and forced to wear a yellow star, and roundups were increasingly common. In desperation, Otto Frank decided to move the family into the unused back rooms of their Prinsengracht premises, first asking some of his Dutch office staff if they would help him with the subterfuge – they bravely agreed. The Franks went into hiding in July 1942, along with a Jewish business partner and his wife and son, the van Pels (renamed the van Daans in the *Diary*). Their new "home" was separated from the rest of the building by a **bookcase** that doubled as a door. As far as everyone else was concerned, they had fled to Switzerland.

So began a two-year incarceration in the **achterhuis**, or rear house, and the two families were joined in November 1942 by a dentist friend, Fritz Pfeffer (Albert Dussel in the *Diary*), bringing the number of occupants to eight. Otto's trusted office staff continued working in the front part of the building, regularly bringing supplies and news of the outside world. In her diary Anne Frank describes the **day-to-day lives** of the inhabitants of the **Secret Annex**: the quarrels, frequent in such a claustrophobic environment, the celebrations of birthdays, or a piece of good news from the war; and of her own, slightly unreal, growing up – some of which was later covered over with brown masking paper prior to publication. In 2018, the hidden text of the diary, which included four "dirty" jokes and 33 lines about sex education and prostitution, was published for the first time to give an insight into Anne as, above all, an ordinary girl despite her talents.

In 1944, the atmosphere was optimistic; the Allies were clearly winning the war and liberation seemed within reach – but it wasn't to be. One day in the summer of that year, a Dutch collaborator betrayed the Franks and thereafter the Gestapo arrived and forced open the bookcase. The occupants of the Secret Annex were arrested and dispatched to Westerbork – the transit camp in the north of the country where all Dutch Jews were processed before being moved to Belsen or Auschwitz. Of the eight from the Annex, only Otto Frank survived; Anne and her sister died of typhus within a short time of each other in **Belsen**, just one week before the German surrender.

Anne Frank's **diary** was among the few things left behind in the Annex after the raid. It was retrieved by one of the family's Dutch helpers and handed to Otto on his return from Auschwitz. In 1947, Otto decided to publish his daughter's diary; since then, it has been translated into over sixty languages and sold many millions of copies. Otto Frank died in 1980 at the age of 91; the identity of the collaborator who betrayed his family has never been confirmed. As for the importance of Anne's diary, **Primo Levi** may well have summed it up best when he wrote "Perhaps it is better that way [that we can concentrate on the suffering of Anne]; if we were capable of taking in all the suffering of all those people, we would not be able to live."

statue of **Anne Frank** by the gifted Dutch sculptor Mari Andriessen (1897–1979), also the creator of the Dokwerker statue outside Amsterdam's Esnoga (see page 87). The second piece, behind the church beside Keizersgracht, consists of three pinkish granite triangles (one each for the past, present and future), which together comprise the **Homomonument**. The world's first memorial to persecuted gays and lesbians, commemorating all those who died at the hands of the Nazis, it was designed by Karin Daan and recalls the pink triangles the Germans made Dutch homosexuals sew onto their clothes during World War II. The monument has become a focus for the city's gay community and the site of ceremonies and wreath-laying throughout the year, most notably on King's Day (April 27) and World AIDS Day (Dec 1). The monument's inscription, by the Dutch writer Jacob Israel de Haan, translates as "Such an infinite desire for friendship".

2

REMBRANDT AND THE WESTERKERK

The Westerkerk was the last resting place of **Rembrandt**, though the exact location of his pauper's tomb is not known. Instead, a small **plaque** in the north aisle commemorates the artist and nearby, in the floor of the nave, is the **tomb** of his son, **Titus** (Grave no. 143). Rembrandt adored his son – as evidenced by numerous portraits – and the boy's death dealt a final crushing blow to the ageing and embittered artist, who died just over a year later in 1669. During renovation of the church in the late 1980s, **bones** were unearthed that could have been those of Rembrandt – a possibility whose tourist potential excited the church authorities no end. Admittedly it was a long shot – paupers' tombs were usually cleared of their accumulated bodies every twenty years or so – but the obvious way to prove it was through chemical analysis: Rembrandt's bones were expected to be unusually high in lead content as lead was a major ingredient of paint. The bones were duly taken to the University of Groningen for analysis, but the tests proved inconclusive.

Westermarkt 6

The French philosopher **René Descartes** (1596–1650) once lodged at **Westermarkt 6**, a handsome building with an attractive neck gable and fancy fanlight. Apparently happy that the Dutch were indifferent to his musings – and that therefore he wasn't going to be persecuted – he wrote, "Everybody except me is in business and so absorbed by profit-making that I could spend my entire life here without being noticed by a soul." However, this declaration may itself have been a deception: it's quite possible that Descartes was spying on the Dutch for the Habsburg King Philip II of Spain, a possibility explored in detail in A.C. Grayling's book entitled *Descartes: The Life and Times of a Genius*. In the event, Descartes spent twenty years in the Netherlands before accepting an invitation from Queen Christina to go to Stockholm in 1649. It turned out to be a poor choice; no sooner had he got there than he caught pneumonia and died.

The Museumhuis Bartolotti

Herengracht 170 • Mon–Sat 10am–4pm, Sun 11am–5pm (the opening time may vary; closed one day a week) • €8 (tickets can be bought online for a specific date and hour) • ☎ 020 427 0750, ⓦ museumhuizen.nl • Tram #13, #14 or #17 to Westermarkt

With a facade of red brick and stone dotted with urns, gargoyles and cherubs, the **Museumhuis Bartolotti** is an excellent illustration of the Dutch Renaissance style. **Hendrick de Keyser** (see box) designed it and a director of the West India Company, a certain Willem van den Heuvel, footed the bill. Van den Heuvel inherited a fortune from his Italian uncle and changed his name in his honour to Bartolotti – hence the name of the house. The famous Dutch harpsichordist Gustav Leonhardt lived here between 1974 and 2012. Now, thanks to the Hendrick de Keyser Association (see page 62), the house is open to visitors, who can experience the life of former inhabitants by sitting on their chairs or opening their drawers.

Herengracht 168

No public access • Tram #13, #14 or #17 to Westermarkt

The Museumhuis Bartolotti (see page 60) is much more ornate than its far more typical neighbour, at **Herengracht 168**, a classic canal house designed by **Philip Vingboons** (1607–78), arguably the most talented architect involved in the creation of the Grachtengordel. The house was built for Michael de Pauw, a leading light in the East India Company in the 1630s, its fetching sandstone facade a suitably grand preamble to an interior that sports a riot of flamboyant stuccowork, verdant Italianate wall paintings and a splendid spiral staircase.

The Woonbootmuseum

Opposite Prinsengracht 296 • Sept–June Tues–Sun 10am–5pm; July–Aug daily 10am–5pm • €4.50 • ☎ 020 427 0750,
Ⓦ houseboatmuseum.nl • Tram #13, #14 or #17 to Westermarkt

Some 2500 barges and houseboats are currently connected to Amsterdam's gas and
electricity networks. The privately owned **Woonbootmuseum** (Houseboat Museum)
is an attractively restored old Dutch houseboat of 1914 that doubles as a tourist
attraction. It's all very low-key and friendly: a handful of explanatory plaques describe
life on the water and, if you are enthused, you can splash out on a book on the subject.

The Felix Meritis building

Keizersgracht 324 • ☎ 020 626 2321, Ⓦ felix.meritis.nl • Tram #13, #14 or #17 to Westermarkt

A Neoclassical monolith dating to 1787, the **Felix Meritis building** was raised to house
Amsterdam's premier science and arts society, which was the cultural focus of the city's
upper crust for nearly one hundred years. Dutch cultural aspirations did not, however,
impress everyone. It's said that when Napoleon visited Amsterdam the entire building
was redecorated for his reception, only to have him stalk out in disgust, claiming that
the place stank of tobacco. Oddly enough, it later became the headquarters of the
Dutch Communist Party, but they sold it to the council, which now leases it to the
Felix Meritis Foundation. As of 2017, the building is closed for renovation, but it's
expected to host a mix of conferences and concerts with a pan-European theme in the
autumn of 2019.

The Cromhouthuizen

Herengracht 364–370 • Tram #1, #2 or #5 to Spui

The graceful and commanding **Cromhouthuizen** consist of four matching stone
mansions embellished with tendrils, garlands and scrollwork, all finessed by charming
little bull's-eye windows and elegant neck gables. Built in the 1660s for one of
Amsterdam's wealthy merchant families, the Cromhouts, the houses were designed by
Philip Vingboons (1607–78), the most inventive of the architects who worked on the
Grachtengordel during the city's expansion. As a Catholic, Vingboons was confined
to private commissions – inconvenient no doubt, but at a time when Protestants and
Catholics were at each other's throats right across Europe, hardly insufferable.

The Cromhouthuis Museum

Herengracht 366–368 • Tues–Fri 10am–5pm, Sat & Sun 11am–5pm • €10 (includes entrance for the Bijbels Museum and a free audio
tour) • ☎ 020 523 1730, Ⓦ cromhouthuis.nl

Two of the Cromhouthuizen have been adapted to accommodate the **Bijbels Museum**
(see page 62) and the **Cromhouthuis Museum**, though they still exhibit several features

---

ARCHITECTURAL INNOVATION: HENDRICK DE KEYSER

Born in Utrecht, the son of a carpenter, **Hendrick de Keyser** (1565–1621) moved to
Amsterdam in 1591. Initially employed as an apprentice sculptor, de Keyser soon ventured
out on his own, speedily establishing himself as one of the city's most sought-after sculptor-
architects. In 1595 he was appointed the city's official stonemason, becoming city architect
too in 1612. His municipal commissions included three churches – the Zuiderkerk (see page
51), the Noorderkerk (see page 56) and the Westerkerk (see page 58) – and the upper
storeys of the Munttoren (see page 72). His domestic designs were, however, more playful
(or at least ornate) and it was here that he pioneered what is often called the **Amsterdam
Renaissance style**, in which Italianate decorative details – tympani, octagonal turrets,
pilasters, pinnacles and arcades – were imposed on traditional Dutch design. The usual media
were red brick and sandstone trimmings – as in the Museumhuis Bartolotti.

2

HERITAGE GUARDIANS: HENDRICK DE KEYSER ASSOCIATION

Founded in 1918, the Hendrick de Keyser Association (ⓦhendrickdekeyser.nl) has been acquiring and restoring historic houses across the Netherlands for over a century. From an impressive Art Nouveau period mansion to a luxurious canal house or a pearl of the De Stijl architectural movement, the specialists open new grounds to the public for a few days at a time every month – see ⓦmuseumhuizen.nl. Bearing the name of the famous seventeenth-century sculptor-architect (see page 61), the association has already renovated over 400 houses from different historical periods. With support from the Dutch culture lottery and the government, it strives to restore interiors as well as exteriors to their original state. Amsterdam gems include the elaborate Museumhuis Bartolotti (see page 60) and the Gemeenlandshuis (at Diemerzeedijk 27) – dating back to 1725, this stately manor is surrounded by water and has a beautiful garden.

---

left over from their original function as bourgeois mansions. The prime examples are on the ground floor and comprise a **painted ceiling** of Classical gods and goddesses by Jacob de Wit and a striking spiral **staircase**. As for the collectors' museum itself, which tells the story of the Cromhouts, the exhibition in the cabinet of curiosities changes every few months but never loses its seventeenth-century origins (also recreated in the two kitchens). Floor two is mostly devoted to temporary exhibitions and displays.

The Bijbels Museum

Herengracht 366–368 • Tues–Fri 10am–5pm, Sat & Sun 11am–5pm • €10 • ☎ 020 624 2436, ⓦ bijbelsmuseum.nl

Spread across the two upper floors is the unusual **Bijbels Museum** (Bible Museum). Here, you'll discover two large and detailed nineteenth-century models, one of the **Tabernacle**, the portable sanctuary in which the Israelites carried their holy of holies, the Ark of the Covenant, and a second of **Jerusalem's Temple Mount**, made when Palestine was still part of the Ottoman Empire. Attempts to reconstruct biblical scenes were something of a cottage industry in the Netherlands in the late 1800s, with scores of Dutch antiquarians beavering away, Bible in one hand and modelling equipment in the other, but the creator of these particular models, a Protestant vicar by the name of **Leendert Schouten** (1828–1905), went one step further, making it his lifetime's work. It was a good move; Schouten became a well-known figure and his models proved a popular attraction, drawing hundreds of visitors to his home. Schouten also assembled an interesting assortment of Middle Eastern **archeological finds** dating from the period when the Israelites were in exile in Egypt, and these are displayed here on Floor 3 too. Finally, the same floor also exhibits an eclectic collection of **antique Bibles**, the most important being two early versions of the official **Statenvertaling** (literally "State's Translation"), published in 1637. Key to the development of Dutch Protestantism, the Statenvertaling was the result of years of study by the leading scholars of the Netherlands, who returned to the original Greek and Hebrew texts for this translation; it sold by the cartload.

Herengracht 380

Tram #1, #2 or #5 to Spui

The gracious symmetries of the Cromhouthuizen contrast with the grandiose pretension of **Herengracht 380**, built in the style of a French chateau for a tobacco planter in 1889. Ornately decorated, the mansion's main gable is embellished with reclining figures and the bay window by cherubs, mythical characters and an abundance of acanthus leaves. It was the first house in the city to be supplied with electricity and it now houses the NIOD Instituut voor Oorlogs-, Holocaust- en Genocidestudies (Institute for War, Holocaust and Genocide Studies; Mon 1–5.30pm, Tues–Fri 9am–5.30pm, ⓦniod.nl). Opposite, across the canal, is the only spot in Amsterdam where the houses come straight out of the water, Venice-like, without the intervention of a pavement.

Herengracht 388 and 394

Tram #1, #2 or #5 to Spui

Herengracht 388 is another handsome **Philip Vingboons** building (see page 61) while neighbouring **Herengracht 394**, the narrow house with the bell gable at the corner of Leidsegracht, bears a distinctive **facade stone** illustrating the legend of the four Aymon brothers, shown astride their trusty steed. The subject of a popular medieval *chanson*, the legend is all about honour, loyalty and friendship, dynastic quarrels and disputes, revolving around the trials and tribulations of the horse. The long, rambling tale ends when the redoubtable beast repeatedly breaks free from the millstones that the brothers have, in a dreadful error of judgement, tied around its neck and refuses to drown; the third time it comes to the surface, the brothers walk away, no longer able to watch the agonies of their animal. Assuming he's been abandoned, the horse cries out and promptly expires.

The Huis Marseille Museum voor Fotografie

Keizersgracht 401 & 399 • Tues–Sun 11am–6pm • €8 • ☎ 020 531 8989, ⓦ huismarseille.nl • Tram #1, #2 or #5 to Keizersgracht

A handsome canal house with an elegant stone gable, the **Huis Marseille** was built for a French merchant, Isaac Focquier, in the 1660s. Focquier made a huge profit exporting goods to Amsterdam from Marseille and to celebrate his good fortune he had a stone tablet showing a map of the eponymous French seaport cut into the front of his new home – a tablet that gave the mansion its name and survives today. Extensively renovated and extended (it took over the neighbouring building at Keizersgracht 399 in 2013), the Huis Marseille now holds the **Museum voor Fotografie**, which offers a rolling programme of exhibitions mostly featuring contemporary photographers and themes.

Leidsegracht

Tram #1, #2 or #5 to Keizersgracht

Appealing **Leidsegracht** is a largely residential canal, lined with chic townhouses and a medley of handsome gables. It's a tranquil scene – or at least it would be were it not for the flat-topped tour boats that use the canal as a short cut as they shunt into and out of Prinsengracht. An eighteenth-century wine merchant by the name of Paling would have welcomed the sight of a boat when he slipped into the Leidsegracht on a dark November evening. Well known as one of the greediest men in Amsterdam, he could apparently shovel down seven pounds of beef, a leg of lamb and thirty herrings in one

---

HAN VAN MEEGEREN AND THE FORGED VERMEERS

Keizersgracht 321, on the other side of the canal from the Felix Meritis building (see page 61), is in itself fairly innocuous, but these routine offices were once the home of the Dutch art forger **Han van Meegeren** (1889–1947). During the German occupation of World War II, Meegeren sold a "previously unknown" **Vermeer** to a German art dealer working for Herman Goering; what neither the agent nor Goering realized was that Meegeren had painted it himself. A forger *par excellence*, Meegeren had developed a sophisticated ageing technique in the early 1930s. He mixed his paints with phenol formaldehyde resin dissolved in benzene and then baked the finished painting in an oven for several hours; the end result fooled everyone, including the curators of the Rijksmuseum, who had bought another "Vermeer" from him in 1941.

The forgeries may well have never been discovered but for a strange sequence of events. In May 1945 a British captain by the name of Harry Anderson discovered Meegeren's "Vermeer" in Goering's art collection. Meegeren was promptly arrested as a collaborator and, to get himself out of a pickle, he soon confessed to this and other forgeries, arguing that he had duped and defrauded the Nazis rather than helping them – though he had, of course, pocketed the money. It was a fine argument and his reward was a short prison sentence – but in the event he died from a heart attack before he could be locked up.

sitting. He also liked his wine, a weakness that prompted his early demise when he fell – or staggered – into the Leidsegracht and no one heard the splash in time.

While you're here on Leidsegracht, be sure to take a gander at **Prinsengracht 681–693**, just round the corner, where an exquisite set of seven neck gables – one for each of the provinces that originally broke away from the Habsburgs – comprises an especially harmonious ensemble that dates back to 1715.

2

Grachtengordel south

Grachtengordel south holds many of Amsterdam's proudest and most extravagant mansions, clustered along **De Gouden Bocht** – the Golden Bend – the curve of Herengracht between Leidsegracht and the River Amstel. It's on this stretch that the merchant elite abandoned the material modesty of their Calvinist forebears, indulging themselves with lavish homes whose fancy facades more than hinted at the wealth within. In the late seventeenth and eighteenth centuries, this elite also forsook brick for stone and the restrained details of traditional Dutch architecture for pompous Neoclassicism, their defeat of the Spanish Habsburgs, allied with their commercial success, prompting them to compare themselves to the Greeks and Romans. In the event, it was all an illusion – the bubble burst when Napoleon's army arrived in 1793 – and, although the opulent interiors of two old mansions, the **Museum Willet-Holthuysen** and the **Museum Van Loon**, still give a flavour of those heady days, for the most part all that's left – albeit a substantial legacy – are the wonderful facades. Few of these big, old houses still act as family homes and most have been recycled as offices and flats, but one has been converted into the delightful purse and bag museum, the **Tassenmuseum Hendrikje**.

Grachtengordel south contains some rather less savoury areas, too, where ill-considered twentieth-century development has blemished the city, especially in the seediness of the **Rembrandtplein** and the mediocrity of Vijzelstraat and **Leidseplein**.

Leidseplein
Tram #1, #2, #5, #7 or #10 to Leidseplein

Lying on the edge of the Grachtengordel, **Leidseplein** is a bustling hub of Amsterdam's nightlife which became pedestrianized, and consequently less frenetic, in 2017. It once marked the end of the road in from Leiden and, as horse-drawn traffic was banned from the centre at the time, it was here that the Dutch left their horses and carts – a sort of equine car park. Today, the surrounding side streets are jammed with bars, restaurants and clubs in a bright jumble of jutting signs and neon lights.

The Stadsschouwburg
Leidseplein 26 • ☎ 020 624 2311, ⓦ stadsschouwburgamsterdam.nl

Leidseplein's architectural highlight is the grandiose **Stadsschouwburg**, a neo-Renaissance edifice dating back to 1894 that was so widely criticized for its clumsy vulgarity that the city council temporarily withheld the money for decorating the exterior. Home to the Nationale Opera and Ballet until the Muziektheater was completed on Waterlooplein in 1986, it is now used for theatre, opera, dance and music performances (see page 186). However, its most popular function is as the place where the Ajax football team gathers on the balcony to wave to the crowds whenever they win anything – as they often do.

American Hotel
Leidsekade 97 • ☎ 020 556 3000, ⓦ edenamsterdamamericanhotel.com

One of the city's oddest buildings, the **American Hotel**, just off Leidseplein, is a monumental and slightly disconcerting rendering of Art Nouveau complete with angular

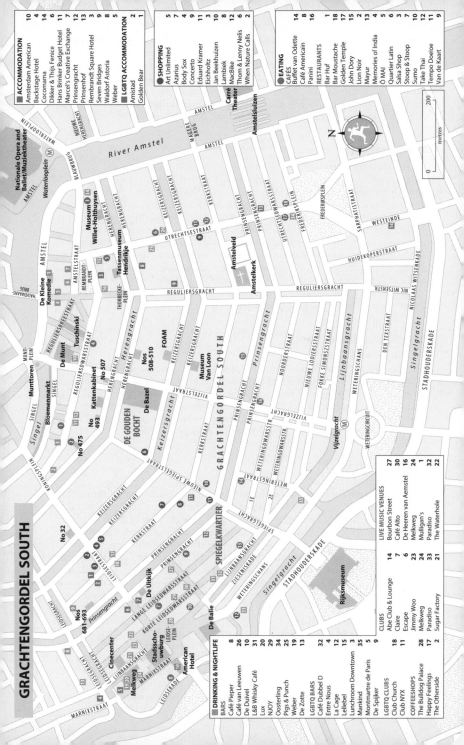

GRACHTENGORDEL SOUTH

turrets, chunky dormer windows and fancy brickwork. Completed in 1902, the present structure takes its name from its demolished predecessor, which was – as the stylistic peccadillo of its architect, one W. Steinigeweg – adorned with statues and murals of North American scenes. Inside the present hotel is the *Café Americain* (see page 159), once the fashionable haunt of Amsterdam's literati, but now a mainstream location for coffee and lunch. Nevertheless, the Art Nouveau decor is still worth a peek – an artful combination of stained glass, shallow arches and geometric patterned brickwork.

Leidsestraat

Tram #1, #2 or #5 to Prinsengracht

Leidsestraat, running northeast from Leidseplein, is one of Amsterdam's principal shopping streets, comprising a long, slender gauntlet of fast food, fashion and shoe shops of little distinction. That said, no. 32, at the junction with Keizersgracht and now home to an Abercrombie & Fitch clothes store, does occupy a splendid stone building of 1891, whose facade is adorned by caryatids and topped by a distinctive corner dome. At the time of its construction, this was the tallest commercial building in the city, one reason why the original owners were able to entice **Gerrit Rietveld** (1888–1964), the leading architectural light of the artistic movement De Stijl, to add a rooftop glass-and-metal showroom in 1933; you can still spy it from the street. As for Rietveld, it is perhaps surprising that he designed just one other building in Amsterdam – the Van Gogh Museum (see page 113).

The Spiegelkwartier

Tram #1, #2 or #5 to Keizersgracht

The chichi end of Amsterdam's antiques and fine arts trade is concentrated in the **Spiegelkwartier**, which runs along the Nieuwe Spiegelstraat and its continuation, Spiegelgracht. It's a pleasant area to wander, though you'll need a wallet full of euros to do more than window-shop. One possible exception are the old glazed tiles – a Dutch speciality – that can be picked up for a (relative) song at Eduard Kramer, Prinsengracht 807 at the corner of Nieuwe Spiegelstraat (see page 191).

De Gouden Bocht

Tram #1, #2 or #5 to Koningsplein

Overlooked by a long sequence of double-fronted mansions, some of the most opulent dwellings in the city, **De Gouden Bocht** (the Golden Bend) stretches along the Herengracht from Leidsegracht to the River Amstel. Most of the houses here were extensively remodelled in the late seventeenth and eighteenth centuries. Characteristically, they have double stairways leading to the entrance, with small doors underneath (originally for servants' use) and large doors above; the majority are topped off with the ornamental cornices that were fashionable at the time. Classical references are common, both in form – pediments, columns and pilasters – and decoration, from scrolls and vases through to geometric patterns inspired by ancient Greece.

Herengracht 475 and 493

Among the bevy of grand houses that make up De Gouden Bocht, look out for **Herengracht 475**, an extravagant stone mansion decorated with allegorical figures and surmounted by a slender balustrade. Typically, the original building was a much more modest affair, dating from the 1660s, but eighty years later the new owner took matters in hand to create the ornate facade of today. Just along the canal to the east, **Herengracht 493** is similarly grand, though here the building is polished off with a flamboyant pediment.

The Kattenkabinet

Herengracht 497 • Mon–Fri 10am–5pm, Sat & Sun noon–5pm • €7 • ☎ 020 626 9040, ⓦ kattenkabinet.nl

By comparison with its immediate neighbours, Herengracht 497 is architecturally plain and restrained, but part of the interior has been turned into the idiosyncratic **Kattenkabinet** (Cat Cabinet), a substantial collection of art and artefacts all relating to cats. They were installed by a Dutch financier whose cherished moggy, John Pierpont Morgan (named after the American financier), died in 1984; feline fanatics will be enraptured.

2

Herengracht 507

Herengracht 507 is an especially handsome house, its Neoclassical pilasters, pediment, mini-balcony and double stairway nicely balanced by the slender windows. This was once the home of **Jacob Boreel** (1630–97), one-time mayor, whose attempt to impose a burial tax in 1690 started a riot during which the mob ransacked his house; Boreel escaped by climbing over his garden fence.

De Bazel

Vijzelstraat 32 • **Conference centre** ☎ 020 723 0560, ⓦ debazelamsterdam.nl • **Stadsarchief and Schatkamer** Tues–Fri 10am–5pm, Sat & Sun noon–5pm • Free, but some temporary exhibitions at the Schatkamer attract an admission fee • ☎ 020 251 1511, ⓦ stadsarchief.amsterdam.nl • Tram #16 or #24 to Muntplein

De Bazel, one of Amsterdam's weirdest and most monumentally incongruous buildings, stretches south down Vijzelstraat from Herengracht as far as Keizersgracht – you can't possibly miss its looming, geometrical brickwork. Dating from the 1920s, this whopper of a structure started out as the headquarters of a Dutch shipping company, the **Nederlandsche Handelsmaatschappij**, before falling into the hands of the ABN-AMRO bank, which was itself swallowed by a consortium led by the Royal Bank of Scotland in 2007 – just before the worldwide banking crisis put paid to their overblown plans. Now home to a conference centre and the **Stadsarchief**, the city archives, the whole caboodle is commonly known as De Bazel after its architect **Karel de Bazel** (1869–1923), whose devotion to theosophy formed and framed his design. Founded in the late nineteenth century, **theosophy** combined metaphysics and religious philosophy, arguing that there was an over-arching spiritual order with reincarnation for all as an added bonus. Every facet of Bazel's building reflects this desire – or search – for order and balance, from the (faded) pink and yellow brickwork of the exterior (representing male and female, respectively) to the repeated use of motifs drawn from the Middle East, the source of much of the cult's spiritual inspiration.

The Schatkamer

At the heart of De Bazel is the magnificent **Schatkamer** (Treasury), a richly decorated Art Deco extravagance that feels rather like a royal crypt. Exhibited here is an intriguing selection of photographs and documents drawn from the city archives – anything from 1970s squatters occupying City Hall to hagiographic tracts on the virtues of the Dutch naval hero Admiral de Ruyter and, perhaps best of the lot, photos of miscreants (or rather the poor and the desperate) drawn from police records. The exhibits are changed regularly and an adjoining film studio shows documentaries about the city, both past and present.

The Museum Van Loon

Keizersgracht 672 • Daily 10am–5pm • €9 • ☎ 020 624 5255, ⓦ museumvanloon.nl • Tram #16 or #24 to Muntplein

Sitting pretty beside Keizersgracht, the **Museum Van Loon** boasts an especially fine interior within a handsome canal house that dates from 1672. The first tenant of the property was the artist Ferdinand Bol, who married an exceedingly wealthy widow

2

and promptly hung up his easel for the rest of his days. The last owners were the van Loons, cofounders of the East India Company and long one of the city's leading families, though they came something of a cropper at the end of World War II. In 1884 a member of the family, Hendrik, purchased this house for his son Willem on the occasion of his marriage to Thora Egidius. Thora had friends and relatives in Germany and during the German occupation she entertained them – unwisely, considering that several of her guests were high-ranking Nazi officials. After the war, allegations of collaboration besmirched Thora's reputation and an embarrassed Queen Wilhelmina fired her as her *dame du palais*, a position she had held since 1898; Thora died two months later.

The **interior** of the house has been returned to something akin to its eighteenth-century appearance, with wood panelling and fancy stuccowork, plus ancestral portraits of stern men and sober women in their be-ruffed Sunday best. Highlights include the ornate copper **balustrade** on the staircase, into which is worked the name "Van Hagen-Trip" (after the former owners of the house); the van Loons filled the spaces between the letters with fresh iron curlicues to prevent their children falling through. The top-floor landing has several pleasant grisaille **paintings** of classical figures – including Alexander the Great and Julius Caesar – and one of the bedrooms, the "painted room", is decorated with a Romantic painting of Italy, depicting a coastal scene with overgrown Classical ruins and diligent peasants. Such artistic conceits were a favourite motif with Amsterdam's bourgeoisie from around 1750 to 1820. The oddest items are the **fake bedroom doors**; the eighteenth-century owners were so keen to avoid any lack of symmetry that they camouflaged the real doors and created imitation, decorative replacements in the "correct" position instead. The other oddity is at the bottom of the garden, where the old **coach house** has trompe l'oeil windows; again, symmetry dictated that the building must have windows, but no self-respecting plutocrat wanted to be watched by his servants – hence the illusion.

FOAM

Keizersgracht 609 • Mon–Wed, Sat & Sun 10am–6pm, Thurs & Fri 10am–9pm • €11, plus additional charge for some exhibitions • ☎ 020 551 6500, ⓦ foam.org • Tram #16 or #24 to Muntplein

In a large and thoroughly refurbished old canal house, Amsterdam's leading photography museum **FOAM** (short for Fotografiemuseum) is achingly fashionable, its temporary exhibitions – of which there are usually four at any one time – featuring the best (or most obscure) of contemporary photographers. FOAM prides itself on its internationalism, though it does give space to famous or up-and-coming Dutch photographers like Carel Willink, Frido Troost and Otto Kaan. FOAM also offers guided, walk-through tours and photography workshops, both of which are extremely popular.

Herengracht 508–510

Tram #16 or #24 to Keizersgracht

The sheer extravagance of the Dutch merchant elite is demonstrated once again at **Herengracht 508–510**, where the grandiose facades of the eye-catching duo are well worth close inspection: both have towering neck gables dating from the 1690s, and sport designs of sea gods straddling dolphins, while tritons – half-men, half-fish – trumpet their conch shells to pacify the tumultuous oceans. No one knows for sure who designed no. 510, but no. 508 was the brainchild of the prolific Pieter Adolfse de Zeeuw, whose wealthy and well-connected patron was Agneta Deutz (1633–92), a second-generation Amsterdammer whose father had moved to the city from Germany.

TULIPS FOR SALE AT THE BLOEMENMARKT

The Tassenmuseum Hendrikje

Herengracht 573 • Daily 10am–5pm • €12.50 • ☎ 020 524 6452, ⓦ tassenmuseum.nl • Metro Waterlooplein, or tram #4, #9 or #14 to Rembrandtplein, or #4 to Keizersgracht

The delightful **Tassenmuseum Hendrikje** (Purse and Bag Museum) holds a superb collection of handbags, pouches, wallets, bags and purses from medieval times onwards, exhibited on three floors of a sympathetically refurbished grand old mansion. It's best to start on the top floor, where a curious miscellany of items from the sixteenth to the nineteenth centuries features examples of bags that preceded the purse – portefeuilles, chatelaines, frame-bags and reticules to name but four. The next floor down focuses on the twentieth century, with several beautiful Art Nouveau and Art Deco handbags and a whole cabinet of 1950s specimens made of "hard plastic", an early form of Perspex. Another display comprises handbags made from animals – the eel, crocodile, leopard and lizard bags look attractive, as long as you don't pause to think about how they were made, but the armadillo bag is rather gruesome. The ground floor is given over to temporary displays, with contemporary bags and purses the favourite theme.

The Museum Willet-Holthuysen

Herengracht 605 • Mon–Fri 10am–5pm, Sat & Sun 11am–5pm • €10 • ☎ 020 523 1822, ⓦ willetholthuysen.nl • Metro Waterlooplein, or tram #4, #9 or #14 to Rembrandtplein

Near the River Amstel, the **Museum Willet-Holthuysen** used to be billed as "the only fully furnished patrician house open to the public", which just about sums it up. The house dates from 1685, but successive members of the coal-trading Holthuysen family remodelled the interior until the last of the line, a certain **Louisa Willet-Holthuysen**, donated her home and its contents to the city in 1895.

The museum entrance is through the old servants' door, leading into the **basement**, which holds a small collection of porcelain, glass and silverware. Up above are the family rooms, most memorably the **Men's Parlour** (or Blue Room), which has been returned to its nineteenth-century Rococo splendour, a flashy and ornate style copied from France and held to be the epitome of refinement and good taste by local merchants. The **Ballroom**, all creams and gilt, is similarly opulent, and the **Dining Room** is laid out for dinner as if Louisa and her husband, **Abraham** (1825–88), were about to entertain – with the family's original Meissen dinner set forming the centrepiece.

The **top floor** displays the fine and applied art collection assembled by Abraham Willet, who fancied himself as a connoisseur. There are Dutch ceramics, pewter and silverware, as well as four finely carved ivory pieces depicting the elements, made in Germany in the eighteenth century. Among the paintings, look out for *Market Day in a Flemish Town* by Sebastian Vrancx (1573–1647) and a distinctly smug self-portrait of Abraham at the age of 28. The exhibits on this floor are, however, occasionally rotated to make way for temporary exhibitions.

At the back of the house lie the formal **gardens**, a geometric pattern of miniature hedges graced by the occasional stone statue.

The River Amstel and the Magere Brug

Tram #4 to Keizersgracht

At its east end, **Herengracht** comes to an abrupt halt beside the wide and windy **River Amstel**, which was long the main trade route into the Dutch interior – goods arriving by barge and boat were traded for the imported materials held in Amsterdam's many warehouses. To the left of Herengracht is the **Blauwbrug** (Blue Bridge) and the old Jewish quarter (see Chapter 4), while in the opposite direction is the **Magere Brug** (Skinny Bridge), the most famous and arguably the cutest of the city's many swing bridges. Legend has it that the current bridge, which dates back to about 1670,

2

THE AMSTELSLUIZEN

The **Amstelsluizen**, the river's locks, are located near both the east end of Prinsengracht and the Magere Brug (see below). Every night, the municipal water department closes these locks to begin the process of **sluicing** out the city's canals via sixteen sluices. A huge pumping station on an island out to the east of the city pumps fresh water from the IJsselmeer into the canal system; similar locks on the west side of the city are left open for the surplus to flow into the IJ and, from there, out to sea via the North Sea Canal. The city's canal water is thus refreshed – though, what with an army of shopping trolleys, rusty bikes and general detritus, the water is only appealing as long as you're not actually in it.

replaced an even older and skinnier version, originally built by two sisters who lived on opposite sides of the river and were fed up with having to walk so far to see each other.

Reguliersgracht

Tram #4, #9 or #14 to Rembrandtplein

Popular for impromptu football games, the **Amstelveld** is a small open space that's overlooked by the squat, seventeenth-century **Amstelkerk**, a simple church made of plain white wood and now used for concerts and special events. Amstelveld also marks the spot where Prinsengracht intersects with **Reguliersgracht**, perhaps the prettiest of the three surviving radial canals that cut across the Grachtengordel – its dainty humpback bridges and green waters overlooked by charming seventeenth- and eighteenth-century canal houses.

Thorbeckeplein

Tram #4, #9 or #14 to Rembrandtplein

Short and stumpy **Thorbeckeplein**, at the north end of Reguliersgracht, hosts an assortment of unexciting bars and restaurants, flanking a statue of **Johan Rudolf Thorbecke** (1798–1872), a far-sighted liberal politician and three-times Dutch premier whose reforms served to democratize the country in the aftermath of the European-wide turmoil of 1848.

Rembrandtplein

Tram #4, #9 or #14 to Rembrandtplein

Rembrandtplein may not be Amsterdam at its most alluring, but it is one of the city's nightlife centres, its bevy of restaurants and bars rammed at weekends. Formerly the city's butter market, the square took its present name in 1876 after it had acquired a **statue of Rembrandt**, a rather prim and proper affair that seems particularly appealing to passing seagulls. The statue now overlooks the life-size, bronze figures of *Nachtwacht 3D*, a sort of replica of Rembrandt's *Night Watch* painting (see page 109), the work of two Russians – Alexander Taratynov and Mikhail Dronov. Completed in 2006, the bronzes have been on a worldwide tour or two, but efforts are now being made to keep them here for good. Otherwise, among the square's hotels, cafés and bars, the *Schiller Hotel*, at no. 26, is the only one to stand out, its original Art Deco interior lit by geometrical chandeliers and decorated with stained-glass windows.

Reguliersbreestraat

Tram #4, #9 or #14 to Rembrandtplein

Pedestrianized **Reguliersbreestraat** is supremely tacky, but here among the fast-food joints, at no. 26, is the city's most extraordinary cinema – the **Tuschinski** (see page

189). Opened in 1921 by a Polish Jew, Abraham Tuschinski, the cinema boasts a marvellously well-preserved Art Deco/Jugendstil facade and interior, which features coloured marble, oodles of wood panelling, elaborate murals and the most ornate of lampstands. Tuschinski himself died in Auschwitz in 1942 at the age of 56. The network of alleys to either side of Reguliersbreestraat was once known as **Duivelshoek** (Devil's Corner), and, although it's been tidied up and sanitized, enough back-street seediness remains to make it a spot to be avoided late at night.

2

The Munttoren
Tram #16 or #24 to Muntplein

Tiny **Muntplein**, where the River Amstel meets the Singel canal, is overshadowed by the **Munttoren**, a sturdy, late-medieval brick tower that is all that has survived from the Regulierspoort, once one of the main gates into the city. In the seventeenth century, the tower was adopted as the municipal mint – hence its name – and to enhance its appearance Hendrick de Keyser (see page 62), in one of his last commissions, added a flashy **spire** in 1620.

The Bloemenmarkt
South side of the Singel between Muntplein and Koningsplein • Mon–Sat 9am–5.30pm, Sun 11.30am–5.30pm • Tram #16 or #24 to Muntplein

Though perhaps past its best, the floating **Bloemenmarkt** (flower market) is one of the main suppliers of flowers to central Amsterdam. Its blooms and bulbs now share stall space with souvenir clogs, garden gnomes and delftware. Come early for the pick of the best.

'T SMALLE BAR, EGELANTIERSGRACHT

The Jordaan and western docklands

Lying to the west of the city centre, the Jordaan (pronounced "your-darn")
is a likeable and easily explored area of slender canals and narrow streets
with a mix of architectural styles from modest modern terraces to handsome
seventeenth-century canal houses. Traditionally the home of Amsterdam's
working class, with its boundaries clearly defined by the Prinsengracht to the
east and the Lijnbaansgracht in the west, the Jordaan's character has been
transformed in recent years by a middle-class influx, and the district is now
one of the city's most sought-after residential neighbourhoods. Before then,
and indeed until the late 1970s, its inhabitants were primarily stevedores and
factory workers, earning a crust among the city's myriad docks, warehouses,
factories and boatyards.

The northern boundary of the **Jordaan** is Brouwersgracht (see page 54), one of Amsterdam's prettiest canals, and beyond that is the pint-sized **Scheepvaartsbuurt** (Shipping Quarter), part of the city's old industrial belt and now a mixed shopping and residential quarter. Just to the north of here lie the **western docklands**, or Westerdok, the oldest part of the sprawling complex of artificial islands that sweeps along the south side of the River IJ. This patch of land was dredged out of the river to provide extra warehousing and dock space in the seventeenth century. The maritime bustle has pretty much disappeared now, but after a long period of neglect the area is finding new life as a chichi residential quarter, with smart apartments installed in its warehouses and its clutch of elegant canal houses revamped and reinvigorated, especially on **Zandhoek**. Finally, the working-class neighbourhood to the west of the Westerkanaal, which marks the limit of the western docklands, is of interest for the **Het Schip** complex, a wonderful example of the Amsterdam School of Architecture and, perhaps more importantly, an example of social housing at its most optimistic.

3

The Jordaan

In all probability the **Jordaan** takes its name from the French word *jardin* ("garden"), since the area's earliest settlers were Protestant Huguenots who fled here to escape persecution in the sixteenth and seventeenth centuries. Another possibility is that it's a corruption of the Dutch word for Jews, *joden*, who also sought refuge here. Whatever the truth, the Jordaan developed from open country – hence the number of streets and canals named after flowers and plants – into a refugee enclave, a teeming, cosmopolitan quarter beyond the pale of bourgeois respectability. Indeed, when the city fathers planned the expansion of the city in 1610, they made sure the Jordaan was kept outside the city boundaries. Consequently, the area was not subject to the rigorous planning restrictions of the main *grachten* and its lattice of narrow streets followed the lines of the original polder drainage ditches, rather than any municipal plan. This gives the district its distinctive, mazy layout and much of its present appeal.

By the late nineteenth century, the Jordaan had become one of Amsterdam's toughest neighbourhoods, a stronghold of the city's industrial **working class**, mostly crowded together in cramped and unsanitary housing. Unsurprisingly, it was a highly politicized area, where protests against poor conditions were frequent, often coordinated by an influential and well-organized Communist Party. In the postwar period the slums were either cleared or renovated, but rocketing property prices in the wealthier parts of the city pushed middle-class professionals into the Jordaan from the early 1980s. This process of gentrification was at first much resented, but today the area is home to many young and affluent "alternative" Amsterdammers, who rub shoulders more or less affably with working-class Jordaaners with long-standing local roots.

THE JORDAAN'S HOFJES

One feature of the Jordaan's varied architectural pleasures is its **hofjes** – almshouses built around a central courtyard and originally occupied by the city's elderly and needy. There were – and are – *hofjes* all over the city, most famously the Begijnhof (see page 40), but there's a real concentration here in the Jordaan. Most date back to the seventeenth or eighteenth centuries, but the majority have been rebuilt or at least overhauled – and all are still lived in, often by the kind of people they were originally built for. The Jordaan's most diverting *hofje* by a long stretch is the **Karthuizerhofje**, on Karthuizersstraat (see page 77).

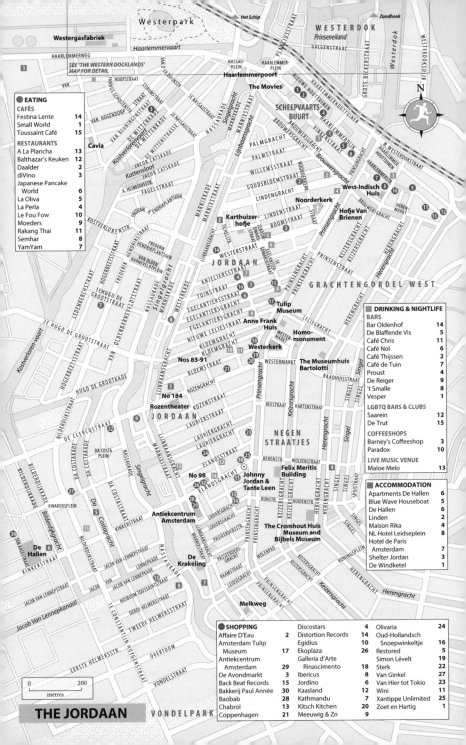

Leidsegracht

Tram #1, #2 or #5 to Prinsengracht

The southern boundary of the Jordaan is generally deemed to be pretty **Leidsegracht**, though this is open to debate: according to dyed-in-the-wool locals the true Jordaaner is born within earshot of the Westerkerk bells, and you'd be hard-pushed to hear the chimes this far south.

Elandsgracht

Tram #7, #10 or #17 to Elandsgracht

The narrow streets and canals just to the north of the Leidsegracht are pleasant, if unremarkable, but **Elandsgracht** does hold, at no. 109, the enjoyable **Antiekcentrum Amsterdam**, an indoor antiques centre that's a good place to pick up Dutch bygones, including tiles and ceramics (see page 191). Football fanatics will also want to take a peek at the Smit-Cruyff sports shop at Elandsgracht 98, where **Johan Cruyff** – star of Ajax in the 1970s and one of the greatest players of all time – bought his first pair of football boots. Nearby, at the east end of Elandsgracht you might pause to look at the **statues** of **Johnny Jordaan** (1924–89) and **Tante Leen** (1912–92) – two singers who were for years the sound of the working-class Jordaan, and whose songs are still remembered and sung in some of the area's more raucous cafés.

Rozengracht

Tram #10 to Rozengracht

Rozengracht lost its canal years ago and is now a busy and somewhat unattractive main road, though it was here at **no. 184** that **Rembrandt** spent the last ten years of his life – a scrolled plaque set high into the wall distinguishes his old home. Rembrandt's last years were scarred by the death of his partner Hendrickje in 1663 and his son Titus five years later, but nevertheless it was in this period that he produced some of his finest work, perhaps most memorably *The Jewish Bride*, a touchingly warm and heartfelt portrait of a bride and her husband, completed in 1668 and now in the Rijksmuseum (see page 106).

Bloemgracht

Tram #10 to Rozengracht

The streets and canals extending north from Rozengracht to Egelantiersgracht form the heart of the Jordaan and provide the district's prettiest moments. Cream of the scenic crop is **Bloemgracht** (Flower Canal), a leafy waterway dotted with houseboats and traversed by dinky little bridges, its network of cross-streets sprinkled with cafés, bars and quirky shops. There's a warm, relaxed community atmosphere here which is really rather beguiling, not to mention a clutch of fine old canal houses. Pride of architectural place goes to **nos. 87–91**, a sterling Renaissance building of 1642 complete with mullion windows, three crow-stepped gables, brightly painted shutters and distinctive facade stones, representing a *steeman* (city-dweller), a *landman* (farmer) and a *seeman* (sailor). **Nos. 83–85** next door were built a few decades later – two immaculately maintained canal houses adorned by the bottleneck gables typical of that period.

Egelantiersgracht

Tram #10 to Rozengracht

The further east you go on **Egelantiersgracht** (Rosehip Canal) the prettier it becomes and at no. 12 – as you near Prinsengracht – is the street's most interesting feature, 't

Smalle (see page 177). An antique bar with a canalside terrace, *'t Smalle* opened in 1786 as a *proeflokaal* – a tasting house for the (long-gone) gin distillery next door. At the time, when quality control was erratic to say the least, each batch of *jenever* (Dutch gin) could turn out very differently, so customers insisted on a taster before they splashed out. As a result, each distillery ran a *proeflokaal* offering free samples, and this is a rare survivor.

The Tulip Museum

Prinsengracht 116 at Egelantiersgracht · Daily 10am–6pm · €5 · ☎ 020 421 0095, ⓦ amsterdamtulipmuseum.com

More of a shop than a museum, the **Tulip Museum** sells all sorts of flower-related items upstairs, while down below is a moderately interesting exhibition on the history of the tulip with some details on the speculative bubble in tulip prices that ripped through the Netherlands in the Golden Age.

The Pianola Museum

Westerstraat 106 · Fri–Sun 11am–5pm · €5 · ☎ 020 627 9624, ⓦ pianola.nl · Tram #3, #5 or #10 to Marnixplein

A busy thoroughfare with the Noordermarkt (see page 54) at its eastern end, workaday **Westerstraat** is home to the small but charming **Pianola Museum**, whose collection of pianolas and automatic music-machines dates from the beginning of the twentieth century. Fifteen have been restored to full working order, and there are usually one or two playing throughout the afternoon. These machines, which work on rolls of perforated paper, were the jukeboxes of their day, and the museum has a vast archive of over 20,000 rolls of music, some of which were "recorded" by famous pianists and composers – Gershwin, Debussy, Scott Joplin, Art Tatum and others. The museum runs a programme of pianola **concerts** throughout the year, where the rolls are played back on the restored machines; times are listed on the website.

The Karthuizerhofje

Karthuizersstraat 89–171 · Daily 10am–8pm · Free · Tram #3, #5 or #10 to Marnixplein

Tucked away behind a white doorway, the **Karthuizerhofje** is the largest of the Jordaan's *hofjes* (see page 74), comprising a substantial courtyard complex established as a widows' hospice in the middle of the seventeenth century. Remodelled on several occasions, the present buildings are much more recent, but with its picket-fenced gardens and old ornate water-pumps, it still makes an appealing, peaceful port of call.

EEL-PULLING IN THE JORDAAN

Horrible as it may sound, **eel-pulling** was a popular pastime hereabouts: a live eel, preferably smeared in soap to make the entertainment last a little longer, was suspended from a rope strung across a canal. Teams took to their boats and tried to pull the poor creature off the rope, the fun being to see who would end up in the water; the winner came away with the eel – or at least a good piece of it. In 1886, a policeman unwisely tried to interfere in the shenanigans and was unceremoniously bundled away by the crowd, but when reinforcements arrived, the whole thing got out of hand and there was a full-scale **riot** – the **Paling-Oproer** (Eel Uprising) – which lasted for three days and cost 26 lives.

Lindengracht

Tram #3, #5 or #10 to Marnixplein

Lindengracht (Canal of Limes) lost its waterway decades ago, and is now a quiet and fairly nondescript thoroughfare flanked for the most part by an indeterminate mix of twentieth-century apartment blocks. Lindengracht has, however, played a prominent role in Jordaan folklore since the day in 1886 when a policeman made an ill-advised attempt to stop an eel-pulling contest (see box above). The east end of Lindengracht intersects with **Brouwersgracht** (see page 54), one of Amsterdam's prettiest streets, which marks the northerly limit of the Jordaan.

The Scheepvaartsbuurt

To the immediate north of Brouwersgracht lies the **Scheepvaartsbuurt** (Shipping Quarter). In the eighteenth and nineteenth centuries, the district bustled with stevedores and merchant ships, maritime activity that extended north across the western docklands (see below). Nowadays it's an unassuming neighbourhood, which focuses on the cafés and food shops that flank the main drag, **Haarlemmerstraat**, and its continuation **Haarlemmerdijk**.

Haarlemmerstraat

A 5min walk from Centraal Station

Before World War II the **Haarlemmerstraat** and its westerly extension, **Haarlemmerdijk**, were congested thoroughfares, but the trams that once ran here were rerouted and this is now a pleasant if unremarkable pedestrianized strip with bars, shops and cafés. The only architectural high points are the grand seventeenth-century facade of the **West-Indisch Huis**, one time headquarters of the West India Company (see page 228), just off Haarlemmerstraat at Herenmarkt 99, and the meticulously restored Art Deco interior of **The Movies** cinema (see page 188), near the west end of the street at Haarlemmerdijk 161.

Haarlemmerpoort

Tram #3 to Haarlemmerplein

Haarlemmerplein, the busy traffic traffic junction at the west end of Haarlemmerdijk, is dominated by the **Haarlemmerpoort**, a grandiose Neoclassical gateway that was built on the site of a medieval entrance to the city in 1840 for the new king William II's triumphal entry into the city. The euphoria didn't last long. William was a distinguished general who had been wounded at Waterloo, but as a king he proved much too crusty and reactionary to be popular, only agreeing to mild liberal reforms after extensive rioting in Amsterdam and elsewhere.

The western docklands

In the eighteenth and nineteenth centuries, the assorted docks, warehouses and shipyards of the **western docklands** stretched across a parcel of land dredged out of the River IJ. The construction of these artificial docklands took the pressure off Amsterdam's congested marine facilities and was necessary to sustain the city's economic success. These riverside wharves, which once belted the River IJ from the western to the eastern docklands, functioned as Amsterdam's heartbeat until the city's shipping facilities began to move away from the centre, a process accelerated by the construction of Centraal Station slap in the middle of the old quayside in the 1880s. The western docklands hung on to some of the marine trade until the 1960s, but today – bar the odd small boatyard – industry has to all intents and purposes disappeared and the area is busy reinventing itself. There is still a vague air of faded grittiness here, but the old, forgotten warehouses – within walking distance of the centre – are rapidly being turned into bijou studios, and dozens of plant-filled houseboats are moored alongside the narrow streets.

Prinseneiland

Tram #3 to Haarlemmerplein

A pleasing mix of houseboats, former warehouses and old canal houses, diminutive **Prinseneiland**, at the heart of the western docklands, is an artificial island a five-minute walk from the Haarlemmerpoort – proceed north from the near (east) side of the gate, walk through the tunnel beneath the railway lines and then turn right along Sloterdijkstraat. Bisecting Prinseneiland is **Galgenstraat** (Gallows St), now guarded by a pair of dainty little bridges and once the site of the municipal gallows, which were clearly visible to passing ships to remind errant mariners of the fate in store for them if they fell foul of the law.

Realeneiland

Tram #3 to Zoutkeetsgracht

East along Galgenstraat, beyond the next canal, **Grote Bickersstraat** slices north to the bridge leading over to **Realeneiland**, another western docklands island, whose houseboats, ex-warehouses and mini-boatyards give it a distinctly nautical flavour. On the island, waterside **Zandhoek** once offered an uninterrupted view over the harbour and was long a favourite with the city's sea captains, who constructed a clutch of fine old canal houses along here in the seventeenth and eighteenth centuries. A number of them have survived and several are decorated with distinctive facade stones, including **De Gouden Reael**, at no. 14, whose stone sports a gold coin. Before Napoleon introduced a system of house numbers, these stones were the principal way for visitors to distinguish one house from another, and many homeowners went to considerable lengths to make theirs unique. Jacob Real, the Catholic tradesman who owned this particular house, also used the image of a *real* – a Spanish coin – to discreetly advertise his sympathies for the Catholic Habsburgs.

At the top of Zandhoek, cross over the canal and then turn left along **Zoutkeetsgracht**; another left turn, this time onto Planciusstraat, returns you to the pedestrian tunnel near the Haarlemmerpoort (see page 78).

The Westergasfabriek

Polonceaukade, off Haarlemmerweg • ☎ 020 586 0710, Ⓦ westergasfabriek.nl • Bus #21 from Centraal Station to stop Van Hallstraat, or tram #10 to Van Limburg Stirumplein

Revamped and replanted, the **Westerpark** is a small slab of greenery that lies sandwiched between a railway embankment and the narrow canal bordering the

Haarlemmerweg. At its far end is the **Westergasfabriek**, a sprawling complex of red-brick nineteenth-century buildings that was formerly a gasworks, then a venue for acid house raves in the 1990s. Mercifully saved from demolition by squatters, it has been renovated and is finding its feet as an arts and entertainment complex (see pages 158, 177 and 200) with an attached leisure park. There are a number of arts- and media-related businesses here, a cinema and a few places to eat and drink.

Het Schip

Spaarndammerplantsoen • Bus #22 from in front of Centraal Station; get off at Spaarndammerstraat and it's a 350m walk to Het Schip (take Hembrugstraat and turn left at the end along Zaanstraat); you can also walk there in 5min from the north side of the Westerpark – a pedestrian tunnel leads under the railway lines to Zaanstraat, where you turn left

Tucked away in a rather glum part of the city is **Het Schip**, a municipal housing block comprising a splendid – and almost pristine – example of the Expressionistic **Amsterdam School** of architecture. Eight years in the making, from 1913 to 1921, the complex takes its name from its ship-like shape and is graced by all manner of fetching decorative details – from the intriguing mix-and-match windows to the wavy brick facades and ornamental sculptures of which the bulging "cigar" turret is the most self-indulgent. The architect responsible was **Michael de Klerk** (1884–1923), who also designed the two other housing blocks on Spaarndammerplantsoen, though Het Schip is easily the most striking. De Klerk reacted strongly against the influence of Berlage, whose style – exemplified by the Beurs (see page 36) – favoured clean lines and functionality, opting instead for much more playful motifs. De Klerk and his architectural allies were politically motivated, eager to provide high-quality homes for the working class, though their laudable aims were often undermined – or at least diluted – by a tendency to over-elaborate. De Klerk's other major commission in Amsterdam was the equally striking De Dageraad housing project (see page 120).

The Museum Het Schip

Spaarndammerplantsoen 140 • Tues–Sun 11am–5pm • €12.50, including hourly guided tour • ☎ 020 686 68595, ⓦ hetschip.nl

De Klerk installed a post office in Het Schip, and the interior, with its multicoloured tiling, now serves as the modest **Museum Het Schip**. The museum is also the starting point for 45-minute **guided tours** that point out the architectural highlights of the complex – which is still used for social housing today – before taking you inside one of the restored residences and proceeding up to the turret, which serves no purpose other than its aesthetics.

The old Jewish quarter and Plantage

Once one of the marshiest parts of Amsterdam, the narrow slab of land between the curve of the River Amstel, Oudeschans and Nieuwe Herengracht was the home of Amsterdam's Jews from the sixteenth century up until World War II. Sadly, the German occupation put paid to the old Jewish quarter, and in 1945 the district lay derelict and sparsely populated. Today, despite some unsympathetic postwar redevelopment, there are some unmissable sights among the cars and concrete, especially the impressive Esnoga (Portuguese synagogue) and the fascinating Joods Historisch Museum, which hold moving reminders of the community that perished here in World War II. The area's other big attractions are the Rembrandthuis, once the artist's home, and Hermitage Amsterdam, used for ambitious exhibitions of fine art.

Immediately to the east of the old Jewish quarter lies the **Plantage**, a well-heeled residential area that's home to the city's botanical gardens – the **Hortus Botanicus** – as well as **Artis Royal Zoo** and the excellent **Verzetsmuseum** (Dutch Resistance Museum).

The old Jewish quarter

Throughout the nineteenth and early twentieth centuries, the **old Jewish quarter** – the Jodenhoek (Jews' Corner) – was a hive of activity, crowded with tenement buildings and smoking factories, its main streets holding scores of open-air stalls selling everything from pickled herrings to pots and pans. Fatefully, it was also surrounded by canals and it was these that the Germans exploited to create the **ghetto** that foreshadowed their policy of starvation and deportation. They restricted movement in and out of the quarter by raising most of the swing bridges (over the Nieuwe Herengracht and the Oudeschans) and by imposing stringent controls on every other access route. From May 1942, the Jews were also obliged to wear the yellow Stars of David that made them readily identifiable and allowed for the rigorous implementation of ever harsher regulations: Jews were not allowed to use public transport, ride bicycles or own telephones, and they were placed under curfew. Meanwhile, roundups and deportations had begun shortly after the Germans arrived, and continued well into 1944. By the winter of that same year, the Jodenhoek was deserted and, as the need for wood and raw materials intensified, many of the houses were raided or dismantled for fuel and supplies.

The Jodenhoek remained a neglected corner of the city well into the 1970s, when the battered remnants took another hit with the large-scale demolition that preceded the construction of the metro beneath Waterlooplein. By these means, the prewar Jodenhoek disappeared almost without trace, the notable exception being the imposing **Esnoga** and the four connected synagogues of the Ashkenazi Jews, now the **Joods Historisch Museum**. The district's other main sight is the **Rembrandthuis**, which features special exhibitions on the artist's work, life and times.

The Oudeschans

Metro Nieuwmarkt

Wide and windy, the **Oudeschans canal** began life as Amsterdam's eastern moat until its original function was usurped when more land was dredged out of the River IJ. Thereafter, the Oudeschans was home to a string of shipyards and, although these are long gone, the canal's defensive origins are still recalled by the **Montelbaanstoren**, a sturdy and conspicuous brick tower built in 1516. The tower's decorative spire was added later when the city felt more secure, to a design by **Hendrick de Keyser** (see page 61), the architect who did much to create Amsterdam's prickly skyline.

The Rembrandthuis

Jodenbreestraat 4 • Daily 10am–6pm • €13 • ☎ 020 520 0400, ⓦ rembrandthuis.nl • Metro Nieuwmarkt or tram #9 or #14 to Waterlooplein

Jodenbreestraat, the "Broad Street of the Jews", was once the hub of Jewish activity in the city. Badly served by postwar development, this ancient thoroughfare is now short on charm, but in these unlikely surroundings stands the fascinating **Rembrandthuis**. Perhaps surprisingly, Rembrandt's old house has survived in good nick, its intricate facade decorated with pretty wooden shutters and a fancy pediment. Rembrandt bought the house at the height of his fame and popularity, living here for almost twenty years and spending a fortune on its furnishings – an expense that ultimately contributed to his bankruptcy (see page 109). An inventory made at the time details the huge collection of paintings, sculptures and art treasures he had amassed, almost all

THE OLD JEWISH QUARTER AND PLANTAGE

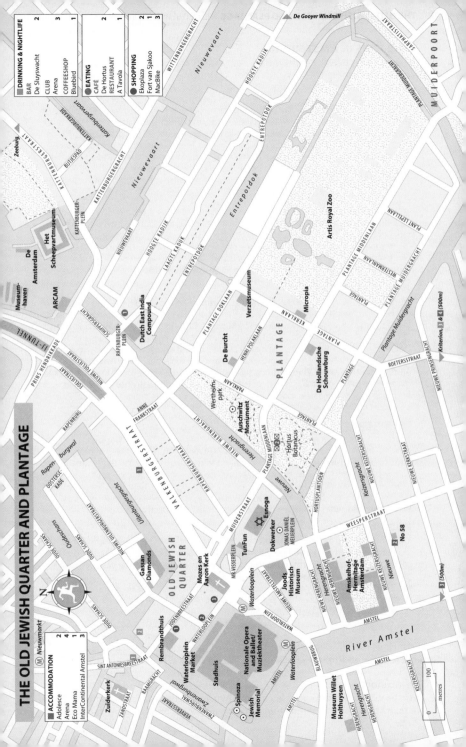

ACCOMMODATION
Adolesce	2
Arena	4
Eco Mama	1
InterContinental Amstel	3

DRINKING & NIGHTLIFE
BAR	
De Sluyswacht	2
CLUB	
Arena	3
COFFEESHOP	
Bluebird	1
EATING	
CAFÉ	
De Hortus	2
RESTAURANT	
A Tavola	1
SHOPPING	
Ekoplaza	2
Fort van Sjakoo	1
MacBike	3

De Gooyer Windmill

Zeeburg

Museum-haven

ARCAM

De Amsterdam

Het Scheepvaartmuseum

Dutch East India Compound

De Burcht

Verzetsmuseum

Artis Royal Zoo

Micropia

Auschwitz Monument

Wertheimpark

Hortus Botanicus

De Hollandsche Schouwburg

Gassan Diamonds

Esnoga

TunFun

Dokwerker

Joods Historisch Museum

Mozes en Aaron Kerk

No 58

Amstelhof Hermitage Amsterdam

Waterlooplein Market

Stadhuis

Nationale Opera and Ballet/Muziektheater

Rembrandthuis

Zuiderkerk

Spinoza

Jewish Memorial

Museum Willet Holthuysen

River Amstel

Kriterion

IJ-TUNNEL

OLD JEWISH QUARTER

PLANTAGE

MUIDERPOORT

N

0   100
metres

THE JEWS IN AMSTERDAM

From the late sixteenth century onwards, Amsterdam was a haven for refugee **Jews** escaping persecution in the rest of Europe. The **Union of Utrecht**, ratified in 1579, signalled the start of the influx. Drawn up by the largely Protestant northern Dutch provinces in response to the invading Spanish army, the treaty combined the United Provinces (later to become the Netherlands) in a loose federation, whose wheels could only be greased by a degree of religious toleration then unknown elsewhere across the continent. Whatever the Protestants may have wanted, they knew that the Catholic minority (around 35 percent) would only continue to support the rebellion against the Spanish Habsburgs if they were treated well – the Jews benefitted by osmosis and consequently migrated here in their hundreds.

TOLERATION – WITHIN LIMITS

This **toleration** did, however, have its limits: Jewish immigrants were forced to buy citizenship; Christian-Jewish marriages were illegal; and, as with the Catholics, Jews were only allowed to practise their religion discreetly behind closed doors. A proclamation in 1632 also excluded them from most guilds – effectively withdrawing their right to own and run most types of business. This forced them either to excel in those trades not governed by the guilds or introduce new non-guild trades into the city. Nonetheless, by the middle of the eighteenth century the city's Jewish community was active in almost every aspect of the economy, especially in bookselling, tobacco, banking and commodity futures.

JEWISH IMMIGRATION

The first major Jewish influx was of **Sephardic Jews** from Spain and Portugal, where persecution had begun in earnest in 1492 and continued throughout the sixteenth century. In the 1630s the Sephardim were joined in Amsterdam by hundreds of (much poorer) **Ashkenazi** Jews from German-speaking central Europe. The two groups established separate synagogues and, although there was no ghetto as such, the vast majority settled on and around what is now Waterlooplein, then a distinctly unhealthy tract of low-lying land that was subject to regular flooding by the River Amstel. Initially known as **Vlooyenburg**, this district was usually referred to as the **Jodenhoek**, or "Jews' Corner", though this was not, generally speaking, a pejorative term and neither did the Dutch eschew living here. Indeed, given the time, the most extraordinary feature of Jewish settlement in Amsterdam was that it occasioned mild curiosity rather than outright hate.

THE NINETEENTH CENTURY

The restrictions affecting both Jews and Catholics were removed during **Napoleon**'s occupation of the United Provinces (see page 227). Freed from official discrimination, Amsterdam's Jewish community flourished and the Jewish quarter expanded, nudging northwest towards Nieuwmarkt and east across Nieuwe Herengracht, though this was just the focus of a community whose members lived in every part of the city. In 1882, the dilapidated houses of the Jodenhoek were razed and several minor canals filled in to make way for **Waterlooplein**, which became a busy and largely Jewish marketplace.

MODERN TIMES

In 1900, there were around 60,000 Jews living in Amsterdam, but **refugees** from Hitler's Germany swelled this figure to around 140,000 in the 1930s. The disaster that befell this community during the **German occupation** is hard to conceive, but the bald facts speak for themselves; when Amsterdam was liberated, there were only 5000 Jews left and the Jodenhoek was, to all intents and purposes, a ghost town. At present, there are about 20,000 Jews resident in – and spread out across – the city, but while Jewish life in Amsterdam has survived, its heyday is gone forever.

of which were confiscated after he was declared insolvent and forced to move to a more modest house on Rozengracht in the Jordaan in 1658.

The interior

Entry to the Rembrandthuis is via the modern annex, but you're soon into the old house, where a string of **period rooms** has been restored to something resembling their appearance when the artist lived here – the reconstruction being based on the inventory. The period furniture is appealing enough, especially the dinky box-beds, and the great man's studio is surprisingly large and well lit, but it's the collection of **seventeenth-century Dutch paintings** that grabs most of the attention. They do vary in quality and interest, but in the Old Entrance Hall look out for several paintings by Rembrandt's master in Amsterdam, **Pieter Lastman** (1583–1633) – not because of their brilliance, but rather because their sheer mawkishness demonstrates just how far Rembrandt soared above his artistic milieu. On the same floor, in the **Salon**, is the museum's one and only Rembrandt painting, his *Portrait of the Preacher Eleazer Swalmius*, an early work currently on long-term loan from Antwerp. The subject's straggly beard and twinkling eyes get the full Rembrandt treatment, though the painting was not attributed to him for many years, largely because its intricacies were hidden by a thick layer of varnish, which has now been removed.

The Art Cabinet and beyond

The intriguing "**Art Cabinet**" is a room crammed with objets d'art and miscellaneous rarities reassembled here in line with the original inventory. There are African spears and shields, Pacific seashells, Venetian glassware and even busts of Roman emperors, all of which were meant to demonstrate Rembrandt's wide interests and eclectic taste. Beyond the Art Cabinet, the rest of the Rembrandthuis is usually given over to temporary exhibitions on the artist and his contemporaries. There's also, space permitting, a collection of **Rembrandt's etchings**, as well as several of the original copper plates on which he worked. It's a large and varied collection, with the biblical illustrations perhaps most appealing of all.

4

Gassan Diamonds

Nieuwe Uilenburgerstraat 173 • Frequent guided tours daily 9am–5pm; 30min • Free • ☎ 020 622 5333, ⓦ gassan.com • Metro Nieuwmarkt or tram #9 or #14 to Waterlooplein

Before World War II, many of Amsterdam's Jews worked as diamond cutters and polishers (see box), and although there's little sign of the industry today, one notable exception, the **Gassan Diamonds** factory, occupies a large and imposing brick building dating from 1897. **Tours** of the factory include a visit to the cutting and polishing areas, as well as a stroll round the diamond jewellery showroom; also on the premises is a large souvenir shop with a substantial range of blue and white delftware.

Waterlooplein

Metro Waterlooplein, or tram #9 or #14 to Waterlooplein

A rectangular parcel of land that was originally swampy marsh, **Waterlooplein** was the site of the first Jewish quarter, but by the late nineteenth century it had become an insanitary slum, home to the poorest of the Ashkenazi Jews. The slums were cleared in the 1880s and thereafter Waterlooplein (and its open-air market) became the centre of Jewish life in the city. During the war, the Germans used the square to round up their victims, but despite these ugly connotations Waterlooplein was revived in the 1950s as the site of the city's main **flea market** – and remains so to this day, albeit on a much smaller scale (Mon–Sat 9am–6pm). As far as the city council was concerned, the market's reappearance was only a stopgap while they mulled over plans to entirely reinvent the area. For starters, whole streets were demolished to make way for the motorist – with Mr Visserplein, for example, becoming little more than a traffic intersection – and then, warming to their theme in the late 1970s, the council announced the construction of the massive new Waterlooplein town and concert hall complex that stands today. Opposition was immediate and widespread, but attempts to prevent the development failed, and nowadays the Stadhuis en Muziektheater complex – or **Stopera** – is accepted if hardly

---

HENRI POLAK, THE CAMPAIGNING RABBI

Traditionally, Amsterdam's **diamond workers** were poorly paid and endured foul working conditions, but all that changed after the creation of the Diamond Workers' Union, the **ANDB** (Algemene Nederlandse Diamantbewerkersbond), at the end of the nineteenth century. Unionized, the diamond workers transformed their pay and conditions, becoming the vanguard of the working class under the leadership of the socialist rabbi **Henri Polak** (1868–1943). The ANDB was also evangelical about members' self-improvement, pushed education and did more to integrate the city's Jews into the mainstream than any other organization. Predictably, the Germans made short work of the union during the occupation, but Polak himself was, for reasons that remain obscure, arrested and then released – before dying of natural causes.

---

admired: it is, as its opponents always insisted, something of an architectural eyesore, its indeterminate modernity impossible to warm to.

Waterlooplein's memorials

Perhaps conscious of the area's architectural deficiencies, the city council has erected two **memorials** outside the Stopera complex at the tip of Waterlooplein, where the River Amstel meets the Zwanenburgwal canal: one honours **Spinoza** (see below), who looks suitably serene above an inscription that reads "The aim of the state is freedom"; the other is a black stone **tribute** to the dead of the Jewish resistance. The inscription from Jeremiah translates "If my eyes were a well of tears, I would cry day and night for the fallen fighters of my beloved people".

The Stopera

Waterlooplein · Stadhuis Mon–Sat 9am–5pm

The main entrance to the **Stopera** complex is on the south side, and in the foyer here is a **sculpture**, a forceful and inventive tribute to the district's Jews, in which a bronze violinist bursts through the floor tiles. To the right of the foyer is the **Muziektheater**, home to the Nationale Opera and Ballet (see page 186), while a covered corridor leads dead ahead to a second, glass-roofed corridor, which is flanked by the assorted offices of the **Stadhuis** (City Hall). This second corridor also holds a minor attraction, a set of **glass columns** that provides a salutary lesson on the fragility of the Netherlands: two contain water indicating the sea levels in the Dutch towns of Vlissingen and IJmuiden (below knee level), while another records the levels recorded during the 1953 flood disaster (way above head height). Next to the columns is a post indicating what is known as "**Normal Amsterdam Level**" (NAP), originally calculated in 1684 as the average water level in the River IJ and still the basis for measuring altitude above sea level across Europe. There's also a small display on NAP in the subterranean gallery next to the glass columns, reached through the turnstile and down the steps.

The Mozes en Aaron Kerk

Waterlooplein 207 · No set opening hours · ☎ 020 233 1522, Ⓦ santegidio.nl

Standing on the corner of Mr Visserplein, the **Mozes en Aaron Kerk** is a rather glum Neoclassical structure built on the site of a clandestine Catholic church in the 1840s. It takes its unusual name from a pair of facade stones bearing effigies of the two prophets that adorned the earlier building. Earlier still, a house stood on this plot and it was here that the philosopher and theologian **Baruch Spinoza** (1632–77) was born. Of Sephardic descent, Spinoza upheld pantheistic views that soon brought him into conflict with the elders of the Jewish community. At the age of 23, he was excommunicated and forced out of the city, moving into a small village where he survived by grinding lenses. After an attempt on his life, Spinoza moved again, eventually ending up in The Hague, where his free-thinking ways proved more acceptable, though he died young – probably of silicosis brought on by inhaling dust from his lens-grinding.

The Esnoga and around

Mr Visserplein 3 • Mon–Thurs & Sun 10am–5pm; Dec–Jan same days 10am–4pm; Fri 10am–4pm; winter Fri 10am–2pm; summer Fri 10am–5pm; closed Yom Kippur & Rosh Hashanah • €15 for combined ticket with Joods Historisch Museum (see page 88) • ☎ 020 624 5351, Ⓦ esnoga.com • Metro Waterlooplein, or tram #9 or #14 to Waterlooplein

Unmissable on the corner of Mr Visserplein is the brown and bulky brickwork of the **Esnoga** (Portuguese Synagogue), completed in 1675 for the city's Sephardic Jews. One of Amsterdam's most imposing buildings, the synagogue, with its grand pilasters and blind balustrade, was built in the broadly Neoclassical style that was then fashionable in Holland. It is surrounded by a courtyard complex of small outhouses, where the city's Sephardim have fraternized for centuries. Barely altered since its construction, the synagogue's lofty interior follows the Sephardic tradition in having the Hechal (the Ark of the Covenant) and *tebah* (from where services are led) at opposite ends. Also traditional is the seating, with two sets of wooden benches (for the men) facing each other across the central aisle – the women have separate galleries up above. A set of superb brass chandeliers holds the candles that remain the only source of artificial light. When it was completed, the synagogue was one of the largest in the world, its congregation almost certainly the richest; today, the Sephardic community has dwindled to just 250 families, most of whom live outside the city centre.

The surrounding **outhouses** illustrate different aspects of the Sephardic tradition – from the mourning room and the rabbi's room to the treasure room with its assortment of ritual vestments and silverware. There's also the intimate **winter synagogue** converted from a classroom in the late 1940s after the disasters of World War II. The mystery to the whole complex is quite why the Germans left it alone – no one knows for sure, but it seems likely that they intended to turn it into a museum once all of the Jews had been deported and slaughtered.

Jonas Daniel Meijerplein

Jonas Daniel Meijerplein, a scrawny triangle of gravel next door to the Esnoga, is named after the lawyer, who in 1796, at the age of just 16, was the first Jew to be admitted to the Amsterdam Bar. It was here on this square in February 1941 that around four hundred Jewish men were forcibly loaded up on trucks and taken to their deaths at Mauthausen concentration camp, in reprisal for the killing of a Dutch Nazi during a street fight. The arrests sparked off the **February Strike** (Februaristaking), a general strike in protest against the Germans' treatment of the Jews. It was organized by the outlawed Communist Party and spearheaded by Amsterdam's transport workers and dockers – a rare demonstration of solidarity with the Jews whose fate was usually accepted without visible protest in almost all of occupied Europe. The strike was quickly suppressed, but is still commemorated by an annual wreath-laying ceremony on February 25, as well as by Mari Andriessen's statue of the **Dokwerker** (Dockworker).

BRAVE RESISTANCE: LODEWIJK VISSER

Mr Visserplein is a busy junction for traffic speeding towards the IJ tunnel. It takes its name from **Lodewijk Ernst Visser** (1871–1942), President of the Supreme Court of the Netherlands in 1939. He was dismissed the following year when the Germans occupied the country, and became an active member of the Jewish resistance, working for the illegal underground newspaper *Het Parool* ("The Password") and refusing to wear the yellow Star of David. He vehemently opposed the Nazi-appointed Judenrat (see box, page 90), publicly denouncing all forms of collaboration and arguing that the Dutch government should take responsibility for all Dutch citizens, Jew and Gentile alike. Visser died from a heart attack shortly after he was threatened with deportation to a concentration camp.

The Joods Historisch Museum

Nieuwe Amstelstraat 1 • Daily 11am–5pm; closed Yom Kippur & Rosh Hashanah • €15 for combined ticket with Esnoga (see page 87) • ☎ 020 531 0310, Ⓦ jhm.nl • Metro Waterlooplein, or tram #9 or #14 to Waterlooplein

The **Joods Historisch Museum** (Jewish Historical Museum) is cleverly shoehorned into four adjacent Ashkenazi synagogues dating from the late seventeenth century. For years after World War II these buildings lay abandoned, but they were finally refurbished – and connected by walkways – in the 1980s, to accommodate a Jewish resource and exhibition centre.

The first major display area, just beyond the reception desk on the ground floor of the **Nieuwe Synagoge**, features temporary exhibitions on Jewish life and culture with vintage photographs usually to the fore – and the same applies to the **Print Room** down below. Moving on, the ground floor of the capacious, late seventeenth-century **Grote Synagoge** holds an engaging display on Jewish life and faith in the Netherlands. There is a fine collection of religious silverware here, plus all manner of antique artefacts illustrating religious customs and practices, alongside a scattering of paintings and portraits. The gallery up above, reached via a spiral staircase, holds a finely judged social history of the country's Jewish population from 1600 to 1900, with an assortment of bygones, documents and paintings tracing their prominent role in a wide variety of industries, both as employers and employees. A complementary history of the Jews in the Netherlands from 1900 onwards occupies the upper level of the neighbouring Nieuwe Synagoge. Inevitably, attention is given to the trauma of World War II, but there is also a biting display on the indifferent or hostile reaction of many Dutch men and women to liberated Jews in 1945. For more on Amsterdam during the German occupation, visit the Dutch Resistance Museum (see page 92). A discrete part of the museum also holds a **children's museum** with interactive educational displays on Jewish themes (see page 210).

The Plantage

Starting at Centraal Station, tram #9 runs along Plantage Middenlaan, passing by or near all the district's main attractions

Laid out in the middle of the nineteenth century, the pleasant, leafy streets of the **Plantage**, falling to either side of **Plantage Middenlaan** boulevard, were developed as part of a concerted attempt to provide good-quality housing for the city's expanding middle classes. Although it was never as fashionable as the older residential parts of the Grachtengordel, the new district did contain elegant villas and spacious terraces, making it the first suburban port of call for many upwardly mobile Jews. Nowadays, the Plantage is still one of the more prosperous parts of the city, in a modest sort of way, and boasts two especially enjoyable attractions – the **Hortus Botanicus** (Botanical Gardens) and the **Verzetsmuseum** (Dutch Resistance Museum). Nearby, just over the **Plantage Muidergracht** canal, and stretching west to the River Amstel, is a small parcel of old Amsterdam, dating back to the late seventeenth century. The main attraction here is **Hermitage Amsterdam**, which showcases temporary exhibitions of fine and applied art loaned from St Petersburg's Hermitage Museum.

The Amstelhof and Hermitage Amsterdam

Amstel 51 • Daily 10am–5pm • €18 • ☎ 020 530 7488, Ⓦ hermitage.nl • Metro Waterlooplein, or tram #9 to Waterlooplein

Occupying the **Amstelhof**, Amsterdam's largest *hofje* (see box, page 91), **Hermitage Amsterdam** displays items, mainly paintings, loaned from the original Hermitage in St Petersburg, with headline exhibitions usually lasting about five months. The Amstelhof also musters a few **additional galleries** (an all-in ticket costs €25) exploring the institution's history – modest stuff perhaps, but still of some interest: the pick are the eighteenth-century kitchen and the old chapel with its mini-organ and twin balconies.

PALM HOUSE AT THE HORTUS BOTANICUS

THE JUDENRAT

In the nineteenth century, many better-off Jews escaped the crowded conditions of the old Jewish quarter to live along Nieuwe Keizersgracht and Nieuwe Prinsengracht, but relative economic success did nothing to stave off the disaster of World War II. One painful reminder of those times still stands at **Nieuwe Keizersgracht 58**, across the canal behind the Amstelhof. From 1940, this house, with its luxurious Neoclassical double doorway set beneath twin caryatids, was the headquarters of the **Judenrat** (Jewish Council), through which the Germans managed the ghetto and organized the deportations. The role of the Judenrat is extremely controversial. Many have argued that they were tainted collaborators, who hoped to save their own necks by working with the Germans and duping their fellow Jews into thinking that the deportations were indeed – as Nazi propaganda insisted – about the transfer of personnel to new employment in Germany. Just how much the council leaders knew about the gas chambers remains unclear, but after the war the surviving members of the Jewish Council successfully defended themselves against charges of collaboration, claiming that they had been a buffer against the Germans rather than their instruments.

The Hortus Botanicus

Plantage Middenlaan 2a • Jul–Aug Mon–Sat 10am–5pm, Sun 10am–7pm; Daily 10am–5pm • €9.50 • ☎ 020 625 9021, Ⓦ dehortus.nl • Metro Waterlooplein, or tram #9 or #14 to Mr Visserplein

The lush **Hortus Botanicus** is an appealing, albeit small, botanical garden. The Hortus was founded in 1682 as **medicinal gardens** for the city's physicians and apothecaries after an especially bad outbreak of the plague. Thereafter, many of the city's merchants made a point of bringing back exotic species from the East, the result being the six-thousand-odd plant species exhibited today – both outside and in a series of hothouses. Botanical specimens also went the other way; in 1848, for instance, two oil palms left the gardens for Java, where they were used to establish the first of that island's many oil palm plantations.

The gardens are divided into several distinct sections, their locations pinpointed on a map available at the entrance. Most of the outdoor sections hold plants, trees and shrubs from temperate and Arctic zones, with many of the more established trees dating back to a major replanting in 1895. The largest of the hothouses is the **Three-Climate Greenhouse**, partitioned into separate zones: subtropical, tropical and desert. The gardens also hold a **butterfly house** and a capacious **palm house** with a substantial collection of cycad palms. The gardens make a relaxing break on any tour of central Amsterdam, especially as the **café**, *De Hortus* (see page 160), in the old orangery, serves tasty lunches and snacks.

The Wertheimpark

Plantage Middenlaan • Open access • Free • Tram #9 or #14 to Mr Visserplein

Bordered by the Nieuwe Herengracht canal, the greenery of the pint-sized **Wertheimpark** is distinguished by the **Auschwitz monument**, a simple affair with symbolically broken mirrors and an inscription that reads *Nooit meer Auschwitz* ("Auschwitz – Never Again"). It was designed by Jan Wolkers (1925–2007), the Dutch author and artist who first came to prominence in the 1960s with a string of barbed novels – *Candyfloss, Oegstgeest Revisited* – railing against his Calvinist upbringing.

De Hollandsche Schouwburg

Plantage Middenlaan 24 • Daily 11am–5pm; closed Yom Kippur & Rosh Hashanah • Free • ☎ 020 531 0310, Ⓦ bit.ly/HollandscheSchouwburg • Tram #9 or #14 to Artis

Originally a theatre where Jewish artists could perform without obstruction, **De Hollandsche Schouwburg** was turned into a Jews-only theatre by the Germans in October 1941 – and was the main assembly point for Amsterdam Jews prior to their deportation in the summer of the following year. Inside, there was no daylight and families were interned in conditions that foreshadowed those of the camps they would soon be transported to. After the war, no one was quite sure what to do with the building, but eventually the facade was restored and the front section refurbished; the ground floor now holds an eternal flame in front of a list of the dead, and four short films tell the story of the theatre and its turbulent history. On the stairs is a small display on the theatre before the war and on the floor above there's an excellent **exhibition** on the plight of the city's Jews, with lots of occupation photos and a number of poignant film clips.

By contrast, the old **auditorium** at the back of the building has been left as an empty, roofless shell. A memorial **column** of basalt on a Star of David base stands where the stage once was, an intensely mournful monument to suffering of unfathomable proportions.

Plantage Kerklaan 36

Tram #9 or #14 to Artis

Plantage Kerklaan 36, across the street from De Hollandsche Schouwburg, once housed the municipal register of births and deaths, records which were extremely helpful to the Germans and their Dutch collaborators in tracking down Jews and young men they wanted to conscript as forced labour. In March 1943, twelve members of the Dutch Resistance, dressed as policemen, entered the building, sedated the guards – who were taken to the zoo next door – then blew the place up. Almost all of the twelve were caught and executed, and their names are on the wall's **commemorative plaque**.

Artis Royal Zoo

Plantage Kerklaan 38–40 • Daily: March–Oct 9am–6pm; Nov–Feb 9am–5pm; June–Aug open till sundown on Sat with special activities • €21 • ☎ 020 523 3670, ⊕ artis.nl • Tram #9 or #14 to Artis

Opened in 1838, **Artis Royal Zoo** is the oldest zoo in the country, though one with a refreshing lack of bars and cages. Despite being one of the city's top attractions for kids, its layout means that it never feels overcrowded. Highlights include an African savanna environment, huge aquariums and an aviary; feeding times always draw a crowd (see page 210). In addition to the usual lions, monkeys and creepy-crawlies, there's also a children's farm where kids come nose-to-nose with sheep, calves and goats, and a new museum, **Micropia**, dedicated to the world of microorganisms (see page 210). The on-site **planetarium** has several shows daily, all in Dutch, though you can pick up a leaflet with an English translation from the desk.

4

EVOLUTION OF THE AMSTELHOF

The conversion of the **Amstelhof** into a gallery follows a curious history. During the second phase of the digging of the Grachtengordel, the three main canals that ringed the city centre were extended beyond the River Amstel up towards the Oosterdok – hence "Nieuwe" Herengracht, Keizersgracht and Prinsengracht. At first, takers for the new land were few and far between and the city had no option but to offer it to charities at discount prices. One result was the establishment of the Amstelhof, a large **hofje** built for the care of elderly women in the 1680s on behalf of the Dutch Reformed Church – with men allowed in from 1719. In time, the Amstelhof, a singularly stern-looking structure, grew to fill most of the chunk of land between Nieuwe Herengracht and Nieuwe Keizersgracht, becoming a fully fledged hospital in the process, but in the 1980s it became clear that its medical facilities were out of date and it went up for sale. Much municipal huffing and puffing ensued until the director of the **Hermitage Museum** in St Petersburg and his Dutch contacts proposed that the Amstelhof be turned into a museum of items on loan from the Hermitage. A very ambitious scheme, it has proved extremely popular – so popular in fact that although the Russian "imports" provide the bulk of the exhibits, they are often boosted by works from elsewhere.

De Burcht

Henri Polaklaan 9 • Open for conferences and special events only • ☎ 020 624 1166, ⓦ deburcht.nl • Tram #9 or #14 to Artis

One of the city's most striking modern buildings, **De Burcht** (The Stronghold) was built for the Diamond Workers' Union (the ANDB) in 1900 to a design by **Hendrik Petrus Berlage** (1856–1934). Berlage incorporated Romanesque features – such as the castellated balustrade and the deeply recessed main door – within an Expressionist framework, but this design was not just about his architectural whims. Acting on behalf of the employers, the police – and occasionally armed scabs – were regularly used to break strikes, and the union believed members would benefit from having a castle-like HQ where they could hole up in relative safety.

The building's brightly coloured **interior** develops these stylistic themes with a beautiful mixture of stained-glass windows, stone arches, painted brickwork and patterned tiles. In the foyer there's also a bust of the remarkable **Henri Polak**, part-time rabbi and founder of the ANDB (see page 86), and up the stairs Floor 1 holds the handsome, wood-panelled **Bestuurskamer** (Union Boardroom), which is kitted out in classic Arts and Crafts style. The room sports three paintings on asbestos cement – one each for sleep, work and relaxation – which celebrate the introduction of the eight-hour working day in 1911, the ANDB's most famous victory. The building is now used for conferences and special events, including weddings, though quite what Polak would have made of this change of use is hard to imagine.

The Verzetsmuseum

Plantage Kerklaan 61 • Mon–Fri 10am–5pm, Sat & Sun 11am–5pm • €11 • ☎ 020 620 2535, ⓦ verzetsmuseum.org • Metro Waterlooplein or tram #9 or #14 to Plantage Kerklaan

The excellent **Verzetsmuseum** (Dutch Resistance Museum) relates the story of the **German occupation** of the Netherlands and the progress of the Resistance in World War II, from the invasion of May 1940 to the liberation of 1945. Thoughtfully presented, the display along the central gangway examines the main themes of the occupation, dealing honestly with the fine balance between cooperation and collaboration. On either side, smaller display areas are devoted to different aspects of the **Resistance**, like the coordinated transport strike towards the end of the war and more ad hoc responses, like the so-called **Melkstaking** (Milk Strike) in the spring of 1943, when hundreds of milk producers refused to deliver, in protest at the Germans' threatened deportation of 300,000 former (demobilized) Dutch soldiers to labour camps in Germany. There is also a particularly interesting section on the Jews, outlining the way in which the Germans gradually isolated them, breaking their connections with the rest of the Dutch population before moving in for the kill. Interestingly, the Dutch Resistance proved especially adept at forgery, forcing the Germans to make the identity cards they issued more and more complicated – but without much success.

Throughout the museum, a first-rate range of old **photographs** illustrates the (English and Dutch) text along with a host of original **artefacts**, from examples of illegal newsletters to signed German death warrants and, perhaps most moving of all, farewell letters thrown from trains heading to Auschwitz. There is also a separate children's section – **Verzetsmuseum Juior** (see page 210) – which traces the stories of four children who witnessed World War II first-hand.

Mass reprisals

Apart from the treatment of the Jews, perhaps the most chilling feature of the occupation was the use of **mass reprisals** to terrify the population. Adopted in 1944, when the Dutch Resistance became a major irritant, this policy of indiscriminate butchery cowed most of the population most of the time, though there was always a minority courageous enough to resist. Some of these brave men and women are commemorated by little metal sheets, which provide potted biographical notes – and it's this mixture of the general and the personal that is the museum's particular strength.

The Dutch East Indies

One intriguing subsection focuses on the **Dutch East Indies**, modern-day Indonesia, where many of the inhabitants initially welcomed the Japanese when they brushed the Dutch aside during the Japanese invasion of the islands in 1942. The Indonesians soon learnt that the Japanese were not to be preferred to their old masters, but when the Dutch tried to reassert their control at the end of World War II in a shoddy and shameful colonial war, the Indonesians fought back, eventually winning independence in 1949.

4

NEMO

The eastern docklands and Amsterdam Noord

Amsterdam's docklands once extended right along the River IJ, comprising a vast maritime complex that incorporated both the western and the eastern docklands, on the south side of the river, and a slew of shipyards on the north side in Amsterdam Noord. Industrial decline set in during the 1880s, but the assorted artificial islands of the eastern docklands – often lumped together as Zeeburg – have now been redefined as a residential and leisure district, featuring some startling modern architecture and cultural hubs. Nonetheless, reminders of the district's nautical heyday are legion, from the warehouses of Entrepotdok to the engaging Scheepvaartmuseum (Maritime Museum).

Amsterdam Noord, stretching out along the far side of the River IJ and reached by ferries from behind Centraal Station, is in an earlier phase of redevelopment. First up for a designer makeover was the motley area around the Buiksloterweg quay, whose whole demeanour has been transformed by the construction of the **EYE Filmmuseum**, Amsterdam's best cinema in the city's proudest new building. Further out along the north side of the river, there's a second patch of cutting-edge redevelopment in the fast-regenerating **NDSM Shipyard**, once an industrial wasteland, now a creative arts and events hub. Finally, just beyond Amsterdam Noord is the rustic **Waterland**, whose dykes and lagoons, meadows and farmland make for pleasant cycling, and stretch as far as Marken (see page 135).

5

The eastern docklands (Oosterdok)

Just to the north of the Plantage district lies the **Oosterdok**, or **eastern docklands**, whose network of artificial islands was dredged out of the River IJ to increase Amsterdam's shipping facilities in the seventeenth and eighteenth centuries. By the 1980s, this mosaic of docks, jetties and islands had become something of a postindustrial eyesore, but since then an ambitious redevelopment programme has turned things around and parts of the area are now occupied by some of the city's most popular housing. It's an enjoyable area to explore and there are three key sights – the **Scheepvaartmuseum** (Maritime Museum), the **NEMO** science and technology centre, which is primarily aimed at kids, and the **De Appel** gallery of contemporary art.

Entrepotdok

Bus #22 or #48 to Kadijksplein

At the northern end of Plantage Kerklaan, just beyond the Verzetsmuseum (see page 92), a footbridge leads over to **Entrepotdok**, on the nearest – and most interesting – of the Oosterdok islands. Old brick **warehouses** stretch along much of the quayside, distinguished by their spout gables, multiple doorways and overhead pulleys. Built by the **Dutch East India Company** (see box) in the eighteenth century, they were once part of the largest warehouse complex in Continental Europe, a gigantic customs-free zone established for goods in transit. On the ground floor, above each main entrance, every warehouse sports the name of a town or island; goods for onward transportation were stored in the appropriate warehouse until there were enough to fill a boat or barge. The warehouses have been tastefully converted into offices and apartments, a fate they share with the central

---

THE DUTCH EAST INDIA COMPANY

Founded in 1602, the **Dutch East India Company** (the VOC – Verenigde Oostindische Compagnie) was the chief pillar of Amsterdam's wealth for nearly two hundred years. Its high-percentage profits came from importing spices into Europe, and to secure its supplies the company's ships ventured far and wide, establishing trading links with India, Sri Lanka, Indochina, Malaya, China and Japan, though modern-day Indonesia was always the main event. Predictably, the company had a cosy relationship with the merchants who steered the Dutch government: the company was granted a trading monopoly in all the lands east of the Cape of Good Hope and could rely on the warships of the powerful Dutch Navy if they got into difficulty. Neither was their business purely mercantile; the East India Company exercised unlimited military, judicial and political powers in those trading posts it established, the first of which was Batavia in Java in 1619.

In the 1750s, the Dutch East India Company went into decline, partly because the British expelled them from most of the best trading stations, but mainly because the company had borrowed too heavily. Napoleon had little time for the privileges and pretensions of the VOC, abolishing its ruling council and ultimately dissolving the company in 1799.

5

Dutch East India Company compound, whose modest brickwork culminates in a chunky Neoclassical entrance at the west end of Entrepotdok on Kadijksplein.

The Scheepvaartmuseum

Kattenburgerplein • Daily 9am–5pm • €16 • ☎ 020 523 2222, ⓦ hetscheepvaartmuseum.nl • Bus #22 or #48 from Centraal Station to Kadijksplein, or a 15min walk from the station

The **Scheepvaartmuseum** (Maritime Museum) occupies the old arsenal of the Dutch Navy, an imposing sandstone structure built on its own mini-islet in the 1650s. It's underpinned by no fewer than 18,000 wooden piles driven deep into the riverbed at enormous expense, a testament to the nautical ambitions of the emergent nation. There's no mistaking the building's serious intentions, its four symmetrical facades suitably dour, its stylistic flourishes limited to some quaint dormer windows and Neoclassical pediments. At the centre, now roofed with a glass canopy, is a wide cobbled courtyard under which was kept a copious supply of fresh water to supply the fleet. At the jetty round the back is a full-scale replica of an East Indiaman merchant ship.

The bulk of the museum's **collection** is displayed in the building's west and east wings, while the north wing is mainly of use as an access point to the jetty. In 2018, the museum launched Dare to Discover, a virtual-reality experience that transports users back to the Dutch Golden Age. The **west wing** is largely devoted to temporary exhibitions, many of which are aimed at children, while the key exhibits are concentrated in the **east wing** on **Floor 2**. It's here you'll find a room full of garish ships' figureheads, a herd of navigational aids and an outstanding assortment of nautical paintings, some trumpeting the achievements of Dutch trading ships, others showing heavy seas and shipwrecks, and yet more celebrating the successes of the Dutch navy, the most powerful fleet in the world for about thirty years from the 1650s onwards. In particular, there's a number of paintings by **Willem van de Velde II** (1633–1707), without doubt the country's finest marine painter.

De Amsterdam

Outside the Scheepvaartmuseum, moored at the museum jetty, is a full-scale replica of an East Indiaman, the 78m **De Amsterdam**. The original ship first set sail in 1748, but came to an ignominious end, getting stuck on the British coast near Hastings. Visitors can wander its decks and galleys, storerooms and gun bays at their leisure, and there are organized activities on board too (see the museum website for details).

ARCAM

Prins Hendrikkade 600 • Tues–Sun 1–5pm • Free • ☎ 020 620 4878, ⓦ arcam.nl • Bus #22 or #48 from Centraal Station to Kadijksplein, or a 15min walk from the station

Sitting pretty on the waterfront, **ARCAM**, the Amsterdam Centre for Architecture, is housed in a distinctive aluminium and glass structure designed by the Dutch

---

JAN VAN SPEIJK: A MARTYR TO THE CAUSE

The Scheepvaartmuseum's layout is something of a moveable feast, but Floor 2 on the east wing is usually home to a cabinet of commemorative souvenirs celebrating the dramatic end of **Jan Carel Josephus van Speijk**, whose misguided heroism made him a folk hero. An Amsterdam orphan, Speijk joined the Dutch Navy, rising through the ranks to become the commander of a munitions ship. In 1830, Speijk and his ship were in Antwerp harbour when that city joined the rebellion against the United Kingdom of the Netherlands (1815–30), the short-lived attempt to combine modern-day Belgium and the Netherlands. The rebellion was to prove successful – leading to the creation of an independent Belgium – but Speijk, seeing the rebels approaching, decided to blow his ship up rather than allow its munitions to fall into their hands, killing himself and most of his crew in the process.

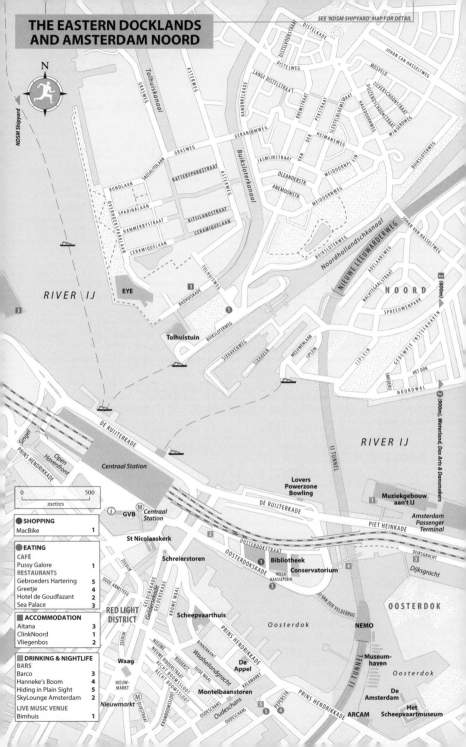

THE EASTERN DOCKLANDS AND AMSTERDAM NOORD

N

NDSM Shipyard

RIVER IJ

EYE

Tolhuistuin

NOORD

3 (800m)

2 (900m), Waterland, Das Arts & Dansmakers

RIVER IJ

DE RUIJTERKADE

Open Havenfront

Centraal Station

Singel

PRINS HENDRIKKADE

Lovers Powerzone Bowling

DE RUIJTERKADE

Muziekgebouw aan't IJ **1**

Amsterdam Passenger Terminal

PIET HEINKADE

IJ TUNNEL

0 ——— 500
metres

(i) GVB **M** Centraal Station

St Nicolaaskerk

Schreierstoren

OOSTERDOKSTRAAT

OOSTERDOKSKADE

Bibliotheek **1**
Conservatorium

HELLA HAASSEPLEIN **3**

DIJKSGRACHT

Dijksgracht

4

IJ VAN DER VELDEBRUG

OOSTERDOK

RED LIGHT DISTRICT

ZEEDIJK
OUDE ARMSTEEG
GELDERSEKADE
KROME WAAL

Scheepvaarthuis

PRINS HENDRIKKADE

Oosterdok

NEMO

Museum-haven

Oosterdok

De Amsterdam

Waag

Nieuwmarkt **M**

NIEUW-MARKT

DIJKSTRAAT

ZEEDIJK

NIEUWE RIDDERSTR
RECHT BOOMSSLOOT
KROMBOOMSSLOOT
OUDESCHANS
OUDESCHANS

BINNENKANT
OUDE WAAL
Waalseilandgracht
KALKMARKT

De Appel

Montelbaanstoren

PEPERSTR
PRINS HENDRIKKADE

5
5   **4**

ARCAM

Het Scheepvaartmuseum

5

architect **René van Zuuk**. The modern design was much praised at the time of its construction, but the building does look rather disconcertingly like the head of a golf club. Inside, a small gallery area is used for an imaginative programme of temporary exhibitions on contemporary architecture in general and future building plans for Amsterdam in particular.

ARCAM also publishes a number of specialist architectural books, maps and leaflets on Amsterdam, and these are on sale here too.

The Museumhaven

Oosterdok • Open access • Free • Bus #22 or #48 from Centraal Station to Kadijksplein, or a 15min walk from the station

Moored on the long jetty between ARCAM and NEMO are the antique boats and barges of the **Museumhaven**, which together make an informal record of the development of local shipping; the earliest boats date from the middle of the nineteenth century, and plaques, in English and Dutch, give the historical lowdown on the more important vessels.

NEMO

Oosterdok • Tues–Sun 10am–5.30pm; mid-Feb to mid-Sept & school holidays also open Mon same hours • €16.50 • ☎ 020 531 3233, ⓦ nemosciencemuseum.nl • Bus #22 or #48 from Centraal Station to Kadijksplein, or Canal Bus (see page 23) from Centraal Station, or a 10min walk via the footbridge spanning the water between NEMO and the Oosterdokskade

Resembling the prow of a ship, the massive, copper-green elevated hood that rears up above the entrance to the River IJ tunnel was designed by the Italian architect Renzo Piano in the 1990s. Inside is **NEMO**, a large and popular science and technology centre whose various interactive exhibits combine to create a (pre-teenage) kids' attraction *par excellence*.

Spread over three main floors, there's plenty of interest here, from interactive exhibits spanning the most distant corners of the globe in the 'Life in Universe' section, to 'Sensational Science' revealing the facts behind common phenomena such as light and sound.

Bibliotheek

Oosterdokskade 143 • Daily 10am–10pm • ☎ 020 523 0900, ⓦ oba.nl • A 5min walk from Centraal Station

Opened in 2007, Amsterdam's principal **Bibliotheek** (Library) occupies a cleverly designed modern block overlooking the waters of the Oosterdok, and across the footbridge from NEMO. The building was designed by Jo Coenon, a Dutch architect and urban planner of repute, and the spacious, subtly lit interior spreads over ten floors; among much else, it includes an auditorium, an exhibition room and a terrace café.

De Appel

Prins Hendrikkade 142 • Tues–Sat noon–6pm • €7 • ☎ 020 625 5651, ⓦ deappel.nl • A 10min walk from Centraal Station

A self-styled international institution for contemporary art, the **De Appel** arts centre offers an ambitious programme of temporary exhibitions in a variety of media and conceptual art forms, from film through to sculpture, installations and paintings.

Housed in an unassuming building, the nineteenth-century premises have had a patchy history – they have previously served as both a spiritual and a meditation centre – but they are large enough to showcase several exhibitions at any one time and there are also performances, film screenings, lectures and debates. There's a vast library and archive, too.

5

Scheepvaarthuis

Grand Hotel Amrâth Amsterdam, Prins Hendrikkade 108, on the corner of Binnenkant • ☎ 020 552 0000, ⓦ amrathamsterdam.com • A 7min walk from Centraal Station

Completed in 1917, the **Scheepvaarthuis** (Shipping Building) is one of the flashiest of the buildings designed by the Amsterdam School of architecture, the work of a certain **Johann Melchior van der Mey** (1878–1949). An almost neurotically decorated edifice covered with a welter of detail celebrating the city's marine connections, it has an entrance shaped like a prow and surmounted by statues of Poseidon and Amphitrite, his wife. Up above them are female representations of the four points of the compass, while slender turrets and Expressionistic carvings playfully decorate the walls. It was built as shipping offices, but is now home to the five-star hotel *Amrâth* – pop in for a glimpse of the immaculately maintained interior.

Zeeburg

To the north and east of the Oosterdok, **Zeeburg** – basically the old docklands between the city library and KNSM Island – has become one of the city's most up-and-coming districts. Actually a series of artificial islands and peninsulas connected by bridges, the docks here date back to the end of the nineteenth century, but like dockland areas all over Europe they fell into disuse and disrepair during the 1970s with the advent of large container ships, which couldn't travel this far upriver. By the early 1990s the area was virtually derelict, and the city council began a massive renovation, which has been rolling on for over twenty years. As a result, this is one of the fastest-developing parts of Amsterdam, with a mixture of renovated dockside structures and new landmark buildings that give it a modern (and very watery) feel that's markedly different from the city centre – despite being just a short walk from Centraal Station. It's the general appearance of the district, rather than any specific sight, which provides its main appeal, so you're best off exploring by bike, especially as distances are – at least in Amsterdam terms – comparatively large: from the library to the east end of KNSM Island is about 4km.

Piet Heinkade

Tram #26 from Centraal Station

The sheer scale of the Zeeburg redevelopment is staggering – and you can get a sense of the city's ambition at two of the district's prime buildings, which are located beside the River IJ just east of Centraal Station – and at the west end of one of the area's new boulevards, **Piet Heinkade**. These two structures are the **Muziekgebouw** (see page 185) and the neighbouring **Amsterdam Passenger Terminal**, a glass-walled behemoth, where visiting cruise ships now berth.

Muziekgebouw aan 't IJ

Piet Heinkade 1 • ☎ 020 788 2000, ⓦ muziekgebouw.nl

A high-spec, multipurpose music auditorium designed by the Danish architects 3XN, the glassy cubes and squares of the **Muziekgebouw** overlook the River IJ. The key to the interior is its flexibility – ceilings, walls and floor are all moveable and adjustable.

Java Island

Bus #48 links Centraal Station with Java, KNSM and Sporenburg islands

The 200m-long **Jan Schaeferbrug** spans the River IJ to reach **Java Island**, a long and narrow sliver of land where tall residential blocks, mostly five storeys high, line up along the four mini-canals that cut across it. In form and layout these high-rises are

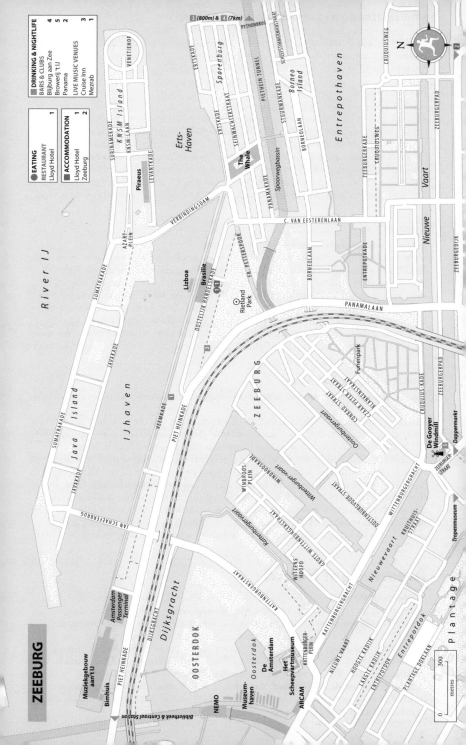

ZEEBURG

River IJ

Muziekgebouw aan't IJ
Bimhuis

Amsterdam Passenger Terminal

Piet Heinkade

Bibliotheek & Centraal Station

OOSTERDOK

Oosterdok

NEMO

Museum-haven

Het Scheepvartmuseum

De Amsterdam

ARCAM

KATTENBURGER-PLEIN

KATTENBURGERGRACHT

NIEUWE VAART

HOOGTE KADIJK

LANGE KADIJK

ENTREPOTDOK

Entrepotdok

PLANTAGE DOKLAAN

Plantage

Tropenmuseum

Doppermarkt

De Gooyer Windmill

ZEEBURGER-STRAAT

WITTENBURGERGRACHT

OOSTENBURGERVOORGRACHT

KRUITHUIS-STRAAT

CRUQUIUS-KADE

ZEEBURGERPAD

Nieuwevaart

WITTENS HOOFD

GROTE WITTENBURGERSTRAAT

KLEINE WITTENBURGERSTRAAT

KATTENBURGERSTRAAT

KORTENBURGERVOORT

WINDROOS-PLEIN

Wittenburger-vaart

Oostenburgervaart

CONRAD-STRAAT

(JAAK PETER STRAAT)

BLANKENSTRAAT

Funenpark

ZEEBURG

PANAMALAAN

Rietland Park

Brasilie

Lizboa

OOSTELIJK HANDELSKADE

Veemkade

PIET HEINKADE

JAN SCHAEFERBRUG

Dijksgracht

DIJKSGRACHT

Java Island

SUMATRAKADE

SUMATRAKADE

JAVAKADE

JAVAKADE

IJhaven

SURINAMEKADE

AZART-PLEIN

Piraeus

KNSM-LAAN

KNSM Island

LEVANTKADE

VENETIEHOF

VERBINDINGSDAM

Erts-Haven

ERTSKADE

ERTSKADE

SEINWACHTERSTRAAT

C. van Eesterenlaan

The Whale

PANAMAKADE

Spoorwegbassin

BORNEOLAAN

BORNEOLAAN

Sporenburg

STUURMANKADE

Borneo Island

PIETHEIN TUNNEL

SCHEEPTIMMERMANSTRAAT

PYTHONBRUG

Entrepothaven

ZEEBURGERKADE

ZEEBURGERKADE

CRUQUIUSWEG

ENTREPOTKADE

Nieuwe Vaart

ZEEBURGERDIJK

ZEEBURGERPAD

CRUQUIUSWEG

ZEEBURGERKADE

3 (800m) & **4** (7km)

EATING
● RESTAURANT	
Lloyd Hotel	1

ACCOMMODATION
■ ACCOMMODATION	
Lloyd Hotel	1
Zeeburg	2

■ DRINKING & NIGHTLIFE
BARS & CLUBS	
Blijburg aan Zee	4
Brouwerij 't IJ	5
Panama	2
LIVE MUSIC VENUES	
Cruise Inn	3
Mezrab	1

0   300
metres

N

5

a successful contemporary take on the seventeenth-century canal houses of the city centre, with a string of quirky, wrought-iron bridges adding panache.

KNSM Island

Bus #48 links Centraal Station with Java, KNSM and Sporenburg islands

The east end of Java Island merges seamlessly with **KNSM Island**, which is named after the shipping company (the Royal Dutch Steamboat Company) that was once based here. Leafy **KNSM-Laan** runs down the centre of the island, flanked by modern blocks, of which the German-designed **Piraeus** apartment building, at the west end of the street, gives the clearest impression of the clumsily monumental nature of much of the architecture here. That said, waterside **Surinamekade**, on the north side of the island, is much prettier, decorated with houseboats, barges and decommissioned fishing smacks.

Sporenburg

Bus #48 links Centraal Station with Java, KNSM and Sporenburg islands

Short and stumpy, the **Sporenburg peninsula** is known for the blunt Modernism of **The Whale**, a large and distinctive residential block standing at the south end of the **Verbindingsdam** causeway, which links the peninsula with KNSM Island. Completed in 1995 to a design by the architect Frits van Dongen, the block takes its name from its size and shape, the sharp outlines of which apparently allow the sun to better warm the building. On the southern edge of Sporenburg is **Panamakade**, where two bridges lead over to the modern, cubic terraces of Borneo Island; the more westerly bridge is flat and ordinary, the other, the precipitous **Pythonbrug**, is named after its curvy, snake-like shape.

Oostelijke Handelskade

Tram #26 runs along Piet Heinkade from Centraal Station to the Rietlandpark tram stop, a 3min walk from Oostelijke Handelskade and the Lloyd Hotel

Running parallel to the IJhaven, **Oostelijke Handelskade** was once a centre of maritime activity, its prime building, now the **Lloyd Hotel** (see pages 150 and 168), starting out in the 1920s as a transit point for passengers travelling onto South America by boat. In the event, this venture did not succeed and the building was subsequently turned into an internment centre by the Germans in World War II and ultimately a borstal – a small display inside the hotel tracks through its bumpy history. Close by are three minor points of interest: the **Brasilie** shopping centre (ⓦwinkelcentrumbrazilie. nl), which occupies a former cocoa warehouse; the **Lizboa**, a replica of a Russian merchant ship, now a restaurant; and the former offices of the **KHL shipping line**, a dinky 1930s building that has been turned into a friendly little café (ⓦdenieuwekhl.nl).

Amsterdam Noord

Amsterdam Noord (North), on the far side of the River IJ, has burgeoned since the construction of the IJ tunnel linked it with the city centre in the 1960s, and more expansion will undoubtedly follow when the Noord-Zuidlijn is finally completed in 2018. The result of all this development is a modern suburban sprawl of little immediate appeal, with a couple of exceptions. The prestigious **EYE Filmmuseum** and cinema, which inhabits a striking building down by the river on the IJpromenade, is the district's main draw. You might also venture across the IJ to go to a gig or event at the regenerated **NDSM Shipyard**. Amsterdam Noord comes to an abrupt end on its eastern side, giving way to the **Waterland**, an expanse of peat meadows, lakes and marshland (see page 103).

CYCLING THE WATERLAND

A chunk of land between Amsterdam Noord and Marken (see page 135), the **Waterland** was an inhospitable marshy fen until the turn of the twentieth century, when it was made more tractable by the digging of drainage canals. These myriad waterways are now home to a wide range of **waterfowl**, as are the area's many lagoons and lakes, the largest of which – abutting the Markermeer – is the **Kinselmeer**. The best way to explore the Waterland is by **bike**, and Amsterdam VVV (see page 30) offers downloadable maps featuring popular cycle routes (⑩ bit.ly/AmsterdamCycleRoutes). One good trip of about 40km begins at the **IJplein ferry dock** on the north side of the IJ, from where you follow Meeuwenlaan to Nieuwendammerdijk. This long lane leads east to meet Schellingwoudedijk, which sticks close to the river before it merges into Durgerdammerdijke at the southern tip of the long dyke that stretches up the coast to Marken. You can return to the dock the same way or travel back a little inland.

GVB, Amsterdam's principal public transport company (⑩ en.gvb.nl), operates half a dozen passenger **ferry services** across the River IJ from the back of Centraal Station. For IJplein, at the start of the Waterland cycle route described above, take the IJpleinveer ferry (daily 6.30am–midnight; every 10–15min; passengers and cycles free; 10min).

The EYE Filmmuseum

IJpromenade 1 · Exhibition space daily 10am–7pm · €10, €16 with a film · ☎ 020 589 1400, ⑩ eyefilm.nl · Take the GVB Buiksloterwegveer passenger ferry service across the River IJ from the back of Centraal Station to the Buiksloterweg quay (daily 6.30am–11pm, till 9pm from Buiksloterweg; every 10–15min; 10min; passengers and cycles free); it's a 5min walk from the ferry dock

Clearly visible from the south side of the River IJ – including parts of Centraal Station – the **EYE Filmmuseum** occupies a superb contemporary building, a graceful shimmering structure whose sleek, angular lines were designed by a Viennese architecture firm, Delugan Meissl. The EYE offers engaging views back over both the river and the city centre from all its three floors, which hold a bar-restaurant, a shop, a film-focused library and four cinema screens (see page 188) showing an enterprising programme of classic and cult films. There is also an **exhibition area** offering four major displays each year, with favourite themes being the interface between film and the visual arts and the evolution of Dutch film and cinematography. One of the most prized parts of the EYE's cinematic collection is the **Jean Desmet** (1875–1956) archive,

NDSM SHIPYARD

●SHOPPING	
Neef Louis	2
Van Dijk & Ko	1

●EATING	
CAFÉS	
Café de Ceuvel	4
Noorderlicht	2
RESTAURANTS	
IJ-Kantine	1
Pllek	3

■ACCOMMODATION	
Amstel Botel	2
DoubleTree by Hilton Hotel Amsterdam	1
Faralda Crane	3

5

comprising over nine hundred films, which the eponymous filmmaker and distributor collected from 1906, until World War I stopped him in his tracks in 1915.

The NDSM Shipyard

Take the GVB passenger ferry service across the River IJ from the back of Centraal Station to the quay at the NDSM Shipyard jetty (daily 6.30am–11.30pm; every 15–30min; 20min; passengers and cycles free)

Until it closed in 1979, the **NDSM Shipyard** was a key part of Amsterdam's industrial economy, its workshops, wharves and engineering plant spreading over a large chunk of land on the north side of the River IJ. After NDSM's demise, no one was quite sure what to do with the site, but very little was demolished and in the last few years the old shipyard – and its distressed industrial buildings – has been revived as an arts and events hub, with a platoon of new or recycled buildings, plus hotels and restaurants (see pages 150, 160 and 169). More will follow, as the work has just begun.

The Museum Quarter and around

During the nineteenth century, Amsterdam burst out of its restraining canals, gobbling up the surrounding countryside with a slew of new residential suburbs, including the Oud Zuid (Old South), at the heart of which was De Pijp, now one of the city's coolest neighbourhoods. Nearby, just to the west, Amsterdam's three leading art museums cluster on the edge of Museumplein in what is commonly known as the Museum Quarter. The largest of the three, the Rijksmuseum, offers a superb sample of Dutch paintings, especially – and most famously – those from Amsterdam's seventeenth-century Golden Age. Similarly impressive is the nearby Van Gogh Museum, which boasts the biggest collection of the artist's paintings in the world, and the wide-ranging contemporary art of the Stedelijk Museum.

Offering a peaceful antidote to the bustle of the Museum Quarter, the leafy **Vondelpark** – the city's most popular green space – is just a few minutes' walk away. East of the museums, the focus of interest in the Oud Zuid is **De Pijp**, a largely working-class neighbourhood with a cosmopolitan population drawn from every corner of the globe. De Pijp's main attractions are the **Heineken Experience**, sited in the company's old brewery, and the sprawling **Albert Cuypstraat open-air market**, while further south, beyond De Pijp, the star turn is the splendid architecture of the **De Dageraad housing estate**.

6

The Rijksmuseum

Museumstraat 1 • Daily 9am–5pm; guided tours take place daily, including the popular "Highlights of the Rijksmuseum" tour (4–8 daily, book in advance if possible) • €17.50; temporary exhibitions extra; guided tours €5 • ☎ 020 6747 000, ✆ rijksmuseum.nl • Tram #2 or #5 to Rijksmuseum, or bus #758 to Rijksmuseum

Facing out towards the Singelgracht canal, at the head of Museumplein, the internationally famous **Rijksmuseum** occupies an imposing pile designed in the early 1880s by **Petrus J.H. Cuypers** (1827–1921). The leading Dutch architect of his day, Cuypers specialized in Neogothic churches, but this commission – along with the one he secured for Centraal Station (see page 33) – called for something more ambitious, the result being a reworking of the neo-Renaissance style then popular in the Netherlands, complete with towers and turrets, galleries, dormer windows and medallions. There's no argument that the building makes a grand statement – and one indeed that matches the museum's collection, an extravagant range of **Dutch paintings**, including many wonderful canvases from the seventeenth-century *Gouden Eeuw* (Golden Age), plus a vast hoard of **applied art and sculpture**.

Floor 2: The Eregalerij (Gallery of Honour)

At the start of the **Eregalerij**, you can expect to see the expansive and finely observed *Marriage Portrait of Isaac Massa and Beatrix Laen* by **Frans Hals** (1582–1666). Relaxing beneath a tree, a portly Isaac glows with contentment as his new wife sits beside him in a suitably demure manner. An intimate scene, the painting also carries a detailed iconography: the ivy at Beatrix's feet symbolizes her devotion to her husband, the thistle faithfulness, the vine togetherness and in the fantasy garden behind them the peacock is a classical allusion to Juno, the guardian of marriage.

Pieter Saenredam

Pieter Saenredam (1597–1665) lived and worked in Haarlem (see page 129), where he became well known for his cool and almost abstract church interiors. The Rijksmuseum has several of his paintings, but the pick is the *Old Town Hall of Amsterdam*, a characteristically precise work in which the tumbledown predecessor of the current building (now the Royal Palace) witnesses the comings and goings of black-hatted townsmen in the stilted manner of a Lowry.

Jan Steen

The prolific **Jan Steen** (1625–79) is well represented by the drunken waywardness of his *Merry Family*, the anarchy of the *Family Scene* and his *Feast of St Nicholas*, which, with its squabbling children, makes the festival a celebration of disorderly greed. Steen knew his bourgeois audience well: his caricatures of the proletariat blend humour with moral condemnation – or at least condescension – a mixture perfectly designed to suit their tastes. Steen was also capable of more subtle works, a famous example being his *Woman at her Toilet*, which is full of associations referring to sexual pleasures just had or about to be taken. For example, the woman is shown putting on a stocking in a conspicuous manner, the point being that the Dutch word for stocking, *kous*, is also a slang word

6

RIJKSMUSEUM ESSENTIALS

In the past few years, the Rijksmuseum has been thoroughly refurbished and is now equipped with an impressive **entrance area**, though the height of this has interfered with the building's original floor plan and as a consequence getting from one section to another can be confusing. **Floor 0** holds the most diverse part of the museum, with early Flemish paintings (1100–1600) on one side and collections of, among much else, delftware, armaments and ship models on the other. **Floor 1**, arguably the Rijksmuseum's weakest, features Dutch art from the eighteenth and nineteenth centuries, with a handful of lesser Van Goghs and a sample of the Hague School of landscape artists being the high points. Up above, **Floor 3** does a quick run-through of twentieth-century art and applied art, with Dutch figures such as Karel Appel and Gerrit Rietveld to the fore. In between, **Floor 2** holds the kernel of the collection, the **Golden Age** paintings, which deservedly attract most visitor attention, with key works displayed in the long and wide **Eregalerij** (Gallery of Honour) – our description follows the order in which the paintings are usually displayed. Temporary exhibitions are held in a separate wing.

In the permanent collection, there is some **rotation** of the paintings, but you can count on seeing all the leading Rembrandts, plus a decent number of canvases by Steen, Hals, Vermeer and their leading contemporaries; be sure to pick up a **free plan** at reception. Bear in mind also that the Rijksmuseum is extremely popular, so it's a good idea to **visit early in the day**, especially during major temporary exhibitions. You can also cut out most of the queuing if you have an I amsterdam card (see page 30), a Museumkaart (see page 30) or have booked online.

---

for a woman's genitalia; incidentally, sometimes this canvas is here, but often it's in rooms 2.24–2.28.

Pieter de Hooch

The paintings of **Pieter de Hooch** (1629–84) are less symbolic than those of Steen – more exercises in lighting – but they're as good a visual guide to the everyday life and habits of the seventeenth-century Dutch bourgeoisie as you'll find: witness both his curious *A Mother's Duty* in which the mother is delousing the child's head, and his *Interior with Women beside a Linen Basket*, showing the women of the house changing the linen while a series of doorways reveals the canal bank in the background.

Johannes Vermeer

The canvases of Pieter de Hooch bear comparison with, and are usually displayed near, the work of **Johannes Vermeer** (1632–75), whose *The Love Letter* reveals a tension between servant and mistress – the lute on the woman's lap was a well-known sexual symbol. *The Kitchen Maid* (also known as *The Milk Maid*), meanwhile, is an exquisitely observed domestic scene, right down to the nail – and its shadow – on the background wall. Similarly, in the precise *Woman in Blue Reading a Letter*, the map behind her hints at the far-flung places her lover is writing from. What you won't find, however, is Vermeer's *Girl with a Pearl Earring* – this is on display in the Mauritshuis gallery in The Hague.

Willem van de Velde II

By contrast, the preoccupations of **Willem van de Velde II** (1633–1707) were nautical, his canvases celebrating either the might of the Dutch navy or the seaworthiness of the merchant marine, as in the churning seas of the superbly executed *Gust of Wind*, whose counterpoint is to be found in the charming *Dutch Ships in a Calm*.

Rembrandt's pupils

The Eregalerij also features some of the work of Rembrandt's better-known pupils, including **Nicholas Maes** (1632–93), whose caring *Young Woman by the Cradle* is not so much a didactic tableau as an idealization of motherhood, his *Old Woman Saying*

Grace doing the same for old age. There are also a couple of canvases by **Gerard Dou** (1613–75), finely realized flashes of everyday life such as his *Old Woman Reading*, while another pupil, **Ferdinand Bol** (1616–80), chips in with the *Portrait of Elizabeth Bas* in a style so close to that of his master that it was regarded as a Rembrandt until the director of the museum proved otherwise in 1911. Perhaps the most talented of Rembrandt's pupils was **Carel Fabritius**, who was killed in 1654 at the age of 32, when Delft's gunpowder magazine exploded. His *Portrait of Abraham Potter* is a restrained, skilful work of soft, delicate hues, contrasting with the same artist's earlier *The Beheading of St John the Baptist*, in which the head is served on a platter in chillingly grisly style.

6

Rembrandt and The Night Watch

For many, **Rembrandt** (see box) is the star turn, and the museum owns several of his early paintings, most memorably an exquisite *Portrait of Maria Trip*, depicting an Amsterdam oligarch kitted out in all her pearls and lace finery. There's also the *Portrait of Johannes Wtenbogaert* in which the sitter's eyes are deep and mournful, suggesting the unbending conscience that had this prominent clergyman in trouble with Maurice, Prince of Orange. Of Rembrandt's later work, look out for the celebrated *Members of the Clothmakers Guild* and a late *Self-Portrait*, with the artist caught in mid-shrug as the Apostle Paul, a self-aware and defeated old man. Also here are the artist's touching depiction of his cowled son, *Titus*, and *The Jewish Bride*, one of his very last pictures, finished in 1667. No one knows who the couple are, nor whether they are actually married (the title came later), but the painting is one of Rembrandt's most telling, the

---

REMBRANDT'S PROGRESS

Born in Leiden to a family of millers, **Rembrandt Harmenszoon van Rijn** (1606–69) picked up his first artistic tips as an apprentice to Pieter Lastman in Amsterdam in the early 1620s, and it was here that the artist developed a penchant for mythological and religious subjects. After his apprenticeship, in around 1625, Rembrandt went back to Leiden to establish himself as an independent master painter and, this achieved, some six years later he returned to Amsterdam, where he was to stay for the rest of his life.

In the early 1630s Rembrandt concentrated on **portrait painting**, churning out dozens of pictures of the bourgeoisie of his day, a profitable business that made him both well-to-do and well known. In 1634 he married **Saskia van Uylenburgh** and five years later the couple moved into a smart house on Jodenbreestraat, now the Rembrandthuis museum (see page 82). All seemed well, and certainly Rembrandt's portraits of his wife are tender and loving, but these years were marred by the death of all but one of his four children in infancy, the sole survivor being his much-loved **Titus** (1641–68).

In 1642 Rembrandt produced what has become his most celebrated painting, **The Night Watch**, but thereafter his career went into decline, essentially because he forsook portraiture to focus on increasingly sombre and introspective **religious works**. Traditionally, Rembrandt's change of artistic direction has been linked to the death of Saskia in 1642, but although it is certainly true that the artist was grief-stricken, he was also facing increased competition from a new batch of portrait artists, primarily Bartholomeus van der Helst, Ferdinand Bol and Govert Flinck. Whatever the reason, there were few takers for Rembrandt's religious works and he made matters worse by refusing to adjust his spending. The crunch came in 1656, when he was formally declared insolvent, and four years later he was obliged to sell his house and goods, moving to much humbler premises in the Jordaan (see page 76). By this time, he had a new cohabitee, **Hendrickje Stoffels** (a clause in Saskia's will prevented them from ever marrying), and, in the early 1660s, she and Titus took Rembrandt in hand, sorting out his finances and his work schedule. With his money problems solved, a relieved Rembrandt then produced some of his finest paintings – for example *The Jewish Bride* – emotionally deep and contemplative works with a rough finish, the paint often daubed with an almost trowel-like heaviness. Hendrickje died in 1663 and Titus in 1668, a year before his father.

paint dashed on freely and the hands touching lovingly – as the art historian Kenneth Clark wrote, in "a marvellous amalgam of richness, tenderness and trust".

The culmination of the Eregalerij is Rembrandt's most famous painting, **The Night Watch** (*De Nachtwacht*) of 1642. Restored after being slashed in 1975, the scene is of a **militia company**, the Kloveniersdoelen, one of the companies formed in the sixteenth century to defend the United Provinces (later the Netherlands) against Spain. As the Habsburg threat receded, so the militias became social clubs for the well-heeled, who were eager to commission their own group portraits as signs of their prestige. Rembrandt charged the princely sum of one hundred guilders for each member of the company who wanted to be in the picture and sixteen – out of a possible two hundred – stumped up the cash. One of them was the company's moneyed captain, **Frans Banningh Cocq**, whose disapproval of Rembrandt's live-in relationship with Hendrickje Stoffels (see page 109) was ultimately to polish off their friendship. Curiously, *The Night Watch* is, in fact, a misnomer – the painting got the tag in the eighteenth century when the background darkness was misinterpreted. There were other misconceptions about the painting too, most notably that it was this work that led to the downward shift in Rembrandt's standing with the Amsterdam elite; in fact, there's no evidence that the militiamen weren't pleased with the picture, or that Rembrandt's commissions dwindled after it was completed.

Though not as subtle as much of the artist's later work, *The Night Watch* is an adept piece, full of movement and carefully arranged. Paintings of this kind were collections of individual portraits as much as **group pictures**, and for the artist their difficulty lay in doing justice to every single face while simultaneously producing a coherent group scene. Abandoning convention in vigorous style, Rembrandt opted to show the company preparing to march off – a snapshot of military activity in which banners are unfurled, muskets primed and drums rolled. There are a couple of **allegorical figures** as well, most prominently a young, spotlit woman with a bird hanging from her belt, a reference to the Kloveniersdoelen's traditional emblem of a claw. Militia portraits commonly included cameo portraits of the artist involved, but in this case it seems that Rembrandt didn't insert his likeness, though some art historians insist that the pudgy-faced figure peering out from the back between the gesticulating militiamen is indeed the artist himself.

The Night Watch's neighbours

Flanking *The Night Watch* are three other Civic Guard group portraits, including **Bartholomeus van der Helst**'s (1613–70) formal and static *Militiamen of the Company of Captain Roelof Bicker*. Rather more accomplished is *The Meagre Company*, started by **Frans Hals** (1580–1666) and finished by **Pieter Codde** (1599–78) due to a dispute. It's a great painting, full of sensitively realized individual portraits, but the more conservative arrangement of Hals's figures forms a striking contrast with Rembrandt's more fluid, dynamic work.

Floor 2: Venne, Avercamp and Goyen (Rooms 2.5 and 2.6)

As religious turmoil intensified in the Low Countries in the sixteenth century, so artists – both Protestant and Catholic – rallied to their particular cause with propaganda paintings. One of the most enjoyable of these is **Adriaen van de Venne**'s (1589–1662) crowded *Fishing for Souls*. There's no mistaking which side van de Venne was on: the Protestants are merrily heaving in souls on the left-hand side of the river, while the disorganized, hierarchical Catholics are stuck on the right. In these rooms also are several paintings by **Hendrik Avercamp** (1585–1634), who specialized in tiny and detailed winter scenes – as in his *Winter Landscape* – and the tonal browns of **Jan van Goyen** (1596–1656), who concentrated on landscapes, with his *Polder Landscape* being a fine example.

THE HEINEKEN EXPERIENCE

6

> ### DELFTWARE
>
> Named after the Dutch city of **Delft**, where it was manufactured, **delftware** traces its origins to fifteenth-century Mallorca, where craftsmen developed **majolica**, a kind of porous pottery that was glazed with metallic oxides. During the Renaissance, these techniques were exported to Italy from where they spread north, first to Antwerp and then to the United Provinces (aka the Netherlands). Initially, delft pottery **designs** featured landscapes, portraits and Bible stories, while the top end of the market was dominated by more ornate Chinese porcelain imported by the Dutch East India Company. However, when a prolonged civil war in China broke the supply line, Delft's factories quickly took over the luxury side of the market by copying Chinese designs. By the 1670s, Delft was churning out blue-and-white tiles, plates, panels, jars and vases of all descriptions by the thousand, even exporting to China, where they undercut Chinese producers. The delft factories were themselves undercut by the British and the Germans from the 1760s onwards, and by the time Napoleon arrived they had all but closed down. There was a modest revival of the delft industry in the 1870s and there are several Dutch producers today, but it's mostly cheap, mass-produced stuff of little originality.

Floor 2: The Treaty of Münster (Room 2.8)

For the Dutch at least, the Treaty of Münster was well worth celebrating: signed in 1648, it ended the Thirty Years' War and recognized the United Provinces (now the Netherlands) as an independent state, free of Habsburg control. No one enjoyed the victory more than Amsterdam's militia companies, and one of them – the Crossbowmen's Civic Guard – paid for **Bartholomeus van der Helst**'s (1613–70) breezily self-confident *The Celebration of the Treaty of Münster*. Later, Van der Helst was to become one of Amsterdam's most popular portraitists after Rembrandt abandoned the normal protocols of portraiture to adopt an introspective, religious style that did not impress the city's burghers one bit. In this room also is a smaller work, by **Gerard ter Borch**, which witnesses the signing of the treaty itself.

Floor 2: Small-scale Dutch painting (Rooms 2.24–2.28)

Widely travelled but mostly based in Holland, **Gerard ter Borch** (1617–81) was a versatile artist whose best work depicts apparently innocent scenes with a distinct subtext. In his *Woman at a Mirror*, for example, the woman glances in a meaningfully anxious manner at her servants, who look on with delicate irony from behind dutiful exteriors. There are yet more subtexts in ter Borch's *Paternal Admonition* – just what exactly is the young woman being told off for? Similarly versatile was **Gabriel Metsu** (1629–67), but his forte was closely observed domestic scenes in strong colours and with a layer of sentimentality – see *The Sick Child*.

Floor 0: The special collections

Perhaps more than anything else, the **special collections** inhabiting **Floor 0** demonstrate and illustrate the country's success as a trading nation and naval power during the Golden Age. This is particularly true of the museum's exemplary collection of **delftware**, from plates and tiles through to vases, chargers and flower holders. Dating from the late sixteenth century, the earlier pieces are comparatively plain, typically decorated with rural, classical or biblical scenes, whereas the later porcelain is more elaborate and often copied from – or in imitation of – Chinese ceramics (see box).

Spare time also for the fancy suits of armour and highly decorated pistols, daggers and swords of the **armaments** section, and the intricate replicas of seventeenth-century Dutch merchantmen among the **ship models**.

The Van Gogh Museum

Museumplein 6 • April–Aug Mon–Thurs & Sun 9am–7pm, Fri & Sat 9am–9pm; Sep–Oct Sat–Thurs 9am–6pm, Fri 9am–9pm; Nov–Mar Mon–Thurs & Sat 9am–5pm, Fri 9am–9pm; Vincent on Friday 9pm–10pm all year • €18 online only, book in advance • ☎ 020 570 5200, Ⓦ vangoghmuseum.nl • Tram #2, #3, #5, #12 or #13 to Van Baerlestraat

Vincent van Gogh (1853–90) is arguably the most popular, most reproduced and most talked about of all modern artists, so it's not surprising that the **Van Gogh Museum**, comprising a fabulous collection of his work, is one of Amsterdam's top attractions.

The museum occupies two modern buildings on the north edge of Museumplein, with the key paintings housed in an angular building designed by a leading light of the De Stijl movement, **Gerrit Rietveld** (1888–1964). This part of the museum, which is spread across four smallish floors, provides an introduction to the artist and his work based on paintings that were mostly inherited from Vincent's art-dealer brother Theo. There are usually small supporting displays here too, mostly putting van Gogh into artistic context with the work of his friends and contemporaries: the museum owns paintings by the likes of Toulouse-Lautrec, Cézanne, Bernard, Seurat, Gauguin, Anton Mauve, Charles Daubigny, Pissarro and Monet.

To the rear of Rietveld's building, connected by a ground-floor escalator, is the ultramodern extension of 1998. This aesthetically controversial structure – financed by the same Japanese insurance company that paid $35 million for one of van Gogh's *Sunflowers* canvases in 1987 – provides temporary exhibition space in its Kurokawa Wing (designed by, and named after, Japanese architect Kisho Kurokawa). Most of the **exhibitions** held here focus on one aspect or another of van Gogh's art and draw heavily on the permanent collection, which means that the paintings displayed in the older building are regularly rotated. The two buildings are connected by a spectacular glass entrance hall, added in 2015.

As you might expect, the museum can get very crowded and the **queues** can be long so come early to avoid the crush or book online.

Before Arles

Inside the Rietveld building, a flight of stairs leads up to the permanent collection, which spreads over three floors and is seemingly in a constant state of flux, with paintings regularly rotated or moved round. That said, the paintings of van Gogh are almost invariably presented in broadly chronological order, with temporary displays providing extra contextual or artistic ballast. The first paintings go back to the artist's **early years** in Holland and Belgium in the early 1880s; dark, sombre works in the main, ranging from an assortment of drab grey and brown still lifes to the gnarled faces and haunting, flickering light of *The Potato Eaters* – one of van Gogh's best-known paintings, and the culmination of hundreds of studies of the local peasantry.

Further along, the sobriety of these early works is easily transposed onto the urban landscape of **Paris** (1886–88), particularly in the *View of Paris*, where the city's domes and rooftops hover below Montmartre under a glowering, blustery sky. But before long, under the sway of fellow painters and the sheer colour of the city itself, van Gogh's approach began to change. This is most noticeable in two of his many self-portraits and in the pictures from **Asnières**, just outside Paris, where the artist used to go regularly to paint. In particular, look out for the surprisingly soft hues and gentle tones of his *Courting Couples*, and the disturbing yellows of *Still Life with Red Cabbages and Onions*. There's also a rare **photograph** of van Gogh in Asnières (though it's only of his back), which shows him in conversation with the artist Emile Bernard.

6

VAN GOGH'S EAR

In February 1888, **Vincent van Gogh** (1853–90) left Paris for **Arles**, a small town in the south of France. At first the move went well, with van Gogh warming to the open vistas and bright colours of the Provençal countryside. In September he moved into the dwelling he called the Yellow House, where he hoped to establish an artists' colony, gathering together painters of like mind. Unfortunately for van Gogh, his letters of invitation were ignored by most, and only **Gauguin**, who arrived in Arles in late October, stayed for long. Initially the two artists got on well, hunkering down together in the Yellow House and sometimes painting side by side, but the bonhomie didn't last. They argued long and hard about art, an especially tiring business for van Gogh, who complained: "Sometimes we come out of our arguments with our heads as exhausted as a used electric battery."

Later, Gauguin would claim that van Gogh threatened him during several of these arguments; true or not, it is certainly the case that Gauguin had decided to return to Paris by the time the two had a ferocious quarrel on the night of December 23. The argument was so bad that Gauguin hotfooted it off to the local hotel, and when he returned in the morning he was faced by the police. After Gauguin's exit, a deeply disturbed van Gogh had taken a razor to his **ear**, severing part of it before presenting the selected slice to a prostitute at the local brothel. Presumably, this was not an especially welcome gift, but in van Gogh's addled state he may well have forged some sort of connection with bullfighting, where the dead bull's ears are cut off and given as a prize to the bullfighter. Hours after Gauguin's return, van Gogh was admitted to hospital, the first of several extended stays, before, fearing for his sanity, he committed himself to the asylum of **St Rémy** in May 1889. Here, the doctor's initial assessment described him as suffering from "acute mania, with hallucinations of sight and hearing"; van Gogh attributed his parlous state to excessive drinking and smoking, though he gave up neither during his year-long stay.

In May 1890, feeling lonely and homesick, van Gogh discharged himself from St Rémy and headed north to Paris before proceeding to the village of **Auvers-sur-Oise**. At first, van Gogh's health improved and he even began to garner critical recognition for his work. However, his twin ogres of depression and loneliness soon returned to haunt him and, in despair, van Gogh shot himself in the chest. This wasn't, however, the end; he took two days to die, even enduring a police visit when he refused to answer any questions, pronouncing: "I am free to do what I like with my own body."

Arles

In February 1888 van Gogh moved to **Arles**, inviting Gauguin to join him a little later (see page 114). With the change of scenery came a heightened interest in colour, and the predominance of **yellow** as a recurring motif; it's represented best in such paintings as *The Harvest*, and most vividly in the disconcerting juxtapositions of *Bedroom in Arles*. Also from this period comes a striking canvas from the artist's *Sunflowers* series, rightly one of his most lauded works, and intensely – almost obsessively – rendered in the deepest oranges, golds and ochres he could find. Gauguin told of van Gogh painting these flowers in a near-trance; there were usually sunflowers in jars all over their house – in fact, they can be seen in Gauguin's portrait of van Gogh from the same period, usually displayed nearby.

St Rémy and after

During his time at the asylum in **St Rémy** (see box, above), van Gogh's approach to nature became more abstract, as evidenced by his unsettling *Wheatfield with a Reaper*, the dense, knotty *Undergrowth* and his palpable *Irises*. Van Gogh is at his most expressionistic here, the paint applied thickly, often with a palette knife, a practice he continued in his final, tortured works painted at **Auvers-sur-Oise**, where he lodged for the last three months of his life. It was at Auvers that he painted the frantic *Wheatfield with Crows*, in which the fields swirl and writhe under weird and dark skies, as well as the organized chaos of *Tree Roots* and the glowering *Wheatfield under Thunderclouds*.

The Stedelijk Museum

Museumplein 10 • Mon–Thurs & Sat 10am–6pm • €17.50 • ☏020 573 2911, ⓦstedelijk.nl • Tram #2, #3, #5, #12 or #13 to Van Baerlestraat

The **Stedelijk Museum**, just along the street from the Van Gogh Museum, has long been Amsterdam's number one venue for modern and contemporary art. It's housed in a big old building that's been dramatically transformed to a design by Benthem Crouwel Architects, though the end result has not been to everyone's liking: the facade looks a little like a giant bathtub. Jarring as it is, the eye-popping building contains the excellent Stedelijk Base, a creative exhibition space designed by Rem Koolhaas and Federico Martelli – thin freestanding walls encourage guests to weave their own route through the 750-plus artworks.

The museum focuses on cutting-edge, temporary exhibitions of **modern art** – from photography through to sculpture and collage – supplemented by a regularly rotated selection from the museum's large and wide-ranging **permanent collection**. Among many highlights, the latter includes a large sample of the work of **Mondriaan** (1872–1944), from his early, muddy abstracts to the boldly coloured rectangular blocks for which he's most famous. The Stedelijk is also strong on Karel Appel, Theo van Doesburg and **Kasimir Malevich** (1878–1935), whose dense attempts at Cubism led to the dynamism and bold primary tones of his "Suprematist" paintings – slices, blocks and bolts of colour that shift around as if about to resolve themselves into some complex computer graphic. Look out too for several paintings by Marc Chagall and a number by American Abstract Expressionists Mark Rothko, Ellsworth Kelly and Barnett Newman, plus the odd work by Lichtenstein, Warhol, Robert Ryman, Willem de Kooning and Jean Dubuffet. The Stedelijk was also the first European museum to start collecting video art, of which it has an extensive range.

Museumplein

Tram #16 to Museumplein, or tram #2, #3, #5, #12 or #13 to Van Baerlestraat

Pancake-flat **Museumplein** is a large open space extending south from the Rijksmuseum to Van Baerlestraat, its wide lawns and gravelled spaces used for a variety of outdoor activities from visiting circuses to political demonstrations. Other than being flanked by the three museums described in this chapter, there's not a great deal to it, though the group of slim steel blocks about three-quarters of the way down on the left-hand side forms a moving **war memorial**, commemorating the women and children who perished in the concentration camp at Ravensbrück near Berlin; Dutch victims included the courageous Corrie ten Boom from Haarlem (see page 129). Ravensbrück has never received the attention given to other, more notorious camps for three likely reasons: no film crew was there at its liberation by the Red Army; the camp was for women only; and Ravensbrück did not fit the usual Holocaust narrative, as most of those that died here – possibly about 60,000 – were special prisoners of some sort or another, for example Communists, Trade Unionists, Poles, prostitutes, spies and SOE agents, but not Jews.

The Concertgebouw

Concertgebouwplein 10 • Regular guided tours (75min) with advance booking required • Guided tours €10 • ☏ 020 573 04 00, ⓦ concertgebouw.nl • Tram #2, #3, #5, #12 or #13 to Van Baerlestraat, or #16 to Museumplein

When the German composer Johannes Brahms visited Amsterdam in the 1870s he was scathing about the locals' lack of culture and, in particular, their lack of an even halfway suitable venue for his music. In the face of such ridicule, a consortium of Amsterdam businessmen got together to fund the construction of a brand-new concert hall, and the result is today's **Concertgebouw**, which was completed in 1888. An attractive structure with a pleasingly grand Neoclassical facade, the Concertgebouw also benefitted from a 1990s facelift that saw the addition of a glass gallery that contrasts nicely with the red brick and stone of the rest of the building. The Concertgebouw has become renowned among musicians and concertgoers for its marvellous acoustics and offers an ambitious programme of classical music (see page 185). It's home to the famed – and much recorded – **Royal Concertgebouw Orchestra** (Koninklijk Concertgebouworkest) and regularly hosts the **Netherlands Philharmonic Orchestra** (Nederlands Philharmonisch Orkest) as well as all manner of visiting orchestras. On offer also are **guided tours**, which take in the Grote Zaal and Kleine Zaal auditoria, as well as various behind-the-scenes activities – control rooms, piano stores, dressing rooms and the like.

The Vondelpark

Multiple entrances, but main entrance on Stadhouderskade • Open access • Free • ⓦ hetvondelpark.net • Tram #1, #2, #5, #7 or #10 to Leidseplein, or bus #145, #753, #754 or #758 to Leidseplein

Amsterdam is short of green spaces, which makes the leafy expanse of the **Vondelpark**, a short distance from both Museumplein and the Concertgebouw, doubly welcome. This is easily the largest and most popular of the city's parks, its network of footpaths well trodden by locals and tourists alike.

The park dates back to 1864, when a group of leading Amsterdammers clubbed together to transform the soggy marshland that lay beyond the old Leidsepoort gateway, on the western edge of Leidseplein, into a landscaped park. The group were impressed by the contemporary English fashion for natural (as distinct from formal) landscaping and they gave the task of developing the new style of park to the Zocher family, big-time gardeners who set about their task with gusto, completing the project in 1865. Named after the seventeenth-century poet **Joost van den Vondel** (see page 44), the park proved an immediate success. It now possesses over a hundred tree species, a wide variety of local and imported plants, and – among many incidental features – a little **bandstand** and a grand **statue** of a pensive Vondel, shown seated with quill in hand, near the park's main entrance. The Zochers didn't forget their Dutch roots: the park is latticed with

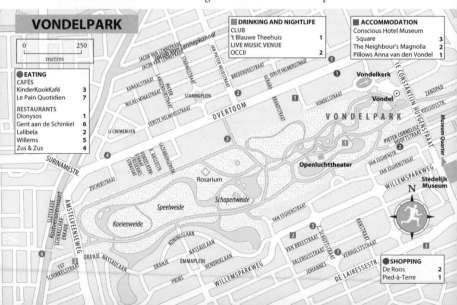

narrow waterways crossed by pretty bridges and ponds that are home to many types of **wildfowl**, including numerous heron, though it's the large colony of (very noisy) bright-green parakeets that grabs the attention. The Vondelpark has several children's **play areas** (see page 209) and a café, *'t Blauwe Theehuis* (⌾blauwetheehuis.nl/en), and during the summer regularly hosts free **concerts** and theatrical performances, mostly in its tiny **open-air theatre**, the Openluchttheater (see page 219), right in the centre of the park.

The Vondelkerk

6

Vondelstraat 120 • No public access • Tram #1 to 1e Con. Huygensstraat

On the edge of the Vondelpark is the lugubrious, brown-brick hull and whopping spire of the **Vondelkerk**, which has had more than its fair share of bad luck. Work on the church began in 1872 to a design by **Petrus J.H. Cuypers** (see page 33), but finances ran out the following year and the building was not completed until the 1880s. Twenty years later, it was struck by lightning and in the ensuing fire its tower was burnt to a cinder – the present one was added much later. The church always struggled to find a decent-sized congregation, but limped on until it was finally deconsecrated in 1979, and turned into offices thereafter.

De Pijp

Just east of the Museum Quarter is the **Oud Zuid**'s most authentic district, **De Pijp** (The Pipe), Amsterdam's first real suburb. New development beyond the Singelgracht began around 1870, but after laying down the street plans of De Pijp, the city council left the actual house-building to private developers, who constructed the long rows of largely featureless five- and six-storey buildings that still dominate the area today. It is these sombre canyons of brick tenements that gave the district its name, as the apartments were said to resemble pipe-drawers: each had a tiny street frontage but extended deep into the building.

The Weteringcircuit

Tram #7 or #10 to Weteringcircuit

At the southern end of Vijzelgracht, across the Singelgracht from De Pijp, is the **Weteringcircuit** roundabout, which has two low-key **memorials** to World War II. On the southwestern corner of the roundabout, by the canal, is a sculpture of a wounded man holding a bugle; it was here, on March 12, 1945, that thirty people were shot by the Germans in reprisal for acts of sabotage by the Dutch Resistance – given that the war was all but over, it's hard to imagine a crueller or more futile action. Across the main street, the second memorial in the form of a brick wall commemorates Hendrik Mattheus van Randwijk (1909–66), a Resistance leader. The restrained wording on the monument translates as:

When to the will of tyrants,
A nation's head is bowed,
It loses more than life and goods –
Its very light goes out.

The Heineken Experience

Stadhouderskade 78 • July & Aug daily 10.30am–9pm; Sept–June Mon–Thurs 10.30am–7.30pm, Fri–Sun 10.30am–9pm; last admission 2hr before closing; allow 1hr 30min for the self-guided tour • €18 • ☎ 020 721 5300, ⌾ heineken.com• Tram #16 or #24 to Marie Heinekenplein

The **Heineken Experience**, a popular attraction beside the Singelgracht on the northern edge of De Pijp, is housed in the former Heineken brewery, a whopping building

6

FREDDY HEINEKEN

Heineken may not be the finest lager in the world, but no other brewer, Guinness apart, has thought up such catchy advertising slogans: "Heineken refreshes the parts other beers cannot reach", for one, is well-nigh impossible to beat. **Alfred ("Freddy") Heineken** (1923–2002) was the mastermind behind the company's rise to alcoholic success, but his route was far from straightforward. The company was founded in 1864 by Alfred's grandfather, Gerard, but his son and successor, Henry Pierre, sold the family's majority stake in 1942. Freddy didn't like this at all, but he bided his time, working his way up through the company ranks before skilfully amassing a majority shareholding in the 1950s. Chairman from 1979, Freddy ran the company with a beady eye for the main chance, increasing its sales dramatically both at home and abroad, while simultaneously developing a reputation as a playboy, or, more euphemistically, "*bon vivant*". Whatever the term, Freddy was hardly subtle: allegedly, the bedroom suite at the back of his office had a four-poster bed, a Jacuzzi and a painting of a naked woman stroking a cat entitled *The Woman with Two Pussies*.

In 1983 Freddy was **kidnapped** by three masked men and held for three weeks before the police finally rescued him. Thereafter, he withdrew from the public eye, but maintained close relations with many of the country's richest and most powerful citizens until his death.

---

that was the company's headquarters from 1864 to 1988, at which time the firm restructured and its brewing moved out of town. Since then, Heineken has developed the site as a tourist attraction, with displays on the history of beer-making in general and Heineken in particular. The old brewing hall is included on the tour, but for many the main draw is the beer itself – although the days when you could quaff unlimited quantities are long gone. Considering it's not a real brewery any more, Heineken makes a decent stab at both entertaining and informing – as well as promoting the brand, of course. There are lots of gimmicky but fun attractions on the **self-guided tour**, including a whole gallery devoted to Heineken's various advertising campaigns and a weird show on what it's like to be a bottle of Heineken, from bottling plant to delivery. You can also order a bottle of Heineken with your name on it and visit the stables to see the brewer's Shire horses. You get a free drink at two bar stops along the way. The second stop – at *The World Bar* – makes a convivial(ish) end to the proceedings and they give you a Heineken glass as a souvenir on the way out.

Albert Cuypstraat

Market Mon–Sat 9am–5pm • ⓦ albertcuypmarkt.nl • Tram #16 or #24 to Albert Cuypstraat

Long and really rather humdrum, **Ferdinand Bolstraat** is De Pijp's main drag, but the east–west thoroughfare of **Albert Cuypstraat** (pronounced "cowp-straat") is its heart. The general **market** held here stretches for over 1km between Ferdinand Bolstraat and Van Woustraat, with a huge range of stalls selling everything from cut-price carrots and raw herring sandwiches to saucepans and day-glo thongs. It's easily the largest market in the city – and some claim it's the largest in Europe. Check out, too, the shops flanking the market on both sides, as they're often cheaper than their equivalents in the city centre.

Sarphatipark

Entrances on every side of the park • ☏ 020 664 1350 • Tram #3 runs along the south side of the park, and tram #4 from Centraal Station travels along Van Woustraat, one block east – get off at Ceintuurbaan

Two blocks south of the Albert Cuypstraat market, the **Sarphatipark** is a welcome splash of greenery among the dense terraces of De Pijp, its mature trees, lawns, footpaths and elongated lake first laid out in the 1880s. The park was named after **Samuel Sarphati**

(1813–66), a doctor of Sephardic Jewish descent, who was so appalled by the living conditions of poor Amsterdammers that he diversified into community projects, establishing a bread factory that produced wholesome, inexpensive bread and a waste collection service. His endeavours made him a much-admired figure – and the park has a fancy colonnaded **monument** in his honour, complete with a bust of the man.

6 De Dageraad

Pieter Lodewijk Takstraat & Burgemeester Tellegenstraat; the visitor centre is at Burgemeester Tellegenstraat 128 • Visitor centre Thurs–Sun 11am–5pm • Free (guided tours €7.50) • ☎ 020 686 8595, ⓦ hetschip.nl • Tram #4 from Centraal Station to the Amstelkade stop, from where it's a 5min walk west to De Dageraad along Jozef Israelskade

Best approached along Jozef Israelskade, which runs along the north side of the Amstelkanaal, **De Dageraad** housing project is a superb and immaculately maintained example of the work of **Michael de Klerk** and **Piet Kramer**. Built between 1919 and 1922 on behalf of the ANDB, the Diamond Workers Union, this was – indeed is – public housing inspired by socialist utopianism, a grand vision built to elevate (and educate) the working class, hence its name – "The Dawn". Overlooking the canal, the handsome brick- and stonework of the **Berlage Lyceum** marks the start of De Dageraad, with 350 workers' houses stretching beyond – to either side of Pieter Lodewijk Takstraat and then Burgemeester Tellegenstraat. The architects used a reinforced concrete frame as an underlay to each house, thus permitting folds, tucks and curves in the brick exteriors – a technique known as "apron architecture" (*Schortjesarchitectuur*). Strong, angular doors, sloping roofs and turrets punctuate the facades, and you'll find a corner tower at the end of every block – it's simply stunning. There's also a small **visitor centre**, which puts some flesh on the architectural bones.

The outer districts

Amsterdam is a comparatively small city, and the majority of its residential outer districts are easily reached from the city centre by public transport or, at a pinch, by bike. Beyond the Oud Zuid and De Pijp (see Chapter 6) stretches the Nieuw Zuid (New South), a well-heeled district at its most diverting among the smart, well-kept houses of Apollolaan. Further south still are the enjoyable woodlands of the Amsterdamse Bos, with plenty of opportunities for outdoor activities such as walking, boating and swimming, and the absorbing Cobra Museum of Modern Art. Also within easy reach of the centre, east of the Oud Zuid, Amsterdam Oost harbours the excellent Tropenmuseum, an ethnographic museum focused on the tropics, as well as the leafy Oosterpark.

The Nieuw Zuid

Beyond the Oud Zuid, the **Nieuw Zuid** (New South) was the first properly planned extension to the city since the concentric canals of the seventeenth century – and it involved several of the leading architects of the day (see box, page 123). Today, the Nieuw Zuid is one of Amsterdam's most sought-after addresses: **Apollolaan** and its immediate environs are especially favoured, with a string of well-maintained apartment blocks interspersed by the occasional larger house designed in a sort of Arts and Crafts-meets-Expressionist style. As with almost any residential area, specific attractions are rare, but points of interest include the **Amsterdam Hilton**, on Apollolaan, where John and Yoko bedded down in 1969, as well as the sprawling parkland of the **Amsterdamse Bos**, just to the southwest of the district (see page 123).

Apollolaan and Beethovenstraat

Trams #5 and #24 from Centraal Station run along Beethovenstraat, which hits Apollolaan at its midway point

Apollolaan, a wide residential boulevard just south of the Noorder Amstelkanaal, is representative of Berlage's intended grand design, with locals popping to the shops on neighbouring **Beethovenstraat**, the main commercial drag. Nonetheless, despite its obvious charms the Nieuw Zuid was far from an instant success with the Dutch bourgeoisie. Indeed, in the late 1930s the district became something of a Jewish

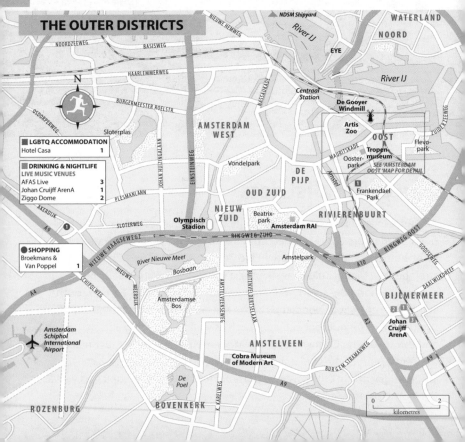

THE OUTER DISTRICTS

LGBTQ ACCOMMODATION
Hotel Casa　　　　　　　　1

DRINKING & NIGHTLIFE
LIVE MUSIC VENUES
AFAS Live　　　　　　　　3
Johan Cruijff ArenA　　　　1
Ziggo Dome　　　　　　　　2

SHOPPING
Broekmans &
Van Poppel　　　　　　　　1

ARCHITECTURAL ELAN: BUILDING THE NIEUW ZUID

When it came to the creation of the **Nieuw Zuid**, the celebrated Dutch architect **Hendrik Petrus Berlage** (1856–1934) was given responsibility for the overall plan, but after his death much of the implementation passed to a pair of prominent architects of the **Amsterdam School**, Michael de Klerk (1884–1923) and Piet Kramer (1881–1961). The two added a playfulness to the scheme – turrets and bulging windows, sloping roofs and frilly balustrades – that you can still see in many of the buildings today. Neither was this architectural virtuosity confined to the houses of the well-to-do. In 1901 a reforming Housing Act forced the city council into a concerted effort to clear Amsterdam's slums, the principal result being the high-quality public housing that still characterizes parts of the Nieuw Zuid, though the prime examples are elsewhere – Het Schip in the western docklands (see page 80) and another, De Dageraad, in the Oud Zuid (see page 120). Later, cutbacks in the city's subsidy meant that the more imaginative aspects of the original scheme for the Nieuw Zuid were toned down, but the area's wide boulevards and narrow side streets were completed as conceived by Berlage. In this, Berlage wanted to reinterpret the most lauded features of the city's seventeenth-century canals – their combination of the grand and spacious with the homely and communal, all in a crisp symmetrical frame.

7

---

enclave – the family of Anne Frank, for example, lived for a time on Merwedeplein just off **Churchilllaan**. This embryonic community was swept away during the German occupation, their sufferings retold in Grete Weil's novel *Last Trolley from Beethovenstraat* (*Tramhalte Beethovenstraat*). A reminder of those terrible times is to be found at the intersection of Apollolaan and Beethovenstraat, where a **monument**, erected in 1954, commemorates the shooting of 29 Resistance fighters here in 1944 in retribution for the killing of a German security officer – a striking memorial showing three sombrely determined victims.

Apollolaan is perhaps best known as the site of the canalside **Hilton Amsterdam**, a modern high-rise hotel at no. 138 (see page 152), where **John Lennon and Yoko Ono** staged their famous, week-long "Bed-In" for peace in 1969. Part celebrity farce, part skilful publicity stunt – "Hair, Peace; Bed, Peace" signs were plastered all over the place – the couple's antiwar proclamations were certainly heard far and wide, but in Britain the press focused on the supposed evil influence of Yoko on John, which satisfied at least three subtexts – racism, sexism and anti-Americanism. The two megastars stayed in what is now known, logically enough, as the "John and Yoko Suite" – as visitors can still do today for upwards of €1600.

The Amsterdamse Bos

Bosbaanweg 5, off Amstelveenseweg • ☎ 020 545 6100, ⊛ amsterdamsebos.nl

Comprising a substantial chunk of wooded parkland, the **Amsterdamse Bos** is the city's largest open space. Planted during the 1930s, the park was a laudable, large-scale attempt to provide gainful work for the city's unemployed, whose numbers had risen alarmingly following the Wall Street Crash of 1929. Originally a bleak area of flat, marshy fields, it's now a mixture of well-tended city park, leafy waterways, deep woodland and grassy meadows, intersected by foot- and cycle paths.

The **main entrance** is on the northeast side of the park off Amstelveenseweg, and from here it's a couple of minutes' walk to **De Boswinkel visitor centre**, a large café and the **Bosbaan** – a dead-straight canal, over 2km long and popular for boating and swimming. Elsewhere in the park there are children's playgrounds, a goat farm (see page 209) and spaces for various sports, including ice-skating, as well as an animal reserve, where a small herd of Scottish Highland cows is allowed to roam in relative solitude.

ARRIVAL AND INFORMATION

THE AMSTERDAMSE BOS

On foot The main entrance to the Amsterdamse Bos is in the northeast corner of the park, just off Amstelveenseweg at its junction with Van Nijenrodeweg.

By tram From Centraal Station, take tram #16 or #24 and get off at the Van Nijenrodeweg/Amstelveenseweg tram stop, one stop before the hospital (every 10min; 30min).

Tourist information Near the main entrance, De Boswinkel visitor centre, Bosbaanweg 5 (Tues–Sun 10am–5pm; ☎ 020 545 6100), has exhibitions on the park's flora and fauna, sells maps and dispenses advice on walking and cycling trails. They will also tell you where to rent bikes, canoes and pedaloes (April–Nov only) – there are outlets close by.

The Cobra Museum of Modern Art

Sandbergplein 1 • Tues–Sun 11am–5pm • €12 • ☎ 020 547 5050, ⓦ cobra-museum.nl • Connexxion bus #347 or #754 from Centraal Station and Leidseplein to Amstelveen bus station, a 5min walk from the museum (every 30min; 40min/20min)

Located well to the south of the city centre, the **Cobra Museum of Modern Art** (Cobra Museum voor Moderne Kunst) displays the work of the artists of the **Cobra movement**, which was founded in 1948. The movement grew out of comparative artistic developments in the cities of Copenhagen, Brussels and Amsterdam – hence the name, **CoBrA**, though nowadays the part capitalization is usually abandoned. The movement's first full exhibition, held at Amsterdam's Stedelijk Museum in 1949, showcased the big, colourful canvases, with bold lines and forms, for which Cobra became famous. Their work displayed a spontaneity and inclusivity that was unusual for the art world of the time and it stirred a veritable hornet's nest of artistic controversy. You'll only

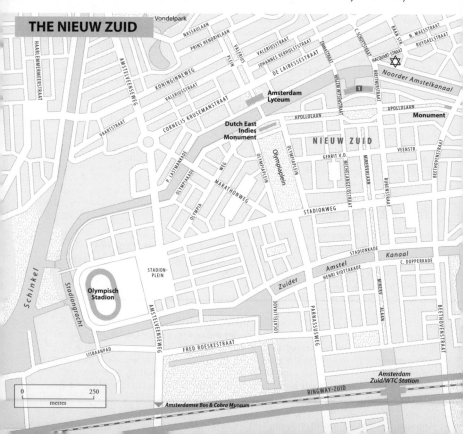

find a scattering of their work here in the gallery, but there's enough to get an idea of what Cobra was about, not least in Karel Appel's (1921–2006) weird, junky bird sculpture outside, and his brash, childlike paintings inside – in many ways Appel was the movement's leading light. Upstairs, the museum hosts regular temporary exhibitions of works by contemporary artists. There's a good shop, too, with plenty of prints and books on the movement, plus a bright café where you can gaze upon Appel's sculpture at length.

Amsterdam Oost

Next door to Amsterdam's Oud Zuid (Old South), **Amsterdam Oost** (East) is a rough-and-ready working-class quarter that stretches out beyond the Singelgracht towards the ring road, with Linnaeusstraat as its long main thoroughfare. The Oost district has one obvious attraction – the excellent **Tropenmuseum**, which is located on the corner of another of the city's municipal parks, the expansive **Oosterpark**.

The Muiderpoort

Alexanderplein • Tram #9 or #14 to Alexanderplein

Amsterdam Oost begins with the city's old eastern gate, the **Muiderpoort**, standing between two canals at the end of Plantage Middenlaan. In the 1770s the gate was revamped in pompous style, a Neoclassical refit complete with a flashy cupola and

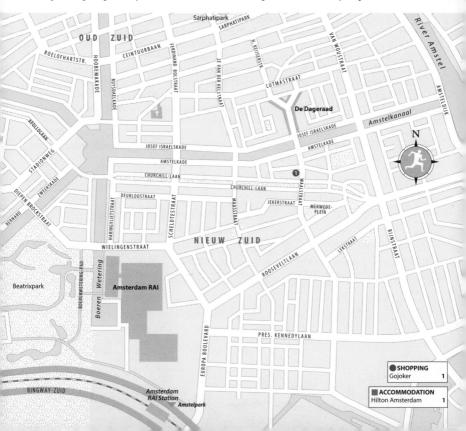

grandiosely carved pediment. Napoleon staged a triumphal entry into the city through the Muiderpoort in 1811, but his arrival was tempered by the behaviour of his half-starved troops, who were so dazzled by a city of (what was to them) amazing luxury that they could barely be restrained from looting.

The Tropenmuseum

Linnaeusstraat 2 • Tues–Sun 10am–5pm; also open Mon in school holidays • €15 • ☎ 088 004 2800, ⓦ tropenmuseum.nl • Tram #9 or #14 to Alexanderplein

The gabled and turreted, red-brick **Royal Tropeninstituut** – formerly the Royal Colonial Institute – is a sprawling complex that runs along Mauritskade on the south side of the Singelgracht canal. Part of the complex now accommodates the **Tropenmuseum**, Amsterdam's popular ethnographic museum, focusing on the world's tropical and subtropical zones – which it does incredibly well. The museum holds a spectacular collection of art and applied art imaginatively displayed in an engaging, modern, yet largely gimmick-free way, and through a variety of media – an audioguide, slides, DVDs and film clips. There are also fun, creative displays devoted to such subjects as music-making, puppetry and traditional storytelling; the labelling is mostly in English and Dutch. The permanent collection is enhanced by an ambitious programme of temporary exhibitions.

Floors 1 and 2

The collection begins in style in the cavernous **central hall**, which is used for large-scale temporary exhibitions. Up above are two floors of gallery space – **Floor 1** for India, New Guinea, the Dutch East Indies and Southeast Asia; and **Floor 2** for Africa, Latin America and the Caribbean, plus Western Asia and North Africa. The strongest collections reflect the Netherlands' colonial connections – primarily with Indonesia, formerly the Dutch East Indies (and including New Guinea), as well as Suriname in South America. Neither does the museum shirk from pointing out some of the more appalling aspects of Dutch colonialism. Highlights in the **New Guinea** section include a whole batch of ancestral and death masks; elaborate carved wooden boats complete with their crews; some incredible ritual poles cut from giant mangroves; and a film showing an early Dutch expedition into the interior of the island. The **Southeast Asia** section is especially wide-ranging with, for example, exhibits on Javanese puppetry, a selection of stone Buddhas and a platoon of Hindu gods.

Floor 3

On the top floor are a battery of studiously authentic **reconstructions** of contemporary life around the world – a mock-up of a Nigerian bar and residential compound, a Middle Eastern teahouse, a South American café, a Swat Valley home and so forth. These exhibits are supported by candid expositions on the problems besetting the developing world, both urban and rural, such as the destruction of the tropical rainforests.

De Gooyer windmill

Funenkade 5 • No public access • Bus #22 from Centraal Station to Oostenburgergracht, or it's about 500m northeast from the Tropenmuseum: walk east along Mauritskade then take Zeeburgerstraat across the canal

Amsterdam was once dotted with windmills, used for pumping water and grinding corn, but most were demolished years ago, which makes the **De Gooyer windmill**, standing tall between two canals just across the water from Amsterdam Oost, something of a rarity. It's also the tallest surviving windmill in the country. If you've come this far, you'll also be pleased to discover that the bar and mini-brewery in the old public baths adjoining the windmill – the **Brouwerij 't IJ** (see page 178) – sells an excellent range of beers and ales.

The Oosterpark

Next to the Tropenmuseum; entrances on every side of the park • ☎ 020 311 4020 • Trams #3 and #7 run along the west side of the park, and tram #9 from Centraal Station travels its eastern perimeter along Linnaeusstraat

Laid out in 1891, the **Oosterpark** is a large slab of greenery whose mature trees, footpaths and bandstand flank a wiggly lake. It's a popular picnic spot and you can hunt out a couple of **monuments** – one to the film-maker Theo van Gogh, who was murdered in Amsterdam in 2004 (see page 237), the other the **National Slavery Monument**, erected in 2002 to commemorate the abolition of slavery in the Netherlands in 1863. The latter is not without its ironies: in 1808, the British had banned the slave trade and stationed their warships off the west coast of Africa to intercept any errant slavers; the British went on to abolish slavery in the British Empire in 1834. Meanwhile, the Dutch, whose South American colony of Suriname was dependent on slave labour, dithered, arguing about the amount slave owners should be compensated and whether their slaves would truly benefit from emancipation – and this despite British pressure. Eventually, they caved in, but only reluctantly.

7

MARKEN LIGHTHOUSE

Day-trips

Amsterdammers always try to persuade you that there's nothing worth seeing outside their city, but the truth is you're spoilt for choice. Amid the urban sprawl is Haarlem, home to the outstanding Frans Hals Museum. Further south are the world-famous Keukenhof gardens, the springtime showcase for the country's flower growers. To the north, there's more countryside and less city; the most obvious targets are the old seaports bordering the former Zuider Zee, whose turbulent waters were once busy with Dutch trading ships. High points are the former island and fishing village of Marken, the old seaport of Volendam and the beguiling, one-time shipbuilding centre of Edam. Further north still is the former Zuider Zee port of Enkhuizen, whose past importance is recalled by one of the country's best open-air museums.

For those with time to travel further afield, the fast and efficient Dutch railway network puts a whole swathe of the Netherlands within easy reach, including all of the **Randstad** (literally "Ring City"), a sprawling conurbation that stretches south of Amsterdam to encompass the country's other big cities, primarily The Hague, Utrecht and Rotterdam.

Haarlem

It's only fifteen minutes from Amsterdam by train, but **HAARLEM** has a very different pace and feel from its big-city neighbour. It's an easy-going, medium-sized town of over 150,000 with a good-looking centre that is easily absorbed in a few hours or on an overnight stay.

Brief history
Founded on the banks of the River Spaarne in the tenth century, the town first prospered when the counts of Holland decided to levy shipping tolls here, but later it developed as a cloth-making centre. In 1572, the townsfolk sided with the Protestant rebels against the Habsburgs, a decision they must have regretted when a large Spanish army besieged them later in the same year. The siege was a desperate affair that lasted for eight months, but finally the town surrendered after receiving various assurances of good treatment – assurances which the Spanish commander, Frederick of Toledo, promptly broke, massacring over two thousand of the Protestant garrison and all their Calvinist ministers. Recaptured by the Protestants five years later, Haarlem went on to enjoy its greatest prosperity in the seventeenth century, becoming a centre for the arts and home to a flourishing school of painters, whose canvases are displayed at the first-rate **Frans Hals Museum**, located in the almshouse where Hals spent his last – and, for some, his most brilliant – years.

8

The Grote Markt
At the heart of Haarlem is the **Grote Markt**, a wide and attractive open space flanked by an appealing ensemble of Neogothic, Gothic and Renaissance architecture, including an intriguing, if exceptionally garbled, **Stadhuis**, whose turrets and towers, balconies, gables and galleries were put together in piecemeal fashion between the fourteenth and seventeenth centuries. At the other end of the Grote Markt stands a **statue** of a certain **Laurens Coster** (1370–1440), who, Haarlemmers insist, is the true inventor of printing. Legend tells of Coster cutting a letter "A" from the bark of a tree, dropping it into the sand by accident, and, hey presto, he realized how to create the printed word. The statue shows him earnestly holding up the letter concerned, though actually most experts agree that it was the German Johannes Gutenberg who invented printing in the 1440s.

The Grote Kerk
Grote Markt • Mon–Sat 10am–5pm; July & Aug also Sun noon–5pm; organ recitals late May to early Oct Tues at 8.15pm; June, July & Aug also Thurs at 4pm & Sat lunch concerts at 1.15–1.45pm • €2.50 • ☎ 023 553 2040, ⊕ bavo.nl

Dominating Haarlem's Grote Markt is the **Grote Kerk** – aka Sint Bavokerk – a soaring Gothic structure supported by mighty buttresses that rise high above the surrounding clutter of ecclesiastical outhouses. If you've been to the Rijksmuseum in Amsterdam (see page 106), the church may seem familiar, at least from the outside, since it turns up in several paintings of Haarlem by the seventeenth-century artists Berckheyde and Saenredam – only the black-coated burghers are missing. Finished in 1538, and 150 years in the making, the church is surmounted by a good-looking lantern tower, which perches above the transept crossing; the tower is made of wood clad in lead, a replacement for a much grander stone tower that had to be dismantled in 1514 when its supports began to buckle.

The nave

Inside the church, the towering beauty of the **nave** is enhanced by the creaminess of the stone and the bright simplicity of the whitewashed walls. The Protestants cleared the church of most of its decoration during the Reformation, but the splendid wrought-iron **choir screen** has survived, as have the choir's wooden **stalls** with their folksy misericords. In front of the screen is the conspicuous Neoclassical **tomb** of Haarlem's own Christiaan Brunings (1736–1805), a much-lauded hydraulic engineer and director of Holland's water board, who devised a strategy for controlling the waters of the lower Rhine.

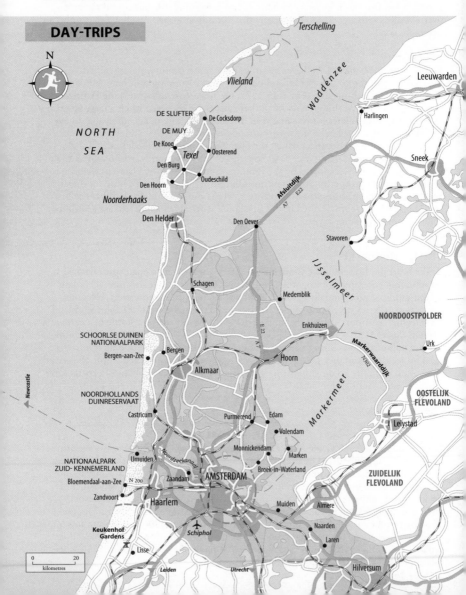

The chapels

Next to the south transept is the **Brewers' Chapel**, sponsored by the brewers' guild, where the central pillar bears two black markers – one showing the height of a local giant, the 2.64m-tall Daniel Cajanus, who died in 1749, the other, at 0.84m, the height of the diminutive Simon Paap from Zandvoort (1789–1828). In the middle of the nave, the **pulpit**'s banisters are in the form of snakes – fleeing from the word of God – and on the far side is the pocket-sized **Dog Whippers' Chapel**, built for the men employed to keep dogs under control in the church, as evidenced by the rings to tether them to, and now separated from the nave by an iron grille.

The organ

At the west end of the church, the mighty Christian Müller **organ** is one of the biggest in Europe, with over five thousand pipes and loads of snazzy Baroque embellishment. Manufactured in Amsterdam in the 1730s, it is said to have been played by Handel and Mozart – the latter on his tour of the country in 1766, at the age of 10. Beneath the organ, Jan Baptist Xavery's lovely group of draped marble figures represent Poetry and Music offering thanks to Haarlem, which is depicted as a patroness of the arts – in return for its generous support in the purchase of the organ. You can hear the organ in action at one of the free recitals held in the summer; the schedule is posted on the church website.

The Corrie Ten Boomhuis

Barteljorisstraat 19 • Tues–Sat: April–Oct 10am–3pm four tours daily in English; Nov–March 11am–2.30pm three tours daily in English; tours 1hr • Free • ☎ 023 531 0823, ⓦ corrietenboom.com

Two minutes from the Grote Markt, the **Corrie Ten Boomhuis** is where a Dutch family – the Ten Booms – hid fugitives, Resistance fighters and Jews alike above their jeweller's shop during World War II. There isn't actually much to look at in the house, but the guided tour is instructive and moving, if a little drawn out. The family, whose bravery sprang from their Christian faith, was betrayed to the Gestapo in 1944, and only one member, Corrie Ten Boom, survived – as does the jeweller's itself, still doing business at street level.

The Frans Hals Museum

Groot Heiligland 62 (Hof) and Grote Markt 16 (Hal) • Tues–Sat 11am–5pm, Sun noon–5pm • €15, including short film on Frans Hals • ☎ 023 511 5775, ⓦ franshalsmuseum.nl • A 5min stroll south of the Grote Markt: take pedestrianized Warmoesstraat and keep going

The **Frans Hals Museum**, Haarlem's biggest draw, occupies the old almshouse complex where the aged Hals lived out his last years on public funds. The collection comprises a handful of prime works by Hals along with an eclectic sample of Dutch paintings from the fifteenth century onwards, all immaculately presented and labelled in English and Dutch. In 2018, the museum merged with De Hallen Haarlem, whose contemporary artworks now sit alongside original Old Masters throughout its two locations.

Highlights include paintings from the **School of Hans Memling** and works by **Jan van Scorel** (1495–1562), including a smooth and polished *Adam and Eve* and a curious *Jerusalem Pilgrims* – one of the country's earliest group portraits. Beyond that, there's a particularly brutal and realistic *Christ Crowned with Thorns* by the Haarlem painter **Marten van Heemskerck** (1498–1574) as well as **Cornelis Cornelisz van Haarlem**'s (1562–1638) giant *Wedding of Peleus and Thetis*, an appealing rendition of what was then a popular subject, though Cornelisz gives as much attention to the arrangement of his elegant nudes as to the subject. This marriage precipitated civil war among the gods and was used by the Dutch as a warning against discord, a call for unity during the long war with Spain. Similarly, the same artist's *Massacre of the Innocents* connects the biblical story with the Spanish siege of Haarlem in 1572.

8

The Haarlem Mannerists

Cornelis van Haarlem (see page 131) was a leading light among the **Haarlem Mannerists**, a coterie of artists that flourished here in Haarlem in the late sixteenth century, adopting an enhanced naturalism, their canvases populated by muscular men and voluptuous women. Perhaps the most talented member of the group was **Hendrik Goltzius** (1558–1617), who is well represented here by three accomplished paintings – of Hercules, Mercury and Minerva. A third member of the group was **Karel van Mander** (1548–1606), a lesser artist perhaps but an influential figure and mentor of many of the city's most celebrated painters, including Hals; the museum owns a number of Mander paintings.

The Frans Hals paintings

The **Hals paintings** begin in earnest with a set of five superb Civic Guard portraits. For a time, Hals was himself a member of the Company of St George, and in the *Officers of the Militia Company of St George* of 1616 he appears in the top left-hand corner – one of his few self-portraits. Look out for a number of exquisite Hals portraits – like those of Cornelia Vooght (1631) and Willem van Warmondt (1640) – plus

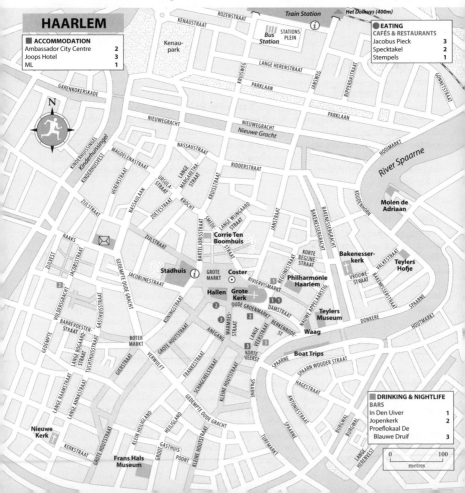

HAARLEM

ACCOMMODATION
Ambassador City Centre	2
Joops Hotel	3
ML	1

EATING
CAFÉS & RESTAURANTS
Jacobus Pieck	3
Specktakel	2
Stempels	1

DRINKING & NIGHTLIFE
BARS
In Den Uiver	1
Jopenkerk	2
Proeflokaal De Blauwe Druif	3

FRANS HALS AND HIS 27 SHADES OF BLACK

Little is known about **Frans Hals** (c.1580–1666), but he was certainly born in Antwerp, the son of Flemish Protestants who fled north to Haarlem to escape Habsburg rule in the late 1580s. In 1610, Hals was admitted to the guild of municipal art restorers and within a few years he was earning money for his own paintings, though, despite his long career, his extant oeuvre is relatively small – some two hundred paintings, and nothing like the number of paintings, sketches and studies left behind by his contemporary, Rembrandt. Hals' outstanding gift was as a **portraitist**, showing a sympathy with his subjects and an ability to capture fleeting expression that some say even Rembrandt lacked. Seemingly quick and careless flashes of colour characterize his work, but they are always blended into a coherent and marvellously animated whole.

Hals is perhaps best known for his **Civic Guard portraits** – group portraits of the militia companies initially formed to defend the country from the Habsburgs, but which later became social clubs for the gentry. Getting a commission to paint one of these portraits was a well-paid privilege – Hals got his first in 1616 – but their composition was a tricky affair and often the end result was dull and flat. With great flair and originality, Hals made the group portrait a unified whole instead of a static collection of individual portraits, his figures carefully arranged, but so cleverly as not to appear contrived. Hals's later paintings are darker, more contemplative works, closer to Rembrandt in their lighting and increasingly sombre in their outlook, reflecting Hals's physical infirmities and financial difficulties: hounded for money by the town's tradesmen and by the mothers of his illegitimate children, Hals became dependent on the public purse, answerable to the stern *Regents and Regentesses of the Oudemannenhuis* whom he portrayed in two famous group portraits that give much meaning to van Gogh's remark that "Frans Hals had no fewer than 27 blacks".

8

the *Regents of St Elizabeth Gasthuis*, a benign group portrait with a palpable sense of optimism, painted in 1641. In stark contrast, the artist's twin *Regents and Regentesses of the Oudemannenhuis*, completed twenty or so years later, with Hals now in his 80s, are dark and broody: these group portraits of those who ran the almshouse where Hals was lodged reveal a set of cold, self-satisfied faces that stare out of the gloom, the women reproachful, the men only marginally more affable. There are those who claim Hals had lost his touch by the time he painted these pictures, yet their sinister, almost ghostly power suggests quite the opposite. Incidentally, although the character just right of centre in the *Regents* painting looks drunk, it is inconceivable that Hals would have painted him in this condition: it's likely that he was suffering from some kind of facial paralysis and his jauntily cocked hat was simply a popular pose of the time.

Pieter Bruegel the Younger

Beyond the Hals paintings, look out for **Pieter Bruegel the Younger**'s (1564–1638) berserk *Dutch Proverbs*, illustrating a whole raft of contemporary proverbs – a detailed key next to the painting gives the lowdown. It was a popular painting and a real money-spinner for Bruegel – who produced no fewer than sixteen versions.

The Teylers Museum

Spaarne 16 • Tues–Fri 10am–5pm, Sat & Sun 11am–5pm • €13.50 • ☎ 023 516 0960, ⊛ teylersmuseum.nl

Founded in 1774 by a wealthy local philanthropist, the **Teylers Museum** occupies a grand Neoclassical building that stands beside the River Spaarne, whose wandering curves mark the eastern periphery of the town centre. The main body of the museum is delightfully old-fashioned, its wooden cabinets crammed with fossils and bones, crystals and rocks, medals and coins, all displayed alongside dozens of antique scientific instruments of lugubrious appearance and uncertain purpose. The finest room is the **rotunda** – De Ovale Zaal – a handsome, galleried affair with splendid wooden panelling, and there are also two rooms of nineteenth-century and early twentieth-century Dutch paintings, featuring the likes of Breitner, Israëls, Weissenbruch and

Wijbrand Hendriks (1774–1831), who was once the keeper of the art collection here. The museum also has a **modern wing**, which features temporary art exhibitions and has a pleasant café overlooking the garden.

Het Dolhuys

Schotersingerl 2 • Tues, Wed & Fri 10am–5pm, Thurs 10am–10pm, Sat & Sun noon–5pm • €8.50 • ☎ 023 541 0670, ⓦ hetdolhuys.nl • A 10min walk north of the train station, on the other side of the old city moat

Haarlem's strangest attraction is **Het Dolhuys**, an imaginative and thought-provoking museum of madness and psychiatric care throughout the ages, housed in a converted lunatic asylum. There are isolation cells, exhibits that tell the stories of "mad" people who have done extraordinary things, as well as displays that show different beliefs about mental illness over the years – from medieval imbalances to possession. The central **Zorgzaal** is the hub of the exhibition, with films, pictures and artefacts from asylums around Holland. Most of it is in Dutch, but a helpful booklet on loan from the reception translates the most important stuff.

ARRIVAL AND INFORMATION   HAARLEM

By train Haarlem's train station is on Stationsplein, just north of the city centre, 10min walk from the Grote Markt. **Destinations** Amsterdam (every 15min; 15min); Enkhuizen (every hour, change at Amsterdam Sloterdijk); Leiden (for the Keukenhof gardens; every 20min; 20min).

Tourist information The VVV is right in the centre of town at Grote Markt 2 (April–Sept Mon–Sat 9.30am–5.30pm, Sun noon–4pm; Oct–March Mon 1–5.30pm, Tues–Fri 9.30am–5.30pm, Sat 10am–5pm; ☎ 023 531 7325, ⓦ haarlemmarketing. nl). They issue free city maps and brochures.

ACCOMMODATION

Ambassador City Centre Oude Groenmarkt 20 ☎ 023 512 5300, ⓦ ambassadorcitycentrehotel.nl; map p.132. Haarlem's best budget option, a modern hotel with an eccentrically decorated lobby and heavy antique furniture, couldn't be more central. Double rooms are simply but well furnished, a few with four-posters, and although bathrooms are on the small side, wi-fi is free and the welcome warm. **€85**

Joops Hotel Lange Veerstraat 36 ☎ 023 512 5300, ⓦ joopshotel.nl; map p.132. Owned by the *Ambassador* (see above), with a mixture of large, antique-filled, slightly

more expensive rooms and good-value, functionally furnished smaller versions. There are apartments too. Check-in is at the *Ambassador*. **€75**

★ **ML** Klokhuisplein 9 ☎ 023 512 3910, ⓦ mlinhaarlem. nl; map p.132. Housed in a former printworks behind the Grote Kerk, Haarlem's best boutique hotel offers 17 comfortably furnished rooms and suites fitted with the latest Hästens beds. The restaurant (closed on Sun and Mon), located in the courtyard, is excellent and there's an all-day brasserie, too. **€120**

EATING AND DRINKING

In den Uiver Riviervismarkt 13 ☎ 023 532 5399, ⓦ indenuiver.nl; map p.132. Just off the Grote Markt, this lively and extremely appealing brown bar, housed in an old fish shop, is decked out in traditional Dutch café style; it has occasional live music too. Tues–Thurs 4pm–1am, Fri &Sat 4pm–2am, Sun & Mon 4pm–midnight.

Jacobus Pieck Warmoesstraat 18 ☎ 023 532 6144, ⓦ jacobuspieck.nl; map p.132. Welcoming and informal café-restaurant that's a good bet for either lunch or dinner, with sandwiches from around €8, and burgers and salads for €10. There's also a short menu of more substantial main courses in the evenings for about €17–24. Tues–Sat 11am–4pm & 5.30–10pm.

Jopenkerk Gedempte Voldersgracht 2 ☎ 023 533 4114, ⓦ openkerk.nl; map p.132. Haarlem used to be known for its beer, and this converted old church is home to the Jopen microbrewery, which is successfully reviving the old

traditions. It's a brewery, bar and restaurant rolled into one, with long benches, comfy sofas and its own cloudy, unfiltered beer. The food is simple rather than splendid, but you should at least try one of the dozen or so Jopen brews at the bar. Tues–Sat 5.30-10pm.

Proeflokaal De Blauwe Druif Lange Veerstraat 7 ☎ 023 531 6568, ⓦ proeflokaaldeblauwedruif.nl; map p.132. Just off the main square, this intimate and amiable bar with boho decor is very Dutch; it does a great line in spirits too. Mon–Thurs 4pm–midnight, Fri & Sat 4pm–2am, Sun 4–9pm.

Specktakel Spekstraat 4 ☎ 023 532 3841, ⓦ specktakel. nl; map p.132. Inventive little place that tries its hand at an international menu, dishing up everything from kangaroo through to antelope and (more reassuringly) cod and beef. Starters €14, mains €22. Tasting menus available for €45–55. Mon, Tues, Thurs & Fri 5.30–10pm, Sat & Sun 5–10pm.

★**Stempels** Klokhuisplein 9 ☎023 512 3910, ⓦmlinhaarlem.nl; map p.132. The best hotel in town also provides the best food – in its brasserie and especially in its restaurant, with great fish and meat prepared in innovative ways. Mains in the restaurant start at around €21, or you'll spend around €10 for the simpler, but just as tasty, dishes in the brasserie. Brasserie daily 8am–10pm; restaurant Tues–Sat 6–10pm.

The Keukenhof gardens

Stationsweg 166, Lisse, 15km north of Leiden • Mid-March to mid-May daily 8am–7.30pm • €18 • ☎0252 465 555, ⓦ keukenhof.nl • From Centraal Station, take the train to Leiden Centraal (every 30min; 40min), then catch the Arriva Keukenhof Express bus #854 (every 15min; 30min) from the adjacent bus station

The largest flower gardens in the world, dating back to 1949, the **Keukenhof gardens** were designed by a group of prominent bulb growers to convert people to the joys of growing flowers from bulbs. Literally the "kitchen garden", its site is the former estate of a fifteenth-century countess, who used to grow herbs and vegetables for her dining table. Several million flowers are on show for their full flowering period, complemented, in case of especially harsh winters, by thousands of square metres of glasshouse holding indoor displays. You could easily spend a whole day here, swooning with the sheer abundance of it all, but to get the most out of it you need to come early, before the tour buses descend on the place. There are several restaurants in the grounds, and a network of well-marked footpaths explores every horticultural nook and cranny.

Marken

8

Once an island in the Zuider Zee, **MARKEN** was, until its road connection to the mainland in 1957, pretty much a closed community, supported by a small fishing industry. Nowadays, it mostly lives off the tourist trade, welcoming day-trippers by

---

THE BULBFIELDS

The pancake-flat fields stretching north from Leiden towards Haarlem (see page 129) are the heart of the Dutch **bulbfields**, whose bulbs and blooms support a billion-euro industry and some ten thousand growers, as well as attracting tourists in their droves. Bulbs have flourished here since the late sixteenth century, when one **Carolus Clusius**, a Dutch botanist and one-time gardener to the Habsburg emperor, brought the first **tulip bulb** over from Vienna, where it had – in its turn – been brought from Asia Minor by an Austrian aristocrat. The tulip flourished in Holland's sandy soil and was so highly prized that it fuelled a massive **speculative bubble**. At the height of the boom – in the mid-1630s – bulbs were commanding extraordinary prices: the artist Jan van Goyen paid 1900 guilders and two paintings for ten rare bulbs, while a bag of one hundred bulbs was swapped for a coach and horses. When the government finally intervened in 1636, the industry returned to reality with a bang, leaving hundreds of investors ruined – much to the satisfaction of the country's Calvinist ministers, who had long railed against such excesses.

Other types of bulbs apart from the tulip have also been introduced, and nowadays the spring flowering season begins in mid-March with **crocuses**, followed by **daffodils** and yellow **narcissi** in late March, **hyacinths** and **tulips** from mid-April through to May, and **irises** and **gladioli** in August. The views of the bulbfields from any of the trains heading southwest from Schiphol airport can often be sufficient in themselves, the fields divided into stark geometric blocks of pure colour, but, with your own transport – either bicycle or car – you can take in their particular beauty by way of special routes marked by hexagonal signposts; local tourist offices sell pamphlets describing the routes in detail. You could also drop by the bulb growers' showpiece, the **Keukenhof gardens**. Bear in mind also that there are any number of local flower festivals and parades in mid- to late April; every local VVV has the details of these too.

BOOM AND BUST ON THE ZUIDER ZEE

The **Baltic trade** was the linchpin of Holland's prosperity in the Golden Age, revolving around the import of huge quantities of grain, the supply of which was municipally controlled to safeguard against famine. The business was immensely profitable, and its proceeds nourished a string of prosperous seaports and fishing villages, including Marken, Volendam and Enkhuizen, but in the eighteenth century the Baltic trade declined, leaving the ports economically stranded, and plans were made to reclaim the Zuider Zee and turn it into farmland. In the event, the Zuider Zee was only partly reclaimed, creating a pair of placid, steel-grey freshwater lakes – the **IJsselmeer**, created when the Afsluitdijk dam cut the former Zuider Zee off from the North Sea in 1932, and the **Markermeer**, calved in 1976 by a complementary dyke linking Enkhuizen with Lelystad.

---

the coachload, but after the crowds have left – or out of season – it's still a rather special place, very peaceful and remote, despite being within just a few kilometres of Amsterdam's urban hubbub.

Marken village

There's no denying the picturesque charms of the island's one and only village – also called **Marken** – where the immaculately maintained houses, mostly painted in deep green with white trimmings, cluster on top of artificial mounds raised to protect them from the waves. There are two old parts to the village, beginning with **Havenbuurt**, around and behind the harbour, which is the bit you see in photos, where many of the waterfront houses are raised on stilts. Although these are now panelled in, they were once open, allowing the sea to roll under the floors in bad weather, enough to terrify most people half to death. In summertime, one or two of the houses are open to visitors, proclaiming themselves to be typical of Marken, and the waterfront is lined by snack bars and souvenir shops, often staffed by locals in traditional costume. Yet, despite the hoopla, you do get a hint of how hard life used to be – both here and in **Kerkbuurt**, the quieter, less visited part of the village just a couple of minutes' walk away, where a huddle of ancient dwellings nestle round the **Grote Kerk**, an ugly 1904 replacement for its sea-battered predecessor.

The Marker Museum

Kerkbuurt 44 • late March to Oct Mon–Sat 10am–5pm, Sun noon–4pm • €3 • ☎ 0299 601 904, ⓦ markermuseum.nl

Squeezed into a set of former eel-smoking houses, the **Marker Museum** outlines the history of the island, detailing the distinctive way of life of its inhabitants. There is a recreation of a fisherman's house as of about 1900, examples of the islanders' traditional dress and homespun crafts, plus a few paintings by two island artists, Jan Moenis and Reinier Pijnenburg.

ARRIVAL AND DEPARTURE   MARKEN

By bus Bus #315, currently operated by EBS (every 30min; 40min; ☎ 0800 0327, ⓦ ebs-ov.nl), links Amsterdam with Marken, departing from the bus station at the back of Centraal Station near the River IJ and dropping off beside the car park on the edge of the village, from where it's a 5min walk to the waterfront. EBS has an information kiosk at the Centraal Station bus station, where you can buy a day pass for all its regional services for €10 (€9 online); tickets

are also available from the driver. Note that there are no buses from Marken to Edam or Volendam.
By ferry The Volendam–Marken Express ferry, Haven 39, Volendam (March–Oct daily 10am–7pm, every 30min– 1hr; Nov–Feb limited service, see website for details; 25min; ☎ 0299 363 331, ⓦ markenexpress.nl), has been a feature of the local tourist industry for many years. Tickets cost €8 one way, €11.50 return; bikes cost €1.50 each way.

ACCOMMODATION AND EATING

★ **Hof van Marken** Buurt II 15 ☎ 0299 601 300, ⓦ hofvanmarken.nl. This small hotel-restaurant, tucked

away in the peaceful backstreets behind Marken's harbour, is filled with just seven simple, stylish rooms, exuding a homely yet contemporary feel. The restaurant serves up great food, with a choice of set menus and dishes like beef tartare with potato confit and horseradish, or leg of lamb with aubergine couscous. Fri 6–9pm, Sat & Sun noon–9pm. **€125**

Land en Zeezicht Havenbuurt 6 ☎ 0299 601 302. Right on the north side of the harbour, this old-fashioned café serves a very decent smoked eel sandwich for €10, as well as more substantial, mainly traditional Dutch dishes. Mon–Thurs 8am–midnight, Fri–Sun 8am–2am.

Volendam

The former fishing village of **VOLENDAM** is the largest of the Markermeer lakeside towns and has seen, by comparison with its neighbours, some rip-roaring, cosmopolitan times. In the early years of the twentieth century it became something of an artists' retreat, with both Picasso and Renoir spending time here, along with their assorted acolytes. Today, evidence of these painterly connections is on show in the public rooms of the waterfront **Hotel Spaander** (see below), whose paintings and sketches were given to the hotel by impoverished artists in exchange for their lodgings. The hotel opened in 1881 and its first owner, Leendert Spaander, had seven daughters, quite enough to keep a whole bevy of artists in lust for a decade or two. The artists are, however, long gone and today Volendam is more or less a tourist target, crammed in season with day-trippers running the gauntlet of the souvenir stalls arranged along the length of the cobbled main street, whose perky gables overlook the harbour.

The Volendams Museum

Zeestraat 41 · Mid-March to mid-Nov daily 10am–5pm · €4 · ☎ 0299 369 258, ⓦ volendamsmuseum.nl

Volendam's only real sight as such is the **Volendams Museum**, which features paintings by many of the artists who have come here over the years. Exhibits also include mannequins in local costume and several interiors – a shop, school and living room – although the museum's crowning glory is a series of mosaics made from 11 million cigar bands: the bizarre lifetime project of a local artist.

ARRIVAL AND INFORMATION

VOLENDAM

By bus Bus #316, currently operated by EBS (every 30min; 30min; ☎ 0800 0327, ⓦ ebs-ov.nl), links Amsterdam with Volendam, departing from the bus station at the back of Centraal Station near the River IJ; get off on Julianaweg, just round the corner from the VVV (see below) and about 400m from the waterfront along Zeestraat. The bus also runs to Edam (10min). EBS has an information kiosk at the Centraal Station bus station, where you can buy a day pass for all its regional services for €10; tickets are also available from the

driver. Note that there are no buses from Volendam to Marken.
By ferry The Volendam–Marken Express ferry, Haven 39, Volendam (March–Oct daily 10am–6pm, every 30min–1hr; Nov–Feb limited service, see website for details; 25min; ☎ 0299 363 331, ⓦ markenexpress.nl) costs €8 one way, €11.50 return; bikes cost €1.50 each way.
Tourist information The VVV is at Zeestraat 37 (April–Oct Mon–Sat 10am–5pm, Sun 11am–3pm; Nov–March Mon–Sat 11am–4pm; ☎ 0299 363 747, ⓦ vvv-volendam.nl).

ACCOMMODATION AND EATING

Hotel Spaander Haven 15–19 ☎ 0299 363 595, ⓦ hotelspaander.com. If you want to stay in Volendam, there's no better place than this wonderfully old-fashioned hotel, with creaking wooden floors and a maze of corridors hung with paintings and sketches. There's a range of decently furnished rooms, the nicest of which overlook the water; the "luxury" rooms are more spacious. A wellness centre, complete with indoor swimming pool, Turkish bath and sauna, is available for guests to use between 7am and 11pm. **€125**

Van den Hogen Haven 106 ☎ 0299 363 775, ⓦ hogen. nl. This is the top pick out of Volendam's handful of harbourside restaurants, serving up an enticing selection of local fish specialities – think day-fresh sole, mussels and cod – or, if you're feeling a little more adventurous, dishes like stewed pike with shrimps. Large windows frame harbour views or, if it's warm, try to nab one of the outdoor tables – the perfect spot to linger on warm days, overlooking the water. Mains start from around €20. Daily 10am–11pm.

8

Edam

You might expect **EDAM** to be jammed with tourists, considering the international fame of the rubbery red balls of cheese that carry its name, but in fact Edam usually lacks the crowds of its Markermeer neighbours. The town is a delightful and good-looking little place of neat brick houses, high gables, swing bridges and slender canals. Founded by farmers in the twelfth century, it experienced a temporary boom in the seventeenth as a shipbuilding centre with river access to the Zuider Zee. Thereafter, it was back to the farm – and the excellent pasture land surrounding the town is still grazed by large herds of cows, though nowadays most **Edam cheese** is produced elsewhere, even in Germany: "Edam" is the name of a type of cheese and not its place of origin. This does, of course, rather undermine the authenticity of Edam's open-air **cheese market**, held every Wednesday morning in July and August on the Kaasmarkt (see page 140) – the only time the town heaves with tourists.

Damplein

At the heart of Edam is **Damplein**, a pint-sized main square that sits beside an elongated, humpbacked bridge vaulting the Voorhaven canal, which connects the town with the Markermeer, and formerly the Zuider Zee. The bridge stopped the canal flooding the town, which occurred with depressing regularity, but local shipbuilders hated the thing as it restricted navigation, and on several occasions they launched night-time raids to break it down, though eventually they bowed to the will of the local council. The proudest building on Damplein is Edam's eighteenth-century **Stadhuis**, a severe Louis XIV-style structure whose plain symmetries culminate in a squat little tower. The ground floor of the Stadhuis is home to the VVV (see page 30), while the first floor holds part of the Edams Museum; the other, larger section is close by at Damplein 8.

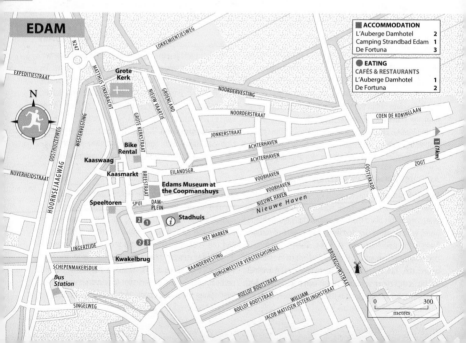

THE EDAM MERMAID

A number of **mermaid legends** have evolved around the coastal towns of northern Holland, but Edam's is the best. In 1403, two milkmaids were rowing across the lake to the north of Edam to get to their cows, when they spied a mermaid, whom they agreed must have been washed up over the sea dyke during a storm. Later, they returned to fish the mermaid out of the lake, and blushes were saved all round by the layer of seaweed and moss protecting the creature's modesty. Back in town, the mermaid slipped into a dress willingly enough and soon picked up all the necessary domestic and devotional skills, learning how to spin, cook and kiss the crucifix, though some versions of the legend feature a less obliging mermaid who didn't take kindly to her chores and was forever trying to escape. The mermaid is supposed to have lived in Edam for fifteen years, and one of the now-demolished town gates was decorated with a mermaid statue in her memory. More important was the municipal subtext; as the legend confirmed, the women of Edam were so kind and the town so pleasant that even a slippery siren was prepared to hole up here.

The Edams Museum at the Stadhuis

Damplein 1 • Tues–Sun 1–4.30pm • €5 for both parts of the museum (see opposite) • ☎ 0299 372 431, ⊛ edamsmuseum.nl

The first floor of the Stadhuis is used for temporary exhibitions by the **Edams Museum**, mostly on Edam's history and evolution. A small and distinctly modest collection of old Dutch paintings is displayed here too, the most curious being the portrait of **Trijntje Kever** (1616–33), a local girl who grew to over 2.5m tall; displayed in front of the portrait is a pair of her specially made shoes.

The Edams Museum at the Steenen Coopmanshuys

Damplein 8 • April to late Oct Tues–Sat 10am–4.30pm, Sun 1–4.30pm • €5 for both parts of the museum • ☎ 0299 372 644, ⊛ edamsmuseum.nl

Facing the bridge on Damplein, the main part of the **Edams Museum** occupies an attractive old merchant's house, whose crow-stepped gables date back to 1530. Inside, a series of cramped and narrow rooms hold a modest display on the history of the town as well as an assortment of local bygones, including a couple of splendid box beds. The museum's pride and joy is, however, its **floating cellar**, long thought to have been built by a retired sea captain who couldn't bear the thought of sleeping on dry land, but actually constructed to stop the house from flooding.

The Grote Kerk

Grote Kerkstraat 57 • Early April to late Oct daily 1.30–5pm • Free • ☎ 0299 371 959, ⊛ grotekerkedam.nl

On the edge of the fields that spread north of town, Edam's rambling **Grote Kerk** is a handsome, largely Gothic structure whose strong lines are disturbed by the almost comically stubby spire, which was shortened to its present height after lightning started a fire in 1602. The church's interior is distinguished by its magnificent stained-glass windows – which date from the early seventeenth century and sport heraldic designs and historical scenes – and by its whopping **organ**.

The Speeltoren and around

From the Kaasmarkt (see page 140), it's a couple of hundred metres south to the fifteenth-century **Speeltoren**, an elegant, pinnacled tower that's all that remains of Edam's second most important medieval church. From here, it's about the same distance again – south along Lingerzijde – to the impossibly picturesque **Kwakelbrug**, an eighteenth-century structure that replaced the medieval original.

EDAM'S CHEESE MARKET

The Kaasmarkt is the site of Edam's summer **cheese market** (July to mid-Aug Wed 10.30am– 12.30pm; ☎0299 315 125, ⓦkaasmarktedam.nl). The produce is laid out in rows before buyers sniff, crumble and taste each cheese, followed by intensive bartering. Once a purchase has been made, the cheese porters, dressed in traditional white costumes and straw boaters, spring into action, carrying off the cheeses on gondola-like trays. Helping to set the scene on the Kaasmarkt is the distinctive **Kaaswaag**, the building where they used to weigh the cheese, which sports the town's coat of arms: a bull on a red field with three stars.

ARRIVAL AND INFORMATION   EDAM

By bus Bus #316, currently operated by EBS (every 30min; 40min; ☎0800 0327, ⓦebs-ov.nl), links Amsterdam with Edam, departing from the bus station located at the back of Centraal Station near the River IJ, and dropping passengers off at Edam's bus station on the southwest edge of town, on Singelweg, around a 5–10min walk from Damplein and the VVV. The bus also goes to Volendam, 3km away (10min). EBS has an information kiosk at the Centraal Station bus station, where you can buy a day pass for all its regional services for €10; tickets are also available to purchase from the driver. There are no buses from Edam to Marken.

Tourist information The VVV is in the Stadhuis, Damplein 1 (Jan–March Mon noon–4pm, Tues–Thurs 10am–3pm, Fri & Sat 10am–4pm; April–Oct Mon–Sat 10am–5pm; Nov–Dec Mon noon–4pm, Tues–Sat 10am–4pm; ☎0299 315 125, ⓦvvv-edam.nl).getting around

By bike Bikes can be rented from Ronald Schot, in the centre at Grote Kerkstraat 7 (☎0299 372 155, ⓦronaldschot.nl); customers get free parking on Kaasmarkt and by the Grote Kerk.

By boat The VVV (see above) takes bookings for local boat trips, both along the town's web of canals and out into the Markermeer.

ACCOMMODATION AND EATING

L'Auberge Damhotel Keizersgracht 1 ☎0299 371 766, ⓦen.damhotel.nl; map p.138. This boutique hotel has an emphasis on old-style opulence, with floor-sweeping drapes and luxuriant fabrics. There's also a cosy bar and a terrace facing the town hall, where you can get a decent lunch – sandwiches, salads, pancakes – for about €10. The upmarket *Auberge* restaurant serves a fantastic and quite ambitious menu; reckon on paying around €16 for a starter like braised oxtail with lobster or duck liver three ways, and €25–30 for saddle of roe or pheasant with herb crust. Daily noon–1pm. **€120**

Camping Strandbad Edam Zeevangszeedijk 7a ☎0299 371 994, ⓦcampingstrandbad.nl; map p.138. East of town on the way to the lakeshore, Edam's nearest campsite

is a 20min walk along the canal from the north side of Damplein. It also has cabins, sleeping two. April–Sept. Camping **€3.75** per person, plus €6 per tent, cabins **€40**

★ **De Fortuna** Spuistraat 3 ☎0299 371 671, ⓦfortuna-edam.nl; map p.138. Just round the corner from the Damplein and abutting a narrow canal, this three-star hotel is the epitome of cosiness, its 23 simple guest rooms distributed among two immaculately restored old houses and three cottage-like buildings round the back. There's also a lively restaurant, decorated in traditional style and serving a tasty French-Dutch menu of dishes made with local ingredients; starters go for about €12, main courses €20–25. Reservations, especially at weekends, are essential. Daily noon–3pm & 6–10pm. **€110**

Enkhuizen

Nudging up against the waters of the IJsselmeer, **ENKHUIZEN** was once one of the country's most important seaports. Nowadays, things are much quieter, but the town centre, with its ancient streets, slender canals and pretty harbours, is wonderfully well preserved, a rough circle with a ring of bastions and moat on one side, and the old sea dyke on the other. Exploring Enkhuizen only takes an hour or two – the centre is about twenty minutes' walk from end to end – and there is also one major attraction, the excellent **Zuiderzeemuseum**.

Brief history

From the fourteenth to the early eighteenth century, when its harbour silted up, Enkhuizen prospered from both the Baltic sea trade and the North Sea herring fishery, its maritime credentials second to none, its citizens renowned for their seamanship. It was also the first town in Noord-Holland to rise against Spain, in 1572, but unlike many of its Protestant allies it was never besieged – its northerly location kept it safely out of reach of the Habsburg army. Subsequently, Enkhuizen slipped into a long-lasting economic lull, becoming a remote and solitary backwater until tourism revived its fortunes.

The Oude Haven

A good place to start an exploration of Enkhuizen's compact centre is the **Oude Haven**, which stretches east in a gentle curve to the conspicuous **Drommedaris**, a heavy-duty brick watchtower built in 1540 to guard the harbour entrance. On the green by the tower there's a modern statue of the seventeenth-century artist **Paulus Potter**, a native of Enkhuizen, painting one of the farm animals he was famous for. Beyond the Drommedaris is the picturesque **Buitenhaven**, with its sailing boats and barges.

The Flessenscheepjesmuseum

Zuiderspui 1 • Mid-Feb to Oct daily noon–5pm; Nov to mid-Feb Fri–Mon noon–5pm • €4 • ☎ 0228 317 762, ⓦ flessenscheepjesmuseum.nl

The pint-sized **Flessenscheepjesmuseum** near the Drommedaris is built above the lock gates at the south end of the Zuiderhaven canal – ask and they'll show you the water flowing beneath the house. The museum itself is devoted to that ubiquitous maritime

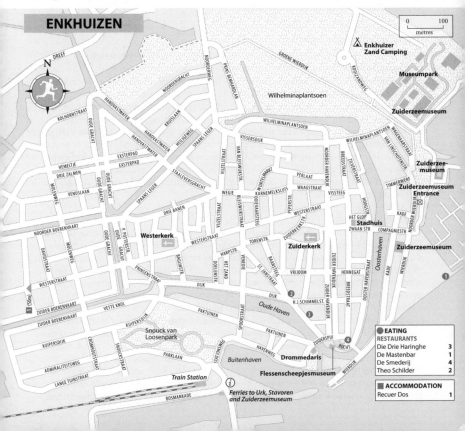

curiosity, the ship-in-a-bottle, and is a well-presented and -labelled collection, with vessels ranging from East Indiamen to steamboats, and containers from light bulbs, even fuses, to a thirty-litre wine flagon. There's also a short film introducing you to the ingenious mysteries of how it's done.

Zuider Havendijk and around

Spreading along and around **Zuider Havendijk** is the oldest part of town, an extraordinarily pretty lattice of alleys, quays, canals and antique houses. Turn left at the north end of Zuider Havendijk to get to the **Zuiderkerk** on Zuiderkerkplein (no fixed opening hours), a hulking Gothic pile with a massive brick tower that was erected in 1518; the octagon and then the cupola on top were added later.

The Westerkerk

Westerstraat 138 • mid-July to mid-Sept Tues–Sat 1.30–5pm; times vary rest of the year • Free • ☎ 228 317 800, ⓦ westerkerkenkhuizen.nl

Enkhuizen's spine is **Westerstraat**, a busy if somewhat humdrum pedestrianized street that is home to most of its shops and stores. About halfway along stands the **Westerkerk**, an early fifteenth-century, red-brick Gothic church with a freestanding wooden tower. The bare interior of the church, with its three naves of equal height, is distinguished by its **rood screen**, a mid-sixteenth-century extravagance whose six intricately carved panels show biblical scenes in dramatic detail – Moses with the Tablets, St John on Patmos and so forth.

The Zuiderzeemuseum

Wierdijk • Indoor museum daily 10am–5pm; Museumpark April to late Oct daily 10am–5pm • €15 • ☎ 0228 351 111, ⓦ zuiderzeemuseum.nl

The **Zuiderzeemuseum** divides into two: an indoor section of around a dozen rooms devoted to annual exhibitions on different aspects of the Zuider Zee (see page 136), and an outdoor section, the Museumpark, which is a collection of original buildings moved here over the last decades. From the centre of Enkhuizen, it's a short walk to the land-bound (indoor) part of the museum. At its heart is the impressive **ship hall**, where you can get up close and personal with a number of traditional sailing barges and other craft. There's an ice-cutting boat from Urk, once charged with the responsibility of keeping the shipping lanes open between the island and the mainland; a dinghy for duck-hunting, complete with shotgun; and some wonderful fully rigged and highly varnished sailing vessels.

The Museumpark

The Zuiderzeemuseum's big draw is the **Museumpark**, whose main entrance is about 100m north of the land-bound section along Wierdijk, and which stretches north along the seaward side of the old dyke that once protected Enkhuizen from the sea. It's a fantastically well-put-together collection of over 130 dwellings, stores, workshops and even streets that have been transported here from every part of the region, and which together provide the flavour of life hereabouts from 1880 to around 1932.

Just about everything is worth seeing, but **highlights** include a reconstruction of Marken harbour as of 1900, a red-brick chapel and assorted cottages from Den Oever, old fishermen's houses from Urk, a post office and a pharmacy that has a marvellous collection of "gapers" – painted wooden heads with their tongues out, which were the traditional pharmacy's sign. The museum strives to be authentic: sheep and goats roam the surrounding meadows, its smokehouses smoke (and sell) real herring and eels, the sweetshop sells real old-fashioned sweets, the beautifully kept schoolrooms offer geography and handwriting classes, and there's even a woman in a 1930s furnished house who will make you a traditional Dutch lunch. There's also a **nature reserve**, where you can take a picnic and walk through the woods for some great views over the water. All in all not be missed, especially if you have children in tow.

ARRIVAL AND INFORMATION

By train Enkhuizen is at the end of the line, and the station is right opposite the head of the main harbour (the Buitenhaven) at the southern end of the town centre. Trains run to Amsterdam's Centraal Station (every 30min; 1hr) and to Haarlem (every 30min; 1hr, change at Amsterdam Sloterdijk).

ENKHUIZEN

Tourist information The VVV is opposite the train station, on the harbourfront at Tussen Twee Havens 1 (April to late Oct daily 9am–5pm; ☎0228 313 164, ⓦ vvvhartvannoordholland.nl). They sell maps and have details of local boat trips and rooms to rent in private houses.

ACCOMMODATION AND EATING

★ **Die Drie Haringhe** Dijk 28 ☎0228 318 610, ⓦ drieharinghe.nl; map p.141. Housed in an immaculately renovated seventeenth-century building down on the harbour, with tables in the courtyard garden outside and by the canal, this is the town's best restaurant, with a menu that's strong on seafood and local specialities. Main courses are in the region of €25; a four-course menu costs €39.50. Reservations advised. Wed–Sun from 5pm.

De Mastenbar Compagnieshaven 3 ☎0228 313 691, ⓦ demastenbar.nl; map p.141. Down on the marina, this modern place is a great spot for a drink or a full meal, with sandwiches, burgers and *uitsmijters*, soups and big salads for lunch, and a good, shortish dinner menu of meat and fish dishes for around €20. It's cosy enough inside, but the outside terrace, from which you can watch the boats chugging by, makes a perfect end to a summer's day. Daily 10am–11.30pm.

★ **Recuer Dos** Westerstraat 217 ☎0228 562 469, ⓦ recuerdos.nl; map p.141. This immaculate Victorian house has three doubles and one single in a series of chalets set in a peaceful and elegant garden. The rooms are clean and comfortable, and there are regular Spanish guitar and other concerts in the hotel's purpose-built music salon – reflecting the owner's occupation as a classical guitar teacher. **€90**

De Smederij Breedstraat 158–160 ☎0228 314 604, ⓦ restaurantdesmederij.nl; map p.141. Inventive, French-Mediterranean cuisine in a smartly renovated building a block back from the harbour, with starters for €12, main courses for around €25. Fri–Tues 5–10pm.

Theo Schilder Dijk 48 ☎0228 317 809, ⓦ schildervis. nl; map p.141. A smashing fish shop serving an array of seafood snacks, with a pint-sized café attached and tables outside. Mon–Sat 9am–6.30pm, Sun noon–6.30pm.

8

THE HOXTON

Accommodation

Almost fifty years since John Lennon and Yoko Ono promoted world peace from room 702 of the Hilton, Amsterdam's hotels are more worthy of the spotlight than ever. Even for seasoned travellers, it's fair to say that the city's accommodation options are among the most exciting in Europe: take your pick from handsomely converted old canal houses, sleek-and-chic boutique B&Bs and luxurious short-stay apartments, while quirkier options include houseboats, a converted train depot and even a crane. Visitors on a budget are catered for too, with bargain beds aplenty in the city's hostels and campsites. However, as in most capitals, prices soar during peak season – July and August, Easter and Christmas – especially last-minute, so booking in advance is a must.

ESSENTIALS

Accessibility Note that many of Amsterdam's buildings have narrow, very steep staircases, and no lifts; indeed, in the older houses the installing of lifts is actually illegal. If this is a consideration for you, check before you book.

Accommodation websites Most of the places listed in this chapter can be booked online direct, or through the major hotel booking sites – try ⓦhotels.nl or ⓦweekendjeweg.nl (the latter in Dutch only). You can also compare prices and availability through the reservation department of the Amsterdam Tourism & Convention Board (☎020 551 2525, ⓦiamsterdam.com). There are also a couple of websites for houseboats and private apartments (see page 154).

Rates, deals and discounts Given the city's popularity, prices tend to be higher than in most other European cities, especially at peak times – July and Aug, Easter and Christmas – but whenever you visit it's advisable to book well ahead as vacant rooms can get very thin on the ground. More positively, prices are very sensitive to demand, so special deals and discounts are commonplace, especially during the week (or at weekends in business-focused hotels). Most hotels post online offers or discounts on their website, so be sure to check individual sites too.

VVV reservations service Once you've arrived, the city's VVVs, or tourist offices (see page 30) will make hotel reservations on your behalf, either in advance or on the same day for a nominal fee, but note that during peak periods and weekends they get extremely busy, with long queues. VVVs also sell an accommodation guide detailing most of the city's hotels.

HOTELS AND B&BS

Amsterdam's **hotels** start at around €80, but at the lower end of the market you have to be careful: some of the least expensive rooms can be very grim, though at least some form of **breakfast** – "Dutch" (ham, bread and jam) or "English" (as above, plus eggs) – is normally included. It's advisable to ask to see the room before you hand over any money, and if you don't like it, refuse it. Note too that in some of the independently run hotels the cheapest rooms

---

WHERE TO STAY

Amsterdam's compactness means that you'll almost inevitably end up somewhere central, or at least within easy reach of the centre; a run-down of the main areas is below. Note that all **directions** given in the listings, including trams and buses, are from Centraal Station (usually abbreviated as "CS"), unless otherwise indicated.

The Old Centre If you choose to stay here, you'll be a short walk from the main sights and the principal shopping and nightlife areas. Cheap hotels abound and this is the first place to start looking if money is tight, although some may find the proximity of the Red Light District off-putting.

Grachtengordel west The canal-laced streets to the west of the Old Centre have a number of quiet waterside hotels, though the least expensive ones are clustered along Raadhuisstraat, one of the city's busiest streets.

Grachtengordel south Ideally positioned for the plethora of clubs, bars and restaurants on and around Leidseplein and Rembrandtplein, this area is on the rise: *Waldorf Astoria* decided to locate their new hotel here in 2014. There are plenty of options for those on a budget too, including a number of very appealing – and occasionally stylish – hotels along the surrounding canals.

The Jordaan Staying in the Jordaan puts you among the locals, well away from the prime tourist areas. There's no shortage of bars and restaurants here either, and some of the city's prettiest canals thread through the district, but you'll be at least a 15min walk from the bright lights. Be aware when looking for a place to stay that Marnixstraat and Rozengracht are busy main roads.

The old Jewish quarter and Plantage Not many tourists stay in this area as it's largely residential, with very few bars or restaurants. Consequently, you're pretty much guaranteed a quiet night's sleep here, and you're only a tram ride away from the leading sights.

The eastern docklands and Amsterdam Noord These up-and-coming districts have some excellent, avant-garde accommodation options, and though their industrial architecture and open expanses might feel a world away from the Old Centre's medieval lanes, they're just a short hop away by ferry or tram.

The Museum Quarter The city's smartest quarter centres around the Van Gogh Museum and the Rijksmuseum – although the buzzy nightlife around Leidseplein is also within easy striking distance. There are no canals, and two of the main drags, Overtoom and 1e Constantijn Huygensstraat, constantly rumble with traffic, but several good hotels are to be found here, plus the leafy Vondelpark.

The outer districts Exciting accommodation options are cropping up in areas such as Amsterdam Oost, offering the opportunity of top-notch digs for less cash – and thanks to reliable and frequent trams, staying here doesn't place you too far from the action.

9

ACCOMMODATION PRICES

The hotel and guesthouse **prices** given in this book are for the **cheapest double room in high season**, and, unless indicated otherwise, include **breakfast**. For hostel accommodation, the price per person for a dorm bed is given. Hotel prices vary enormously with availability and season, so doing a bit of research before you go is well worthwhile.

often have **shared facilities**, and en-suite rooms, if available, could be an extra €10–20. A significant number of hotels in Amsterdam have large three- or four-bed **family rooms**, though if there's a few of you it's generally cheaper to book an apartment (see page 154). **Wi-fi** is widely available, and is generally included in the price. **B&Bs** are on the increase, and the city also has a good number of **LGBTQ accommodation** options (see page 205).

THE OLD CENTRE

Art'otel Prins Hendrikkade 33 ☎020 719 7200, ⬥artotels.com; right opposite CS; map p.34. As you might have guessed from the name, this new hotel is filled with art. It even has its own gallery, with a curator on hand and a monthly cultural programme. All 107 rooms contain a unique piece of art, and are comfortable too, sleekly styled and moodily lit, with Elemis products in the bathroom. Downstairs you'll find a pool, sauna and gym. **€237**

The Crown Oudezijds Voorburgwal 21 ☎020 626 9664, ⬥hotelthecrown.com; 5min walk from CS; map p.34. This is really a hotel for lone travellers or groups of friends as the rooms are mainly singles, triples and quads, but there is a double on the top floor, as well as a six-person room. The rooms at the back are dark and a bit austere; those at the front are nicer, but prone to noise from the busy canal outside. It's very safe, despite its location right in the middle of the Red Light District, and the 24hr bar has amiable staff and a pool table. **€120**

The Exchange Damrak 50 ☎020 523 0080, ⬥hoteltheexchange.com; 7min walk from CS; map p.34. Rooms at this boutique hotel in the heart of the Old Centre are dressed with all manner of fashiony details. Options range from tiny, pared-back one-star rooms for those on a budget, to pricier, spacious, five-star rooms with great city views (€273). **€110**

France Amsterdam Oudezijds Kolk 11 ☎020 535 3777, ⬥francehotel.nl; 5min walk from CS; map p.34. This friendly 55-room hotel is located on a tiny and little-trafficked canal just off the burgeoning Zeedijk; both the lobby and the rooms are decorated in a brisk Scandi style. **€150**

The Grand Oudezijds Voorburgwal 197 ☎020 555 3111, ⬥sofitel-legend-thegrand.com; tram #4, #9, #16 or #24 to the Dam; map p.34. Originally a royal inn dating from 1578, and after that the Amsterdam Town Hall, this fine classical building is one of the city's architectural high points. The rooms are large, well appointed and boldly decorated in crisp, modern style. There are all the usual facilities you'd expect from a five-star hotel, including a spa with indoor pool and Turkish bath, and a fine dining restaurant on site. Breakfast costs a whopping €30 extra. Deals are often available; check the website. **€370**

★ **Hotel de l'Europe** Nieuwe Doelenstraat 2–14 ☎020 531 1777, ⬥deleurope.com; tram #4, #9, #16 or #24 to Muntplein; map p.34. This elegant old-timer has plenty of *fin-de-siècle* charm and an attractive and central riverside location. The large, opulent rooms each feature a replica Dutch Master painting chosen by the Rijksmuseum, and there's also a two-Michelin-star restaurant, *Bord'Eau*, a spa and the glamorous *Freddy's Bar*. You'll pay an extra €50 for a River Amstel view, but this is about as luxurious as the city gets, and last-minute bargains are plentiful. **€381**

Hotel des Arts Rokin 154–156 ☎020 620 1558, ⬥hoteldesarts.nl; tram #4, #9, #16 or #24 to Muntplein; map p.34. This seventeenth-century townhouse that started life as an orphanage for Catholic girls is now a two-star hotel with 22 classical-style rooms. Wi-fi is only available in the lounge and guests are charged a set fee of €12.50. **€150**

INK Sofitel Nieuwezijds Voorburgwal 67 ☎020 627 5900, ⬥sofitel.com; 5min walk from CS; map p.34. In a historic building, formerly the headquarters of the *De Tijd* newspaper, the 149 rooms at this hotel have extremely comfortable beds and quirky chalkboard-style wallpaper. There's a nice downstairs bar, too. **€194**

Le Coin Nieuwe Doelenstraat 5 ☎020 524 6800, ⬥lecoin.nl; tram #4, #9, #16 or #24 to Muntplein; map p.34. In a good location opposite the swanky *Hotel de l'Europe*, but a quarter of the price, *Le Coin's* modern rooms all have kitchenettes and lounge areas with a TV. Breakfast costs extra. **€170**

Misc Kloveniersburgwal 20 ☎020 330 6241, ⬥misceat drinksleep.com; Metro Nieuwmarkt or a 10min walk from CS; map p.34. Very friendly hotel on the edge of the Red Light District with six good-sized rooms, each elegantly decorated on a different theme. The bright breakfast area overlooks the canal and is great for people-watching. Canal-view rooms cost roughly €30 more. **€205**

Nes Kloveniersburgwal 137–139 ☎020 624 4773, ⬥hotelnes.nl; tram #4, #9, #16 or #24 to Muntplein; map p.34. A pleasant and quiet hotel with helpful staff, well positioned away from noise, but close to shops and nightlife. The size of the 39 functional rooms can vary quite a bit, so don't be afraid to ask to see other rooms if yours looks on the small side. Breakfast not included. **€180**

9

NH City Centre Spuistraat 288–292 ☎020 420 4545, ⓦnh-hotels.com; tram #1, #2 or #5 to Spui; map p.34. Well situated for the cafés and bars of the Spui and the Museum Quarter, this appealing hotel occupies a sympathetically renovated 1920s Art Deco building that was once the HQ of the Gerzon fashion house. Rooms vary in size; some have canal views, all boast comfy beds and good showers. Bike rental available. Breakfast costs extra. €225

NH Collection Amsterdam Doelen Nieuwe Doelenstraat 26 ☎020 554 0600, ⓦnh-hotels.com; tram #4, #9, #16 or #24 to Muntplein; map p.34. Famous as the site of building where Rembrandt painted *The Night Watch* (see page 109), and with an old-fashioned stately elegance about it, this hotel is smaller than it looks from the outside, and has a nice breakfast room overlooking the water. €230

Park Plaza Victoria Damrak 1–5 ☎020 623 4255, ⓦparkplaza.com; 2min walk from CS; map p.34. This tall, elegant building opposite Centraal Station is geared towards business travellers and split into two sections: the 306-room Victoria Wing, with rooms suited to the classical style of the old building; and the new 164-room Urban Wing, whose rooms have a more modern, fashionable edge. Amenities include a lounge bar with occasional live jazz, restaurant, fitness centre and pool. It's pricey, but there are often bargains to be had. Breakfast not included. €331

Rho Nes 5–23 ☎020 620 7371, ⓦrhohotel.com; tram #4, #9, #16 or #24 to the Dam; map p.34. Built as a theatre in 1908, this hotel has a lovely, high-ceilinged, *fin-de-siècle* lobby, which gives a slightly misleading impression: the rooms are on the small side and have been unimaginatively modernized. Still, it's pleasant enough, and in a central location just off the Dam. Bike rental available. €140

Rokin Rokin 73 ☎020 626 7456, ⓦwww.rokinhotel. com; tram #4, #9, #16, #24 to Rokin; map p.34. This conveniently located three-star family hotel has small, modern doubles with exposed beams, as well as singles and triples. Lift access to three of the four floors. The private car park is a handy bonus. €134

Sint Nicolaas Spuistraat 1a ☎020 626 1384, ⓦhotel nicolaas.nl; 5min walk from CS; map p.34. With more character than many of the other mid-range hotels in the area, and very conveniently located. The cosy downstairs bar-reception gives way to 27 smartly refurbished en-suite rooms, all with flatscreen TVs. €175

Vijaya Oudezijds Voorburgwal 44 ☎020 638 0102, ⓦhotelvijaya.com; 10min walk from CS; map p.34. Right in the heart of the Red Light District, next door but one to the Ons' Lieve Heer Op Solder (see page 47), this is a warren of rooms spread over a couple of old canal houses. It's rather threadbare and there's no lift, but the rates are reasonable. €120

Winston Warmoesstraat 129 ☎020 623 1380, ⓦwinston.nl; 10min walk from CS; map p.34. This self-consciously young and cool budget art hotel has funky rooms and dorms individually decorated with wacko art, a busy ground-floor bar and restaurant (hotel guests get a 25 percent discount on the food menu) and, next door, the *Winston Kingdom* nightclub. It's a formula that works a treat: the *Winston* is popular and often full – though this is probably also due to its low prices. Rooms are light and airy, some en suite, some with a communal balcony. Erotic images abound in some, so if you're travelling as a family you might want to check first to prevent any embarrassing questions. Lift and full disabled access. Dorms €42, doubles €72

GRACHTENGORDEL WEST

Agora Singel 462 ☎020 627 2200, ⓦhotelagora.nl; tram #1, #2 or #5 to Koningsplein; map p.55. Handily located and amiable small hotel near the flower market and close to the Spui. The guest rooms, of which there are just sixteen, are kitted out in simple, basic style and vary greatly in size. As well as doubles, three- and four-bed rooms are available; rooms with a canal view cost more and are noisier. There's a large breakfast room, too. No lift. €174

★**Ambassade** Herengracht 341 ☎020 555 0222, ⓦambassade-hotel.nl; tram #1, #2 or #5 to Spui; map p.55. Eminently appealing hotel that occupies a series of cleverly renovated seventeenth-century canal houses. There are sixty-odd rooms, each decorated in period-meets-country-house style, mostly in pastel shades and with big beds and high-spec bathrooms. There's also a well-stocked library and a study room with modern art. Breakfast is taken in an elegant panelled room, where the original merchant-owners once surveyed the scene; a restaurant is in the offing. Guests get discounts at a nearby "Float & Massage" centre. €283

★**b&nb Herengracht** Herengracht 21 176 ☎020 820 8670, ⓦbandnbherengracht.com; tram #1, #2 or #5 to Leidseplein for Hotel Vondel; map p.55. Owned by the same entrepreneur responsible for *De Hallen* (see page 149), this oh-so-central bed (and no breakfast) has three double rooms: subterranean bolthole, canal view or garden view. They're all snug, but come with an en-suite rainshower, iPod docking station, a Nespresso coffee machine and flatscreen TV with DVD player. Check-in is at the *Hotel Vondel* on Vondelstraat; you'll then be taken by taxi to the Herengracht. €270

Chic & Basic Herengracht 13–19 ☎020 522 2345, ⓦchicandbasic.com/amsterdam; 10min walk from

---

TOP 5 BUDGET CHOICES

ClinkNoord see page 154
Cocomama see page 154
Eco Mama see page 154
Lloyd Hotel see page 150
Prinsenhof see page 149

9

CS; map p.55. The Dutch branch of this funky Spanish concept offers 26 country-chic rooms, some of which overlook the canal, with folksy quilted bedspreads, upcycled fittings and a lighting system that you can adjust according to your mood. Breakfast costs extra. **€209**

Clemens Raadhuisstraat 39 ☎ 020 624 6089, ⓦ clemens hotel.nl; tram #13 or #17 to Westermarkt; map p.55. Close to the Anne Frank Huis, this well-run two-star budget hotel, with a friendly, knowledgeable owner, is one of the better options along this busy main road. The rooms, all en suite, are decorated in fairly uninspiring monochrome, but come with a mini-fridge and LCD TV. **€152**

★ **Dylan** Keizersgracht 384 ☎ 020 530 2010, ⓦ dylan amsterdam.com; tram #1, #2 or #5 to Leidsestraat/ Keizersgracht; map p.55. Hip without being pretentious, the *Dylan* has earned itself many repeat guests. This stylish hotel is housed in a seventeenth-century building that centres on a beautiful courtyard and terrace. The 40 sumptuous rooms come in shades of white and oatmeal, and have a flatscreen TV, Bose stereo and an Illy espresso maker, and there's a Michelin-star restaurant on site, serving up modern French cuisine. Breakfast costs extra. **€470**

Estheréa Singel 303–309 ☎ 020 624 5146, ⓦ estherea. nl; tram #1, #2 or #5 from CS to Spui; map p.55. This enjoyable and very comfortable four-star occupies a pair of sympathetically modernized old canal houses in a great location, a brief stroll from the Spui. There's no attempt at modern minimalism here – the carpets are thick and plush, the public areas rich in browns and reds. The rooms, all accessed via lift, are equally flamboyant, with beds that you can sink into; the pick of them overlook the canal. Free iPad and DVDs on request. Breakfast costs extra. **€210**

Hegra Herengracht 269 ☎ 020 623 7877, ⓦ hotelhegra. nl; tram #1, #2 or #5 to Spui; map p.55. On a handsome stretch of canal near the Spui, this hotel has a welcoming atmosphere and small but comfortable rooms, either en suite or with shared facilities. Relatively inexpensive for the location, but breakfast costs extra. **€240**

't Hotel Leliegracht 18 ☎ 020 422 2741, ⓦ thotel.nl; tram #13 or #17 to Westermarkt; map p.55. Extremely appealing hotel located in an old high-gabled house along a quiet stretch of canal, run by friendly staff. The eight spacious rooms – three with canal views – are imaginatively decorated, from the Delft tile-themed "Amstel" to the Dutch art-themed "Bloemgracht". All rooms have large beds, a TV, fridge and either a bath or shower. Minimum two-night stay at weekends (Fri & Sat). **€209**

The Hoxton Herengracht 255 ☎ 020 888 5555, ⓦ thehoxton.com; tram #1, #2 or #5 to the Dam; map p.55. Five conjoined seventeenth-century canal houses comprise this sexy hotel, which oozes Modernist style. It was the first opening outside London of this cool mini-chain, and its 111 rooms follow the same winning formula, ranging from the very snug "Shoebox" to the palatial

"Roomy", as well as a few "Concept" rooms with stunning period features. Downstairs is *Lotti's* restaurant – with a cool retractable roof for sunny days – serving a mix of Italian and Dutch specialities and elegant cocktails. In the morning a breakfast goodie bag is hung outside your door. **€129**

Pax Raadhuisstraat 37b ☎ 020 624 9735, ⓦ hotel-pax. hoteleamsterdam.net; tram #13 or #17 to Westermarkt; map p.55. Straightforward city-centre cheapie with a mixture of fair-sized rooms sleeping one to four people; all are very sparsely furnished. As with most of the hotels along this busy stretch, ask for a room at the back. No lift and no breakfast. **€95**

Pulitzer Prinsengracht 323 ☎ 020 523 5235, ⓦ pulitzer amsterdam.com; tram #13 or #17 to Westermarkt; map p.55. Gorgeous in their own right, these combined seventeenth-century canal houses were made all the more famous by Brad Pitt and George Clooney when they filmed scenes for *Ocean's Twelve* here. Smack in the centre of the Negen Straatjes shopping quarter, the rooms in this prestigious five-star are all done up in soft tones following a 2016 renovation, some overlooking the inner courtyard, others with canal views. There's a good restaurant too. **€305**

Singel Hotel Singel 13–17 ☎ 020 626 3108, ⓦ singelhotel.nl; 5min walk from CS; map p.55. Pleasant hotel located in three charming canal houses right next to the old Lutheran church. The rooms are rather small and functional, but well equipped, and some overlook the Singel. Minimum two-night stay at weekends. **€191**

The Times Hotel Herengracht 135 ☎ 020 330 6030, ⓦ thetimeshotel.nl; tram #1, #2 or #5 to Spui; map p.55. Colourful design hotel with a wink to the old Dutch Masters – each room contains a gigantic painting of Vermeer, Rembrandt or van Gogh. Excellent quality for the price, though breakfast costs extra. **€161**

★ **The Toren** Keizersgracht 164 ☎ 020 622 6033, ⓦ thetoren.nl; tram #13 or #17 to Westermarkt; map p.55. Cosy, retro-chic boutique hotel, converted from two elegant canal houses (one of which was once the home of the Dutch prime minister), with an emphasis on intimacy and comfort. There's a sumptuous bar/breakfast room downstairs, and they offer a few snacks for lunch and dinner. Very attentive and friendly staff, too. **€332**

Wiechmann Prinsengracht 328–332 ☎ 020 626 3321, ⓦ hotelwiechmann.nl; tram #2, #13 or #17 to Westermarkt; map p.55. Family-run for over fifty years, this mid-sized hotel occupies an attractively restored canal house close to the Anne Frank Huis, with dark wooden beams. The large, bright rooms – with a TV and shower – are a bit bare, but spotlessly clean. **€157**

GRACHTENGORDEL SOUTH

Amsterdam American Leidsekade 97 ☎ 020 556 3000, ⓦ amsterdamamericanhotel.com; tram #1, #2 or #5 to Leidseplein; map p.65. This landmark Art

Deco hotel, dating from 1902, was once the height of chic; the high rollers have since moved on, and the bedrooms are now standard-issue modern affairs, but they are large and comfortable, with double-glazed windows (a useful addition, since the hotel is just off Leidseplein). **€250**

Backstage Hotel Leidsegracht 114 ☎020 624 4044, ⓦbackstagehotel.com; tram #1, #2 or #5 to Prinsengracht; map p.65. This hotel accommodates musicians playing at the nearby Melkweg or Paradiso; furnishings such as theatre mirrors, PA spotlights and flight cases in the 22 rooms, and guitars and amps in the bar, are bound to make them feel at home, but non-musicians are also welcome. Facilities include a 24hr bar and pool table. Breakfast costs extra. **€145**

Dikker & Thijs Fenice Prinsengracht 444 ☎020 620 1212, ⓦdikkerandthijshotelamsterdam.com; tram #1, #2 or #5 to the corner of Prinsengracht and Leidsestraat; map p.65. Once a shop purveying fine foods, this small and stylish hotel continues the tradition with an excellent seasonal-food restaurant. The modern rooms are a little blander, but have a minibar, tea- and coffee-making facilities and TV. Those on the top floor offer a good view of the city. Breakfast costs extra. **€198**

Marcel's Creative Exchange Leidsestraat 87 ☎020 622 9834, ⓦmarcelamsterdam.nl; tram #1, #2 or #5 to Prinsengracht; map p.65. Named after the owner – graphic designer and artist Marcel van Woerkom – this stylishly restored house is a relaxing haven from the buzz of the city, with regulars returning year after year, so you'll need to book well in advance in high season. Three en-suite doubles, including one with a private patio garden, are available for two, three or four people sharing. No breakfast, but there are tea- and coffee-making facilities. **€190**

★ **Prinsenhof** Prinsengracht 810 ☎020 623 1772, ⓦhotelprinsenhof.com; tram #4 to Prinsengracht; map p.65. This small one-star has been offering bed and board since 1813. Rooms are spacious and tastefully decorated, making it one of the city's top budget options, but with only eleven rooms, booking ahead is essential. Rooms don't have TVs, but there is wi-fi. **€90**

Rembrandt Square Hotel Rembrandtplein 24 ☎020 620 0652, ⓦrembrandtsquarehotel.com; tram #4, #9 or #16 to Rembrandtplein; map p.65. A one-star hotel with an urban feel, located just off busy Rembrandtplein. The rooms are tastefully decorated in white and green shades, with comfy beds and shared bathrooms. There's a lively coffeeshop on the ground floor, too. **€80**

Seven Bridges Reguliersgracht 31 ☎020 623 1329, ⓦsevenbridgeshotel.nl; tram #16, #24 or #9 to Keizersgracht; map p.65. Excellent value for money, this hotel takes its name from its canalside location, which affords a view of no fewer than seven quaint little bridges. The hotel is beautifully decorated in antique style, its spotless rooms regularly revamped. It's small and popular,

TOP 5 LUXURY CHOICES   9
Conservatorium see page 151
Dylan see page 148
The Grand see page 146
Hotel de l'Europe see page 146
Waldorf Astoria see page 149

so advance reservations are pretty much essential. Breakfast is served in the rooms. **€250**

★ **Waldorf Astoria** Herengracht 542–556 ☎020 718 4600, ⓦwaldorfastoria3.hilton.com; tram #4 to Rembrandtplein; map p.65. The iconic *Waldorf Astoria* set up shop in Amsterdam in 2014, the hotel housed within a series of conjoined seventeenth-century canal houses in one of the city's most prestigious neighbourhoods. The 93 rooms and suites come in tasteful, calming neutral shades, with either canal or garden views. There's a variety of dining options, including the two-Michelin-star *Librije's Zusje*, plus a chic Guerlain spa. It's hard to fault, except for the eye-watering cost. **€800**

Weber Marnixstraat 397 ☎020 627 2327, ⓦhotelweber. nl; tram #1, #2 or #5 to Leidseplein; map p.65. This boutique hotel offers seven spacious rooms with sleek black decor, kitchenette, Nespresso coffee machine and breakfast delivered to your mini-fridge. It sits above a popular bar, mainly attracting a youthful clientele. No lift. **€200**

THE JORDAAN AND WESTERN DOCKLANDS

Blue Wave Houseboat De Costakade 342 ☎065 0667 7760, ⓦbluewavehouseboat.com; tram #7 or #17 to Bilderdijkstraat/Kinkerstraat; map p.75. Hosts Elizabeth, Hans and their daughter Maya rent out two cosy double bedrooms with en-suite mosaic-tiled bathrooms aboard their houseboat. The floating terrace has serene canal views and there's internet, a piano, guitar and a DVD collection for entertainment too. **€290**

★ **De Hallen** Bellamyplein 47 ☎020 820 8670, ⓦhoteldehallen.com; tram #7 or #17 to Ten Katestraat; map p.75. There's plenty of buzz surrounding the stunning conversion of this 1902 tram depot. Original features, such as rails in the dining-room floor, and the vaulted glass ceiling, have been kept intact, and the 57 rooms seem to be suspended within the structure. The small but smart rooms – all fresh green tones and white linens – are split over two floors, and arranged around a central area dotted with sofas and modern art from the owner's private collection. The bar and *Remise47* restaurant are good too. Six apartments are also available (see page 154). **€175**

Linden Lindengracht 251 ☎020 622 1460, ⓦlinden hotel.nl; bus #18 to Willemstraat or tram #3 or #10 to Marnixplein, or a 15min walk from CS; map p.75. This 25-room hotel, in the heart of the Jordaan, is on a corner, so

9

some of the rooms have sweeping views of the canal and its adjoining streets. The functional rooms, which sleep two to four people, are rather nondescript, with small beds and a shower room. **€215**

★ **Maison Rika** Oude Spiegelstraat 12 ☎020 330 1112, ⓦrikastudios.com; tram #1, #2 or #5 to Spui; map p.75. Housed in a former art gallery, this boutique option has two beautifully furnished queen-sized bedrooms on the second and third floors and is owned by fashion designer Ulrika Lundgren, who has a shop across the street. There's free water, chocolates, tea and coffee, but breakfast isn't available. Two-night minimum stay on weekends. **€295**

Hotel de Paris Amsterdam Marnixstraat 372 ☎020 622 5587, ⓦhoteldeparisamsterdam.nl; tram #1, #2 or #5 to Leidseplein; map p.75. A three-star hotel set in a fuchsia-pink townhouse near Leidseplein, within walking distance of Vondelpark, the Van Gogh Museum, Rijksmuseum and Stedelijk Museum. There are forty comfortably furnished rooms, with lots of glossy wood and neutral colours, overlooking either the Marnixstraat or the hotel's patio. Bike rental also available. **€166**

THE OLD JEWISH QUARTER AND PLANTAGE

Adolesce Nieuwe Keizersgracht 26 ☎020 626 3959, ⓦen.adolesce.nl; tram #9 or #14 to Waterlooplein; map p.83. Popular and welcoming four-storey hotel (no lift) in an old canal house not far from Waterlooplein. There are ten neat, if a little dated, rooms and a communal seating area. No breakfast, but coffee, tea, juice and waffles are available all day. Closed Nov–March. **€130**

Arena 's Gravesandestraat 51 ☎020 850 2400, ⓦhotelarena.nl; Metro Weesperplein, then an 8min walk; map p.83. A little way east of the centre, in a renovated former orphanage on the edge of the Oosterpark, this hip four-star hotel has split-level rooms in tranquil grey or cream. There's a lovely, relaxed vibe in the bar and the intimate restaurant with garden terrace, and a lively late-night club (Fri & Sat) located within the former chapel. Bike rental and in-room massages are also available. Breakfast costs extra. **€129**

InterContinental Amstel Professor Tulpplein 1 ☎020 520 3189, ⓦihg.com; Metro Weesperplein; map p.83. One of the city's most enduring top-class hotels, the *InterContinental* occupies a grand, chateau-style, nineteenth-century mansion beside the Singelgracht canal, and is favoured by visiting celebrities. There's an excellent French restaurant, plus a health club with pool and Jacuzzi. If you have the means, splash out – there are lots of deals available, too. **€462**

THE EASTERN DOCKLANDS AND AMSTERDAM NOORD

Aitana IJdok 6 ☎020 891 4800, ⓦroom-matehotels. com/en/aitana; 10min walk from CS; map p.97. Built on an artificial island just metres from Centraal Station, this ultramodern hotel has light, bright rooms that come with a LCD TV and rainshower, plus access to the on-site gym. The breakfast buffet doesn't finish until noon – perfect for late risers. **€215**

Amstel Botel Moored at NDSM Pier 3 ☎020 626 4247, ⓦbotel.nl; 5min ferry ride from CS; map p.103. This three-star floating hotel in the up-and-coming NDSM district has 175 en-suite rooms, "waterside" or "landside", with a TV and free in-house movies. Rooms are fairly functional – staying here might feel like spending your holiday on a cross-Channel ferry – but the bar has internet access, a pool table, juke box and pinball machine. **€110**

DoubleTree by Hilton Hotel Amsterdam NDSM-Plein 28 ☎020 722 0666, ⓦdoubletree3.hilton.com; 10min ferry ride from CS; map p.103. The first hotel to set up in the hip NDSM district, this plush boutique option may have icy front-desk staff, but the luxurious rooms, fitness centre, brasserie and bar should more than make up for it. **€240**

Faralda Crane NDSM-Plein 78 ☎020 760 6161, ⓦfaralda.com; 10min ferry ride from CS; map p.103. Ever slept 50m in the air? The world's first hotel in a crane offers three ultra-contemporary suites with knee-buckling city views. Bungee jumping from the top costs €87.50 a go (ⓦbungeeamsterdam.com), or there's the more relaxing spa pool. As you'd expect, there's a long waiting list, so book well in advance. **€435**

★ **Lloyd Hotel** Oostelijke Handelskade 34 ☎020 561 3607, ⓦlloydhotel.com; tram #26 to Rietlandsparken, then a 3min walk; map p.101. Situated in the Oosterdok (eastern docklands) district, this ex-prison and refugee workers' hostel has been renovated to become a "cultural embassy", with an arts centre which puts on regular exhibitions, readings and performances, as well as an art library. The hotel serves all kinds of travellers, with rooms ranging from one-star affairs with a shared bathroom to five-star suites. Some rooms are great, others not, so don't be afraid to ask to change. The pleasantly bustling, airy restaurant and lobby area on the ground floor is another plus. **€114**

THE MUSEUM QUARTER AND AROUND

Bicycle Hotel Van Ostadestraat 123 ☎020 679 3452, ⓦbicyclehotel.com; tram #16 or #24 to Van de Helststraat; map p.107. Youthful, eco-conscious place located down a quiet residential street. Two-, three- and four-bed rooms, plus one with bunk beds, are bright and clean. During the winter months they usually offer free bike rental; otherwise it's €8/day. If you book direct via their website there's a 7.5 percent discount; cash is preferred on site. **€135**

Bilderberg Hotel Jan Luyken Jan Luykenstraat 58 ☎020 573 0730, ⓦbilderberg.nl; tram #2 or #5 to Van Baerlestraat or Rijksmuseum; map p.107. A please-all boutique hotel whose smart rooms all have the same cream linens and wood finish. There's a nice lounge and bar downstairs. Pets allowed. **€134**

★ **College** Roelof Hartstraat 1 ☎ 020 571 1511, ⓦ thecollegehotel.com; tram #5 or #24 to junction of Roelof Hartstraat and Van Baerlestraat; map p.107. Converted from a nineteenth-century schoolhouse, the *College* is an elegant boutique hotel run by hotel-school students. It has tasteful modern rooms, a first-rate restaurant, a swanky bar and a chic terrace planted with olive trees – perfect for sunny days. **€189**

★ **Conscious Hotel Museum Square** De Lairessestraat 7 ☎ 020 671 9596, ⓦ conscioushotels.com; tram #16 to Jacob Obrechtstraat; map p.116. Right in the heart of the Museum Quarter, this hotel is 100 percent sustainable, from the living plant wall by reception to the 36 rooms, which feature photographic forest wallpaper, Mongolian goat-hair carpet that's anti-static (and good for your feet, apparently), desks made out of recycled yoghurt pots, and ergonomic beds. Other pluses are the scrumptious organic breakfast, bike rental and hotel garden. **€170**

★ **Conservatorium** Van Baerlestraat 27 ☎ 020 570 0000, ⓦ conservatoriumhotel.com; tram #5 to Van Baerlestraat; map p.107. The capital's most jaw-dropping hotel, this heritage building – once the Sweelinck Music Conservatorium – has been transformed into a contemporary design wonderland. Standard guestrooms come with Nespresso machine and free newspapers, plus access to Akasha – the city's largest and most opulent spa. There's a great on-site brasserie too (see page 160). Check website for packages. **€489**

Fita Jan Luijkenstraat 37 ☎ 020 679 0976, ⓦ fita.nl; tram #2 or #5 to Van Baerlestraat; map p.107. Mid-sized hotel decorated with Brecht Swaanswijk art and offering unremarkable but comfortable en-suite doubles, though some of them are very snug indeed. **€199**

Maxime P.C. Hooftstraat 63 ☎ 020 676 5306, ⓦ maxime amsterdam.nl; tram #2 or #5 to Van Baerlestraat; map p.107. Unusual boutique hotel, this one: there's no reception, no staff and no breakfast. Instead, there are twelve dark and moody high-spec rooms accessed via a lift and your own individual pin code emailed to you upon booking. **€141**

The Neighbour's Magnolia Willemsparkweg 205 ☎ 020 676 9321, ⓦ magnoliahotelamsterdam.com; tram #2 to Cornelis Schuytstraat; map p.116. This colourful family-run hotel on a busy street near the Vondelpark has 21 spotless rooms with cheery pink carpet, Fairtrade toiletries and flatscreen TV. There's an honesty bar, living room and business area too. Breakfast costs extra. Deals are often available. **€142**

NL Hotel Leidseplein Nassaukade 368 ☎ 020 689 0030, ⓦ hotel368.com; tram #1, #2 or #5 to Leidseplein and then a 5min walk; map p.75. These thirteen rooms, some with canal views, are a fusion of Dutch and Asian influences, with plenty of orange, Buddhas and tulips. The hospitable owners are a good source of advice on the area's trendier spots. Breakfast costs extra. **€130**

Okura Ferdinand Bolstraat 333 ☎ 020 678 7111, ⓦ okura.nl; tram #12, #13, #16 or #24 to Cornelis Troostplein; map p.107. Don't be fooled by the concrete, purpose-built facade: this deluxe hotel comes with a spa, pool and fitness centre (complete with personal trainers), plus an astonishing three Michelin-starred restaurant. Its 300 rooms boast huge marble walk-in bathrooms, and mod cons abound in its suites. If you're feeling particularly flush you could book "The Suite", set over two floors with a suspended glass staircase, cinema and private butler; a night here will set you back a cool €12,500. **€234**

Piet Hein Vossiusstraat 51–53 ☎ 020 662 7205, ⓦ hotelpiethein.nl; tram #1, #2 or #5 to Leidseplein, then a 5min walk; map p.107. This sleek three-star has large rooms with views over the entrance to the Vondelpark; the slightly pricier rooms in the modern annex overlook its peaceful back garden. There's also a comfy bar that's normally open until 1am, and a smart garden. **€100**

Max Brown Museum Square Jan Luijkenstraat 40-46 ☎ 020 662 0526, ⓦ maxbrownhotels.com; tram #2 or #5 to Hobbemastraat; map p.107. Conveniently located just a block away from the Van Gogh Museum, this contemporary hotel is situated in a string of four beautifully converted canal houses. Simple yet comfortable rooms are adorned with wood furniture and panels, and a plant-strewn bar also serves light bites throughout the day. **€148**

Roemer Roemer Visscherstraat 10 ☎ 020 589 0800, ⓦ hotelroemer.com; tram #1, #2 or #5 to Leidseplein, then walk across the bridge; map p.107. This high-end, stylish boutique option, dotted with contemporary art and with its own garden, caters for discerning business travellers, but will suit non-business types too. They offer a "Roemer Inclusive" rate, which includes all alcoholic drinks, snacks in the afternoon and a scrumptious breakfast (otherwise a pricey €19.95). **€170**

Pillows Anna van den Vondel Anna van den Vondelstraat 6 ☎ 020 683 3013, ⓦ pillowshotels.com/amsterdam-vondel; tram #7, #13 or #17 to Jan Pieter Heijestraat; map p.116. Thoroughly revamped and reopened in 2017, this modern boutique hotel boasts 31 minimalist-chic rooms decked out with natural colours and softly textured fabrics. They offer views out over the lovely backyard garden or the city, and are equipped with Nespresso coffee machines, smart HD TVs and wireless sound systems. Some even have their own terrace or French balcony. Breakfast not included. **€330**

The Student Hotel Wibautstraat 129 ☎ 020 214 9999, ⓦ thestudenthotel.com; metro to Jan van Galenstraat; map p.107. Students can book a modern, hotel-standard

9

TOP 5 QUIRKY CHOICES
Art'otel see page 146
Blue Wave Houseboat see page 149
Faralda Crane see page 150
De Hallen see page 149
De Windketel see page 155

Vondel Vondelstraat 26 ☎020 612 0120, ⊛hotelvondel. com; tram #1, #2 or #5 to Leidseplein, then walk across the bridge; map p.107. Seven conjoined townhouses form this cool and sleek boutique option with plush public areas. Rooms – available as singles, doubles, triples and an apartment (see page 155) – are more pared back, with light, natural wood and minimalist furniture. Rooms are good value, but breakfast – albeit delicious – is expensive (€19.95). **€208**

en-suite room with a flatscreen TV, desk and access to a shared kitchen, plus state-of-the-art café, games room, gym and restaurant, from one night to a few months (discounts apply). **€147**

Volkshotel Wibautstraat 150 ☎020 2612 100, ⊛volkshotel.nl; metro to Wibautstraat; map p.107. These unique digs were once a newspaper headquarters, but don't be deterred by the bland 1970s exterior: the 172 rooms are a quirky hybrid of wood, glass and concrete. Nine "special" rooms take things to another level entirely: the "Soixante Neuf" even has a bed suspended from the ceiling. Other perks include a rooftop sauna and hot tub, plus yoga lessons three times a week for €11. **€140**

HOSTELS

Handy if you're on a tight budget, the least expensive central option is to book a dorm bed in a **hostel**. Most hostels will provide clean **bed linen**, but may charge extra for a towel. Many places also lock guests out for a short period each day to clean, and a few demand a minimum two-night stay at weekends. Many hostels also offer triples, doubles and singles for much less than you'd pay in a regular hotel – though the quality and size varies dramatically. All of the hostels listed below have free **wi-fi**, at least in the public areas. Most include some sort of **breakfast**, with white bread, jam, cereals, tea and coffee, but it's usually pretty basic.

THE OLD CENTRE

Bob's Youth Hostel Nieuwezijds Voorburgwal 92 ☎020 623 0063, ⊛bobsyouthhostel.nl; 10min walk from CS; map p.34. An old favourite with backpackers, *Bob's* is a lively place with small, basic four- to twenty-bed dorms livened up with graffiti. Breakfast is taken in the artsy coffeeshop on the ground floor. However, they kick everyone out at 10.30am to clean, which is not so good if you want a lie-in. Walk-ins welcome. Dorms **€30**

Flying Pig Downtown Nieuwendijk 100 ☎020 420 6822, ⊛flyingpig.nl; 5min walk from CS; map p.34. Clean, large and well run by ex-travellers familiar with the needs of backpackers. Free use of kitchen facilities, no curfew, shuttles to the beach in summer, and the hostel bar is open practically all night. It's justifiably popular, and a very good deal, with mixed dorms, some of which have queen-sized bunks sleeping two. During peak season you'll

THE OUTER DISTRICTS

Hilton Amsterdam Apollolaan 138, Nieuw Zuid ☎020 710 6000, ⊛bit.ly/HiltonAmsterdamHotel; tram #5 or to Apollolaan; map p.124. Way outside the centre by a canal in the distinctly upmarket Nieuw Zuid district, this hotel has all the facilities you could hope for, from lounge bar, café and health club through to an Italian restaurant. Mainly attracting a business-oriented clientele, it's only really worth considering if you can afford to soak up a bit of 1960s nostalgia in its stunning "John and Yoko" suite (€1499), where the couple held their famous 1969 "Bed-In" for peace (see page 123). **€230**

need to book well in advance. There's another branch of the *Flying Pig* near the Vondelpark (see page 154). Dorms **€40**, doubles **€72**

Meeting Point Warmoesstraat 14 ☎020 627 7499, ⊛hostel-meetingpoint.nl; 10min walk from CS; map p.34. One of the city's oldest hostels, *Meeting Point* is somewhat faded and worn, but it still offers the cheapest sleep in town in eight- to eighteen-bed dorms. There's a private bar with pool table for guests. Breakfast costs extra, but it's probably best to go elsewhere. Dorms **€25**

Shelter City Barndesteeg 21 ☎020 625 3230, ⊛shelterhostelamsterdam.com; Metro Nieuwmarkt; map p.34. A non-evangelical Christian youth hostel smack in the middle of the Red Light District. You might be handed a booklet on Jesus when you check in, but you'll get a quiet night's sleep, the sheets are clean and they cook pancakes for breakfast. Dorms are single sex; towel rental costs €1, lockers are free. There's a second *Shelter* in the Jordaan (see page 154). Dorms **€25**

Stayokay Stadsdoelen Kloveniersburgwal 97 ☎020 624 6832, ⊛stayokay.com; Metro Nieuwmarkt or Waterlooplein, or tram #4, #9, #16 or #24 to Muntplein; map p.34. The closest to Centraal Station of the three official hostels – see also *Stayokay Vondelpark* (see page 154) and *Stayokay Zeeburg* (see page 154). There are dorm rooms as well as private twins, and the price includes linen, breakfast and locker, plus use of communal kitchen. There's a good bar with pool table downstairs, and guests get a range of discounts on activities in the city. Dorms **€31.50**, doubles **€102**

9

GRACHTENGORDEL SOUTH

★ **Cocomama** Westeinde 18 ☎020 627 2454, ⓦcocomamahostel.com; tram #4 or #7 to Stadehouderskade; map p.65. Amsterdam's first boutique hostel, with upmarket two- to six-bed wooden-bunk dorms, four double rooms, and a family room planned. There's also a super communal kitchen, a lounge with movies and games, and a lush garden. A minimum two- or three-night stay in high season. Dorms €50, doubles €140

Hans Brinker Budget Hotel Kerkstraat 136–138 ☎020 622 0687, ⓦhansbrinker.eu/amsterdam; tram #1, #2 or #5 to Keizersgracht; map p.65. Raucously popular hostel with around five hundred beds – some of the cheapest in town. The four- to eight-bed dorms are basic and clean; singles, doubles and triples are also available, all en suite. The facilities are good: restaurant selling fast food, basement bar and club, and it's near to the buzz of Leidseplein, too. A hostel to head for if you're out for a good time (and not too bothered about getting a solid night's sleep). Over-35s not permitted. Dorms €28.50, doubles €78

THE JORDAAN AND WESTERN DOCKLANDS

Shelter Jordan Bloemstraat 179 ☎020 624 4717, ⓦshelter.nl; tram #13 or #17 to Marnixstraat; map p.75. The second of Amsterdam's two Christian *Shelter* hostels (see page 152), situated in a particularly attractive and quiet part of the Jordaan, close to the Lijnbaansgracht canal. Great-value beds in single-sex dorms (sleeping four to eighteen); rates include breakfast, sheets, shower and locker. There's a decent café downstairs. Dorms €30

THE OLD JEWISH QUARTER AND PLANTAGE

★ **Eco Mama** Valkenburgerstraat 124 ☎020 770 9529, ⓦecomamahotel.com; tram #9 to Mr Visserplein then 2min walk, or Metro Waterlooplein; map p.83. Superb light, bright eco-hostel with green roof, water-saving system and rooms that range from "El Cheapo" twelve-bed dorms to very stylish private en-suite doubles; there's a ladies-only dorm too. Dorms €50, doubles €160

THE EASTERN DOCKLANDS AND AMSTERDAM NOORD

ClinkNoord Badhuiskade 3 ⓦclinkhostels.com; 5min by ferry from CS; map p.97. This brand-new hostel housed in the 1920s former headquarters of Shell offers four- to ten-bed dorms (including girls-only dorms) and private en-suite rooms. Facilities include a free cinema, self-catering kitchen, café and library, plus a bar with live music. Dorms from €15, doubles from €71

THE MUSEUM QUARTER AND AROUND

Flying Pig Uptown Vossiusstraat 46–47 ☎020 400 4187, ⓦflyingpig.nl; tram #1, #2 or #5 to Leidseplein, then a short walk; map p.107. A cut above *Flying Pig Downtown* (see page 152), this branch of the chain faces the Vondelpark and is close to the city's most important museums. It's also immaculately clean and well maintained by a staff of travellers. Dorms sleep from four to fourteen, and a few have queen-sized bunks that can be shared. There's free use of kitchen facilities, no curfew and good tourist information, as well as a strong party atmosphere – it's no coincidence they serve the cheapest beer in town. Dorms €40, doubles €80

Stayokay Vondelpark Zandpad 5 ☎020 589 8996, ⓦstayokay.com; tram #1, #2 or #5 to Leidseplein, then a 5min walk; map p.107. With 536 beds, this is one of the largest hostels in Europe, with good facilities such as a bar, restaurant, secure lockers, bike rental and shed, plus various discounts on tours and museums and no curfew. To be sure of a place in high season (when there's a minimum stay of two nights if you want to stay on a Sat), you'll need to book at least two months ahead. Members receive €2.50 discount on every night's stay, plus ten percent discount on bar orders and bike rental. Rates vary enormously, but include use of all facilities, shower (though not towels), sheets and breakfast. Dorms €45, doubles €110

THE OUTER DISTRICTS

Stayokay Zeeburg Timorplein 21, Amsterdam Oost ☎020 551 3190, ⓦstayokay.com; train to Amsterdam Muiderpoort; map p.126. Located in a former school in a residential area on the eastern outskirts of the city, this hostel has its own bar/restaurant, bike rental and laundry, and is wheelchair accessible. It shares the building with Studio/K, a multipurpose venue that shows arthouse films and has a decent restaurant. In high season a minimum of two nights is required if you want to stay a Sat. Dorms €36, doubles €130

APARTMENTS AND HOUSEBOATS

For groups or families, short-term **apartment** rentals can work out cheaper than staying in a hotel, with the further advantages of privacy and the convenience (or at least relative cheapness) of self-catering. Apartments sleeping four or five can often be found for the same price as a double room in a hotel. **Houseboats** tend to be significantly more luxurious and expensive; several options are listed on airbnb (ⓦairbnb.nl), as well as ⓦhouseboatrental.amsterdam.

City Mundo (ⓦamsterdam.citymundo.com/) is a local booking service for private accommodation, including rooms, apartments and houseboats. Alternatively, the following are reliable city-centre options.

Apartments De Hallen Bellamyplein 47, Jordaan ☎020 820 8670, ⓦapartmentsdehallen.com; tram #13 to Geuzenveld (stop Willem de Zwijgerlaan) or #17 to Bellamyplein (stop Ten Katestraat); map p.75. Six high-spec stylish apartments for two or four people, with original artwork and the sort of amenities you'd find in a luxe boutique hotel such as Nespresso machines and underfloor bathroom heating. Minimum-stay restrictions. €270

Hoksbergen Singel 301, Grachtengordel west ☎020 626 6043, ⓦhotelhoksbergen.com; map p.55. Apartments sleeping up to six people in various locations around town; minimum three-night stay required. €150

Prinsengracht Prinsengracht 540–542, Grachtengordel south ☎020 589 0800, ⓦprinsengrachtapartments. com; tram #1, #2 or #5 to Leidseplein, then a 2min walk; map p.65. Owned by the same entrepreneur responsible for trendy De Hallen (see page 149) and b&nb Herengracht (see page 147), these five high-quality apartments sleep up to four and have a bathroom with underfloor heating, washer and dryer, a sleek kitchen, free wi-fi and daily housekeeping. Minimum seven-night stay. €150

Vondel Vondelstraat 26, Museum Quarter ☎020 612 0120, ⓦhotelvondel.com; tram #1 to Leidseplein, then walk across the bridge; map p.107. This luxury apartment is superbly furnished, with herringbone wooden floors and chic black walls, with pops of colour in the outsized paintings. A minimum-night stay applies during some periods. €170

De Windketel Watertorenplein 8c, western docklands ⓦwindketel.nl/en; tram #13 or #17 to Westerpark/Van Hallstraat, then tram #10; map p.75. An apartment in an octagonal 1890s converted water tower, De Windketel is split over three floors. There's a well-equipped kitchen on the ground floor, a living room with floor-to-ceiling windows on the second, and tucked away in the eaves, a bedroom with built-in bathtub and wooden ceiling. A unique chance to stay in a historic building. Minimum three-night stay. €375

CAMPING

Vliegenbos Meeuwenlaan 138, Amsterdam Noord ☎020 636 8855, ⓦamsterdam.nl/vliegenbos; bus #32 or #33 (10min), or ferry to Buiksloterweg and then a 15min walk; by car, take Exit S116 off the A10; map p.97. A relaxed and friendly site with places for campervans and tents, as well as trekkers' cabins with bunk beds (sleeping bags required) and basic cooking facilities, and a "camping hotel" – a new area of canvas tents with bunk beds and a central festival-style open-air kitchen; phone ahead to check availability. There's also a general shop, bar and restaurant, and wi-fi and hot showers are included in the price. Car parking costs €7. Closed 23 Oct to 30 March. Camping (2 people) €22, caravans €31, hotel doubles €75, cabins €80

Zeeburg Zuider IJdijk 20, eastern docklands ☎020 694 4430, ⓦcampingzeeburg.nl; tram #26 to Zuiderzeeweg, then a 10min walk; by car, take Exit S114 off the A10; map p.101. Environmentally friendly, well-equipped campsite located in the eastern docklands with tent and caravan pitches, plus a handful of brightly coloured, heated wagonettes (summer only) that sleep one to two or three to four people, and equally cheery eco-cabins; both come with linen, electricity and wi-fi. There's also a bar, restaurant, laundry, kayak and bike rental, plus a petting zoo and nearby outdoor pool. Shower coins cost €0.80. Open all year. Camping (2 people) €32, caravans €50, wagonettes €160, cabins €95

GREENWOODS

Cafés and restaurants

Amsterdam may not be at Europe's gastronomic cutting edge, but the food in the average Dutch restaurant has improved by leaps and bounds in recent years. Traditionally, Dutch food has been a bit of a meat-and-two-veg affair, with potatoes a staple, as well as filling stews, sausages, steaks and the like. More recently, however, many restaurants have introduced more of a Modern European menu, with influences from French and Mediterranean cuisine, as well as from the Nordic kitchen; the city also has an array of ethnic restaurants, especially Indonesian, Surinamese and Thai. Amsterdam's numerous cafés and bars – often known as *eetcafés* – serve hearty, reasonably priced food in an unpretentious atmosphere, and there are plenty of tempting street food options too, from herring rolls to apple pie.

If you just want lunch, or a bite between sights, there are plenty of places throughout the city – **cafés and tearooms** – where you can just grab a cup of coffee and a sandwich or light lunch. **Bars** (see page 174) almost always serve sandwiches, and usually something more substantial as well; those that serve good-quality food are indicated in the listings. **Vegetarian** dining isn't a problem: many *eetcafés* and restaurants have at least one meat-free dish on the menu, and the city has a growing number of veggie restaurants.

With Amsterdam's singular approach to the sale and consumption of cannabis, you might choose to enjoy a joint after your meal, rather than a beer; included in this chapter is a selection of "**coffeeshops**" where you can buy grass or hash. Be aware that smoking tobacco inside bars and coffeeshops is no longer permitted, although tobacco substitutes and pure joints are still available.

10

ESSENTIALS

Credit cards Almost all of the larger or smarter restaurants take credit cards, but don't assume this to be the case at smaller or cheaper places.

Meal times and opening hours Dutch meal times are a little idiosyncratic; breakfast tends to be later than you might expect, and other meals tend to be earlier. If you choose to eat breakfast away from your hotel, you'll find very few cafés open before 8am or 8.30am. The standard Dutch lunch hour is from noon to 1pm, with sandwiches the staple. Full-blown restaurants, on the other hand, tend to open in the evening only, usually from around 5.30pm or 6pm until around 10pm, with the busiest time for dining being between 7pm and 8pm. The majority of bars serve food – everything from sandwiches to a full menu – in which case they may be known as *eetcafés*. This type of place is usually open all day, serving both lunch and evening meals, as well as coffee and drinks.

Prices The cost of eating out in Amsterdam can be higher than in many other European capital cities. However,

intense competition keeps prices fairly manageable, and in all but the ritziest of joints you can expect to pay no more than €20–25 for a main course, often less. If you're on a budget, stick to the *dagschotel* (dish of the day) wherever possible, for which you pay around €10–15 for a meat or fish dish, with generous sides.

Reservations Due to Amsterdam's rising popularity as an emerging gastronomic destination, reservations are increasingly necessary – especially for bookings on Fri and Sat nights. To be on the safe side, call ahead or book online for any day of the week. Some of the most popular restaurants are now also operating on a two-shifts system, which means you may only be able to get a table at either 6.30pm or 8.30pm.

Tipping A tip of about ten percent is pretty much expected in proper restaurants. In Amsterdam's cafés and bars, the custom is generally to round up the bill to the nearest couple of euros.

CAFÉS AND TEAROOMS

Amsterdam has plenty of **cafés and tearooms**, serving good coffee, sandwiches, light snacks and cakes at very affordable prices throughout the day. Some may serve alcohol but you wouldn't class them as bars.

DUTCH CHEESE

Dutch **cheeses** have a somewhat unjustified reputation abroad for being bland and rubbery, but in fact they can be delicious, even if there isn't the variety you find in French cheeses, for example. Most Dutch cheeses are a variation on the familiar pale yellow, semisoft **Gouda**, within which differences in taste come from the varying stages of maturity: *jonge* (young) cheese has a mild flavour, *belegen* (mature) has a fuller flavour, and *oude* (old) can be pungent and strong, with a grainy, flaky texture. Generally, the older they get, the saltier they are. Best-known among the other cheeses is **Edam**, also semisoft in texture but slightly creamier than Gouda; it's usually shaped into balls and coated in red wax ready for export – it's not eaten much in the Netherlands. **Leidse** is simply a type of Gouda laced with cumin or caraway seeds, with most of its flavour coming from the seeds; **Maasdam** is a Dutch version of a Swiss-style cheese – strong, creamy and full of holes, sold under brand names such as Leerdammer and Maasdammer. You'll also come across Dutch-made Emmental and Gruyère.

Amsterdam has several specialist **cheese shops** (see page 196), and there's also a good range of cheeses on sale at the Saturday farmers' market on the Noordermarkt (9am–4pm). Finally, Amsterdam is within easy striking distance of two world-famous cheese markets, one at Edam (see page 140), the other at Alkmaar.

10

TOP 5 HISTORIC CAFÉS AND BARS

Café Americain See page 159
Café de Dokter See page 174
Gartine See page 158
Hoppe See page 175
Café Papeneiland See page 176

THE OLD CENTRE

De Bakkerswinkel Warmoesstraat 69 ☎020 489 8000, ⍟debakkerswinkel.com; map p.34. Part of an immensely popular chain where you can expect to queue for a table at lunchtime. Mouthwatering home-made scones with lemon curd and jam, muffins, cakes, quiches and pies for €5–10. Other branches at Roelof Hartstraat in the Oud Zuid and at the Westergasfabriek complex in Westerpark. Mon–Fri 8am–5.30pm, Sat & Sun 9am–6pm.

Bistro Berlage Beursplein 1 ☎020 530 4146, ⍟bistro berlage.nl; map p.34. The best chance to glimpse the interior of the Beurs – former stock exchange (see page 36) – and an elegantly furnished restaurant serving modern classics, including dry aged sirloin with red wine jus or fillet of red mullet with parsley root mousseline. A large island bar in the middle of the bistro is perfect for a quick drink or two. Daily 10am–10pm.

Café Esprit Spui 10 ☎020 639 2589, ⍟caffeesprit.nl; map p.34. Attached to the chain clothes shop, this is a modern, minimalist café that overlooks the Spui square (with a huge terrace to boot). They serve interesting, generously filled sandwiches and superb salads, as well as more substantial meals. Daily 10am–6pm.

Café de Jaren Nieuwe Doelenstraat 20 ☎020 625 5771, ⍟cafedejaren.nl; map p.34. One of the grandest of the grand cafés, overlooking the Amstel next to the university, with three floors, two terraces and a cool, light feel. A great place to read the Sunday paper – unusually, you'll find English ones here. There's reasonably priced food too, and a great salad bar. There are sandwiches and snacks downstairs and a full restaurant upstairs. Mon–Thurs & Sun 8.30am–1am, Fri & Sat 8.30am–2am.

★ **Gartine** Taksteeg 7 ☎020 320 4132, ⍟gartine. nl; map p.34. Tucked down an alleyway just off the Kalverstraat shopping street, *Gartine* is an oasis of civilized calm. Most of the ingredients in their delicious sandwiches, salads and afternoon teas are grown in their own allotment. Wed–Sat 10am–6pm.

Gebr. Niemeijer Nieuwendijk 35 ☎020 707 6752, ⍟gebroedersniemeijer.nl; map p.34. A great spot for continental breakfast before hitting the shops, *Gebr. Niemeijer* serves wonderful pastries and bread (also available to take away) with top-quality organic hams, cheeses, jams and more. The coffee is excellent too. Tues–Fri 8.15am–5.30pm, Sat 8.30am–5pm, Sun 9am–5pm.

Greenwoods Singel 103 ☎020 623 7071, ⍟greenwoods.eu; map p.34. Pocket-sized English-style tearoom serving up a tasty line in salads, omelettes and cakes. Look out for the daily specials and order an uber-English pot of tea, perhaps with some scones and jam. Second branch at Keizersgracht 465. Mon–Thurs 9am–4.30pm, Fri–Sun 9am–7pm.

Hofje van Wijs Zeedijk 43 ☎061 368 7866, ⍟wijsenzonen. com; map p.34. A hidden treasure, this eighteenth-century courtyard café-restaurant sells Indonesian coffee, countless different tea blends and even beer with names like Spicy Ginseng and Kopi Luwak. The home-made delicacies are mainly made with organic ingredients. Daily noon–10pm.

Koffieschenkerij de Oude Kerk Oudekerksplein 27 ☎065 265 3302; map p.34. Located in a converted part of the Oude Kerk (see page 46), this café exudes a sense of divine calm. It has a beautiful little garden outside for sunny days, too. The selection of sandwiches is small, but they're home-made, and the coffee and cakes are delicious. Mon–Sat 9am–6pm, Sun 9am–5pm.

Puccini Staalstraat 21 ☎020 620 8458, ⍟puccini. nl; map p.34. This lovely café serves great salads, sandwiches, cakes and pastries, a few doors down from its sister chocolate shop (see page 198). For the chocoholics, there are also Puccini chocolate shops located at Oudekerksplein 17 and Singel 184. Mon–Fri 8.30am–6pm, Sat & Sun 9am–6pm.

Staalmeesters Kloveniersburgwal 127 ☎020 623 4218, ⍟diningcity.net/destaalmeesters; map p.34. Cosy, if slightly cramped, café, with wooden tables and a large replica of Rembrandt's *The Syndics of the Clothmaker's Guild* on the wall. Breakfast until 4.30pm for the genuine nightcrawler and delicious *glühwein* (mulled wine) in winter. Mon–Thurs & Sun 10am–1am, Fri & Sat 10am–3am).

GRACHTENGORDEL WEST

★ **Madame de Pompadour** Huidenstraat 12 ☎020 623 9554, ⍟pompadour.amsterdam; map p.55. This patisserie and chocolatier sells dozens of different sorts of bonbons as well as a mouthwatering selection of cakes and candied fruits, to take out or eat in. Mon–Fri 10am–6pm, Sat 9am–6pm, Sun noon–6pm.

★ **Singel 404** Singel 404 ☎020 428 0154; map p.55. A favourite among students for decades, *Singel 404* serves arguably the best sandwiches in Amsterdam. Try the smoked chicken, avocado, sun-dried tomatoes and brie – lunch heaven. But get there early or be prepared to wait for a table. Daily 10.30am–6pm.

Spanjer & van Twist Leliegracht 60 ☎020 639 0109; ⍟spanjerenvantwist.nl; map p.55. Hip café-bar with an arty air and brisk modern fittings. Tasty snacks and light meals, including daily specials of soup, quiche and pasta. The terrace right on the canal is a gorgeous place to people-watch during the summer. Daily 9am–1am.

Van Harte Hartenstraat 24 ☎020 625 8500 ⓦ; map p.55. Crowded and cheerful spot for lunch, dinner and drinks, with tasty sandwiches, a large tea selection, home-made pies and bonbons from *Pompadour* (see page 198). Good pan-European three-course dinner menu for €25. Mon & Sun 10am–6pm, Tues–Thurs 10am–11pm, Fri & Sat 10am–midnight.

Winkel 43 Noordermarkt 43 ☎020 623 0223, ⓦwinkel43.nl; map p.55. Queue up along with the rest of Amsterdam (or so it seems) for delicious, chunky apple pie, home-made in the basement of this sober but agreeable lunchroom-cum-restaurant. There's great coffee and fresh mint tea to go with it. Mon 7am–1am, Tues–Thurs 8am–1am, Fri 8am–3am, Sat 7am–3am, Sun 10am–1am.

GRACHTENGORDEL SOUTH

Buffet van Odette Prinsengracht 598 ☎020 423 6034, ⓦbuffet-amsterdam.nl; map p.65. Neat little place decorated in attractive, modern style and serving tasty snacks and light meals, from home-made quiches, soups and pastas through to fruit tarts; cheese omelettes are the house speciality. Wed–Mon noon–midnight.

Café Americain Hampshire Hotel – Amsterdam American, Leidsekade 97 ☎020 556 3010, ⓦcafea mericain.nl; map p.65. There was a time when this café was the trendiest spot in the city, attracting – at one time or another – artists, poets and TV folk. Nowadays, it's mainly tourists and business people, but the fanciful Art Nouveau decor, coordinated down to the doorknobs, has survived intact and makes a visit worthwhile. Daily 7am–10pm.

Panini Vijzelgracht 3–5 ☎020 626 4939, ⓦrestaurantpanini.nl; map p.65. Formica may be a thing of the past almost everywhere else, but not here, giving this split-level, Italian café-restaurant a vaguely beatnik air. Great coffee, sandwiches, pasta and snacks during the day; reasonably priced meat, fish and pasta dishes at night. Mon–Sat 8.30am–11pm.

10

SNACKS AND STREET FOOD

Chips/fries (*friet* or *patat*) are the most common **fast food** standby. *Vlaamse* or "Flemish-style", sprinkled with salt and smothered with lashings of mayonnaise (*frietsaus*), are the most common, while other accompaniments include curry, goulash, tomato or *saté* (peanut) sauce. If you want your fries plain, ask for *patat zonder*; fries with mayonnaise are *patat met*. You'll also come across *bitterballen* – a savoury meatball-shaped snack filled with minced beef, covered with breadcrumbs and deep-fried – and *frikandel*, a sausage of somewhat dubious origin. All these are available all over the counter at fast-food outlets, or, for a euro or two, from coin-op heated glass compartments on the street and in train stations (look out for Febo signs for the quintessential Dutch fast-food experience).

One of the pleasures of Amsterdam is sampling the delicious **fish and seafood specialities** sold from stalls dotted around the city centre: **raw herring** (*haring*) with onions and pickles, **smoked eel** (*gerookte paling*), **mackerel in a roll** (*broodje makreel*), **mussels** (*mosselen*) and various kinds of **deep-fried fish chunks** (*kibbeling*). Look out, too, for the **Hollandse Nieuwe** – the fresh catch of herring brought in from the North Sea, usually around the start of June. An absolute delicacy, try eating it Dutch-style: hold the fish by the tail, tip your head back and dangle it into your mouth. Among other places, there are stalls at the following city-centre locations: Nieuwmarkt, Westermarkt, Stromarkt, Haarlemmerplein and Albert Cuypstraat.

Another snack you'll see everywhere is **shwarma** or *shoarma* – another name for a doner kebab: shavings of lamb pressed into a pitta bread. They're sold in numerous Middle Eastern restaurants and takeaways for about €4. Other street foods include **pancakes** (*pannenkoeken*), sweet or savoury, also widely available in restaurants; waffles filled with syrup (*stroopwafels*); and, in winter, *oliebollen*, deep-fried doughnuts sometimes filled with fruit (often apple) or custard (known as *Berliners*) and traditionally eaten during the festive season.

Bars often serve **sandwiches and rolls** (*boterham* and *broodjes*) – often open, and varying from a slice of tired cheese on old bread to something so embellished it's a complete meal – as well as more substantial dishes. A sandwich made with a baguette is known as a *stokbrood*. In winter, *erwtensoep* (or *snert*) – thick pea soup with smoked sausage – is available in many places, and at about €5 a bowl makes a cheap but hearty lunch. Alternatively, there's the *uitsmijter* (a "kicker-out", derived from the practice of serving it at dawn after an all-night party to prompt guests to depart); now widely available at all times of day, it comprises one, two, or three fried eggs on buttered bread, topped with a choice of ham, cheese or roast beef. At under €10, it's another good budget brunch or lunch option.

SWEET TREATS

Dutch **cakes and biscuits** are always good, best eaten in a *banketbakkerij* (patisserie); stand at the counter or buy to take away and munch them on the hoof. Top of the list is the ubiquitous Dutch speciality **appelgebak** – chunky, memorably fragrant apple-and-cinnamon pie, served warm in huge wedges, often with whipped cream (*slagroom*). Other sweet nibbles include **speculaas**, a crunchy cinnamon cookie with a gingerbread-like texture; **stroopwafels**, thin waffles sandwiched together with sweet and spicy syrup; and **amandelkoek**, cakes with a crisp biscuit outside and melt-in-the-mouth almond paste inside.

10

THE JORDAAN AND WESTERN DOCKLANDS

Festina Lente Looiersgracht 40b ☏020 638 1412, ⓦcafefestinalente.nl; map p.75. Relaxed neighbourhood café-bar with mismatched furniture and armchairs to laze in. The outside tables overlooking the canal are a suntrap in the summer when the locals come out to relax with friends for the afternoon; inside is cosy in the winter, and has a good selection of board games. Mon & Thurs 9am–1am, Fri–9am–3am, Sat 10am–3am, Sun 10am–1am.

★ **Small World** Binnen Oranjestraat 14 ☏020 420 2774, ⓦsmallworldcatering.nl; map p.75. Tiny Australian-run café and deli with a few chairs inside and a few more on the pavement outside. Amazing sandwiches, salads, savoury pies and juices, as well as a mouthwatering selection of cakes and muffins. Tues–Fri 10.30am–7pm, Sat 10.30am–6pm, Sun noon–6pm.

THE OLD JEWISH QUARTER AND PLANTAGE

De Hortus Plantage Middenlaan 2a ☏020 625 9021, ⓦdehortus.nl; map p.83. The pleasant café in the orangery of the Hortus Botanicus (see page 90) serves a good range of tasty sandwiches and rolls – plus cakes and tarts supplied by the famous Patisserie Kuyt. Unfortunately, you have to pay entry for the gardens (€9.50) to get to the café. Daily 10am–5pm.

THE EASTERN DOCKLANDS AND AMSTERDAM NOORD

★ **Café de Ceuvel** Korte Papaverweg 4 ☏020 229 6210, ⓦcafedeceuvel.nl; map p.103. This genial vegetarian café, opened in June 2014, is well worth the walk. The friendly owners have transformed a polluted shipyard into a sustainable green "business" park, of which the café – constructed entirely from recycled materials – forms the hub. The quiches, salads and sandwiches (€8) include ingredients and herbs grown from their converted houseboat garden; don't miss the home-made lemonade. Tues–Thurs & Sun 11am–midnight, Fri & Sat 11am–2am.

Noorderlicht Plein 102 ☏020 492 2770, ⓦnoorderlicht cafe.nl; map p.103. The first café to make its mark in the regenerating NDSM district, *Noorderlicht* was the brainchild of a group of squatters who built the entire café from recycled materials and focused on seasonal dishes and sustainably sourced fish and meat. It comes alive on summer weekends with a programme of live music, DJs and storytelling. Sandwiches €6.50, mains €9–11. Mon–Fri 11am–midnight, stays open later Sat & Sun.

Pussy Galore Tolhuisweg 2 ☏063 633 1828; ⓦopen coop.nl; map p.97. Part of a co-op, this vintage-decorated café – with its own on-site roaster – also functions as a shared working space for professionals. At 1pm they serve a lunchtime buffet (€3–10, depending on how much you take) that's very popular, so turn up early. Kids will like the pet chickens and rabbits in the front garden. Mon–Fri 9am–5pm.

THE MUSEUM QUARTER AND AROUND

Brasserie Keyzer Van Baerlestraat 96 ☏020 675 1866, ⓦbrasseriekeyzer.nl; map p.107. In operation since 1905, and right next to the Concertgebouw, this café-restaurant exudes a *fin-de-siècle* charm, with ferns, gliding bow-tied waiters and a dark, carved-wood interior. It's open all day, and you can come here for dinner, but these days it's best as a venue for lunch or coffee. Daily 10am–11pm.

Conservatorium Brasserie & Lounge Van Baerlestraat 27 ☏020 570 0000, ⓦconservatoriumhotel.com; map p.107. Inside the gorgeously renovated *Conservatorium* hotel, the *Brasserie* serves an all-day menu including salads, sandwiches and seasonal dishes at lunchtime. It may not be cheap, but it's worth it for the amazing glass-roofed courtyard venue. Daily 6.30am–11pm.

CT Coffee & Coconuts Ceintuurbaan 282–284 ☏020 354 1104, ⓦcoffeeandcoconuts.com; map p.107. Housed in a former 1920s cinema, *CT Coffee & Coconuts* is a huge venue by Amsterdam standards, and is a favourite among students and freelancers. The coffee is excellent and plentiful, and the menu an international fusion of flavours. Daily 8am–11pm.

KinderKookKafé Vondelpark 6B ☏020 625 3257, ⓦkinderkookkafe.nl; map p.116. A café entirely dedicated to making kids happy (see page 211) with a help-yourself bar where they can top their own sandwich, pizza or cake; the food is simple but tasty. Daily 10am–5pm.

Le Pain Quotidien Johannes Verhulststraat 104 ☏020 379 5900, ⓦlepainquotidien.nl; map p.116. Part of the chain of French bakeries and cafés, *Le Pain Quotidien* serves up super-fresh bread and pastries, which come topped with continental staples like ham, cheese or jam, or more adventurous choices like hummus, smoked salmon or avocado and tomato salsa. Daily 8am–6pm.

★ **Little Collins** 1e Sweelinckstraat 19F ☎ 020 753 9636, Ⓦ littlecollins.nl; map p.107. A fantastic brunch spot run by Australian expats. Although the menu changes regularly, you can expect to find options like kimchi toasties, baked *kasundi* eggs and spiced roasted cauliflower. Mon 9am–4pm, Wed–Thurs 10.30am–10pm, Fri–Sun 9am–10pm.

Omelegg Ferdinand Bolstraat 143 ☎ 20 370 1134, Ⓦ omelegg.com; map p.107. The first omelette specialist in Amsterdam, *Omelegg* serves eggs in all manner of different ways – all of which are delicious. The café itself has a fun, kitsch decor that's a little like a Swiss chalet. Mon–Fri 7am–4pm, Sat & Sun 8am–4pm.

Toussaint Café Bosboom Toussaintstraat 26 ☎ 020 685 0737, Ⓦ cafe-toussaint.nl; map p.75. This cosy, very friendly café not far from the Vondelpark is a pleasant spot for lunch – excellent sandwiches, toasties and *uitsmijters*, as well as tapas-style options. Mon–Thurs & Sun 10am–midnight, Fri & Sat 10am–1am.

THE OUTER DISTRICTS

Maxwell Café Beukenplein 27, Amsterdam Oost ☎ 020 772 6748, Ⓦ maxwellcafe.nl; map p.126. *Maxwell* is a great addition to the Beukenplein, an up-and-coming little square. Come here for light bites – think soups, salads, shakes and sandwiches – at lunchtime, or for a beer or a cocktail in the evening. There's a fun atmosphere, representative of the new wave of good venues opening in Amsterdam Oost. Mon–Thurs & Sun 11am–1am, Fri & Sat 11am–2/3am.

RESTAURANTS

THE OLD CENTRE

CHINESE

Golden Chopsticks Oude Doelenstraat 1 ☎ 020 620 7040, Ⓦ goldenchopsticks.nl; map p.34. Cheap and cheerful canteen-style Chinese food on the edge of the Red Light District. Very central, and, despite the spartan interior, some of the best Chinese food you'll find in Amsterdam. Mon–Sat 11am–1am, Sun 11am–midnight.

Nam Kee Zeedijk 111–113 ☎ 020 624 3470, Ⓦ namkee.nl; map p.34. Made famous by the Dutch film *Oysters at Nam Kee*, this Amsterdam institution has been going strong for years and has a loyal clientele thanks to its great food and quick service. There are two other branches: one at Geldersekade 117, the other at Marie Heinekenplein 4. Daily 11.30am–10.30pm.

New King Zeedijk 115–117 ☎ 020 625 2180, Ⓦ newking.nl; map p.34. Slightly posher than some of the other Chinese restaurants along the Zeedijk, *New King* attracts locals and visitors alike for its authentic Mandarin cuisine. Daily 11am–10.30pm.

Oriental City Oudezijds Voorburgwal 177-179 ☎ 020 626 8352, Ⓦ oriental-city.com; map p.34. Located just a ten-minute walk from the central station, this multi-floor restaurant serves traditional Chinese food with an innovative twist. Hong Kong-born chefs rustle up specialities including Chongqing boiled beef (a Sichuan staple famed for its tenderness) and traditional roasted suckling pig. Mon–Sun 11.30am–10.30pm.

DUTCH AND MODERN EUROPEAN

★ **Blauw aan de Wal** Oudezijds Achterburgwal 99 ☎ 020 330 2257, Ⓦ blauwaandewal.com; map p.34. A haven of calm amid the hustle and bustle of the Red Light District, *Blauw aan de Wal* lies down an alleyway in the heart of de Wallen. It serves tremendous French-Dutch food that's a little on the pricey side (three courses for €45, five for €67) but absolutely worth it. Mon–Sat 6–11.30pm.

Restaurant Vermeer Prins Hendrikkade 59-72 ☎ 020 428 2222, Ⓦ restaurantvermeer.nl; map p.34. Part of the NH Collection Amsterdam Barbizon Palace hotel, this sleek Michelin-starred restaurant is run by British chef Christopher Naylor who transforms everyday ingredients (pigeon, mackerel, radish, rosemary) into complex dishes full of distinctive flavours. Once a month on a Wednesday, Naylor cooks a simple family-style sharing dinner – think beef wellington or game pie – which you can even eat at the chef's table in the kitchen while chatting to the team at work. Otherwise, choose between a four- (€65), five- (€75) or six-course menu (€85). Mon–Sat 16.30–10pm.

Hemelse Modder Oude Waal 11 ☎ 020 624 3203, Ⓦ shemelsemodder.nl; map p.34. Friendly restaurant serving mostly Dutch food in an informal atmosphere. Service is very attentive (they'll even let you speak Dutch if you want to practise), and the food is tasty and reasonably priced. Main courses €20, three-course menu €37. Daily 6–10pm.

★ **Lastage** Geldersekade 29 ☎ 020 737 0811, Ⓦ restaurantlastage.nl; map p.34. Awarded a Michelin star (and deservedly so), *Lastage* is serving up some of the most creative modern Dutch food in Amsterdam. Prices range from €47 for three courses to €89 for a "flight" of courses that lets you try pretty much the entire menu. Needless to say, booking well in advance is essential. Tues–Sun 6.30–9pm.

De Silveren Spiegel Kattengat 4 ☎ 020 624 6589, Ⓦ desilverenspiegel.com; map p.34. There's been a restaurant in this location since 1614, and "The Silver

10

DUTCH (AND NON-DUTCH) CUISINE

Traditionally at least, **Dutch cuisine** lacks a certain finesse, with its origins firmly rooted in the meat, potato and cabbage school of cooking. That said, many restaurants are now offering modern interpretations of Dutch cuisine, which include a healthy selection of vegetarian and seafood dishes. Nonetheless, it's the city's non-Dutch restaurants that usually steal the gastronomic limelight – especially the abundance of outstanding Indonesian and Surinamese restaurants, owing to the Netherlands' colonial history. The Dutch are particularly partial to **Indonesian** staples, such as *Nasi goreng* and *Bami goreng* (fried rice or noodles with meat), but there are normally more exciting items on the menu too, some very spicy; chicken or beef in peanut sauce (*saté*) is always a favourite. Or you could order a **rijsttafel** – a sampler meal, comprising rice and/or noodles served with ten or twelve small dishes at varying spice levels, with hot *sambal* sauce on the side. Usually ordered for two or more people, a *rijsttafel* will cost around €20–30 per person. **Surinamese** restaurants are less numerous, but they offer a distinctive, essentially Creole cuisine – try *roti*, flat, pancake-like bread served with a spicy curry, hard-boiled egg and vegetables. **Italian** food is ubiquitous, with pizzas and pasta dishes starting at a fairly uniform €10 or so in most places.

We've listed restaurants by **type of cuisine**, but there's an alphabetical list of restaurants in the index.

Mirror" is one of the best in the city, with a delicately balanced menu of Dutch cuisine. The food is spectacular – the proprietor lives on the coast and brings in the fish himself – and there's a cellar of 350 wines. Their tasting menus range from €52 to €152, depending on number of courses and whether you opt for the paired wines to go with them. Mon–Sat 6–10.30pm.

Skek Zeedijk 4 ☎ 020 427 0551, ⓦ skek.nl; map p.34. A no-nonsense cultural *eetcafé* run by students. Cheap but seasonal mains (around €14) range from hearty salads to pimped-up burgers. Check the website for their frequent live music and exhibitions. Mon 4pm–1am, Tues–Thurs & Sun noon–1am, Fri & Sat noon–3am.

Supperclub Ruyterkade Steiger 14 ☎ 020 344 6400, ⓦ supperclub.amsterdam; map p.34. More than just a restaurant, the *Supperclub* is a full-blown dining experience featuring a five-course set menu served to customers on enormous white beds, usually while taking in some form of entertainment, or on board a cruise liner gazing out over the water from the candlelit deck bar. The fusion food is decent, though some may find the whole concept pretentious or downright disconcerting – it's not the most comfortable way to eat dinner. It's expensive: you have to order the set dinner at €65 The *Supperclub Cruise* leaves from De Ruyterkade, Pier 14, behind Centraal Station (☎ 020 344 6403). Supperclub Mon–Weds & Sun 7.30pm–2am, Thurs–Sat 7.30pm–5am; cruises Fri & Sat from 6.45pm.

Van Beeren Koningsstraat 54 ☎ 020 622 2329, ⓦ eetcafevanbeeren.nl; map p.34. This *eetcafé* serves a satisfying mixture of Dutch staples and Modern European dishes in relaxed surroundings. The food is good, the setting cosy, and it remains a moderately priced choice (main courses €17–21). Mon–Thurs 5pm–1am, Fri 5pm–3am, Sat 4pm–3am, Sun 4pm–1am.

Van Kerkwijk Nes 41 ☎ 020 620 3316, ⓦ caferestaurant vankerkwijk.nl; map p.34. It looks like a café but is more of a restaurant these days, serving steaks, fish and so on from an ever-changing menu that isn't written down, but heroically memorized by the attentive waiting staff. Good food, and reasonably priced – mains around €15. Daily 11am–1am.

D' Vijff Vlieghen Spuistraat 294–302 ☎ 020 530 4060, ⓦ caferestaurantvankerkwijk.nl; map p.34. One of the city's best Dutch restaurants, "The Five Flies" occupies immaculate ground-floor premises kitted out in a smart version of traditional Dutch style, from the tiled and wood-panelled walls to the beamed ceiling and antique embossed leather hangings. Intimate and very cosy, with an enterprising menu that features imaginative renditions of traditional dishes, with plenty of excellent fish. Main courses €22–28. Daily 6–10pm.

FISH

Lucius Spuistraat 247 ☎ 020 624 1831, ⓦ lucius.nl; map p.34. This long-established, bistro-style restaurant, with its high-varnish wooden panelling, is one of the best fish restaurants in town. The lemon sole, when it's on the menu, is excellent, and so are the seafood platters. Mains €25–30, and a three-course menu for €39.50. Daily 5pm–midnight.

FRENCH, BELGIAN AND SWISS

Brakke Grond Nes 43 ☎ 020 622 9014, ⓦ brakkegrond. nl; map p.34. Modern, high-ceilinged *eetcafé* specializing in Belgian beer and food (mains €14–17), often full of people discussing the performance they've just seen at the adjacent Flemish Cultural Centre. Daily 11.30am–10pm.

★ **De Compagnon** Guldenhandsteeg 17 ☎020 620 4225, ⓦdecompagnon.nl; map p.34. This traditional restaurant serves very good French food to a discerning clientele in an old-fashioned atmosphere. There's a great, if not especially cheap, wine list, too. It's expensive – reckon on €25-plus for a main course – and tends to be fully booked well in advance, but you might get in for lunch at short notice. Mon–Sat noon–1.30pm & 6–9.30pm. A five-course menu costs €45.

INDONESIAN

Kantjil en de Tijger Spuistraat 291–293 ☎020 620 0994, ⓦkantjil.nl; map p.34. This airy Indonesian restaurant has been something of an institution for over twenty years. The traditional *rijsttafels* start at €27.50/person and are served in a stylish wood-panelled setting. Daily noon–11pm.

Sampurna Singel 498 ☎020 625 3264, ⓦsampurna.com; map p.34. Intimate but relaxed, *Sampurna* has been serving classic Indonesian dishes for decades in its cosy location just off the flower market. *Saté* skewers are under €10, main dishes around €20–27, or order a bunch of small dishes to share in the form of a *rijsttafel*. Daily noon–11pm.

ITALIAN

Mappa Nes 59 ☎020 528 9170, ⓦrestaurantmappa.nl; map p.34. Classic Italian food with some inventive twists, incorporating good home-made pasta dishes and excellent service in an unpretentious and modern environment. Pastas cost around €13–17, while meat and fish dishes will set you back€17–21. Mon–Wed & Sun 11am–midnight, Thurs–Sat 11am–1am.

Vasso Roozenboomsteeg 10/14 ☎020 626 0158, ⓦvasso.nl; map p.34. Genuine, creative Italian food served in three curvy, sixteenth-century buildings off a corner of the Spui. Polite and attentive service and semi-steep prices – around €25 for a main course. Mon–Sat 5–11pm.

JAPANESE

Kobe House Nieuwezijds Voorburgwal 77 ☎020 622 6458, ⓦkobehouse.nl; map p.34. Not a lot of

atmosphere, partly because it's a big restaurant that rarely seems to get full. But if you're craving sushi or other Japanese treats, this is the place. Order a set menu for two people for €75. Daily noon–10.30pm.

PANCAKES

★ **Pannenkoekenhuis Upstairs** Grimburgwal 2 ☎020 626 5603, ⓦupstairspannenkoeken.nl; map p.34. Minuscule place in a tumbledown house opposite the university buildings, accessible via an extraordinarily steep staircase (think: ladder) and with dozens of teapots hanging from the ceiling. They serve hearty sweet and savoury pancakes at low prices. Mon–Sat noon–6pm, Sun noon–5pm.

SPANISH AND PORTUGUESE

Catala Spuistraat 299 ☎020 623 1141, ⓦtapasbar catala.com; map p.34. With Serrano hams hanging from the ceiling and surprisingly authentic tapas for a location so close to the Spui square, *Catala* specializes in – you guessed it – Catalan food, and has a large selection of Torres wine and Spanish liqueurs. Menu for around €30. Daily 1–11pm.

THAI

★ **Bird** Zeedijk 72–74 ☎020 620 1442, ⓦthai-bird.nl; map p.34. This Thai restaurant is always packed, and rightly so, drawing people from far and wide for its authentic Thai fare. Its sister snack bar across the road (also called *Bird*) serves much the same food but in cheap-and-cheerful snack-bar surroundings. Daily noon–11pm.

Me Naam Naan Koningsstraat 29 ☎020 423 3344, ⓦmenaamnaan.nl; map p.34. Just off the Nieuwmarkt, this slightly more upmarket Thai restaurant serves award-winning food from northeast Thailand. Mains cost around €15–20 and feature meat, fish and vegetarian curries, salads and other dishes. Thurs–Sun 5–10.30pm.

GRACHTENGORDEL WEST

DUTCH AND MODERN EUROPEAN

Belhamel Brouwersgracht 60 ☎020 622 1095, ⓦbelhamel.nl; map p.55. Beautiful restaurant with

---

RESTAURANTS ON THE INTERNET

Among the many websites providing information on Amsterdam's restaurant scene, one of the most useful is ⓦ **iens.nl**, an independent index of all the major restaurants in Amsterdam and most other Dutch cities. The reviews are user-generated and of mixed quality, but the opening hours and telephone numbers are regularly updated, and there is an easy-to-follow grading system for the quality of the food and service.

In the past few years, a host of **food and restaurant blogs** has also sprung up in Amsterdam – many of which are in English. One of the most established is ⓦamsterdamfoodie.nl – with a large database of restaurants, the blog has recommendations based on price, location and type of cuisine.

10

lovely Art Nouveau decor and an extremely well chosen menu, mixing French and Italian dishes with Dutch influences. Main courses €15–25. The prime tables have charming canal views, and the overall experience makes for a very romantic evening. Daily noon–10pm.

★ **Café de Klepel** Prinsenstraat 22 ☎020 623 8244, ⓦcafedeklepel.nl; map p.55. Brown café turned gorgeous restaurant, airy but intimate *Café de Klepel* has delicious French-inspired dishes on its short but perfectly balanced menu, plus an extensive wine list. Three courses for €36.50; four courses for €42.50. A delightful evening out. Mon–Thurs 6pm–midnight, Fri–Sun 4pm–midnight.

De Luwte Leliegracht 26 ☎020 625 8548, ⓦrestaurant deluwte.nl; map p.55. This friendly restaurant is attractively kitted out, featuring old wooden benches and a fireplace. The small but well-chosen menu offers first-rate French-inspired cuisine, but without much in the way of vegetarian options. Mains average around €23. Daily 6–10pm.

Prego Herenstraat 25 ☎020 638 0148, ⓦrestaurant prego.nl; map p.55. Informal Mediterranean restaurant with modern decor offering an inventive menu of rich dishes, including such delights as *confit de canard*, grilled fish and fresh pasta. Mains cost around €20. Daily 6–10pm, Sat & Sun also 12.30–3pm.

Stout Haarlemmerstraat 73 ☎020 616 3664, ⓦrestaurantstout.nl; map p.55. This lively and fashionable café-restaurant, popular with locals, serves up great sandwiches and salads in the daytime, and everything from duck to fresh oysters in the evening. Mains are €19–24, but you can also sample ten sharing dishes for only €30/person. The comfortable cushions outside are good for lounging. Mon–Thurs & Sun 10am–1am, Fri & Sat 10am–3am.

Struisvogel Keizersgracht 312 ☎020 423 3817, ⓦrestaurantdestruisvogel.nl; map p.55. *Struisvogel* means "ostrich" in Dutch, and this is often a speciality of the house. This cosy restaurant is in the basement of a canal house, and serves a limited but reasonably priced menu, considering the location (three courses for €28.50). Daily 5.30pm–midnight.

FRENCH AND BELGIAN

★ **Beulings** Beulingstraat 9 ☎020 320 6100, ⓦbeulings.nl; map p.55. The kind of restaurant you want to take your parents to, *Beulings* is a sophisticated but intimate place serving elegant French food. Five-course chef's tasting menu €55. Wed–Mon from 7pm.

Bordewijk Noordermarkt 7 ☎020 624 3899, ⓦbordewijk.nl; map p.55. Upmarket French-Mediterranean restaurant in an eclectically decorated venue overlooking the Noordermarkt church and square. Deservedly good reputation for its food, including seasonal game dishes. Mains from around €28, or choose the chef's menu from €40 (three courses, plus dessert) upwards. Tues–Sat 6.30–10.30pm.

Spingaren Herengracht 88 ☎020 624 9635, ⓦspingaren. nl; map p.55. Located in a historical building with wonderful views, this rustic restaurant and tasting room has gained a reputation for its artisanal charcuterie since opening in 2017, serving up excellent sausages, pastrami, cured meats and pâté (also available for takeaway). Guests can compose their own charcuterie plates or pick from a menu of fish and meat dishes (butcher's board costs €22); a small selection of vegetarian dishes includes sticky cauliflower and red curry (around €15). Tues–Sat 5.30–10pm.

ITALIAN

Bussia Reestraat 28–32 ☎020 627 8794, ⓦbussia.nl; map p.55. Everything at this top-notch Italian restaurant is home-made using fresh ingredients, from the original Italian *gelato* to the pasta. Many wines sold by the glass. Four courses for around €50 and up. Lunch Thurs–Sat noon–2pm, Sun noon–3pm; Dinner Tues–Sun 6–9.30pm.

Quattro Gatti Hartenstraat 3 ☎020 421 4585, ⓦquattrogatti.nl; map p.55. Tables for two are slotted every which way into this tiny Italian in the Negen Straatjes. The food is delicious and authentic, but portions are huge, and the prices reflect that (mains around €24, less for pasta). A three-course menu for two costs €55. Tues 7–10pm, Wed–Sat noon–2.30pm, Thurs–Sat also 7–10pm.

JAPANESE

Kagetsu Hartenstraat 17 ☎020 427 3828, ⓦkagetsu. nl; map p.55. Excellent Japanese restaurant for sushi and other traditional Japanese fare in the Negen Straatjes (translating as the "Nine Little Streets", which crisscross between the canals in this area of the canal belt). The freshness of *Kagetsu*'s fish is second to none. There is also a branch at Kastelenstraat 268. Daily noon–10.30pm.

PANCAKES

Pancake Bakery Prinsengracht 191 ☎020 625 1333, ⓦpancake.nl; map p.55. Located in the basement of an old canal house, this long-established restaurant offers a mind-boggling range of fillings for its pancakes and is very popular with tourists. Pancakes go for €13–16, depending on toppings. Daily 9am–9.30pm.

VEGETARIAN

Bolhoed Prinsengracht 60 ☎020 626 1803; map p.55. Something of an Amsterdam institution, this popular vegan and vegetarian restaurant features quirky local artwork and a frequently changing dish of the day, plus organic drinks to wash it all down with. Main courses around €15–20. Daily noon–9.30pm.

10

GRACHTENGORDEL SOUTH

DUTCH AND MODERN EUROPEAN

Bar Huf Reguliersdwarsstraat 43 ☎020 303 9561, ⓦbarhuf.nl; map p.65. A handy place for late-night dining, *Bar Huf* is Amsterdam's answer to a gastropub. Burgers, ribs, mac'n'cheese and salads are all on the menu – all given a modern, creative twist that elevates them above their humble origins. Main courses average around €10–15. Mon–Thurs & Sun 5pm–1am, Fri & Sat 5pm–3am.

Lion Noir Reguliersdwarsstraat 28 ☎020 627 6603, ⓦlionnoir.nl; map p.65. Fashionably decorated and lit, *Lion Noir* is a place to see and be seen. While the dinner menu offers flashy mains like duck breast, veal and Black Angus beef for around €26, the restaurant also serves lighter bites for lunch, snacks at the bar, and a range of delicious cocktails. Daily 6–10pm, also Mon–Fri noon–2.30pm.

Stoop & Stoop Lange Leidsedwarsstraat 82 ☎020 620 0982, ⓦstoopenstoop.nl; map p.65. *Stoop & Stoop* has been going strong just off the bustling Leidseplein for decades, and (uniquely for the area) it attracts both locals and visitors. Don't expect anything fancy; this cosy *eetcafé* serves up simple, generous dishes at affordable prices (mains €13–20). Daily 5pm–midnight.

John Dory Prinsengracht 999 ☎020 622 9044, ⓦjohndory.nl; map p.65. Set in a former 17th-century warehouse, this canalside restaurant specialises in dishes made with fresh fish and seafood caught locally. Aside from this so-called 'fishtronomy', the menu also caters for meat-lovers and vegetarians. The lower-level dining room offers a view of the kitchen, while the upper floor is more elegant with white-linen tablecloths and glassware. Menus range from four (€39) up to ten courses (€85/person). Tues–Sat 5.30–10.30pm, also Fri noon–2pm.

FRENCH AND BELGIAN

Quartier Latin Utrechtsestraat 49 ☎020 622 7419, ⓦrestaurantquartierlatin.nl; map p.65. Split-level, intimate, bistro-style restaurant serving up a (broadly) French menu – dishes include *tournedos* with Roquefort sauce. Main courses €18–24. Tues–Sun 5–11pm.

Van de Kaart Prinsengracht 512 ☎020 625 9232, ⓦvandekaart.com; map p.65. Excellent French/Mediterranean basement restaurant decorated in chic minimalist style and featuring an inventive, ever-changing

menu, along with excellent service. Three courses cost €37.50. Daily 11am–10pm.

INDIAN

Mayur Korte Leidsedwarsstraat 203 ☎020 623 2142, ⓦmayur.nl; map p.65. Undoubtedly one of the city's best Indian restaurants, if not one of the cheapest. The quality of the food is outstanding – try especially the tandoori dishes at around €24–34. The classic north Indian curries are also served, and there's a wide range of vegetarian dishes. Tasting menus from €36.50. Daily 5–11pm.

Memories of India Reguliersdwarsstraat 88 ☎020 623 5710, ⓦmemoriesofindia.nl; map p.65. Given its location near the Rembrandtplein and its nightlife, *Memories of India* is a surprisingly calm and quiet affair. The menu is extensive, with all the usual suspects, but the food is a cut above the average. Main courses from around €15. Daily 5–11pm.

INDONESIAN

Tempo Doeloe Utrechtsestraat 75 ☎020 625 6718, ⓦtempodoeloerestaurant.nl; map p.65. A buzzing place packed full of tables serving excellent *rijsttafels* whose component parts come in several spice levels. Beware the "very hot" dishes – they can be eye-watering. Reservations are a must, but don't expect to get seated on time. Mon–Sat 6pm–midnight, Wed–Sat also noon–4pm.

ITALIAN

Bar Moustache Utrechtsestraat 141 ☎020 428 1074, ⓦbarmoustache.nl; map p.65. One of Amsterdam's many hipster hangouts, *Bar Moustache* is a fun place for groups – not least because of the fantastic platters of *antipasti* it serves to start your meal (€19.50 for two). Follow with pasta for around €15 or a main dish for €18. Mon–Thurs 8am–1am, Fri & Sat 9am–3am, Sun 9am–1pm.

JAPANESE

Sumo Kleine Garmanplantsoen 17 ☎020 423 5131, ⓦrestaurantsumo.com; map p.65. The first of what's quickly becoming a nationwide chain of sushi restaurants, *Sumo* attracts both Leidseplein tourists and thrifty locals. The all-you-can-eat concept (usually to be avoided but not in this case) offers varied sushi and other dishes for €18–28, depending on the day and time. Daily noon–10pm.

MEXICAN

★ Salsa Shop Amstelstraat 32a ☎020 205 1040, ⓦsalsashop.com; map p.65. The Mexican cuisine scene is relatively new in Amsterdam, and this is one of the best newcomers. *Tacos* are the speciality – you assemble your own from a variety of different fillings for around €8 for three. Not surprisingly, the salsas are amazing. Mon–Thurs & Sun 11.30am–10pm, Fri & Sat 11am–11pm.

THAI

Take Thai Utrechtsestraat 87 ☎020 622 0577, ⓦtakethai.com; map p.65. Modern and minimalist, *Take Thai* is worlds away from the usual kitsch interiors of Thai restaurants. Fresh and authentic curries, soups and classic Thai starters are all on the menu. Main courses around €20. Daily 5.30–9.30pm.

VEGETARIAN

Golden Temple Utrechtsestraat 126 ☎020 626 8560, ⓦrestaurantgoldentemple.com; map p.65. Laidback place with a little more soul than the average Amsterdam veggie joint. Inexpensive, well-prepared, lacto-vegetarian food and attentive service. No alcohol. Daily 5–9.30pm.

VIETNAMESE

★ **Ô MAI** Utrechtsestraat 12 ☎064 359 8740, ⓦomai. nl; map p.65. Vietnamese restaurants have recently taken off in Amsterdam, and this is one of the finest. The fresh spring rolls, soups and noodle dishes are all delightful, with mains costing around €10. Daily noon–midnight.

THE JORDAAN AND WESTERN DOCKLANDS

AFRICAN

Semhar Marnixstraat 259–261 ☎020 638 1634, ⓦsemhar.nl; map p.75. This small and popular restaurant's simple but authentic Ethiopian menu features meat, fish or vegetable dishes, such as lamb, catfish or chickpeas, soaked up with a large, spongy flatbread. Try the African beer flavoured with banana or coconut – nicer than it sounds. Mains around €15. Tues–Sun 4–10pm.

DUTCH AND MODERN EUROPEAN

Balthazar's Keuken Elandsgracht 108 ☎020 420 2114, ⓦbalthazarskeuken.nl; map p.75. As the name suggests (*keuken* means kitchen), this restaurant makes you feel like you've accidentally stumbled into someone's kitchen. The weekly changing four-course dinner menu is more sophisticated, made with only the freshest ingredients. Book ahead, as tables tend to fill up quickly. Tues–Sun 6–10.30pm.

★ **Daalder** Lindengracht 90 ☎020 624 8864, ⓦdaalderamsterdam.nl; map p.75. *Daalder* may look like a brown café, but behind the scenes is a seriously ambitious chef turning out exquisite Modern European food. Despite Michelin-starred status, a five-course menu with wine costs €107 at the time of writing. On weekends a €30 deposit is requested for all dinner reservations. Mon–Fri & Sun noon–2.30pm and 6–10pm, Sat 5–10pm.

Moeders Rozengracht 251 ☎020 626 7957, ⓦmoeders. com; map p.75. Cosy restaurant whose theme is obvious from the moment you step inside – mothers (*moeders*), photos of thousands of whom plaster the walls. You're welcome to bring your own mother along, but if not then just savour the moderately priced Dutch staples and daily specials – traditional food, well presented and with the odd modern twist. Mains €15–21. Mon–Fri 5pm–midnight, Sat & Sun noon–midnight.

ITALIAN

★ **diVino** Boomstraat 41a ☎6 5344 6392, ⓦwijnbardivino.nl; map p.75. Although it calls itself a wine bar, *diVino* is as much a simple Italian restaurant as it is a bar – perfect for *aperitivo* o'clock. Order some of their cured meats and cheeses as *antipasti*, then move onto their delicious but affordable fresh pasta dishes for around €13. A three-course menu will set you back €35. Daily 4–11pm.

La Perla Tweede Tuindwarsstraat 14 & 53 ☎020 624 8828, ⓦpizzaperla.nl; map p.75. Arguably serving the best pizza in Amsterdam, *La Perla* comes in two parts: on one side of the street (at no. 53) there's a sit-down restaurant, and on the other (at no. 14) is a takeaway. Pizzas cost around €13-14. Daily: restaurant 10am–10pm; takeaway 5–10pm.

YamYam Frederik Hendrikstraat 88–90 ☎020 681 5097, ⓦyamyam.nl; map p.75. Top pizzeria and

10

FOOD TOURS

While **food tours** (guided walks involving several local tastings en route) have been growing in popularity in the UK and US for a few years, they've only fairly recently arrived in Amsterdam. One of the most well-reputed and diverse companies, **Eating Amsterdam Tours** (☎020 894 3068 ⓦeatingamsterdamtours.com), offers a Dutch food walking tour through the Jordaan, a food and canals tour (including a 1hr boat cruise), also through the Jordaan, and tailor-made private tours for groups. Tours for six to twelve are led by local guides, last three to four hours, and cost €79–106 per person. Also popular are the **Hungry Birds** food tours (ⓦhungrybirds.nl), which take place during the daytime in De Pijp, sampling a range of street food and visiting a local market. They also offer bike tours, if you feel like working off some calories at the same time, or a cooking experience with a local chef. Tours cost from €79 per person and last four hours.

10

trattoria in a simple, traditional dining room with an open kitchen. It attracts the couples and hip young parents of the neighbourhood with its excellent pizza toppings, including fresh *rucola* and truffle sauce. Pizzas €8–14. Booking strongly advised. Tues–Sun 5.30–10pm.

JAPANESE

Japanese Pancake World 2e Egelantiersdwarsstraat 24 ☎020 320 4447, ⊛japanesepancakeworld.com; map p.75. The clue in in the title: this cute little café serves up excellent Japanese pancakes filled with a variety of ingredients: choose from jumbo shrimps, scallop, pork, salami, cheese and shiitake mushrooms. Sit at the back to watch the chef in action. Pancakes €10–20. Thurs–Tues noon–10pm.

★ **Le Fou Fow** Elandsgracht 2a ☎020 845 0544, ⊛foufow.nl; map p.75. Authentic and extremely tasty *ramen* (noodle soup) made with a base of chicken, pork or miso broth. The *ramen* itself costs around €10–15 (depending on size) but be aware that sides and drinks are on the pricey side. Tues–Sun 5–9pm and noon–3pm.

SPANISH

A La Plancha 1e Looiersdwarsstraat 15 ☎020 420 3633, ⊛alaplancha.nl; map p.75. A tiny and tightly packed Jordaan tapas bar serving authentic Spanish dishes to share. Their website promises a "holiday feeling" and that's exactly what you get – transported straight to sunny Spain. Mon–Thurs & Sun 5pm–1am, Fri & Sat 5pm–3am.

La Oliva Egelantiersstraat 122–124 ☎020 320 4316, ⊛laoliva.nl; map p.75. This sleek Jordaan eatery specializes in *pintxos*, the delectable Basque snacks on sticks that make Spanish bar-hopping such a delight. With a nod to Dutch tastes perhaps, this is more of a restaurant than a bar, and the *pintxos* anything but bite-sized. But you're more than welcome to sit at the bar and sample one or two with a drink. Mon–Wed & Sun noon–10pm, Thurs–Sat noon–11pm.

THAI

Rakang Thai Elandsgracht 29–31 ☎020 627 5012, ⊛rakang.nl; map p.75. Richly decorated restaurant with striking paintings and glassware. The Thai food is fresh and delicious and not too highly spiced. The adjacent takeaway is of the same good quality. Main courses around €15–25. Daily 6–10.30pm.

THE OLD JEWISH QUARTER AND PLANTAGE

ITALIAN

A Tavola Kadijksplein 9 ☎020 625 4994, ⊛atavola restaurant.nl; map p.83. On a quiet spot overlooking the water, *A Tavola* serves up simple but delicious Italian food, including a lovely selection of *antipasti*, pasta, meat and fish. Mains average around €25, but you can have a bowl of pasta for €15. Wed–Sun 5.30–10pm.

THE EASTERN DOCKLANDS AND AMSTERDAM NOORD

CHINESE

Sea Palace Oosterdokskade 8 ☎020 626 4777, ⊛seapalace.nl; map p.97. A floating Chinese ersatz pagoda, *Sea Palace* has become an iconic feature of Amsterdam's east dock. Due to its sheer size and wow factor, it does attract a lot of tourists and can be expensive. Stick to the dim sum, which are delicious and won't break the bank at €4–6 apiece. Daily noon–midnight.

DUTCH AND MODERN EUROPEAN

Gebroeders Hartering Peperstraat 10 ☎020 421 0699, ⊛gebr-hartering.nl; map p.97. Run by two brothers, *Gebroeders Hartering* serves up a feast for a special occasion. Choose from five courses for €55; up to seven courses for €80. Menus are always seasonal and frequently adventurous, with offal and unpasteurized cheeses frequently appearing. Daily 6pm–midnight.

★ **Greetje** Peperstraat 23–25 ☎020 779 7450, ⊛restaurantgreetje.nl; map p.97. A cosy, busy restaurant serving traditional Dutch dishes with a modern twist. A changing menu reflects the seasons and the favourite dishes of the owner's mother – a native of the southern Netherlands – for €23–29. Deluxe tasting menu costs €53/person. Superb home cooking with great service. Daily 6–1am.

Hotel de Goudfazant Aambeeldstraat 10 ☎020 636 5170, ⊛hoteldegoudfazant.nl; map p.97. It's worth taking the ferry northbound from Centraal Station to try the French-inspired dishes in the industrial setting of this former garage. A three-course menu with seasonal produce will set you back a little over €30. It's very trendy, so bookings are essential. Tues–Sun 6–11pm.

IJ-Kantine Ondinaweg 15–17 ☎020 633 7162, ⊛ijkantine.nl; map p.103. This hip industrial open space with exposed vents serves up a please-all menu of burgers (€14.50), pasta and the like. There's also a small indoor play area for kids. Daily 9am–11pm; bar till midnight.

Lloyd Hotel Oostelijke Handelskade 34 ☎020 561 3677, ⊛lloydhotel.com/restaurant; map p.101. Situated in the eastern docklands, just 5min by tram from Centraal Station, this is one of Amsterdam's most unusual hotels (see page 150). It comes complete with an airy, canteen-like, café-restaurant on the ground floor, where they serve a wide range of European dishes made with local ingredients. The burgers are reputed to be the best in Amsterdam. Mains cost €15–21, sandwiches €5–10. Daily 7am–1am.

★ **Pllek** Tt. Neveritaweg 59 ☎ 020 290 0020, ⓦ pllek. nl; map p.103. One of several hip venues to have sprung up at the NDSM wharf, *Pllek* is arguably the best. Dishes are inventive, international and affordable: mains like wild boar stew will set you back around €19. Mon–Thurs & Sun 9.30am–1am, Fri & Sat 9.30am–3am.

THE MUSEUM QUARTER AND AROUND

AFRICAN

Lalibela 1e Helmersstraat 249 ☎ 020 683 8332, ⓦ lalibela.nl; map p.116. Take tram #1 or #6 along Overtoom to Jan Pieter Heijstraat to eat at this first-rate Ethiopian restaurant. You'll eat authentic, well-spiced dishes, all served with delicious sides of lentils and vegetables. Mains €10–15. Daily 5–11pm.

DUTCH AND MODERN EUROPEAN

Canvas op de 7e Wibautstraat 150, Amsterdam Oost ☎ 020 261 2110, ⓦ volkshotel.nl/en/canvas; map p.107. Located in the canteen of a former national newspaper office, *Canvas* is on the seventh floor, so panoramic views are guaranteed. Mains like bavette steak or sea bream hover around the €16 mark and are served at long picnic tables. DJs play at *Club Canvas* on Fri and Sat. Daily 7am–1am (Club Canvas Fri & Sat 11pm–4am).

De Duvel 1e van der Helststraat 59–61 ☎ 020 675 7517, ⓦ deduvel.nl; map p.107. Immensely popular and always crowded (so book ahead), *De Duvel* serves up mains like chicken *saté* and beef *carpaccio* for around €16. It's also a fashionable spot for after-dinner drinks. Mon–Thurs & Sun 11am–1am, Fri & Sat 11am–3am.

★ **Loetje** Johannes Vermeerstraat 52 ☎ 020 662 8173, ⓦ loetje.nl; map p.107. Excellent steaks, fries and salads are the order of the day at this *eetcafé*. The pleasant outdoor terrace in the summer is a bonus. *Loetje* has other branches in Amsterdam (although this is the original) including Centraal Station (Stationsplein 10), Parnassusweg 1021 and Ruyschstraat 15. Daily 10am–10.30pm.

Zus & Zus Overtoom 548 ☎ 020 616 5825, ⓦ restaurant zusenzus.nl; map p.116. This family-run restaurant serves a monthly-changing seasonal menu of Mediterranean-inspired meat, fish and vegetarian dishes. Though a little off the beaten track, *Zus & Zus* is well worth the tram ride from the centre – friendly and affordable, with mains at €17–20. Mon–Sat 12.30–10pm.

FRENCH AND BELGIAN

Gent aan de Schinkel Theophile de Bockstraat 1 ☎ 020 388 2851, ⓦ gentaandeschinkel.nl; map p.116. Situated just past the southernmost end of the Vondelpark, a 2min walk across the pedestrian bridge, this lovely corner restaurant overlooking the Sloterkade canal serves mainly Belgian food, and there's a huge range of bottled Belgian

---

TOP 5 CHEAP EATS
Bird See page 163
Le Fou Fow See page 168
Pannenkoekenhuis Upstairs See page 163
Salsa Shop See page 166
Small World See page 160

10

beers to enjoy on the summer terrace. Mon–Thurs & Sun 10am–1am, Fri & Sat 10am–2am.

Le Garage Ruysdaelstraat 54–56 ☎ 020 679 7176, ⓦ restaurantlegarage.nl; map p.107. This elegant restaurant, with an eclectic French and Italian menu, is popular with a media crowd, since it's run by the well-known Dutch TV chef Joop Braakhekke. Call to reserve at least a week ahead and dress to impress. Most mains are €22–€30, so the house menu coming in at €37 for three courses seems to be a good option for getting your money's worth. Mon–Sat 6–11pm, Thurs & Fri noon–2pm.

Willems Willemsparkweg 177 ☎ 020 752 1973, ⓦ restaurantwillems.nl; map p.116. Classic French fare – including steak *tartare*, foie gras and crème brûlée – nestles up against some more modern Italian influences. Popular with the affluent Oud-Zuid set, *Willems* also has a cool, minimalist interior and a nice terrace in summer. Mains average around €20. Mon 6pm–1am, Tues–Thurs 11am–1am, Fri & Sat 11am–2am, Sun 3pm–1am.

GREEK

Dionysos Overtoom 176 ☎ 020 689 4441; map p.116. Inexpensive Greek restaurant just west of the Vondelpark, with a good selection of *meze* (you can eat well for around €20) and occasional live Greek music – dancing is encouraged. Tues–Sun 5.30–11pm.

INDONESIAN

Sama Sebo P.C. Hooftstraat 27 ☎ 020 662 8146, ⓦ samasebo.nl; map p.107. One of Amsterdam's best-known Indonesian restaurants, especially for its *rijsttafel* (€31.50). If this seems a little pricey, it's easy to eat more economically by choosing à la carte dishes, and there's a reasonable set lunch for €18 a head too. Mon–Sat noon–3pm & 5–10pm.

ITALIAN

★ **Spaghetteria** Van Woustraat 123 ☎ 020 000 0000, ⓦ spaghetteria-pastabar.nl; map p.107. A very informal pasta bar with long communal wooden tables, *Spaghetteria* serves up six frequently changing but always excellent pasta dishes. Slow-cooked deer *ragù* with tagliatelle is a favourite when in season, and most pastas come in at around €10–15. House wine is the only kind on offer, but the lack of a list only adds to the family-style

10

DE FOODHALLEN

De Foodhallen ("The Food Halls"; Mon–Thurs & Sun 11am–11.30pm, Fri & Sat 11am–1am; ⓦ foodhallen.nl) opened in the Oud West district in 2014, and immediately set Amsterdam on the map as a bona fide foodie destination. Best described as a giant indoor **street-food market**, there are dozens of stalls selling everything from Vietnamese *banh mi* to Spanish *jamón* to Indian tandoori – all from the best purveyors in the city. Several bars are dotted around too, so it's easy to spend an entire afternoon or evening munching and drinking your way round. There are live DJs every Friday and Saturday until late. To get there, take tram #17 from Centraal Station, or tram #7 from Leidseplein, and get off at Bilderdijkstraat, Kinkerstraat or Ten Katemarkt.

dining atmosphere. No reservations. There are three more branches at Jan Hanzenstraat 32 in the Oud West district, at Pretoriusstraat 72 and at Olympiaplein 176. Daily 5–10.15pm.

JAPANESE

Yamazato and Teppanyaki Sazanka Ferdinand Bolstraat 333 ☎ 020 678 7450, ⓦ okura.nl/culinary; map p.107. The swanky *Okura Hotel* (see page 151) has four restaurants, three of which have Michelin stars: this is the swankiest experience of Japanese food you'll find in the city. Dating back over thirty years, *Yamazato* was the first place to serve Japanese haute cuisine in the Netherlands. It's a traditional *kaiseki* restaurant whose menu features expertly prepared sushi, tempura, sashimi and *sukiyaki*; reckon on paying upwards of €100/person. *Teppanyaki Sazanka* is the renowned grill restaurant, where the chef prepares fish, steaks and vegetables on a hot plate in front of you (seasonal menu €110; booking essential). Daily 6–9.30pm.

MIDDLE EASTERN

Artist 2e Jan Steenstraat 1 ☎ 020 671 4264, ⓦ libanees-artist.nl; map p.107. This small Lebanese restaurant, just off Albert Cuypstraat in De Pijp, has a good selection of hot and cold *meze*. Expect to pay around €19 for a set menu; smaller dishes cost around €7. Daily noon–midnight.

SURINAMESE

Spang Makandra Gerard Doustraat 39 ☎ 020 670 5081, ⓦ spangmakandra.nl; map p.107. Cheap and cheerful Surinamese-Javanese *eetcafé*, going strong since 1978 (so much so that they've opened three other branches at Tussenmeer 227, Gerard Doustraat 39 and Boerhaaveplein

3). Most dishes are under €10, and you can get delicious Surinamese sandwiches for €4.50. Great flavours, and an excellent budget choice. Mon–Sat 11am–10pm, Sun 1–10pm.

THAI

Sawaddee Ká Overtoom 49 ☎ 020 612 7537, ⓦ sawaddeeka.nl; map p.107. A welcoming northeast Thai restaurant serving the usual curries, noodles, Thai soups and salads. Given that *Sawaddee Ká* is at the Leidseplein end of the Overtoom, prices are reasonable at around €12–15 for mains. Also does takeaway and delivery. Daily 4–11pm.

TURKISH

Orontes Albert Cuypstraat 40-42 ☎ 020 679 6225, ⓦ restaurantorontes.nl; map p.107. Excellent Turkish restaurant in De Pijp, serving a wide range of hot and cold starters to share (€5–8.50), and delicious meat and veggie skewers with plenty of side dishes for around €18–20. Or keep it simple and order a *meze tafel* for two people at €36.50. There's a second branch on the Hugo de Grootplein near Westerpark. Mon–Sat 3–11pm.

VEGETARIAN

De Waaghals Frans Halsstraat 29 ☎ 020 679 9609, ⓦ waaghals.nl; map p.107. Well-prepared, organic, vegetarian dishes are the order of the day at this cooperative-run restaurant near the Albert Cuypmarkt. The menu changes twice a month, and though food takes a while to prepare, portions are generous. Mains cost around €20. It's popular, so book ahead to be sure of a table. Daily 5–9.30pm.

COFFEESHOPS

THE OLD CENTRE

Dampkring Handboogstraat 29 ☎ 020 638 0705, ⓦ dampkring-coffeeshop-amsterdam.nl; map p.34. Colourful coffeeshop set to a soundtrack of loud music and flaunting a laidback atmosphere, known for its good-quality hash. There's a second branch on the

Haarlemmerstraat, just west of Centraal Station. Daily 10am–1am.

Grasshopper Oudebrugsteeg 16 ☎ 020 423 2424, ⓦ thegrasshopper.com/nl; map p.34. This multilevel coffeeshop, with bar, sports screen and restaurant, has tried to steal some thunder from *The Bulldog* (see page 172) in

COFFEESHOP ESSENTIALS

This is the one Western country where the purchase of **cannabis** is tolerated, the most conspicuous result of which is the existence of licensed **coffeeshops**, selling bags of dope in much the same way as bars sell glasses of beer. The seedier coffeeshops are concentrated in and around the Red Light District; the more congenial in the Grachtengordel and the Jordaan.

LAWS AND REGULATIONS

The Dutch government's attitude to soft drugs is more complex than you might think: the use of cannabis is not technically legal, but is tolerated, resulting in a rather complicated set of rules and regulations that can safely be ignored as long as you buy very small amounts for **personal use only** – which means possession of up to 30g and sales of up to 5g per purchase in coffeeshops, though in practice this is pretty relaxed. They're not allowed to sell alcohol.

10

A serious hurdle for coffeeshops was the law introduced in July 2008, banning the smoking of tobacco in public areas. Many of the coffeeshops feared closure, but they bounced back with creative solutions, such as selling **pure weed joints** (not for the faint-hearted) or joints mixed with **tobacco substitutes**. Vaporizers are another such solution: they heat the weed to a high temperature, capture the vapour in a type of balloon, and allow you to inhale it pure (rather like a bong). The larger coffeeshops have also built designated smoking areas.

Another major setback was a law passed to close down coffeeshops located within 250m of primary schools and 350m of secondary schools. Several coffeeshops have already closed as a result, but many are still open (albeit some with reduced operating hours), and the fight against the ban continues. Another law, which came into effect in 2014, makes it illegal to help people grow marijuana. The legislation not only targets "grow shops", which sell seeds, lamps, fertilizer and other supplies, but any transport firms, landlords and electricians that facilitate illegal marijuana production.

Meanwhile, the government frequently toys with laws stopping **tourists and foreigners** from buying cannabis, making a Dutch identity or residency permit a condition of purchase. Although this has not yet been enforced in Amsterdam, it is a possibility. In general, the legislation is slowly but steadily toughening up, meaning there are fewer coffeeshops now (about 190 as of 2017) than there were just a couple of years ago – a trend that is bound to continue. Check Ⓦ coffeeshopdirect.com for up-to-date information on what's open.

Finally, never, ever buy dope **on the street** – if you do, you'll likely become a magnet for some pretty unsavoury characters, plus you may find yourself not buying something that isn't dope at all. Needless to say, you should also not attempt to take any form of cannabis out of the country.

THE MENU

When you first walk into a coffeeshop, it isn't immediately apparent how to buy the stuff – it's illegal to advertise cannabis in any way, so you'll have to ask to see the **menu**, which is normally kept behind the counter. The menu will list all the different hashes and grasses on offer, along with (if it's a reputable place) exactly how many grams you get for your money. Current **prices** per gram range from €10 for low-grade stuff up to €30 for top-quality hash, and as high as €60 for really strong grass. The **hash** on sale originates in various countries and is pretty self-explanatory, apart from Pollem, which is compressed resin and stronger than normal. **Marijuana** is a different story, and the old days of imported Colombian, Thai and sensimilia are fading away; taking their place are limitless varieties of **Nederwiet** – Dutch-grown under UV lights and more potent than anything you're likely to have come across. Skunk, Haze and Northern Lights are all popular types of Dutch weed, and should be treated with caution – a smoker of low-grade British draw will be laid low (or high) for hours by a single spliff of skunk. You would be equally well advised to take care with **space-cakes** (cakes or biscuits baked with hash), which are widely available: you can never be sure exactly what's in them and they tend to have a delayed reaction (up to two hours before you notice anything strange – don't get impatient and gobble down another one!). Once they kick in, they can bring on an extremely intense, bewildering high – ten to twelve hours is not uncommon.

10

recent years. It is one of the more welcoming places for visitors, although its proximity to Centraal Station means that at times it can be overwhelmed by tourists. Mon–Thurs 9am–1am, Fri & Sat 9am–3am.

Kadinsky Rosmarijnsteeg 9 ☎020 624 7023, ⓦkadinsky.nl; map p.34. Small and cosy, this coffeeshop weighs out strictly accurate deals to a background of jazz dance music. The chocolate chip cookies are to die for. Second branch at Zoutsteeg 14. Daily 10am–1am.

★ **Rusland** Rusland 16 ☎020 845 6434, ⓦbit.ly/RuslandCafe; map p.34. One of the first Amsterdam coffeeshops, this is a cramped but vibrant place that's a favourite with both dope fans and tea addicts (it has forty different kinds). A cut above the rest. Daily 8am–12.30am.

GRACHTENGORDEL WEST

Amnesia Herengracht 133 ☎020 427 7874; map p.55. Stylish and dimly lit coffeeshop with a canalside terrace. Daily 9am–1am.

La Tertulia Prinsengracht 312 ☎020 623 8503, ⓦcoffeeshoptertulia.com; map p.55. Tiny corner coffeeshop, complete with indoor rockery and tinkling fountain. It's much better outside, though, as it's on a particularly fine stretch of canal. Tues–Sat 11am–7pm.

Siberië Brouwersgracht 11 ☎020 623 5909, ⓦcoffeeshopsiberie.nl; map p.55. Bright, modern coffeeshop set up by the former staff of *Rusland* (see above) and notable for having avoided the over-commercialization of the larger chains. Very relaxed, very friendly, and worth a visit whether you want to smoke or not; has a good selection of magazines as well as a chessboard. Mon–Thurs & Sun 11am–11pm, Fri & Sat 11am–midnight.

GRACHTENGORDEL SOUTH

The Bulldog Palace Leidseplein 15 ☎020 422 3444, ⓦthebulldog.com; map p.65. The biggest and most famous of the coffeeshop chains, and a long way from its poky Red Light District origins, the main branch of *The Bulldog* is on the Leidseplein, housed in a former police station. It has a large cocktail bar, coffeeshop, juice bar

and souvenir shop, all with separate entrances. It's big and brash, not at all the place for a quiet smoke, though the dope they sell (packaged up in neat little brand-labelled bags) is reliably good. Mon–Thurs 9am–1am, Fri & Sat 9am–3am, Sun 9am–2am.

Happy Feelings Kerkstraat 51 ☎020 777 9898, ⓦhappyfeelingsamsterdam.com; map p.65. Formerly a hippie hangout, this is now a fresh and trendy coffeeshop with flatscreen TVs on the walls, attracting a selective crowd. Mon–Sat 9am–1am.

The Otherside Reguliersdwarsstraat 6 ☎020 421 1014, ⓦtheotherside.nl; map p.65. Popular with (but not exclusively occupied by) gay smokers due to its location on the Reguliersdwarsstraat (a popular gay street; in Dutch, "the other side" is a euphemism for homosexuality), this is a crowded and fun coffeeshop near the Rembrandtplein and Muntplein. Daily 10am–midnight.

THE JORDAAN AND WESTERN DOCKLANDS

Barney's Coffeeshop Haarlemmerstraat 102 ☎020 625 9761, ⓦbarneysamsterdam.com; map p.75. This extremely popular café-cum-coffeeshop is one of the most civilized places in town to enjoy a big hit with a fine breakfast – at any time of day. A few doors down, at no. 98, *Barney's Farm* is a nice sunny spot in the morning and serves alcohol, while across the street *Barney's Uptown* has good cocktails in a trendier environment. Daily 9.30am–1am.

Paradox 1e Bloemdwarsstraat 2 ☎020 623 5639, ⓦparadoxcoffeeshop.com; map p.75. If you're fed up with the usual coffeeshop food offerings, let *Paradox* satisfy your munchies with outstanding natural food, including spectacular fresh fruit smoothies and veggie burgers. Daily 10am–8pm.

THE OLD JEWISH QUARTER AND PLANTAGE

Bluebird Sint Antoniesbreestraat 71 ☎020 622 5232; map p.83. With comfy sofas as well as tall stools, the *Bluebird* serves food, coffees and other non-alcoholic drinks, and you can get your smoking fix here too. Daily 9.30am–1am.

THE MELKWEG

Bars, clubs and live music venues

Amsterdam is famous for its traditional, old-style bars or brown cafés – cosy, intimate places so-called because of the dingy colour of their walls, stained by years of tobacco smoke, and their antique-verging-on-rickety furnishings and fittings. In complete contrast are its buzzing riverside terraces, wow-factor rooftop bars and elegant wine bars. Once the go-to city for a wild night out, Amsterdam has grown up a little, balancing the rowdy with refined options: from the lively, somewhat touristy, pubs and clubs clustered around Leidseplein, Spui and Rembrandtplein to the chic cocktail bars housed in converted synagogues or jazzed-up shipping containers. The city also puts on an impressive array of live music, partly due to its youthful population, and partly thanks to generous government subsidies.

BARS

A drink in a cosy **brown café** (*bruin café* or *bruine kroeg*) is an Amsterdam must. At the other extreme are the slick **designer bars**, which tend to be as un-brown as possible and geared towards a largely young crowd, though many students are loyal to the brown cafés. In between are a host of bars that pick and mix the old and the new. Another type of drinking spot – though there are very few of them left – is the **tasting house** (*proeflokaal*), selling only spirits – *jenever* – and often closing early, around 8pm. For **gay bars** see Chapter 14. Many bars – often designated **eetcafés** – offer a complete food menu; those that specialize more in food than drink are listed in the "Cafés and restaurants" chapter (see page 156). **Prices** are fairly standard everywhere, and the only time you'll pay through the nose is in the tourist traps around Leidseplein, Rembrandtplein and along the Damrak.

THE OLD CENTRE

BeerTemple Nieuwezijds Voorburgwal 250 ☎ 020 627 1427, ⓦ beertemple.nl; map p.34. While American beers may not enjoy the greatest reputation in Europe, *BeerTemple* is changing all that by serving up the best selection of US craft beers (thirty beers on draft and sixty-plus bottled) in Amsterdam. Mon–Thurs & Sun 2pm–1am, Fri & Sat 2pm–3am.

De Bekeerde Suster Kloveniersburgwal 6 ☎ 020 423 0112, ⓦ debekeerdesuster.nl; map p.34. Don't waste your time in the unappealing bars of the Red Light District proper; this place is a few steps away and offers home-brewed beer, a good bar menu and a very convivial atmosphere, just off the Nieuwmarkt. Mon–Thurs & Sun noon–midnight, Fri & Sat noon–2am.

Bubbles & Wines Nes 37 ☎ 020 422 3318, ⓦ bubbles andwines.com; map p.34. Over fifty wines are available by the glass in this intimate and elegant wine and champagne bar. The knowledgeable staff are on hand to advise you on drinks to suit your taste. Mon–Sat 3.30pm–1am, Sun 2–9pm.

De Buurvrouw St Pieterspoortsteeg 29 ☎ 020 625 9654, ⓦ debuurvrouw.nl; map p.34. This dark, noisy bar with a wildly eclectic crowd is a great alternative place to head for if you're looking for music late at night in the city centre. Mon–Thurs & Sun 10pm–3am, Fri & Sat 10pm–4am.

Café Belgique Gravenstraat 2 ☎ 020 625 1974, ⓦ cafe-belgique.nl; map p.34. Tiny and very appealing bar behind the Nieuwe Kerk that specializes in brews from Belgium; sample them with plates of Dutch and Trappist cheese. Mon–Thurs & Sun 3pm–1am, Fri & Sat 3pm–3am).

★ **Café de Dokter** Roozenboomsteeg 4 ☎ 020 626 4427, ⓦ cafe-de-dokter.nl; map p.34. Small, dark, brown café with stained glass and furnishings about as old as the clientele, who look as though they've been here for centuries. Liqueurs fill the shelves behind the tiny bar, and the *ossenworst* (raw smoked beef sausage) is to die for. Wed–Sat 4pm–1am.

BEER, WINE AND SPIRITS

Amsterdam's favourite tipple is **beer**, mostly Pilsener-style lager, usually served in a relatively small measure (just under a half-pint, with a foaming head) – asking for *een biertje* will get you a regular lager if you don't specify anything else. The three leading Dutch brands – Amstel, Grolsch and Heineken – are worldwide bestsellers, but are available here in considerably more potent formats than the insipid varieties shunted out for export. Different beers come in different glasses – white beer (*witbier*), which is light, cloudy and served with lemon, has its own tumbler; and most of the speciality Dutch and Belgian beers have their own distinctive glasses with stems of different shapes and sizes. Try the seasonal bock beers for something a little different from the usual lagers. Reckon on paying around €2.50 for a standard-measure small draught beer, €3–5 for wheat and bottled beer.

 Wine is reasonably priced – expect to pay around €8 or so for an average bottle of white or red in a supermarket, €18 in a restaurant, or €3–5 for a glass. As for spirits, **jenever**, the Dutch precursor to gin and also made from juniper berries, is a bit weaker and a little oilier than English gin. It's served in a small glass and is traditionally sipped straight from the bar to stop it spilling over the sides. There are a number of varieties, principally *oude* (old), which is smooth and mellow, *jong* (young), which tastes more like English gin, and *korenwijn* (literally translated as corn wine), which has a malty, oaked flavour. Ask for a *borreltje* (straight *jenever*), a *bittertje* (with Angostura bitters) or, if you've a sweeter tooth, try one of the many varieties of fruit-flavoured *jenever*. A glass of beer with a *jenever* chaser is a *kopstoot*.

 Other drinks you'll come across include numerous Dutch **liqueurs**, notably *advocaat* (eggnog), and the Dutch-produced **brandy**, *Vieux*, which tastes as if it's made from prunes but is in fact grape-based.

Café de Gaeper Staalstraat 4 ☎020 623 3895, ⓦ cafedegaeper.com; map p.34. This convivial brown café (located in a former pharmacy) is packed during term time with students from the university across the canal. There's tasty food, plus outdoor seating that's good for people-watching in warm weather. Mon–Thurs 10am–1am, Fri & Sat 10am–3am, Sun 11am–1am.

Café het Paleis Paleisstraat 16 ☎020 626 0600, ⓦ cafe hetpaleis.nl; map p.34. This bar is a favourite with students from the adjoining university buildings. Trendily refurbished, it also serves food – focaccia sandwiches, salads and such like. Mon & Sun 9.30pm–midnight, Mon–Thurs & Sun 9.30pm–1am, Fri & Sat 9.30am–3am.

Dante Spuistraat 320 ☎020 774 7473, ⓦ amsterdam dante.com; map p.34. Right in the heart of the city's densest concentration of watering holes, *Dante* has a "grand café" feel about it that's reminiscent of Paris or New York. Come here for coffee, drinks, snacks, lunch or dinner, but expect to pay for the prime location. Mon–Fri 11am–1am, Sat & Sun 10am–1am.

De Engelbewaarder Kloveniersburgwal 59 ☎020 625 3772, ⓦ cafe-de-engelbewaarder.nl; map p.34. Once the meeting place of Amsterdam's bookish types, this is still known as a literary café. It's relaxed and informal, with live jazz on Sun afternoons. Mon–Thurs 10am–1am, Fri & Sat 10am–3am, Sun 11am–1am.

★ **Gollem** Raamsteeg 4 ☎020 612 9444, ⓦ cafe gollem.nl; map p.34. Small, cosy, split-level bar with rickety furniture, wood panelling and a generous selection of Belgian beers, plus a few Dutch brews for variety – and with the correct glasses to drink them from. There are now also three other branches at Overtoom 160, Daniel Stalpertstraat 74 and Amstelstraat 34. Mon–Thurs 4pm–1am, Fri & Sat noon–3am, Sun noon–1am.

Hoppe Spui 18–20 ☎020 420 4420, ⓦ cafehoppe.com/nl; map p.34. One of Amsterdam's longest-established and best-known bars, and a likeable, scruffy joint, popular with the city's business folk. It's especially good in summer, when the throng spills out onto the street. Mon–Thurs 8am–1am, Fri & Sat 8am–2am.

In 't Aepjen Zeedijk 1 ☎020 626 8401, map p.34. This building has been a bar since the days when the Zeedijk was a haunt for sailors gambling away their last few guilders and having to barter rather than pay cash. Its name – literally "In the Monkeys" – refers to the fact that monkeys were once the stock in trade here. There are no monkeys now, but not much else has changed. Mon–Thurs & Sun noon–1am, Fri & Sat noon–3am.

★ **In de Wildeman** Kolksteeg 3 ☎020 638 2348, ⓦ indewildeman.nl; map p.34. One of the centre's most appealing beer-tasting houses, this lovely old-fashioned watering hole has a barely changed wood-and-tile interior that still boasts its original low bar and shelving: a peaceful escape from the tacky shops of nearby Nieuwendijk. Mon–Thurs noon–1am, Fri & Sat noon–2am.

Lokaal 't Loosje Nieuwmarkt 32 ☎020 627 2635, ⓦ loosje.nl; map p.34. Quiet, old-style brown café that's been here for two hundred years and looks it, with an attractive old tiled interior. It has a pleasant atmosphere, and is always busy. Daily 8.30am–1am.

Mata Hari Oudezijds Achterburgwal 22 ☎020 205 0919, ⓦ matahari-amsterdam.nl; map p.34. A breath of fresh air at the northern end of the Red Light District, *Mata Hari* is a spacious, trendy bar with vintage styling that's popular with locals as well as tourists. It also does good food. Mon–Thurs & Sun 11am–1am, Fri & Sat 11am–3am.

De Ooievaar Sint Olofspoort 1 ☎06 3158 6941, ⓦ proeflokaaldeooievaar.nl; map p.34. This old *proeflokaal* (tasting house) is a civilized escape from the nearby sleaze of the Red Light District – and it's handily situated for Centraal Station. Boiled eggs at the bar go down well with the *jenever*, and there's beer, too. Daily from noon.

Poco Loco Nieuwmarkt 24 ☎020 624 2937, ⓦ dining city.net/pocoloco; map p.34. One of the liveliest cafés on the Nieuwmarkt, with a cheerful retro interior attracting a matching clientele. Also a good selection of tapas and other snacks. Mon–Thurs & Sun 10am–1am, Fri & Sat 10am–3am.

Schuim Spuistraat 189 ☎020 638 9357; map p.34. A popular and spacious bar-café with retro furniture, *Schuim* is very popular with a young and unpretentiously boho crowd, as well as students from the nearby university. Mon–Thurs 11am–1am, Fri & Sat 11am–3am, Sun noon–1am.

★ **Tales & Spirits** Lijnbaanssteeg 5 ☎065 535 6467, ⓦ talesandspirits.com; map p.34. Down an alleyway just off the Singel canal, *Tales & Spirits* does a great line in cocktails, which make a delicious predinner aperitif or a good start to a night out on the town. The food is also creative and not too pricey for its central location, with dishes coming in at around €10–20. Tues–Sun 5.30pm–1am, Fri & Sat 5.30pm–3am.

The Tara Rokin 85–89 ☎020 421 2654, ⓦ thetara.com; map p.34. Amsterdam has quite a few Irish pubs these days, but this is one of the better ones for several reasons: decent food (including a great all-day breakfast), regular football and other sports on TV, and occasional live music.

11

TOP 5 COCKTAIL BARS

Bar Oldenhof See page 177
Hiding in Plain Sight See page 178
NJOY See age 176
Tales & Spirits See page 175
Vesper See page 177

It's very spacious for its central location, too. Mon–Thurs & Sun 10am–1am, Fri & Sat 10am–3am.

★ **Wynand Fockink** Pijlsteeg 31 ☎020 639 2695, ⊛wynand-fockink.nl; map p.34. This small, intimate bar, hidden just behind the *Krasnapolsky* hotel off the Dam, is one of the city's oldest *proeflokaalen*, and it offers a vast range of its own flavoured *jenevers* that were once distilled down the street. It's standing-room only here – you bend down at the counter and sip your *jenever* from a glass filled to the brim. Daily 2–9pm.

GRACHTENGORDEL WEST

't Arendsnest Herengracht 90 ☎020 421 2057, ⊛arendsnest.nl; map p.55. In a handsome old canal house, this bar boasts impressive wooden decor – from the long bar to the tall wood-and-glass cabinets – and specializes in Dutch beers, of which it has over one hundred varieties, thirty on tap. Mon–Thurs & Sun noon–midnight, Fri & Sat noon–2am.

Café Het Molenpad Prinsengracht 653 ☎020 625 9680, ⊛cafehetmolenpad.nl; map p.55. Revamped to maintain its brown café charm, *Het Molenpad* hasn't lost its laidback atmosphere. It fills up with a young, professional crowd after 6pm. Daily from noon–late.

★ **Café Papeneiland** Prinsengracht 2 ☎020 624 1989, ⊛papeneiland.nl; map p.55. With its wood panelling, antique Delft tiles and ancient stove, this rabbit warren of a place is one of the cosiest (and oldest, founded in 1642) bars in the Grachtengordel. It gets jam-packed late at night with a garrulous crew of locals and tourists. Mon–Thurs & Sun 10am–1am, Fri & Sat 10am–2am.

Café Pieper Prinsengracht 424 ☎020 626 4775, ⊛cafepieper.com; map p.65. Laidback neighbourhood brown bar, at the corner of Leidsegracht, with rickety old furniture and a mini-terrace beside the canal. It has a surprisingly large selection of liqueurs plus a genial, sometimes rather tipsy, proprietor. Mon, Wed & Thurs noon–1am, Tues 4pm–midnight, Fri & Sat noon–2am, Sun 2–10pm.

Café de Prins Prinsengracht 124 ☎020 624 9382, ⊛deprins.nl; map p.55. With its well-worn decor and chatty atmosphere, this popular and lively bar offers a wide range of drinks and a reasonably priced bar menu, with food served from 10am to 10pm. Large – at least in Amsterdam terms – and airy, it's popular with 20-somethings. Mon–Thurs & Sun 10am–1am, Fri & Sat 10am–2am.

Van Puffelen Prinsengracht 377 ☎020 624 6270, ⊛restaurantvanpuffelen.com; map p.55. This long-established and popular spot is divided into two, with a brown café-bar on one side and an *eetcafé* on the other. The café-bar is an appealing place to drink, with a good choice of international beers, while the restaurant side concentrates on Dutch(ish) dishes with occasional Mediterranean leanings. Main courses average around

€18–20. Mon–Thurs from 4pm, Fri–Sun noon–midnight.

GRACHTENGORDEL SOUTH

Café van Leeuwen Keizersgracht 711 ☎020 625 8215, ⊛cafevanleeuwen.nl; map p.65. This convivial café gets jam-packed with the local in-crowd after a day at the office. There's also a good selection of food (mains for around €15), lots of wines by the glass and occasional live jazz on Sun. Mon–Thurs 8.30am–1am, Fri 8.30am–3am, Sat 9am–3am, Sun 10am–1am.

De Duivel Reguliersdwarsstraat 87 ☎063 083 2404, ⊛cafededuivel.amsterdam; map p.65. Tucked away on a street of bars and coffeeshops, this is the best hip-hop bar in Amsterdam, with nonstop beats and a faithful clientele. Daily 8pm–3/4am.

L&B Whisky Café Korte Leidsedwarsstraat 82 ☎020 625 2387, ⊛whiskyamsterdam.nl; map p.65. With literally hundreds of whiskies on offer, *L&B* has the biggest selection in the Netherlands: from Scotch to Irish, and from Bourbon to Japanese varieties, you'll find it all here. Mon–Thurs & Sun 8pm–3am, Fri & Sat 8pm–4am.

Lux Marnixstraat 403 ☎020 422 1412, ⊛barlux.nl; map p.65. Designer bar aimed at the pre-club crowd, with a good line in full-volume house and regular DJs, attracting a young, alternative clientele. Mon–Thurs & Sun 7pm–3am, Fri & Sat 7pm–4am.

★ **NJOY** Korte Leidsedwarsstraat 93, ⊛njoycocktails. com; map p.65. You have to ring a buzzer to get into *NJOY* (make sure you're not wearing trainers or a baseball cap) but for all that, once you're inside it's not at all pretentious, and a lively spot. The cocktails are excellent (and on the strong side). Mon–Thurs & Sun 5pm–3am, Fri & Sat 5pm–4am.

Oosterling Utrechtsestraat 140 ☎020 623 4140, ⊛cafeoosterling.nl; map p.65. Intimate neighbourhood bar that's been plying its trade for donkeys' years. Kitted out in attractive traditional style, it specializes in *jenever*, with dozens of brands and varieties on offer. Mon & Tues 3pm–midnight, Wed–Sat noon–1am, Sun 1–8pm.

Pigs & Punch Utrechtsestraat 30A ☎020 330 2994, ⊛pigsandpunch.nl; map p.65. Formerly known as Mystique, this cool new bar has a modern decor and offers all the drinks you might want, plus hearty food at reasonable prices. Among the highlights are excellent spare ribs (€15). The cocktails are also fantastic, and the list changes regularly – try one of the punch bowls if they have them on offer. Mon–Sat 5pm–1am.

Weber Marnixstraat 397 ☎020 422 1412, ⊛barweber. nl; map p.65. Next door to (and run by the same people as) *Lux*, *Weber* is an equally popular local hangout, attracting musicians, students and young professionals. It gets crowded and noisy at weekends. Mon–Thurs & Sun 7pm–3am, Fri & Sat 7pm–4am.

11

★ **De Zotte** Raamstraat 29 ☎ 020 626 8694, ⊛ dezotte. nl; map p.65. Down a tiny street tucked behind the Leidseplein, this laidback bar specializes in Belgian beer, of which it has numerous varieties. Their chips and mayo are pretty outstanding too. Daily 4pm–1am.

THE JORDAAN AND WESTERN DOCKLANDS

★ **Bar Oldenhof** Elandsgracht 84 ☎ 020 751 3273, ⊛ bar-oldenhof.com; map p.75. Beautiful old-fashioned bar, decorated with opulent velvet, leather armchairs and deer antlers on the wall. *Oldenhof* does a great line in cocktails, as well as single malt whiskies and fine wines. Settle in for an evening, and leave feeling like Ernest Hemingway. Mon–Thurs 6pm–1am, Fri 6pm–3am, Sat 5pm–3am, Sun 5pm–1am.

De Blaffende Vis Westerstraat 118 ☎ 020 625 1721; map p.75. Something of an institution, this typical neighbourhood bar has oodles of atmosphere and a well-priced bar menu. Mon–Thurs 8.30am–1am, Fri & Sat 9am–3am, Sun 10am–1am.

Café Chris Bloemstraat 42 ☎ 020 624 5942, ⊛ cafechris. nl; map p.75. Very proud of being the Jordaan's oldest bar (and, arguably, Amsterdam's too – although opinions differ), dating from 1624, this place has a comfortable, homely atmosphere, and it has a pool table too. Mon–Thurs 3pm–1am, Fri & Sat 3pm–2am, Sun 3–9pm.

Café Nol Westerstraat 109 ☎ 020 624 5380, ⊛ cafenol-amsterdam.nl; map p.75. A raucous but jolly Jordaan singing bar, this luridly lit dive closes late – very late at weekends, when the back-slapping joviality and drunken sing-alongs keep you rooted until the small hours. Wed, Thurs & Sun 9pm–3am, Fri & Sat 9pm–4am.

Café Thijssen Brouwersgracht 107 ☎ 065 236 9146, ⊛ cafethijssen.nl; map p.75. An old-time favourite with neighbourhood locals, this bar is nothing fancy, but perfect for lingering over coffee or fresh mint tea with a magazine during the day, or a beer and a portion of *bitterballen* in the evening. The tiny terrace gives good views of the bustling market. Mon–Thurs 8am–1am, Fri 8am–3am, Sat 7.30am–3am, Sun 8am–midnight.

Café de Tuin 2e Tuindwarsstraat 13 ☎ 020 624 4559, ⊛ cafedetuin.nl; map p.75. The Jordaan has some marvellously unpretentious bars, and this is one of the best: agreeably unkempt and always full of locals. Mon–Thurs 10am–1am, Fri & Sat 10am–3am, Sun 11am–1am.

Pacific Parc Polonceaukade 23 ☎ 020 488 7778, ⊛ pacificparc.nl; map p.77. Part of the imaginative redevelopment of the Westergasfabriek (former gas factory), this bar-restaurant has outdoor seating overlooking the canal on one side and the Westerpark on the other. It's a cool summer hangout for food or just drinks, with live music and/or DJs several nights of the week. Daily from 11am.

Proust Noordermarkt 4 ☎ 020 623 9145, ⊛ proust. nl; map p.75. Trendy design bar – the focal point is a giant lamp in the shape of a revolver – but the laidback Jordaan atmosphere attracts students and young urban professionals. There's a reasonably priced bar menu too. Mon 9am–1am, Tues–Thurs & Sun 11am–1am, Fri 11am–3am, Sat 9am–3am.

De Reiger Nieuwe Leliestraat 34 ☎ 020 624 7426, ⊛ dereigeramsterdam.nl; map p.75. In the thick of the Jordaan, this is one of the area's many meeting places: an old-style brown café filled with modish Amsterdammers, and with faded portraits on the walls. Mains for around €20. Tues–Fri 5pm–11.30pm, Sat 6–11.30pm, Sun 4pm–11.30pm.

★ **'t Smalle** Egelantiersgracht 12 ☎ 020 623 9617, ⊛ t-smalle.nl; map p.75. Candlelit and laidback café-bar, with a pontoon on the canal out front for relaxed summer afternoons. In winter, be sure to try the *glühwein*. Mon–Thurs & Sun 10am–1am, Fri & Sat 10am–2am.

★ **Vesper** Vinkenstraat 57 ⊛ vesperbar.nl; map p.75. On a quiet street sandwiched between the lovely Brouwersgracht canal and the Haarlemmerdijk shopping street, *Vesper* is an intimate little cocktail bar that's perfect for a predinner aperitif or a late-night tipple – try the Vesper Martini. Tues–Thurs 8pm–1am, Fri & Sat 5pm–3am.

THE OLD JEWISH QUARTER AND PLANTAGE

De Sluyswacht Jodenbreestraat 1 ☎ 020 625 7611, ⊛ sluyswacht.nl; map p.83. This pleasant little bar occupies an old and now solitary gabled house that stands sentry by the lock gates opposite the Rembrandthuis. A great spot to nurse a beer on a warm summer's night, with a lovely view down the canal towards the Montelbaanstoren. Mon–Thurs 12.30pm–1am, Fri & Sat 12.30pm–3am, Sun 12.30pm–7pm.

THE EASTERN DOCKLANDS AND AMSTERDAM NOORD

Barco Korte Geuzenstraat 98 ☎ 069 274 9009, ⊛ cafebarco.nl; map p.97. Located on a converted boat, *Barco* is a lovely little spot overlooking the IJ. As well as a small but decent selection of cocktails, they also serve tapas (€3–5 each) and wines by the glass, carafe and bottle. Mon–Thurs 4pm–midnight/1am, Fri 4pm–midnight/3am, Sat 3pm–midnight/3am, Sun 3pm–10pm/1am.

TOP 5 BEER BARS

't Arendsnest See page 176
Brouwerij 't IJ See page 178
Gollem See page 175
In de Wildeman See page 175
De Zotte See page 177

11

Blijburg aan Zee Muiderlaan 1001 ☎020 416 0330, ⓦblijburg.nl; map p.101. Amsterdam's city beach itself, situated on the IJsselmeer, might be something of a disappointment, but its *Blijburg aan Zee* bar is very cool, with DJs in summer and live music in winter. Mon–Thurs 8.30am–11pm, Fri & Sat 8.30am–1am.

★ **Brouwerij 't IJ** Funenkade 7 ☎020 622 8325, ⓦbrouwerijhetij.nl; map p.101. Long-established brewery in the old public baths adjoining the Gooyer windmill, serving up an excellent range of their own home-made beers and ales, from the thunderously strong (9 percent) Columbus amber ale to the easier-drinking Natte (6.5 percent). Daily 2–8pm.

Hanneke's Boom Dijksgracht 4 ☎020 419 9820, ⓦhannekesboom.nl; map p.97. Right on the waterfront between Centraal Station to the west and the NEMO science centre to the east, *Hanneke's Boom* is a hipster hangout that's especially popular in summer. Grab a beanbag or a bench and soak up the sun. Mon–Thurs & Sun 10am–1am, Fri & Sat 10am–3am.

★ **Hiding in Plain Sight** Rapenburg 18 ☎062 529 3620, ⓦhpsamsterdam.com; map p.97. Arguably the best cocktail bar in Amsterdam, *Hiding in Plain Sight* is decorated in the style of an old American speakeasy. The drinks menu is ever-changing; if you find it impossible to choose, the extremely knowledgeable bar staff are on hand to advise. Also has a large selection of Mezcal. Mon–Thurs & Sun 6pm–1am, Fri & Sat 6pm–3am.

SkyLounge Amsterdam Oosterdoksstraat 4 ☎020 530 0875, ⓦskyloungeamsterdam.com; map p.97. Located on the top floor of the *DoubleTree by Hilton* hotel right next to Centraal Station, the *SkyLounge* affords some of the best views of Amsterdam – particularly at sunset. Inevitably, drinks are pricey, but the service is slick, and the extra euros are worth it just for the photos. Mon, Tues & Sun 11am–1am, Wed & Thurs 11am–2am, Fri & Sat 11am–3am.

THE MUSEUM QUARTER AND AROUND

Bazar Albert Cuypstraat 182 ☎020 675 0544, ⓦhotelbazar.nl; map p.107. This cavernous converted synagogue is usually buzzing with activity long after the market traders have packed up. A lively place to share a bottle of wine over a platter of *meze*. Mon–Thurs 8am–midnight, Sat 8am–1am, Sun 9am–midnight.

Café Krull Sarphatipark 2 ☎020 662 0214, ⓦcafekrull.com; map p.107. With rustic wooden tables, old posters on the wall and magazines strewn around, *Café Krull* has a homely, casual vibe that makes it popular with students and anyone else looking to chill out over a coffee or something stronger. Mon–Fri 9am–1am, Sat & Sun 9am–3am.

Café Wildschut Roelof Hartplein 1–3 ☎020 676 8220, ⓦcafewildschut.nl; map p.107. Just around the corner from the *College Hotel*, this busy bar-café is famous for its congenial, spacious Art Deco interior and outdoor seating in summer. By far the nicest place to drink in the area, with a decent menu too. Mon–Fri from 9am, Sat & Sun 10am–late.

Chocolate Bar 1e Van der Helststraat 62a ☎020 675 7672, ⓦchocolate-bar.nl; map p.107. Cool, disco-inspired café-bar that's open for tasty food and cocktails at any time of the day. Perch at the bar on leather stools or lounge in the cosy room out back. Mon–Thurs & Sun 9am–1am, Fri & Sat 9am–3am.

Ebeling Overtoom 52 ☎020 777 2005, ⓦde-ebeling.nl; map p.107. This dark and cosy lounge bar converted from an old bank (the toilets are in the vaults) is a pretty far cry from the traditional brown café. There's Guinness on tap, decent music and a modern, comfortable vibe. Mon–Wed 10am–3am, Thurs 10am–3am, Fri & Sat 10am–4am.

Kingfisher Ferdinand Bolstraat 24 ☎020 671 2395, ⓦwww.kingfishercafe.nl; map p.107. This amiable neighbourhood café is good for lunch, or just a drink if you want to continue imbibing after the Heineken Experience (see page 117) – it's right around the corner. Mon–Thurs 10am–1am, Fri & Sat 10am–3am, Sun noon–1am.

Pilsvogel Gerard Douplein 14 ☎020 664 6483, ⓦpilsvogel.nl; map p.107. A favourite drinking spot for style-conscious 30-somethings, with a laidback atmosphere and decent tapas, and a good selection of Spanish wines. Mon–Thurs & Sun 10am–1am, Fri & Sat 10am–3am.

THE OUTER DISTRICTS

Bar Bukowski Oosterpark 10, Amsterdam Oost ☎020 370 1685, ⓦbarbukowski.nl; map p.126. Inspired by the eponymous writer and legendary drinker, *Bar Bukowski* has literary quotes on the menus and giant typewriter art above the bar. Its sister bar next door, *Henry's*, serves great cocktails to a buzzing young crowd. Mon–Thurs 8am–1am, Fri 8am–3am, Sat 9am–3am, Sun 9am–1am.

CLUBS

After a long lull, **clubbing** in Amsterdam has been reinvigorated by a good range of venues that bear comparison with clubs in any other European city, plus plenty of bars hosting regular DJs – most playing variations on house, trance, garage and techno. Although all the places listed below **open** at either 10pm or 11pm, there's not much point turning up anywhere before midnight; unless stated otherwise, everywhere stays open until around 5am on Fri and Sat nights, 4am on other nights. For gay and lesbian clubs see Chapter 14.

CLUBBING IN AMSTERDAM

Most clubs charge for entry, with **ticket prices** hovering between €5 and €20 at weekends and dropping to around €7 during the week. To save money, you could consider buying an Amsterdam Nightlife Ticket, which costs €10 or €20 and grants entry to over 20 nightclubs for two or seven days, respectively – see ⓦamsterdamnightlifeticket.com. A singular feature of Amsterdam clubbing, however, is that you're expected to tip the bouncer if you want to get back into the same place next week; €1 or €2 in the palm of his hand will do nicely. **Drinks** prices are just slightly more expensive than in cafés, at around €3–4. **Dress up** if you want to get into some of the smaller, hipper clubs where space is limited and door staff have carte blanche about who they let in. **Smoking** is not allowed inside, but most clubs have purpose-built smoking lounges. As far as **drugs** go, smoking joints in the designated area is generally fine. Should you need reminding, ecstasy, acid, speed and cocaine are all illegal, and you can expect less than favourable treatment from the bouncers (and the law) if you're caught consuming.

11

THE OLD CENTRE

Bitterzoet Spuistraat 2 ☎020 421 2318, ⓦbitterzoet.com; map p.34. Spacious but cosy two-floored bar and theatre hosting a mixed bag of events: DJs playing punk, hip-hop, r'n'b, reggae and disco, film screenings and occasional urban poetry nights. Mon–Thurs & Sun 8pm–3am, Fri & Sat 8pm–4am.

Club NL Nieuwezijds Voorburgwal 169 ☎020 622 7510, ⓦclubnl.nl; map p.34. What was the city's first lounge bar is now a posh and opulent house club, frequented by the rich and famous. Mon, Wed, Thurs & Sun 11pm–3am, Fri & Sat 11pm–4am.

Disco Dolly Handboogstraat 11 ☎020 620 1779, ⓦdiscodolly.nl; map p.34. The reincarnation of the *Dansen bij Jansen* club, this two-floor disco-ball club plays a soundtrack of soul, boogie-woogie, disco, deep house and occasional hip-hop. Very popular with students. Mon–Thurs & Sun 11pm–4am, Fri–Sat 11pm–5am.

Winston Kingdom Warmoesstraat 129 ☎020 623 1380, ⓦwinston.nl; map p.34. This small venue adjacent to the *Winston hotel* (see page 147) puts on eclectic club nights featuring electronica, drum'n'bass and hip-hop. A good place to catch upcoming bands. Mon–Thurs 9pm–late, Fri & Sat 11pm–late, Sun 10pm–late.

GRACHTENGORDEL SOUTH

Abe Club & Lounge Amstelstraat 30 ☎06 2448 2590, ⓦclubabe.com; map p.65. This sophisticated club pays homage to a nineteenth-century banker and philanthropist named Abraham Carel Wertheim, who remodelled the bank building in eclectic style; the club's stylish decor follows suit. A mixed line-up of DJs play varied beats, from house to old-school hip-hop. Thurs & Sun 11pm–3.30am, Fri & Sat 11pm–4am.

Claire Rembrandtplein 17 ⓦstudio-80.nl; map p.65. Right on the Rembrandtplein, this radio station-turned-club once hosted the popular Studio 80 nightclub, which attracted a fashionable, scene-y crowd with techno, gritty hip-hop and electro acid, and was a breeding ground for

young and upcoming DJs and bands. Now *Claire* is following in its footsteps with wild music events every weekend. Thurs 11pm–4am, Fri & Sat 11pm–8am.

Escape Rembrandtplein 11 ☎020 622 1111, ⓦescape.nl; map p.65. A feature of Amsterdam's clubbing scene since the 1980s, this vast club can hold two thousand people. It has undergone renovations to stay modern, with an impressive sound system and visuals, and the opening of the *Escape* café and lounge should pull in the crowds. Mon–Thurs & Sun 11pm–4am, Fri & Sat 11pm–5am.

Jimmy Woo Korte Leidsedwarsstraat 18 ☎020 626 3150, ⓦjimmywoo.com; map p.65. This exclusive club is spread over two floors: upstairs, the black lacquered walls, Japanese lamps and cosy booths with leather couches have an intimate, sexy vibe, while downstairs a packed dancefloor throbs under the oscillating light from hundreds of light bulbs studded into the ceiling. It's popular with young, well-dressed locals, so look smart if you want to join in. Thurs 11pm–3am, Fri & Sat 11pm–4am, Sun 8pm–midnight.

Melkweg Lijnbaansgracht 234a ☎020 531 8181, ⓦmelkweg.nl; map p.65. After the bands have finished (see page 181), excellent, offbeat disco sessions go on well into the small hours, sometimes featuring the best DJs in town, with anything from dancehall to indie pop on Sat. The *Melkweg* also plays host to some of the most enjoyable theme nights around, ranging from African dance to experimental jazz-trance. Opening times vary; check the website; however, the club was closed for renovation at the time of writing.

Paradiso Weteringschans 6–8 ☎020 626 4521, ⓦparadiso.nl; map p.65. One of the principal venues in the city, this converted church just around the corner from the Leidseplein is popular with an alternative crowd. On Wed and Thurs eclectic dance night "Noodlanding" continues to draw in the crowds, and look out for DJ sets featuring live performances on Sat.

Sugar Factory Lijnbaansgracht 238 ☎020 627 0008, ⓦsugarfactory.nl; map p.65. Opposite the *Melkweg* and considered its little sister, *Sugar Factory* pulls in a young, trendy crowd and has an underground vibe. Regular nights include Techno Tuesday, Wednesday's "Night Shift" (hip-hop, disco and house) and Sunday's "Wicked Jazz", with DJs and musicians putting on a mix of jazz, r'n'b and funk. Daily 6pm–5am.

THE EASTERN DOCKLANDS AND AMSTERDAM NOORD

★ **Panama** Oostelijke Handelskade 4, Zeeburg ☎ 020 311 8686, ⓦ panama.nl; map p.101. One of Amsterdam's coolest clubs, *Panama* overlooks the River IJ and plays host to top-name international DJs Thurs–Sun. Dress to impress. Mon–Wed noon–1am, Thurs & Sun noon–3am, Fri & Sat noon–4am.

ROCK AND POP VENUES

As far as **live music** goes, Amsterdam is a regular tour stop for many major artists – so keep an eye on the listings magazines (see box, below). **Dutch rock and pop** bands are often worth seeking out too. Look out for the celebrated Zuco 103, with a distinctive Brazilian sound, Junkie XL and other members of the dance/hip-hop scene, singer-songwriter Anouk and experimental Spinvis, or rock bands such as BLØF. The city's biggest **venue** for concerts is Ziggo Dome, capable of seating 17,000 people. Second largest, in the southeastern suburbs, is the 50,000-seater Johan Cruijff Arena (formerly named Amsterdam ArenA). Close by, the AFAS Live, a simple but acoustically impressive black box, hosts medium-sized acts, while the two dedicated music venues in Amsterdam city centre – the *Paradiso* and the *Melkweg* – are on a much smaller scale, and supply a daily programme of music to suit all tastes (and budgets). Alongside the main venues, the city's clubs, bars and multimedia centres host occasional performances by live bands. As far as **prices** go, for big names you'll pay anything between €30 and €60 a ticket; ordinary gigs cost €8–20, although some places charge a membership fee (*lidmaatschap*) on top.

MAJOR VENUES

Johan Cruijff Arena Boulevard 1, Amsterdam Oost ☎ 020 311 1333, ⓦ johancruijffarena.nl; metro or train

THE MUSEUM QUARTER AND AROUND

't Blauwe Theehuis Vondelpark 5 ☎ 020 662 0254, ⓦ blauwetheehuis.nl; map p.116. There's free open-air dancing with DJs throughout the summer in the Vondelpark, usually at weekends, but check the website for the programme. Mon–Fri 9am–7pm, Sat & Sun 9am–8pm.

THE OUTER DISTRICTS

AFAS Live ArenA Boulevard 590, Amsterdam Oost ☎ 0900 687 42 42, ⓦ afaslive.nl; metro or train to Bijlmer station; map p.122. One of the best concert venues in the country, *AFAS Live* hosts a variety of dance events featuring well-known Dutch DJs, as well as Stilo Latino parties.

to Bijlmer station; map p.122. The Ajax soccer stadium also plays host to world-class music acts such as the Rolling Stones and Madonna.

★ **Melkweg** Lijnbaansgracht 234a, Grachtengordel south ☎ 020 531 8181, ⓦ melkweg.nl; map p.65. The *Melkweg* (Milky Way) is probably Amsterdam's most respected entertainment venue. A former dairy (hence the name) just round the corner from Leidseplein, it has two separate halls for live music, hosting a broad range of genres, from reggae to rock. There's also a café-restaurant (Marnixstraat entrance; Wed–Sun noon–9pm).

Paradiso Weteringschans 6–8, Grachtengordel south ☎ 020 626 4521, ⓦ paradiso.nl; map p.65. This converted church near the Leidseplein, revered by many for its atmosphere and excellent programme, features local and international bands, ranging from the newly signed to the more established.

Ziggo Dome De Passage 100, Amsterdam Oost ☎ 0900 235 3663, ⓦ ziggodome.nl; bus, metro or train to Bijlmer station; map p.122. The city's biggest venue for concerts and shows, hosting major international artists and bands.

SMALLER VENUES

Akhnaton Nieuwezijds Kolk 25, Old Centre ☎ 020 624 3396, ⓦ akhnaton.nl; map p.34. Various organizers host popular dance nights here (see page 183). Daily from noon.

11

WHAT'S ON INFORMATION

The quickest way to find up-to-date **events listings** is to visit ⓦ iamsterdam.com. Alternatively, the I amsterdam store inside the IJ-hal (see page 30) and I amsterdam visitor centres (see page 30) have information about what's on, as well as tickets and listings magazines. You can pick up a copy of the excellent English-language *I amsterdam Magazine*, published every two months, from visitor centres too (€4.95), as well as free copies of *Uitkrant*, which has comprehensive listings of all concerts, festivals and theatre events, but is only published in Dutch. You could also try the Wednesday entertainment supplement of the daily newspaper *Het Parool*.

SUMMER MUSIC FESTIVALS

The Vondelpark is a popular venue for **summer concerts in the city**, with the Summer Breeze Latin Festival at the end of May (ⓦmysummerbreeze.nl) and events at *'t Blauwe Theehuis* (see page 181). Frankendael Park in Amsterdam Oost hosts the free Roots Open Air (ⓦamsterdamroots.nl), a huge one-day event usually held around July 5. It attracts over 60,000 people and is the culmination of the Amsterdam Roots Festival – an international music festival starting on June 30 and spanning a variety of genres in a series of venues around the city, including the *Melkweg*, *Paradiso* and *Bimhuis*. Summer folk, jazz and rock concerts are hosted by *Noorderlicht* café (see page 160) in the NDSM district, a short ferry ride from Centraal Station. Other day- or weekend-long summer festivals include the Pacha Festival in May, Nomads Festival and Red Light Jazz Festival in June, Pitch Festival in July and Encore Festival in August (see Chapter 17 for details).

Of the music festivals **outside the city**, the most famous is Pinkpop Festival (May/June; ⓦpinkpop.nl), down in the south in Landgraaf, near Maastricht. Others include Lowlands (Aug; ⓦlowlands.nl), held in Flevoland province, and Parkpop (June; ⓦparkpop.nl), Europe's largest free festival, taking place at The Hague's Zuiderpark. Major **dance festivals** include Dancevalley (first weekend in Aug; ⓦdancevalley.com), which takes place in Spaarnwoude between Haarlem and Amsterdam, Mysteryland (end Aug; ⓦmysteryland.nl) in Hoofddorp near Haarlem, and Extrema Outdoor (mid-July; ⓦxofestival.nl) near Eindhoven in the south. Dates vary, so check the websites before making plans.

11

De Buurvrouw St Pieterspoortsteeg 29, Old Centre ☎020 625 9654, ⓦdebuurvrouw.nl; map p.34. An eclectic, alternative bar that's open till late (see page 174). A DJ plays 60s classics and rock 'n' roll from a booth suspended from the ceiling, and they occasionally host local bands too. Mon–Thurs & Sun 10pm–3am, Fri & Sat 10pm–4am.

Cruise Inn Zuiderzeeweg 29, eastern docklands ☎020 692 7188, ⓦcruise-inn.com; map p.101. This volunteer-run clubhouse was set up over twenty years ago by a group of enterprising rockabillies. It's located somewhat off the beaten track in Zeeburg, to the northeast of the Oosterdok (tram #14 to Flevopark), but worth the trek, with jam sessions and great live band nights, putting on music from the 1950s and 1960s. Sat 9pm–3am.

De Heeren van Aemstel Thorbeckeplein 5, Grachtengordel south ☎020 620 2173, ⓦdeheerenvanaemstel.nl; map p.65. This warm, atmospheric café hosts live bands every Fri and Sat, playing a mixture of excellent covers, jazz, rock and Netherlands classics. Mon, Tues & Sun upon request, Wed–Thurs & Sat 5pm–3am, Fri 3pm–5am.

Mezrab Veemkade 576, eastern docklands ☎020 419 3368, ⓦmezrab.nl; map p.101. This cultural centre hosts regular gigs, mainly on Sat. On the second Thurs there's a special get together of musicians from the Mezrab Collective and further afield, while storytelling nights are held on Fri (slots open to the public; contact in advance). Wed–Sun from 7pm (events start at 8pm).

Mulligan's Amstel 100, Grachtengordel south ☎020 622 1330, ⓦmulligans.nl; map p.65. Irish bar that's head and shoulders above the rest for atmosphere and authenticity, with Gaelic musicians and storytellers most nights for free. Mon–Thurs 4pm–1am, Fri & Sat 4pm–3am.

OCCII Amstelveenseweg 134, Vondelpark ☎020 671 7778, ⓦoccii.org; map p.116. This former squat bar opposite the western entrance of the Vondelpark organizes live alternative music, from indie pop to electro-punk. Mon–Thurs & Sun 9pm–2am, Fri & Sat 10pm–3am.

'Skek Zeedijk 4–8, Old Centre ☎020 427 0551, ⓦskek.nl; map p.34. Frequent performances from Thurs to Sun by singer-songwriters and hip-hop, rock and jazz acts in this pleasant *eetcafé* run by students (see page 162). Mon 4pm–1am, Tues–Thurs & Sun noon–1am, Fri & Sat noon–3am.

The Waterhole Korte Leidsedwarsstraat 49, Grachtengordel south ☎020 620 8904, ⓦwaterhole.nl; map p.65. Late-night bar with live music every night, ranging from punk and rock to jazz and blues. It's popular for its regular Monday "new bands" sessions, which attract a raucous but friendly crowd, and for its pool table and cheap beer. Mon–Thurs & Sun noon–3am, Fri & Sat noon–4am.

Winston International Warmoesstraat 129, Old Centre ☎020 623 1380, ⓦwinston.nl; map p.34. Part of the arty *Winston* hotel (see page 147), this adventurous small venue attracts an eclectic crowd and offers a mix of live bands, electro, drum'n'bass and cheesy pop nights. Mon–Thurs & Sun 10pm–3am, Fri & Sat 10pm–4am.

JAZZ, BLUES AND LATIN VENUES

For **jazz** fans, Amsterdam can be a treat. Ever since the 1940s and 1950s, when American jazz musicians began moving to Europe, the city has had a soft spot for freestyle form. Paris stole much of the limelight, but Chet Baker lived and died in Amsterdam, and he and any number of legendary jazzbos could once be found jamming into the

FOLK AND WORLD MUSIC

The Dutch **folk music** tradition is virtually extinct in Amsterdam, except for occasional performances. There are still one or two touring folk singers who perform traditional *smartlappen* (torch songs) at the Carré Theater (see page 185) and a few other sympathetic venues, but the best place to catch these traditional songs – a brash and sentimental adaptation of French *chanson* – is *Café Nol* (see page 177), in the heart of the Jordaan, where they made their name. More accessible is **world music**, for which there are several good venues, including the *Akhnaton* (see below) and the *Melkweg* (see page 181). The latter also doubles as a venue for the **Amsterdam Roots Festival** held in July (see page 182).

small hours at *Casablanca* on Zeedijk. Venues have changed a lot since then, varying from tiny bars staging everything from Dixieland to avant-garde, to the large, modern *Bimhuis* – the city's major jazz venue – which plays host to both international names and home-grown talent. Pianist Michiel Borstlap, cellist Ernst Reijseger and sought-after percussionist Han Bennink – member of the acclaimed contemporary jazz collective, ICP – are among the **Dutch musicians** you might come across, and they're well worth catching if you get the chance. The **jazz season** runs from September to July, with concerts and festivals held all over the country, with the North Sea Jazz Festival (see box) a highlight. The Dutch connection with **Suriname** – a former colony tucked in between Venezuela and Brazil – means that there's a sizeable **Latin American** community in the city, and plenty of authentic salsa and other Latin sounds to be discovered; the best venue for this type of music is the *Akhnaton*. The *Melkweg* (see page 181) and the *Paradiso* (see page 181) put on occasional salsa nights.

Akhnaton Nieuwezijds Kolk 25, Old Centre ☎ 020 624 3396, Ⓦ akhnaton.nl; map p.34. This crowded, lively "Centre for World Culture" is your best bet for Latin music, hosting a wide-ranging programme of events from salsa nights to Turkish dance parties. Daily from noon.

Bimhuis Piet Heinkade 3, eastern docklands ☎ 020 788 2150, Ⓦ bimhuis.nl; map p.97. The city's premier jazz and improvised music venue is located right next to the Muziekgebouw, beside the River IJ to the east of Centraal Station. There are gigs from Dutch and international artists throughout the week, as well as jam sessions and workshops, plus a bar and restaurant for concertgoers, with pleasant views over the river. You get a 25 percent discount on tickets with the I amsterdam card. Mon–Thurs & Sun 6.30pm–1am, Fri & Sat 6.30pm–3am.

Bourbon Street Leidsekruisstraat 6–8, Grachtengordel south ☎ 020 623 3440, Ⓦ bourbonstreet.nl; map p.65. Friendly bar with a relaxed atmosphere, walls covered with memorabilia, and quality blues and jazz played nightly – and it's free before 11pm. Daily 10pm–3am.

Café Alto Korte Leidsedwarsstraat 115, Grachtengordel south ☎ 020 626 3249, Ⓦ jazz-cafe-alto.nl; map p.65. It's worth hunting out this legendary little jazz bar just off Leidseplein for its quality modern jazz every night; though slightly cramped, it's big on atmosphere. Entry is free, and you don't have to buy a beer to hang out and watch the band. Live jazz every night from 9pm.

Casablanca Zeedijk 26e, Old Centre ☎ 020 776 7407, Ⓦ cafecasablanca.nl; map p.34. When it's not putting on variety and cabaret shows, this venerable old-timer hosts live jazz most nights of the week. Mon–Sat 8pm–3am.

De Engelbewaarder Kloveniersburgwal 59, Old Centre ☎ 020 625 3772, Ⓦ cafe-de-engelbewaarder.nl; map p.34. This literary café (see page 175) hosts excellent live jazz sessions every Sun afternoon (4.30–7pm), except July and August. Mon–Thurs 10am–1am, Fri & Sat 10am–3am, Sun noon–1am.

Kapitein Zeppos Gebed Zonder End 5, Old Centre ☎ 020 624 2057, Ⓦ zeppos.nl; map p.34. This hangout is tucked away down a tiny street off Grimburgwal and is very easy to miss. It's a live music bar and a restaurant, which boasts a theatricality worthy of its place at the top end of Amsterdam's small theatre district. Mon–Thurs 11am–1am, Fri & Sat noon–3am, Sun noon–1am.

Maloe Melo Lijnbaansgracht 163, Jordaan ☎ 020 420 4592, Ⓦ www.maloemelo.com; map p.75. You can catch lively local blues acts every day of the week in the small back room of this dimly lit, low-ceilinged bar. Mon–Thurs & Sun 9pm–3am, Fri & Sat 9pm–4am.

11

JAZZ FESTIVALS

The Netherlands boasts one of the best jazz festivals in the world, the **North Sea Jazz Festival** (Ⓦ northseajazz.com), held in July at the Ahoy arena in Rotterdam. Comprising three days and nights of continuous jazz on fourteen stages, the event involves around 1200 musicians, among them world-class performers. **Tickets** cost from €79 a day, with supplements for the big names.

Arts and culture

Amsterdam is at the cutting edge of the arts scene, with an impressive roster of concerts and shows organized year-round, plus some world-class festivals and offbeat fringe events. Lovers of the performing arts are particularly well catered for, with venues such as the state-of-the-art Muziekgebouw aan't IJ and the prestigious Concertgebouw top of the list, not to mention an array of concert halls, theatres and churches hosting all manner of cultural happenings, from modern dance to stand-up comedy. Film-lovers are also in for a treat, with venues running the gamut from handsome Art Deco cinemas to the cutting-edge EYE Filmmuseum across the IJ. And with opportunities to snap up discount tickets readily available, there's nothing to stop even those on the tightest of budgets enjoying the city's arts scene.

ESSENTIALS

Discounts and entertainment passes If you're under 30 and plan to take in a few events, you might want to buy a Cultureel Jongeren Passport (CJP; ⓦcjp.nl), which costs €17.50 and gets you reductions on entry to theatres, concerts and *filmhuizen*, and can be bought online. Aside from CJP cardholders, the only people generally eligible for discounts at cultural events and venues are students and over-65s (though most places will only accept Dutch ID).

Listings information The quickest way to find up-to-date listings of events is to visit ⓦiamsterdam.com. Alternatively, the I amsterdam store inside the IJ-hal (see page 30) and I amsterdam visitor centres (see page 30) have information about what's on, as well as tickets and

listings magazines. You can pick up a copy of the excellent English-language *I amsterdam Magazine*, published every two months, from visitor centres too (€4.95), as well as free copies of *Uitkrant*, which has comprehensive listings of all concerts, festivals and theatre events, but is only published in Dutch. You could also try the Wednesday entertainment supplement of the daily newspaper *Het Parool*.

Tickets Tickets for most concerts and events can be bought from the I amsterdam visitor centres (see page 30). The Last Minute Ticket Shop (ⓦlastminuteticketshop.nl) sells half-price seats from 10am on the day of the performance. You can buy tickets from the Stadsschouwburg (see page 186) and the Bibliotheek (see page 98).

CLASSICAL AND OPERA

There's no shortage of **classical music** concerts in Amsterdam, with two major orchestras based in the city. The **Royal Concertgebouw Orchestra** remains one of the most dynamic in the world, and occupies one of the finest concert halls to boot. The other resident orchestra is the **Netherlands Philharmonic**, also based in the Concertgebouw. Among visiting orchestras, the Rotterdam Philharmonic has a world-class reputation, as does the Radio Philharmonic Orchestra, based in Hilversum outside Amsterdam. As well as the main concert halls, a number of churches host occasional performances of classical and chamber music at very reasonable prices. Some are listed below, but you could also try the Nieuwe Kerk on the Dam, the Westerkerk, the Noorderkerk, the Mozes en Aaronkerk on Waterlooplein and the tiny Amstelkerk on Kerkstraat. Visiting companies perform at the Stadsschouwburg, the Carré Theater and the Nationale Opera & Ballet. **Tickets** aren't as expensive as in some European cities, starting from as little as €7.50 for matinee concerts, rising to €70 for big-name performers. As far as **contemporary classical music** goes, the Muziekgebouw aan't IJ is the city's leading showcase for musicians from all over the world. Local talent is headed by the Asko ensemble, as well as the Nieuw Ensemble. Look out for the Grachtenfestival, when classical music is performed from the city's canals (see page 220).

VENUES

Beurs van Berlage Damrak 243, Old Centre ⓣ020 530 4141, ⓦbeursvanberlage.com. The splendid interior of the former stock exchange is the setting for regular exhibitions and concerts, though nowadays it's used most for conferences. The resident Netherlands Philharmonic rehearse in the huge Amvest Zaal, the former Corn Exchange Hall, a glassed-in pavilion.

Carré Theater Amstel 115–125, Grachtengordel south ⓣ0900 252 5255, ⓦcarre.nl. This splendid late

nineteenth-century structure (originally built for a circus) represents the ultimate venue for Dutch folk artists, and hosts all kinds of international performances: anything from Antony and the Johnsons to *Carmen*, with reputable touring orchestras and opera companies in between.

Concertgebouw Concertgebouwplein 2–6, Museum Quarter ⓣ0900 671 8345, ⓦconcertgebouw.nl. Going to a concert at the Concertgebouw (see page 115), one of the most impressive-looking – and -sounding – venues in the city, is a great experience, especially when the Netherlands Philharmonic Orchestra are performing. The acoustics of the Grote Zaal (Great Hall) are unparalleled, while the smaller Kleine Zaal regularly hosts chamber concerts. Though both halls boast a star-studded international programme, prices are very reasonable, ranging from €23 to €50. Free 30min Wed lunchtime concerts are held from Sept to May (doors open 12.15pm; arrive early), and in July and Aug there's a heavily subsidized series of summer concerts.

Conservatorium Oosterdokskade 151, eastern docklands ⓣ020 527 7777, ⓦahk.nl. Students perform free classical recitals almost daily at the state-of-the-art Amsterdam School of the Arts. Check the website for details or call for times.

Engelse Kerk Begijnhof 48, Old Centre ⓣ020 672 2288, ⓦercadam.nl. The Engelse Kerk is the church with the biggest programme: three to four performances a week. Tickets are available from the church 30min before the start of the performance. Check the website for details.

Marionetten Theater Nieuwe Jonkerstraat 8, Old Centre ⓣ020 620 8027, ⓦmarionettentheater.nl. This puppet theatre maintains an old European tradition with its performances of operas by Mozart and Offenbach. Although they tour the Netherlands and the rest of Europe for most of the year, the wooden marionettes return to Amsterdam in spring and Oct, and at Christmas. Call for details of performances, and to find out about their opera dinners.

Muziekgebouw aan't IJ Piet Heinkade 1, eastern docklands ⓣ020 788 2000, ⓦmuziekgebouw.nl. East

12

CLASSICAL MUSIC FESTIVALS

By far the most prestigious multi-venue Dutch festival for contemporary classical music is the annual **Holland Festival** (hollandfestival.nl) in June, which takes place in major venues around Amsterdam and attracts the best of the country's mainstream and fringe performers in all areas of the arts, as well as an exciting international line-up. Otherwise, one of the more interesting, music-oriented events is the popular **Grachtenfestival** (grachtenfestival.nl), held in mid-August, a ten-day classical music extravaganza that concludes with a piano recital on a floating stage outside the *Pulitzer* hotel on Prinsengracht, with the whole area floodlit and filled with small boats; it can be a wonderfully atmospheric evening. In early September, Utrecht holds **Gaudeamus Muziekweek** (gaudeamus.nl), a forum for debate and premiere performances of cutting-edge contemporary music.

12

of Centraal Station, the Muziekgebouw (see page 100) – Amsterdam's newest concert hall for over a hundred years – has given new impetus to the redevelopment going on along the IJ, with two medium-sized concert halls, state-of-the-art acoustics, and a café and bar. Its top-quality programme of contemporary music, opera and orchestral music draws a highbrow crowd to this part of town, but it's worth a visit for the building alone; the café offers great views over the water. The same development also includes the Bimhuis (see page 183). 25 percent discount on tickets with the I amsterdam card. Box office Mon–Sat noon–6pm.

Nationale Opera & Ballet Amstel 3, old Jewish quarter ☎020 625 5455, ⓦoperaballet.nl. The Nationale Opera & Ballet joined forces with the closely associated Muziektheater in 2013, and the €150 million complex, which includes the city hall, now offers the fullest, and most reasonably priced, programme of opera in Amsterdam; not surprisingly, tickets go very quickly. 25 percent discount on tickets with the I amsterdam card.

Oude Kerk Oudekerksplein 23, Old Centre ☎020 625 8284, ⓦoudekerk.nl. In the heart of the Red Light District, this church is the oldest building in Amsterdam and hosts carillon recitals – sit outside and listen for free.

Paradiso Weteringschans 6–8, Grachtengordel south ☎020 626 4521, ⓦparadiso.nl. This converted church, located near the Leidseplein, though usually a pop and rock venue (see page 181), has also been known to host classical concerts.

Stadsschouwburg Leidseplein 26, Grachtengordel south ☎020 624 2311, ⓦstadsschouwburgamsterdam. nl. Connected to the *Melkweg*, the municipal theatre stages significant opera, theatre and dance performances. Thurs performances are subtitled in English. Box office Mon–Sat noon–6pm.

Waalse Kerk Oudezijds Achterburgwal, Walenpleintje 159, Old Centre ☎020 623 2074, ⓦdewaalsekerk. nl. This church puts on weekend afternoon and evening concerts of early classical and chamber music.

THEATRE, CABARET AND COMEDY

Surprisingly for a city that functions so much in English, there is next to no **English-language drama** to be seen in Amsterdam, though a handful of amateur companies put on English productions in summer, and there are also occasional performances by touring groups at the theatres listed below and at other venues dotted around town. English-language **comedy** and **cabaret**, on the other hand, has gained more ground, spearheaded by the resident and extremely successful "Boom Chicago" comedy company. During the summer, a number of small venues host mini-seasons of English-language stand-up comedy and cabaret, featuring touring British performers and tourist-geared material. Most of Amsterdam's **larger theatre companies** concentrate either on foreign works in translation or Dutch-language theatre, neither of which is likely to be terribly interesting for the non-Dutch speaker.

ARTS AND THEATRE FESTIVALS

The main event to watch out for, apart from the mainstream Holland Festival (see page 186), is July's **Over Het IJ Festival** (☎020 492 2229, ⓦoverhetij.nl), a showcase for all kinds of performance art, often in outdoor locations in the NDSM district; the involvement of many interesting small companies pushes the standard of the average production well above that of the usual fringe festival acts. In June, the **International Theatre School Festival** sees eight theatres – several on Nes, a tiny alley running from the Dam parallel to Rokin – host productions by local and international theatre schools. Discounted tickets can be bought online – check ⓦitsfestival.com.

DANCE FESTIVALS

Julidans (Ⓦ julidans.nl) is a twelve-day festival dedicated to contemporary dance, hosting both established and up-and-coming choreographers. It's held at numerous locations around the Leidseplein, with the Stadsschouwburg as its main focus. The Hague – just a 45-minute train ride from Centraal Station – hosts two biennial dance festivals: the **Holland Dance Festival** (Ⓦ holland-dance.com; next in 2020), which attracts leading international companies; and **CaDance** (Ⓦ cadance.nl; next in 2019), which premieres contemporary dance works.

However, there are some **avant-garde** theatre groups whose work often relies on visual rather than verbal impact. Look out also for puppetry performances at the Marionetten Theater (see page 185).

MAJOR VENUES AND ACTS

De Balie Kleine-Gartmanplantsoen 10, Grachtengordel south ☎ 020 553 5151, Ⓦ debalie.nl. This multimedia centre for arts and culture located off the Leidseplein often plays host to drama, debates, international symposia and the like, sometimes in conjunction with the *Paradiso* next door. It also has a lovely, roomy, mezzanine bar.

★ **Boom Chicago** Rozengracht 117, Jordaan ☎ 020 217 0400, Ⓦ boomchicago.nl. Something of a phenomenon in Amsterdam, this rapid-fire improv comedy troupe hailing from America performs nightly at the Rozentheater to crowds of both tourists and locals, and receives rave reviews. Inexpensive food, cocktails and beer served in pitchers. You get 25 percent discount on tickets with the I amsterdam card.

Carré Theater Amstel 115–125, Grachtengordel south ☎ 0900 252 5255, Ⓦ carre.nl. A chunky old building on the eastern bank of the Amstel which, aside from its folk associations, hosts all kinds of top international acts, with an emphasis on hit musicals.

Comedy Café IJdok 89, Haarlem ☎ 020 722 0827, Ⓦ comedycafe.nl. The Comedy Café puts on stand-up four nights a week, with comedy in Dutch and English. Wednesday is open-mic night – a good chance to spot new talent.

De Kleine Komedie Amstel 56–58, Grachtengordel south ☎ 020 624 0534, Ⓦ dekleinekomedie.nl. One of Amsterdam's oldest theatres, established in 1786, De Kleine Komedie occasionally hosts a few English-language comedy shows.

★ **Melkweg** Lijnbaansgracht 234a, Grachtengordel south ☎ 020 531 8181, Ⓦ melkweg.nl. At the centre of the city's cultural scene, this is often the first-choice venue for foreign touring theatre companies. There's also a café-restaurant (under renovation at the time of writing).

Stadsschouwburg Leidseplein 26, Grachtengordel south ☎ 020 624 2311, Ⓦ stadsschouwburgamsterdam.nl. The Stadsschouwburg occasionally hosts productions on tour from London or New York.

AVANT-GARDE VENUES

De Brakke Grond Nes 45, Old Centre ☎ 020 622 9014, Ⓦ brakkegrond.nl. One of the theatres to host the International Theatre School Festival (see page 186), De Brakke Grond shows mainly Flemish productions.

DasArts Jodenbreestraat 3, Center ☎ 020 527 7837, Ⓦ atd.ahk.nl. This student theatre puts on international workshops and performances.

Felix Meritis Keizersgracht 324, Grachtengordel west ☎ 020 627 9477, Ⓦ felixmeritis.nl. This eighteenth-century centre for arts and sciences hosts theatre, debate, music and visual arts events; it's been under renovation and is set to reopen in autumn 2018.

Mezrab Veemkade 576, eastern docklands ☎ 020 419 3368, Ⓦ mezrab.nl. This cultural centre hosts storytelling nights on Fri evenings, with all performances in English; comedy nights take place on the first Fri of the month. Comedy nights and storytelling sessions are free, but donations are welcome.

12

DANCE

Amsterdam's largest and most prestigious dance company is the **Dutch National Ballet** (Ⓦ operaballet.nl). For fans of **folk dancing**, the excellent Internationaal Danstheater (Ⓦ intdanstheater.net) is based in the city. Among the most innovative of the other leading **Dutch dance companies** that tour Amsterdam – or visit nearby Rotterdam and The Hague – is the Nederlands Dans Theater (Ⓦ ndt.nl), with a repertoire of ballet and modern dance. Amsterdam also has many experimental dance groups, and small productions staged by dance students abound – look out for performances by the Dansmakers. Modern dance and movement theatre companies from outside Amsterdam that often perform in the city include the Dance Works Rotterdam (Ⓦ danceworksrotterdam.nl) and Introdans (Ⓦ introdans.nl).

VENUES AND ACTS

Dansmakers Gedempt Hamerkanaal 203–205, Amsterdam Noord ☎ 020 689 1789, Ⓦ dansmakers.nl. A dance company staging productions by young, up-and-coming choreographers.

Internationaal Danstheater Kloveniersburgwal 87, Old Centre ☎ 020 623 9112, Ⓦ intdanstheater.net. Folk dancing from around the world, featuring a number of international choreographers.

FILM FESTIVALS

Amsterdam's flagship film event is the excellent **International Documentary Film Festival** in November (⊛idfa.nl), when up to three hundred documentaries from all over the world are shown over ten days in various locations around Rembrandtplein, making it the largest documentary festival in the world. The **Netherlands Film Festival** (⊛filmfestival.nl), held each September in Utrecht, just thirty minutes by train from Amsterdam, features home-grown productions only. There are also numerous local, albeit less famous, film festivals such as the open-air Pluk de Nacht (Seize the Night), World Cinema Amsterdam and On the Roof Film Festival – check ⊛iamsterdam.com for details.

★**Melkweg** Lijnbaansgracht 234a, Grachtengordel south ☎020 531 8181, ⊛melkweg.nl. Upstairs in this pop and world music venue, there's a little theatre that puts on modern dance productions.
Nationale Opera & Ballet Amstel 3, old Jewish quarter ☎020 625 5455, ⊛operaballet.nl. Home of the esteemed National Ballet, but with a third of its dance schedule given over to big-name international companies to put on their own performances.
Stadsschouwburg Leidseplein 26, Grachtengordel south ☎020 624 2311, ⊛stadsschouwburgamsterdam. nl. This theatre is the principal host of the Julidans dance festival in July (see page 187), and also stages a number of regular productions.

FILM

All foreign **films** playing in Amsterdam (Dutch movies are something of a rarity) are shown in their **original language** and subtitled in Dutch. If you're interested in seeing a non-English-language movie, check with the venue whether it's been **subtitled** in English (*Engels Ondertiteld*) before you go. Films are almost never dubbed into Dutch; if they are, *Nederlands Gesproken* will be printed in the listings. Check ⊛filmladder.nl for **listings**; weekly programmes change on Thursdays.

CINEMAS

De Balie Kleine-Gartmanplantsoen 10, Grachtengordel south ☎020 553 5100, ⊛debalie.nl. Cultural centre for theatre, politics, film and new media, showing movies a few evenings of the week, often with English subtitles.
Cavia Van Hallstraat 52, western docklands ☎020 681 1419, ⊛filmhuiscavia.nl. This is one of the best of the small *filmhuizen*, with an eclectic and noncommercial programme of international and arthouse movies.
Cinecenter Lijnbaansgracht 236, Grachtengordel south ☎020 623 6615, ⊛cinecenter.nl. Opposite the *Melkweg*, this cinema shows independent and quality commercial films, the majority originating from non-English-speaking countries, shown with an interval.
★**EYE Filmmuseum** IJpromenade 1, Amsterdam Noord ☎020 589 1400, ⊛eyefilm.nl. The stunning Eye Filmmuseum, across the water from Centraal Station, screens a mixture of blockbusters and arthouse films every other day or so.
Filmhallen Hannie Dankbaarpassage 12, De Hallen, Amsterdam West ☎020 820 8122, ⊛filmhallen.nl. Part of the 1902 converted tram depot housing the *Foodhallen* (see page 170) and *De Hallen* hotel (see page 149), this stylish cinema screens the latest films.

Kriterion Roeterstraat 170, Plantage ☎020 623 1708, ⊛kriterion.nl; Metro Weesperplein. Cool duplex cinema showing arthouse and quality commercial films, with late-night cult favourites. There's a bar attached.
Melkweg Lijnbaansgracht 234a, Grachtengordel south ☎020 531 8181, ⊛melkweg.nl. As well as music, art and dance, the *Melkweg* manages to maintain a consistently good monthly film programme, ranging from mainstream fodder through to more obscure imports.
The Movies Haarlemmerdijk 161–163, western docklands ☎020 638 6016, ⊛themovies.nl. A beautiful Art Deco cinema, and a charming setting for independent films. It's worth visiting for the bar and restaurant alone, fully restored to their original appearance. "Filmdinner" nights include a three-course meal and film from €35, and there are late showings (11.45pm) of classic or cult films at weekends.
De Munt Vijzelstraat 15, Grachtengordel south ☎0900 1458, ⊛pathe.nl/bioscoop/demunt. This huge, multi-screen cinema has up to six showings a day of mainstream films, as well as a few home-grown productions.
Pathé Cinemas Boulevard 600, Amsterdam Oost ☎0900 1458, ⊛pathe.nl/bioscoop/arena; metro or train to Bijlmer station. With multiple screens (including IMAX), this is the largest cinema in Amsterdam, located right next to the Johan Cruijff Arena.
Rialto Ceintuurbaan 338, De Pijp ☎020 662 3488, ⊛rialtofilm.nl. The only fully authentic art-house cinema in Amsterdam, showing an enormously varied programme of European and world movies supplemented by themed series and classics. The cinema boasts a large café, and the place has a friendly, welcoming atmosphere.
Studio/K Timorplein 62, eastern docklands ☎020 692 0422, ⊛studio-k.nu. Studio/K is a cultural hub run

12

solely by students and containing a small cinema showing mainstream and arthouse films.

Tuschinski Theater Reguliersbreestraat 26–34, Grachtengordel south ☎0900 1458, ⊛pathe.nl/bioscoop/tuschinski. This fabulous Art Deco theatre shows the artier offerings from the mainstream list.

De Uitkijk Prinsengracht 452, Grachtengordel south ☎020 223 2416, ⊛uitkijk.nl. Pronounced "out-kike", the oldest cinema in the Netherlands is set in a converted canal house with no bar, no ice cream and no popcorn – but low prices. It also shows popular movies for months on end.

12

AMSTERDAM FRIDGE MAGNETS

Shops and markets

If you're looking for a souvenir of Amsterdam to remind you of your trip, you'll be spoilt for choice: this is a city geared up for shopping, selling everything from bikes to antiques, and from tulip bulbs to Dutch cheese. There are, of course, the obligatory malls and chain stores, but where the city scores is in its excellent, unusual speciality shops, almost always owned by a family or individual. Amsterdam's compactness also works in the shopper's favour: whereas in other cities you can spend days trudging far-flung neighbourhoods in search of something interesting, here you'll find every kind of store packed into a relatively small area. An array of vibrant street markets, selling organic produce, bric-a-brac and everything in between, completes the picture.

ANTIQUES

Affaire D'Eau Haarlemmerdijk 148–150, western docklands ☎020 422 0411, ⓦaffairedeau.com; map p.75. Antique bathtubs, taps, sinks and toilets, as well as lamps, mirrors and posh soaps. Mon–Sat 10.30am–6pm.

Antiekcentrum Amsterdam Elandsgracht 109, Jordaan ☎020 624 9038, ⓦantiekcentrumamsterdam. nl; map p.75. This indoor antiques centre is the largest in the Netherlands, with more than fifty dealers and an enormous choice, with everything from vintage watches to 1960s ceramics. Mon & Wed–Fri 11am–6pm, Sat & Sun 11am–5pm.

Eduard Kramer Prinsengracht 807, Grachtengordel south ☎020 626 1116, ⓦantique-tileshop.nl; map p.65. A wonderful selection of Dutch tiles from the fifteenth century onwards; there's online ordering too. Mon 11am–6pm, Tues–Sat 10am–6pm, Sun 1–6pm.

Harrie van Gennip Govert Flinckstraat 402, De Pijp ☎020 679 3025, ⓦwww.harrievangennip.nl; map p.107. A huge collection of old and antique stoves from all parts of Europe, lovingly restored and all in working order. Thurs 1–6pm, Sat 11am–4pm.

Jan Beekhuizen Nieuwe Spiegelstraat 49, Grachtengordel south ☎020 626 3912, ⓦjanbeekhuizen. nl; map p.65. In the heart of Amsterdam's antiques quarter, this shop sells European pewter from the fifteenth to the nineteenth centuries. Mon–Sat 10am–6pm.

Neef Louis Papaverweg 46–48, Amsterdam Noord ☎020 486 9354, ⓦneeflouis.nl; map p.103. Jam-packed with good-quality vintage signs, sofas, furniture, vases and much more, this warehouse is worth the ferry trip across the water. It sits opposite the equally good Van Dijk & Ko (see below). Tues–Fri 10am–6pm, Sat 10am–5pm.

Thom & Lenny Nelis Keizersgracht 541, Grachtengordel south ☎062 184 1710, ⓦnelisantiques.com; map p.65. Fascinating collection of medical antiques, spectacles, tribal artefacts and other curiosities; some of the jars would make unusual vases. Thurs–Sat 11am–5pm, or by appointment.

★ **Van Dijk & Ko** Papaverweg 46, Amsterdam Noord ☎020 684 1524, ⓦvandijkenko.nl; map p.103. Opposite Neef Louis (see above), this antiques warehouse is a treasure-trove of reasonably priced vintage furniture, books, school supplies, glassware – you name it – and they deliver worldwide. If you've worked up an appetite rummaging for bargains, try the bohemian café at the end of the cul-de-sac. Tues–Sat 10am–6pm, Sun noon–6pm.

Van Hier tot Tokio Prinsengracht 262, Jordaan ☎020 428 2682, ⓦjapaneseantiquestore.com; map p.75. This split-level shop has a good selection of modern and antique Japanese furniture, crafts, kimonos and the like. Tues–Sat 11am–6pm, Sun–Mon 11am–5pm.

WHERE TO SHOP

The busiest shopping districts in Amsterdam are in Grachtengordel west and the Old Centre. In the latter, the action is concentrated along **Damstraat**, **Nieuwendijk**, **Kalverstraat** and **Rokin**, running south and north of the Dam. These are home to high-street fashion shops and **Magna Plaza** (ⓦmagnaplaza.nl), a mainstream department store; crowded Saturday afternoons here can be grim.

Grachtengordel west is altogether more appealing, especially the eclectic shops round the **Negen Straatjes** (Nine Little Streets; ⓦtheninestreets.com), clustered around Herengracht (see map, page 55). The nine streets concerned are bordered by Reestraat, Hartenstraat and Gasthuismolensteeg to the north and Runstraat, Huidenstraat and Wijdeheisteeg to the south. They're lined with upmarket boutiques and quirky clothing stores, and affordable antiques, art and homeware shops. **Haarlemmerstraat**, running west from Centraal Station in the Jordaan, is another street with appealing independently owned shops.

South of the Negen Straatjes, **Leidsestraat** offers a good selection of affordable designer clothes and shoe stores. Further into Grachtengordel south, pricier antiques – the cream of Amsterdam's renowned trade – can be found in the **Spiegelkwartier** along Nieuwe Spiegelstraat and Spiegelgracht, while in the Museum Quarter further south, **P.C. Hooftstraat**, **Van Baerlestraat** and **Cornelis Schuytstraat**, and, **Beethovenstraat** further south in the Nieuw Zuid, are excellent hunting grounds for designer clothes and upmarket ceramics, with top-notch confectioners and delicatessens into the bargain.

If you venture out to the Amsterdam West district, seek out the **De Hallen** complex (see page 170; ⓦdehallen-amsterdam.nl), which has a lovely covered arcade of independent shops selling clothes and knick-knacks.

ARTS AND CRAFTS

13

ART GALLERIES

Amsterdam has a small but thriving commercial art scene and some great private galleries, and these are well worth visiting either to check out their exhibitions or to buy some art.

Arti et Amicitae Rokin 112, Old Centre ☎ 020 624 5134, ⓦ arti.nl. Part of a private art academy, this is one of the city's most prestigious exhibition spaces, with a gallery at the top of a Berlage-designed staircase, usually given over to exhibitions of modern art in a variety of media. Tues–Sun noon–6pm.

Chiellerie Raamgracht 58, Old Centre ☎ 06 1474 0152, ⓦ amsterdampainter.tictail.com. Cutting-edge gallery off Kloveniers-burgwal that focuses on photography and has regular temporary exhibitions. Call for viewing.

FOAM Keizersgracht 609, Grachtengordel south ☎ 020 551 6500, ⓦ foam.org. One of the city's major exhibition spaces for photography, with regular large-scale exhibitions (entrance €11) and a small collection of material that's always on view. Mon–Wed, Sat & Sun 10am–6pm, Thurs & Fri 10am–9pm).

Huis Marseille Keizersgracht 401, Grachtengordel west ☎ 020 531 8989, ⓦ huismarseille.nl. The city's prime photography exhibition space, housed in a fabulous location in a restored, mid-seventeenth-century canal house that was once the home of a French merchant – hence the name. It hosts quarterly exhibitions, to which admission is usually around €8. Tues–Sun 11am–6pm.

Mokum Oudezijds Voorburgwal 334, Old Centre ☎ 020 624 3958, ⓦ galeriemokum.com. This historic Amsterdam gallery, named after the Jewish word for the city and a famous magical realist shop, exhibits both fantastical and modern realist works. Thurs–Sun noon–5pm.

Reflex Modern Art Gallery Weteringschans 79a, Grachtengordel south ☎ 020 627 2832, ⓦ reflex amsterdam.com. You'll always find something interesting in this gallery, which represents some big international names, most notably some of the artists of the Cobra school – Appel, Corneille and others. Tues–Sat 11am–6pm.

Torch Lauriergracht 94, Jordaan ☎ 020 626 0284, ⓦ torchgallery.com. One of the city's most thought-provoking contemporary galleries. Thurs–Sat noon–6pm.

W139 Warmoesstraat 139, Old Centre ☎ 020 622 9434, ⓦ w139.nl. Long-established yet ahead-of-the-curve art gallery located in the heart of Amsterdam that can always be relied upon to take a chance on new, up-and-coming artists. Daily noon–6pm.

ART SUPPLIES, CRAFTS AND GIFTS

Akkerman Langebrugsteeg 13, Old Centre ☎ 020 623 1649, ⓦ pwakkerman.nl; map p.34. The city's poshest pen shop, with an excellent selection of writing accessories. Mon–Fri 9.30am–6pm, Sat 10am–5pm, Sun 1–5pm (closed Sun July–Aug).

Art Unlimited Keizersgracht 510, Grachtengordel south ☎ 020 624 8419, ⓦ artunlimited.com; map p.65. Sprawling shop selling postcards, cards and posters, with excellent stock and all kinds of images: good for communiqués home that avoid windmills and clogs. Mon & Sun noon–6pm, Tues, Wed, Fri & Sat 10.15am–6pm, Thurs 10.15am–7pm.

Beadazzled Sarphatipark 6, De Pijp ☎ 020 673 4587, ⓦ beadazzled.nl; map p.107. Beads in all shapes and colours as well as bags, cheerfully decorated lamps and other accessories. Mon 1–6pm, Tues–Fri 10.30am–6pm, Sat 10.30am–5pm.

Blond Gerard Doustraat 69, De Pijp ☎ 020 428 4929, ⓦ blond-amsterdam.com; map p.107. Popular gift shop with a selection of hand-painted and personalized pottery, bed linen, towels and notepads, mainly in the colour pink. Mon noon–6pm, Tues–Fri 10am–6pm, Sat 10am–5pm.

Coppenhagen Rozengracht 54, Jordaan ☎ 020 624 3681, ⓦ coppenhagenbeads.nl; map p.75. The only thing you'll find in this shop is beads and beady accessories – including everything you need to make your own jewellery. Mon 1–6pm, Tues–Fri 10am–6pm, Sat 10am–5pm.

Posthumus Sint Luciensteeg 23, Old Centre ☎ 020 625 5812, ⓦ posthumuswinkel.nl; map p.34. A selection of upmarket stationery, cards and, best of all, hundreds of rubber stamps. Tues–Fri 10am–5.30pm, Sat 11am–5.30pm.

Van Beek Stadhouderskade 62–65, De Pijp ☎ 020 658 2222, ⓦ vanbeekart.nl; map p.107. Long-established outlet for every kind of high-quality art material you can imagine. Mon 1–6pm, Tues–Fri 9am–6pm, Sat 10am–5pm.

Van Ginkel Bilderdijkstraat 99, Amsterdam West ☎ 020 618 9827, ⓦ petervanginkel.nl; map p.75. Supplier of art materials, with an emphasis on print-making. Mon–Sat 10am–6pm.

BOOKS

Virtually all of Amsterdam's many **bookshops** stock at least a small selection of English-language books, though prices are always inflated (sometimes dramatically). The city is particularly strong on **secondhand and antiquarian** bookshops, where you can pick up classics and one-off literary finds.

GENERAL

★ **American Book Center** Spui 12, Old Centre ☎ 020 625 5537, ⓦ abc.nl; map p.34. This store has a vast stock of books in English, as well as lots of US magazines. Mon noon–8pm, Tues–Sat 10am–8pm, Sun 11am–6pm.

13

ON YOUR BIKE

While in Amsterdam you may want to buy a **bike**, but don't be tempted by anything you're offered on the street or in a bar – more often than not you'll end up with a stolen edition. Try instead the shops listed below, which sell, rent and repair bikes of all qualities; a well-worn boneshaker will set you back around €100, maybe less, while €150 and up should get you a fairly decent secondhand machine. To rent one you'll need to show ID and/or pay a €50 or €100 deposit, or leave a credit card.

MacBike De Ruijterkade 34B, Old Centre ☎020 624 8391, map p.34; Oosterdokskade 63A, eastern docklands ☎020 811 5110, map p.97; Waterlooplein 199, old Jewish quarter ☎020 428 7005, map p.83; Weteringschans 2 on the edge of Leidseplein, Grachtengordel south ☎020 528 7688, map p.65; ⓦmacbike.nl. Several locations of this well-established and very popular bike sales, rental and repair firm are dotted around town. They also organize city tours and rentals (see page 22). Daily 9am–8pm.

Rent a Bike Damstraat 20–22, Old Centre ☎020 625 5029, ⓦrentabike.nl; map p.34. Traditional Dutch bikes for sale, both used and new, as well as scooters, tandems and cargo bikes for rent. Daily 9am–6pm.

★**Athenaeum** Spui 14–16, Old Centre ☎020 514 1460, ⓦathenaeum.nl; map p.34. Perhaps the city's most appealing bookshop, and although it's relatively short on stuff in English, its array of books about Amsterdam is always current, and its selection of international newspapers and magazines one of the best in the city. Mon–Sat 9am–7pm, Sun 11am–6pm.

Martyrium Van Baerlestraat 170–172, Oud Zuid ☎020 673 2092, ⓦhetmartyrium.nl; map p.107. Good general bookshop with lots of material in English. Mon–Fri 9am–6pm, Sat 9am–5.30pm, Sun noon–5pm.

Scheltema Rokin 9–15, Old Centre ☎020 523 1411, ⓦscheltema.nl; map p.34. Amsterdam's biggest and arguably best bookshop, with six floors of absolutely everything (mostly in Dutch). Mon–Wed & Fri–Sun 11am–7pm, Thurs 11am–9pm.

Waterstones Kalverstraat 152, Old Centre ☎020 638 3821, ⓦwaterstones.com; map p.34. Amsterdam branch of the UK high-street chain, with four floors of books and magazines. A predictable selection, but prices are sometimes cheaper here than elsewhere. Mon 10am–6.30pm, Tues–Wed 9.30am–6.30pm, Thurs 9.30am–9pm, Fri & Sat 10am–7pm, Sun 11am–6.30pm.

SECONDHAND AND ANTIQUARIAN

A. Kok Oude Hoogstraat 14–18, Old Centre ☎020 623 1191, ⓦkok.nvva.nl; map p.34. Vintage and secondhand bookstore, especially strong on prints and maps. Mon–Fri 9.30am–6pm, Sat 9.30am–5pm.

Boekenmarkt Spui, Old Centre ☎065 106 9630, ⓦdeboekenmarktophetspui.nl; map p.34. Open-air book market on the Spui, selling lots of secondhand books, as well as prints and posters. Fri 10am–6pm.

The Book Exchange Kloveniersburgwal 58, Old Centre ☎020 626 6266, ⓦbookexchange.nl; map p.34. Large and rambling old shop headed up by a friendly American proprietor, and a large selection of secondhand books published in English. Mon–Sat 10am–6pm, Sun 11.30am–4pm.

Brinkman Singel 319, Old Centre ☎020 623 8353, ⓦantiquariaatbrinkman.nl; map p.34. A stalwart of the Amsterdam antiquarian book trade, *Brinkman* has occupied the same premises for over fifty years, and has lots of good stuff – much of it in English. Tues–Fri 10am–5pm, Sat 11am–5pm.

Egidius Haarlemmerstraat 87, western docklands ☎020 624 3255; ⓦbit.ly/Egidius; map p.75. A good selection of literature, art and poetry, plus a gallery selling lithographs. Tues–Fri 11am–6pm, Sat 11am–5pm.

Fenix Frans Frans Halsstraat 88, De Pijp ☎020 673 9459, ⓦfenixbooks.com; map p.107. General secondhand bookstore, with piles of stuff stacked up on the floor. There's a good range of books in English, with an emphasis on Celtic literature, history and culture. Mon–Sat noon–6pm.

Oudemanhuispoort Book Market Oudemanhuispoort, Old Centre; map p.34. This lovely open-air book market, set up underneath the covered walkways of historic university buildings, sells a mix of secondhand books, sheet music and prints. Mon–Sat 8am–5pm.

SPECIALIST

Boekholt A la Carte Ferdinand Bolstraat 147-HDe Pijp ☎020 625 0679, ⓦboekholtalacarte.nl; map p.107. Large and friendly travel bookshop, with lots of English-language titles. They have a good selection of maps too. Mon–Sat 10am–6pm, Sun noon–5pm.

Architectura & Natura Leliegracht 22h, Grachtengordel west ☎020 623 6186, ⓦarchitectura.nl; map p.55. An eclectic collection of books on architecture and interior design, with many English titles. Mon noon–5pm, Tues–Fri 10.30am–6.30pm, Sat 10.30am–5pm, Sun noon–5pm.

13

★ **Boekie Woekie** Berenstraat 16, Grachtengordel west ☎020 639 0507, ⓦboekiewoekie.com; map p.55. Books on – and by – leading Dutch artists and graphic designers. Entertaining postcards too. Daily noon–6pm.

Cine-Qua-Non Houtkopersdwarsstraat 6 ☎06 440 34480, ⓦcinequanon.eu; map p.34. Film and cinema books, posters and other movie paraphernalia.

Evenaar Korsjespoortsteeg 2, Grachtengordel west ☎020 624 6289, ⓦevenaar.net; map p.55. This travel bookshop concentrates less on guidebooks and more on travel literature, of which it has an exemplary selection in both English and Dutch. Tues–Sat noon–6pm.

Fort van Sjakoo Jodenbreestraat 24, old Jewish quarter ☎020 625 8979, ⓦsjakoo.nl; map p.83. Anarchist bookshop stocking a wide selection of radical political publications. Mon–Fri 11am–6pm, Sat 11am–5pm.

Gojoker Waalstraat 26, ☎020 620 5078; map p.124. Classic and contemporary comic store, with some American publications too. Tues–Sun noon–7pm.

Lambiek Koningsstraat 27 ☎020 626 7543, ⓦlambiek. net; map p.65. The city's largest and best comic bookshop and gallery, opened in 1968 and still going strong, with international stock. Their website has an excellent "comiclopedia". Mon–Fri 11am–6pm, Sat 11am–5pm, Sun 1–5pm.

Mendo Berenstraat 11, Grachtengordel west ☎020 612 1216, ⓦmendo.nl; map p.55. Stylish, à la mode bookshop specializing in architecture, art, interior design, photography and graphic design. Mon–Fri 10am–5pm.

★ **Pied-à-Terre** Overtoom 135–137, Vondelpark ☎020 308 0080, ⓦpiedaterre.nl; map p.116. The city's best travel bookshop, with knowledgeable staff and a huge selection of books and maps. They also sell hiking maps for Holland and beyond, mostly in English. Mon 1–6pm, Tues, Wed & Fri 10am–6pm, Thurs 10am–9pm, Sat 10am–5pm.

Robert Premsela Van Baerlestraat 78, Museum Quarter ☎020 662 4266, ⓦpremsela.nl; map p.107. Great art and architecture book specialist, with lots of stuff in English, plus books on photography and travel. Mon noon–6pm, Tues–Fri 10am–6pm, Sat 10am–5pm, Sun noon–5pm.

De Roos P.C. Hooftstraat 183, Vondelpark ☎020 689 0081, ⓦroos.nl; map p.116. New Age bookshop with a wide selection of esoteric books, crystals, yoga accessories and alternative remedies. Part of a larger centre with a café and training courses. Mon–Fri 8am–10pm, Sat & Sun 8am–5.30pm.

Xantippe Unlimited Prinsengracht 290, Jordaan ☎020 623 5854, ⓦxantippe.nl; map p.75. Amsterdam's foremost women's bookshop, with a wide selection of new feminist titles in English, plus literature, biographies, cookbooks, children's books and postcards. Tues–Sat 10am–6pm, Sun noon–5pm.

CLOTHES, SHOES AND ACCESSORIES

In many ways, Amsterdam is an ideal place for **clothes shopping**; prices aren't too high and the city is sufficiently compact to save lots of shoe leather. On the other hand, don't expect the huge choice of, say, London or New York. There's a fair range of **secondhand clothing shops** dotted around the Jordaan, on **Oude and Nieuwe Hoogstraat**, and along the Negen Straatjes, the narrow streets that connect the major canals in **Grachtengordel west**. The **Waterlooplein** flea market (see page 200) is also a great hunting ground for vintage bargains. For children's clothes, see Chapter 15.

HIGH-STREET AND DESIGNER

Agnès B Rokin 126, Old Centre ☎020 627 1465, ⓦbit. ly/AgnesAmsterdam; map p.34. Amsterdam city-centre shop of the chic French designer who produces relaxed yet chic pieces for everyday wear. Mon 1–6.30pm, Tues–Sat 10am–7pm, Sun 12.30–5.30pm.

Body Sox Leidsestraat 35, Grachtengordel south ☎020 422 3544, ⓦbodysox.nl; map p.65. Socks, tights and stockings in every conceivable colour and design. Mon 10am–6pm, Tues, Wed, Fri 9.30am–6pm, Thurs 9.30am–9pm, Sat 9.30am–5pm, Sun noon–5pm.

Cora Kemperman website only ⓦcorakemperman. shop. A Dutch brand producing a line of well-made,

elegant, relaxed designer womenswear that won't break the bank.

★ **Denham** Hobbemastraat 8, Grachtengordel west ☎020 681 3524, ⓦdenhamthejeanmaker.com; map p.55. Founded in Amsterdam in 2008 by Englishman Jason Denham, whose jean and clothing designs are now gaining worldwide recognition. Also at Prinsengracht 531 (☎020 303 2825). Mon noon–7pm, Tues–Fri 10am–7pm, Thurs 8am–8pm, Sat 10am–6pm, Sun noon–6pm.

HoodLamb website only ⓦhoodlamb.com. Not all hemp is like sackcloth – check out the silky hemp shirts, fleeces and jeans in this clothing store that sells nothing but clothes made from the stuff.

I Love Vintage Prinsengracht 201, Grachtengordel west ⓦilovevintage.nl; map p.55. This highly popular online shop now has its own physical store, with a select collection of vintage-inspired clothes, lingerie and accessories. Mon–Sat 11am–7pm, Sun noon–5pm.

Laundry Industry Sint Luciënsteeg 18 ☎020 362 1832, ⓦlaundryindustry.com; map p.34. This high-end Dutch clothing brand does chic, youthful clothes for women and men, with jumpers around the €150 mark. Mon & Sun noon–6.30pm, Tues–Sat 11am–6.30pm.

Local Service Keizersgracht 400, Grachtengordel west ☎020 626 6840; map p.55. Stocks expensive men's and

EUROPE'S BEST DENIM

If you're after a new pair of jeans, you've come to the right place: Amsterdam excels in **denim**. G-Star and Tommy Hilfiger all have their European headquarters here, and a Denim City workshop – dedicated to denim education and research – has been established in the De Hallen complex (see page 170). And with home-grown brands like Denham (see above) making a splash on the fashion scene, and the Amsterdam Denim Days festival (ⓦamsterdamdenimdays.com) held annually, the city is well on its way to becoming the denim capital of Europe.

women's designer labels, with an ultra-trendy, alternative twist. Mon 1–6pm, Tues–Fri 10am–6pm, Sat 10am–5.30pm, Sun 1–5.30pm.

Margriet Nannings Prinsenstraat 8, Grachtengordel west ☎020 620 7672, ⓦmargrietnannings.com; map p.55. Pricey designer clothes for women, mostly casual chic, with classy handbags and jewellery too. There's a menswear shop next door at Prinsenstraat 6. Mon 1–6pm, Tues, Wed, Fri & Sat 10.30am–6pm, Thurs 10.30am–8pm.

Marlies Dekkers Berenstraat 18, Grachtengordel west ☎020 421 1900, ⓦmarliesdekkers.com; map p.55. Holland's most successful lingerie designer, known for her daring collection and stylish shop displays. Mon 1–6pm, Tues–Sat 11am–6pm, Sun noon–5pm.

Sissy-Boy Nieuwezijds Voorburgwal 182, Magna Plaza, Old Centre ☎020 740 1230, ⓦsissy-boy.com; map p.34. Simply designed but classy and affordably priced clothes for men and women. A number of designer labels are featured alongside the Sissy Boy label. Mon 11am–7pm, Tues, Wed, Fri & Sat 10am–7pm, Thurs 10am–9pm, Sun noon–7pm.

SECONDHAND AND VINTAGE

1953 retro & chic Staalstraat 2, old centre ☎062 493 3582; map p.34. Small but brimming with really interesting clothes and retro accessories dating from the 1900s to the 1980s. Mon noon–6.30pm, Tues–Sat 11am–6.30pm, Sun 1–6pm.

Episode Berenstraat 1, Grachtengordel west ☎020 626 4679, ⓦepisode.eu; map p.55. One of the larger secondhand stores, with everything from army jackets to hats, fur coats, shoes and belts, specializing in clothes from the 1970s and 1980s. There are also branches at Nieuwe Spiegelstraat 61, Grachtengordel south (☎020 330 4847), Waterlooplein 1, Old Centre (☎020 320 3000) and Spuistraat 37 & 96, Old Centre (☎020 358 5022). Mon–Wed 11am–6pm, Thurs 11am–8pm, Fri 11am–7pm, Sat 10am–7pm, Sun noon–6pm.

★ **Laura Dols** Wolvenstraat 7, Grachtengordel west ☎020 624 9066, ⓦlauradols.nl; map p.55. Top dog on the vintage fashion scene, Laura Dols has rails groaning under the weight of countless dresses, all sorted according to colour. There's a multitude of vintage pieces for both women and men, including some excellent swimwear,

1920s flapper dresses, 1930s hats and 1950s skirts, stunningly printed fabrics from the 1960s, piles of vintage pillowcases, tablecloths and tea towels, and a superb selection of children's and baby clothes. Prices are high, but not unaffordable. Mon–Wed & Sat 11am–6pm, Thurs & Fri 11am–7pm, Sun noon–6pm.

Second Best Singel 281, Grachtengordel west ☎020 422 0274, ⓦsecond-best.nl; map p.55. Most things here are from the last fifteen years, so don't expect to dig out a 1950s prom dress from the racks of classy cast-offs. There is, however, some great modern(ish) stuff to be found if you're prepared to rummage – and pay a little over the odds. Tues–Sat 11am–6pm.

Wini Haarlemmerstraat 29, western docklands ☎020 427 9393, ⓦwinivintage.nl; map p.75. Best known for their vintage dresses, but with a few men's and kids' options too. They also have a selection of vintage fabrics, which you can buy by the metre to make your own creations. Mon–Sat 10.30am–6pm, Sun noon–6pm.

Zipper Huidenstraat 7, Grachtengordel west ☎020 623 7302, ⓦzipperstore.nl; map p.55. Zipper has mainly cheap and cheerful stuff from the 1960s, 1970s and 1980s, and is great for jeans. Pay attention though, as they stock new clothes alongside the vintage ones, and that 1960s-style shift dress may not be all that it seems. They also have a good selection of accessories, both vintage and modern. There's a second branch at Nieuwe Hoogstraat 8, Old Centre (☎020 627 0353). Mon noon–6.30pm, Tues, Wed, Fri & Sat 11am–6.30pm, Thurs 11am–8pm, Sun 1–6.30pm.

SHOES, BAGS AND OTHER ACCESSORIES

Appenzeller Grimburgwal 1, Old Centre ☎020 626 8218, ⓦappenzeller.nl; map p.34. Designer of state-of-the-art modern jewellery, watches and spectacles. Tues–Sat 11am–5.30pm.

The English Hatter Heiligeweg 40, Old Centre ☎020 623 4781, ⓦenglish-hatter.nl; map p.34. Ties, hats and various other accessories, alongside classic menswear from shirts to cricket sweaters. Mon noon–6pm, Tues, Wed, Fri & Sat 9.30am–6pm, Thurs 9.30am–9pm, Sun 11am–5.30pm.

Fred de la Bretonière St Luciensteeg 20, Old Centre ☎020 623 4152; ⓦfreddelabretoniere.com; map p.34. This designer is famous for his high-quality

13

handbags and shoes, all sold at affordable prices. There's another branch at Utrechtsestraat 77, Grachtengordel south (☎020 626 9627). Mon 1–6pm, Tues, Wed, Fri & Sat 10am–6pm, Thurs 10am–7pm, Sun noon–5pm.

De Grote Tas Oude Hoogstraat 6, Old Centre ☎020 623 0110, ⓦdegrotetas.nl; map p.34. A family-owned store now run by the third generation, selling a wide selection of businesslike bags, briefcases and suitcases. Mon–Wed 10am–6pm, Thurs 10am–9pm, Fri & Sat 10am–7pm, Sun 11am–6pm.

Hoeden M/V Herengracht 422, Grachtengordel west ☎020 626 3038, ⓦhoeden-mv.com; map p.55. Need something for the races? You're sure to find it among this selection of pricey designer hats, from felt Borsalinos to straw Panamas. They stock gloves and umbrellas too. Mon 1–6pm, Tues & Sat 10am–6pm, Wed 11am–6pm, Thurs & Fri 10am–7pm.

't Klompenhuisje Nieuwe Hoogstraat 9a, Old Centre ☎020 622 8100, ⓦbit.ly/tKlompenhuisje; map p.34. Amsterdam's best and brightest array of clogs and kids' shoes. Mon–Sat 10am–6pm.

Linhard Van Baerlestraat 50, Museum Quarter ☎020 679 0755, ⓦlinhard.nl; map p.107. Stocks a variety of fashionable, fairly priced bags, shoes, bracelets, jeans and coats made by different designers. Mon 11am–6pm, Tues–Sat 10am–6pm, Sun noon–5pm.

Patta Zeedijk 67, Old Centre ☎020 331 8571, ⓦpatta. nl; map p.34. The trendiest trainers store in town, selling high-street brands, plus clothes by Alife, Rockwell and Reigning Champ. Mon–Wed & Fri noon–7pm, Thurs noon–9pm, Sat 11am–7pm, Sun 1–6pm.

Restored Haarlemmerdijk 39, western docklands ☎020 337 6473, ⓦrestored.nl; map p.75. Visually intriguing store stocked with all manner of handmade items from leather bags and jewellery to trinkets for the home – all with limited availability. Mon 1–6pm, Tues– Sat 11am–6pm, Sun 1–5pm.

Shoebaloo P.C. Hooftstraat 80, Vondelpark ☎020 671 2210, ⓦshoebaloo.nl; map p.107. The city's coolest shoe shop for both men and women, with a space-like interior. They also sell designer accessories. There's also a men's branch at Koningsplein 5–7, Grachtengordel south (☎020 626 7993) and a women's and children's branch at C. Schuystraat 9, Grachtengordel south (☎020 662 5779). Mon & Sun noon–6pm, Tues, Wed, Fri & Sat 10am–6pm, Thurs 10am–9pm.

Tikal Hartenstraat 2a, Grachtengordel west ☎020 623 2147; map p.55. Colourful jewellery and textiles from Mexico and Guatemala. Mon 1–6pm, Tues–Fri 11am– 6pm, Sat 11am–5.30pm.

DEPARTMENT STORES AND SHOPPING MALLS

De Bijenkorf Dam 1, Old Centre ☎088 245 3333, ⓦdebijenkorf.nl; map p.34. Dominating the northern corner of the Dam, this is the city's top department store with an interesting history (see page 37). A huge, bustling place – the name means "beehive" – it's spread over six floors and is good for designer clothes, accessories and kids' stuff. Mon & Sun 11am–9pm, Tues–Sat 10am–9pm.

HEMA Nieuwendijk 174–176, Old Centre ☎020 623 4176, ⓦhema.nl; map p.34. A cross between Woolworths and Marks & Spencer, HEMA is great for stocking up on all the important things – underwear, toiletries and other essentials – with occasional designer delights thrown in for good measure. Surprises include wine and salami at the back of the shop, a good bakery and cheese counter, and great sweets. There's another branch at Kalverstraat 212, Old Centre (☎020 422 8988). Mon–Sat 9am–9pm, Sun 10am–7pm.

Magna Plaza Nieuwezijds Voorburgwal 182, Old Centre ⓦmagnaplaza.nl; map p.34. This large shopping mall is

imaginatively sited in the old Neogothic post office building behind the Dam, though even here the shops themselves – comprising the usual big-brand stuff – don't match the setting. Mon 11am–7pm, Tues–Sat 10am–7pm, Thurs 10am–9pm, Sun noon–7pm.

Peek & Cloppenburg Dam 20, Old Centre ☎020 623 2837, ⓦpeek-cloppenburg.nl; map p.34. Less a department store than a multistorey clothes emporium featuring some very middle-of-the-road styles. Nonetheless, this remains an Amsterdam institution. Mon– Wed, Fri & Sat 10am–8pm, Thurs 10am–9pm, Sun 10am–8pm.

Stadshart Rembrandtweg 41a, Amstelveen ☎020 426 5805, ⓦstadshartamstelveen.nl; tram #5 from Museumplein to Amstelveen. Large covered shopping centre south of the city with two hundred high-street- brand shops, restaurants and bars. It also hosts an organic food market on Tues. Mon & Sun 1–6pm, Tues, Wed, Fri & Sat 10am–6pm, Thurs 10am–9pm.

FOOD AND DRINK

SPECIALIST AND GOURMET STORES

Amazing Oriental Nieuwmarkt 27, Old Centre ☎020 626 2797, ⓦamazingoriental.com; map p.34. Large and warren-like Chinese supermarket, with all sorts of stuff

squirrelled away in corners – seaweed, water chestnuts, spicy prawn crackers. Get there early so you don't miss for the handmade tofu. Mon 11am–6pm, Tues–Sat 9.30am–6pm.

13

NIGHT SHOPS

Most **night shops** (*avondwinkels*) open when other stores are starting to think about closing up, and they stay open until well into the night – which sounds great, but you have to pay for the privilege: essentials can cost three times the regular price. With a couple of exceptions, they're located a fair walk from the city centre and may take time to seek out. For a complete list, check the Gouden Gids (Yellow Pages; ⓦdetelefoongids.nl) under "*avondverkoop*". Bear in mind also that Albert Heijn supermarkets (see page 200) are mostly open until 10pm Monday to Saturday.

De Avondmarkt De Wittenkade 96, Jordaan ☎020 686 4919, ⓦdeavondmarkt.nl; map p.75. One of the largest and cheapest night shops in town, with a good selection of fresh produce, spirits and home-made takeaway meals. Mon–Fri 4pm–midnight, Sat 3pm–midnight, Sun 2pm–midnight.

Sterk De Clercqstraat 7, Jordaan ☎020 618 1727, ⓦsterk.amsterdam; map p.75. This city-centre institution has a variety of breads and pastries baked on the premises, a large fresh produce section, a deli and friendly staff. Beats the pants off most regular supermarkets. Mon–Thurs & Sun 9am–1am, Fri & Sat 9am–3am.

Arxhoek Rokin 66, Old Centre ☎6 200 12721, ⓦarxhoek-fromager.com; map p.34. Centrally situated cheese shop (previously located in Damstraat 19) with handmade rounds of *kaas* from the Netherlands and abroad. Besides excellent cheese, it offers other delicacies such as Spanish hams, sausages and fine wines. Mon–Fri 9.30am–8pm, Sat 10am–8pm, Sun 11am–8pm.

Bakkerij Paul Année Bellamystraat 8, Amsterdam West ☎020 618 3113, ⓦbakkerijpaulannee.nl; map p.75. The best wholegrain and sourdough breads in town, bar none – all made from organic grains. Mon & Wed–Sat 9am–5pm.

Eichholtz Leidsestraat 48, Grachtengordel south ☎020 622 0305, ⓦeichholtzdeli.com; map p.65. Old-fashioned store specializing in imported foods from Britain and the US – the place to find Oreo cookies, Pop Tarts and Heinz beans. Mon 10am–6.30pm, Tues, Wed, Fri & Sat 9am–6.30pm, Thurs 9am–9pm, Sun noon–6.30pm.

★ **Ibericus** Haarlemmerstraat 93, western docklands ☎020 223 6573, ⓦiberdeli.nl/nl/ibericus; map p.75. High-quality Spanish cured hams hang from the ceiling of this atmospheric shop run by Paul Gonzalez. If you're feeling peckish he offers sampler menus for €9.50, otherwise you're welcome to try before you buy. Mon–Sat 10am–6pm, Sun 11am–5pm.

Jordino Haarlemmerdijk 25a, western docklands ☎020 420 3225, ⓦjordino.nl; map p.75. You can sample some of Amsterdam's best ice cream and chocolates at this Haarlemmerdijk institution. Mon & Sun 1–6.30pm, Tues–Sat 10am–6.30pm.

De Kaaskamer Runstraat 7, Grachtengordel west ☎020 623 3483, ⓦkaaskamer.nl; map p.55. Friendly shop with a comprehensive selection of Dutch cheeses, plus international wines, cheeses and olives. Mon noon–6pm, Tues–Fri 9am–6pm, Sat 9am–5pm, Sun noon–5pm.

Kaasland Haarlemmerstraat 2, western docklands ☎020 422 1715, ⓦkaasland.com; map p.75. As the name suggests, this shop offers a huge selection of cheeses, plus bread and sandwiches. Mon–Fri 8am–8pm, Sat 8am–7pm, Sun 10am–7pm.

Kaldi Herengracht 300, Grachtengordel west ☎020 428 6854, ⓦkaldi.nl; map p.55. Kaldi sells more than fifty varieties of organic tea, as well as Smit & Dorlas roasted coffee; it doubles as a coffeeshop, so you can try them all. Mon–Thurs 8.30am–5.30pm, Fri 8.30am–6pm, Sat & Sun 11am–5.30pm.

Lanskroon Singel 385, Grachtengordel west ☎020 623 7743, ⓦlanskroon.nl; map p.55. A famously good pastry shop, with a small area for on-the-spot consumption. Mon–Fri 8am–7pm, Sat 9am–7pm, Sun 10am–7pm.

Meeuwig & Zn. Nieuwe Hemweg 6K, western docklands ☎020 626 5286, ⓦmeeuwig.nl; map p.75. Oil specialists Meeuwig & Zn. stock oils from all over the world, sold from large silver canisters. They also have a wide selection of vinegar, over thirty kinds of mustard and tasty fresh olives. Sat noon–5pm.

Rembrandt Hoeve, Amsteldijk Noord 127, Amstelveen, ☎085 208 4292; ⓦrembrandthoeve-amsterdam.nl. Located on the outskirts of Amsterdam, this farm has been producing the finest Dutch cheeses for over 30 years. It specialises in flavoured cheeses, adding different ingredients such as garlic, chives or mustard seeds to traditional Gouda. Join a tour for a behind-the-scenes glimpse into the cheese-making process, or simply pick up some goodies at the farm shop. Daily 8am–6pm.

Olivaria Hazenstraat 2a, Jordaan ☎06 8194 9655; map p.75. Olive oil – and nothing but. Incredible range of oils, all imported from small- and medium-sized concerns around the world. Expert advice and a well-stocked tasting table. Mon 2–6pm, Tues–Fri 11am–6pm, Sat 11am–5pm.

Oud-Hollandsch Snoepwinkeltje Tweede Egelan tierdwarsstraat 2, Jordaan ☎020 420 7390, ⓦsnoepwinkeltje.com; map p.75. All kinds of mouthwatering Dutch sweets, stacked up in floor-to-ceiling

13

TOP 5 SHOPS FOR ONLY-IN-AMSTERDAM SOUVENIRS

Amsterdam Tulip Museum for locally grown Dutch tulips. See page 202

De Bierkoning for Dutch speciality beers, such as Johnny and Raggle Taggle. See page 198

Condomerie Het Gulden Vlies for marshmallow-flavoured condoms. See page 202

Denham for handmade denim jeans. See page 194

Oud-Hollandsch Snoepwinkeltje for Dutch salted liquorice. See page 197

glass jars and attracting hordes of neighbourhood kids. The ideal place to try the traditional Dutch salted liquorice. Tues–Sat 11am–6.30pm.

Pompadour Chocolaterie Huidenstraat 12, Grachtengordel west ✆020 623 9554, ⊕pompadour.amsterdam; map p.55. Delicious chocolates and lots of home-made pastries (usually smothered in or filled with chocolate). Mon–Fri 10am–6pm, Sat 9am–6pm, Sun noon–6pm.

★ **Puccini Bomboni** Singel 184, Grachtengordel west ✆020 427 8341, ⊕puccinibomboni.com; map p.55. Arguably the best chocolatier in town, selling a wonderfully creative range of chocolates in all shapes and sizes. This mini-chain has also abandoned the tweeness of the traditional chocolatier for brisk, modern decor. There's another branch at Staalstraat 17, Old Centre (✆020 626 5474). Mon & Sun 11am–6pm, Tues–Sat 9am–6pm.

Simon Lévelt Prinsengracht 180, Jordaan ✆020 624 0823, ⊕simonlevelt.nl; map p.75. This specialist tea and coffee company has occupied the same premises for over 150 years and, although there are now Lévelts dotted across the city, this is the best. Friendly service too. Mon–Fri 10am–6pm, Sat 10am–5pm, Sun 1–5pm.

★ **Zoet en Hartig** Haarlemmerdijk 158, western docklands ✆020 767 0434; map p.75. Rustic chocolatier famous for their handcrafted chocolates and signature "hotchocspoon" (chocolate spoon for stirring into milk), available in sixty flavours. They also do home-made cheese biscuits and sausage rolls for those less sweet of tooth. Mon–Sat 9.30am–5.30pm, Sun 11am–5pm.

SUPERMARKETS

Supermarkets are thin on the ground in central Amsterdam and most – apart from Albert Heijn's flagship store (see below) – are crowded and cramped. If you're buying fruit and vegetables, note that you'll usually need to weigh and price them yourself (unless a price is given per item, *per*

stuk); put them on the scale, press the little picture, then press BON to print out a sticky barcode. If you're buying beer, juice or water in bottles (either glass or plastic), a charge of €0.10–0.50 will be added on at the checkout; you get it back when you return the empties – to a different store if you like.

De Aanzet 1e Jacob van Campenstraat 10, De Pijp ✆020 673 3415, ⊕de-aanzet.nl; map p.107. Small, organic cooperative supermarket serving the local community since 1982. It stocks ecofriendly toiletries and household products too. Mon–Fri 8.30am–7pm, Sat 8.30am–6pm.

Albert Heijn Nieuwezijds Voorburgwal 226, Old Centre ✆020 421 8344, ⊕ah.nl; map p.34. Located just behind the Dam, this is the biggest of the city's forty-odd Albert Heijn supermarkets. There are other central branches at Koningsplein 4 and Vijzelstraat 113, both Grachtengordel south; Westerstraat 79, Jordaan; Haarlemmerdijk 1, western docklands; and Overtoom 454, Vondelpark. Daily 8am–10pm.

Dirk van den Broek Marie Heinekenplein 25, De Pijp ✆08 8313 4315, ⊕dirk.nl; map p.107. Beats Albert Heijn hands down in everything except image: it's cheaper across the board and bigger too. More branches dotted around the suburbs. Daily 8am–10pm.

Ekoplaza Elandsgracht 118, Jordaan ✆04 1331 3502, ⊕ekoplaza.nl; map p.75. This all-organic chain has much better-tasting fruit and veg than anywhere else; also grains, pulses, Bonbon Jeanette chocolates and superb bread. There are other branches around town, including Waterlooplein 131 (✆020 624 1765). Elandsgracht: Mon–Fri 8am–8pm, Sat 8am–7pm.

WINE, BEER AND SPIRITS

De Bierkoning Paleisstraat 125, Old Centre ✆020 625 2336, ⊕bierkoning.nl; map p.34. The "Beer King" is aptly named, with 1500 different beers on the shelves, plus the appropriate glasses to drink them from. Mon–Sat 11am–7pm, Sun noon–6pm.

Chabrol Haarlemmerstraat 7, western docklands ✆020 622 2781, ⊕chabrolwines.com; map p.75. Stocks an excellent selection of wine and champagne, recommended by an extremely knowledgeable staff. Daily noon–7pm.

Gall & Gall Nieuwezijds Voorburgwal 226a, Old Centre ✆020 421 8370, ⊕gall.nl; map p.34. The most central branch of the largest chain of wine merchants in Amsterdam, with a good choice of wines, as well as *jenevers* (Dutch gin). Regular tastings are held here too. Among others, there are also outlets at Jodenbreestraat 23, old Jewish quarter (✆020 428 7060) and Overtoom 468 (✆020 618 1332). Daily 8am–10pm.

Le Cellier Spuistraat 116, Old Centre ✆020 638 6573, ⊕lecellier.nl; map p.34. The largest wine,

13

AMSTERDAM'S MARKETS

Amsterdam's markets offer so much more than just flowers, from antiques to gourmet nibbles. As with all markets, they can open and close at different times depending on the weather and the mood of the sellers.

Albert Cuypmarkt Albert Cuypstraat, De Pijp ⓦ albertcuyp-markt.amsterdam. In existence since 1905, this is the city's principal street market, with over 260 stands selling everything from luggage to fish, and some great bargains to be had. Mon–Sat 9.30am–5.30pm.

Biologische Borenmarkt Haarlemmerplein, western docklands ⓦ bewustbiologisch.nl. Organic farmers' market selling all kinds of produce, including amazing fresh breads, wine, cheese and meat. Wed 10am–5pm.

Bloemenmarkt Singel, between Koningsplein and Muntplein, Grachtengordel south. Locals have all but abandoned Amsterdam's famous floating flower market because the choice and quality has wilted considerably over the years, but it's still an obligatory stop for many. Mon–Sat 9am–5.30pm, Sun 11am–5.30pm.

Boerenmarkt Noordermarkt, Grachtengordel west ⓦ boerenmarktamsterdam.nl. This vibrant organic farmers' market is a good place to pick up foodie souvenirs (see page 54). Sat 9am–4pm.

Dappermarkt Dapperstraat 279, Amsterdam Oost ⓦ dappermarkt.nl. Culturally diverse market with two hundred stalls selling plants, food and appliances. Mon–Sat 10am–5pm.

IJ-Hallen Vlooienmarkt TT Neveritaweg 15, Amsterdam Noord ⓦ ijhallen.nl. Housed in a huge warehouse in the trendy NDSM district a ferry ride from Centraal Station, this is one of Europe's biggest and best flea markets, with over 750 stalls; you won't leave empty-handed. Twice monthly; check website for dates.

Lindengracht Lindengracht, south of Brouwersgracht, Jordaan. This rowdy and raucous general household supplies market, with over two hundred stands, has been in operation since 1894. A great slice of working-class Amsterdam. Sat & Sun 9am–4.30pm.

Nieuwmarkt Nieuwmarkt, Old Centre. From Mon–Fri it's a small collection of stalls selling veg and cheese, on Sat it's a full-blown organic farmers' market. There's also a flea market here on summer Sundays. Mon–Sat from 9am–5pm.

Noordermarkt Noordermarkt, Grachtengordel west, ☎ 020 552 4074. Part organic food market, part junk-lover's gold mine, the Noodermarkt is full of all kinds of bargains – oriental rugs, jewellery and old books, among other treasures – tucked away beneath piles of seemingly useless rubbish. Get there early. Flea market Mon 9am–2pm; organic market Sat 9am–5pm.

Stadshart Rembrandtweg 37, Amstelveen ☎ 020 426 5800, ⓦ stadshartamstelveen.nl; tram #5 from Museumplein to Amstelveen. An organic market is held every Fri (8am–5pm) in this covered shopping arcade (see page 196).

Sunday Market Cultuurpark Westergasfabriek, Westerpark, western docklands ⓦ sundaymarket.nl. This monthly art, fashion and design market is a platform for designers to sell their wares. You're likely to find jewellery, customized T-shirts, ceramics and art, as well as some interesting food stalls. First Sun of month noon–6pm.

Ten Katemarkt Ten Katestraat 97-99, Amsterdam West ⓦ tenkatemarkt.nl. This lovely local food market, selling olives, roast chicken and fruit, among other goodies, is the ideal place to stock up for a picnic in the nearby Vondelpark. Mon–Sat 10am–5pm.

Waterlooplein Waterlooplein, old Jewish quarter ⓦ waterloopleinmarkt.nl. A real Amsterdam institution, this is the city's best central flea market by far. Sprawling and chaotic, it's the final resting place for many a pair of yellow corduroy flares; but there are more wearable clothes to be found too, as well as some wonderful antiques and bric-a-brac stalls, and some secondhand vinyl to root through. Mon–Sat 9am–6pm.

beer and spirits shop in the centre of Amsterdam, with a huge selection of bottles, along with regular tastings

and workshops organized on Fri evenings. Mon–Sat 9.30am–5.30pm.

FURNITURE AND HOMEWARE

Baobab Elandsgracht 105, Jordaan ☎ 020 626 8398, ⓦ baobab-aziatica.nl; map p.75. Atmospheric store selling jewel-toned textiles and ceramics sourced from Indonesia and the Far East. It also stocks a ginormous selection of well-priced silver jewellery. Mon–Sat 11am–6pm.

★ **Droog Design** Staalstraat 7b, Old Centre ☎ 020 523 5050, ⓦ droog.com; map p.34. Founded in 1993, the ahead-of-the-curve Droog Design has made a serious contribution to contemporary design. Some of their innovative products, such as their milk-bottle chandelier, have ended up in museum collections; here, you'll find their gallery, café and extremely stylish shop. Daily 9am–7pm.

★ **Frozen Fountain** Prinsengracht 645, Grachtengordel south ☎020 622 9375, ⓦfrozen fountain.nl; map p.55. Contemporary furniture and interior design with an emphasis on Dutch designs. Mon 1–6pm, Tues–Sat 10am–6pm, Sun noon–5pm.

★ **Galleria D'Arte Rinascimento** Prinsengracht 170, Jordaan ☎020 622 7509, ⓦdelft-art-gallery. com; map p.75. If you're after that elusive present and don't want to settle for tourist tat, this is the place – a great selection of new and antique delftware, from small ashtrays to large vases. Daily 9am–6pm.

Kitsch Kitchen Rozengracht 8–12, Jordaan ☎020 462 0050, ⓦkitschkitchen.nl; map p.75. Crammed

full of chunky furniture, bowls and kitsch homeware, plus bags, aprons, umbrellas and diaries, all in bright primary colours. Mon–Sat 10am–6pm, Sun noon–5pm.

Saskya & Co Stromarkt 5, Old Centre ☎020 420 0840; map p.34. A better class of Dutch souvenir, with ceramics, textiles and other bits and pieces that are a cut above the stuff you find elsewhere around the centre. Not cheap though. Tues–Sun 11am–6pm.

Wonderwood Rusland 3, Old Centre ☎020 625 3738, ⓦwonderwood.nl; map p.34. Wonderwood claims to be a cross between a shop and a gallery, and it certainly is a good place to browse, packed as it is with vintage furniture designs in wood from the 1940s to the 1960s – as well as its own creations based on the classics. Wed–Sat noon–6pm, or by appointment.

MUSIC

Amsterdam boasts lots of small, low-key independent shops specializing in one type of **music** or another and it's here you can uncover vintage items unavailable elsewhere. If it's **vinyl** you're after, though, you've come to the wrong city. Some places still sell records, most notably Distortion Records (see below), but it's very much taken for granted that music comes on CD. The main exception is the Waterlooplein flea market (see page 200), which has stacks of old records – and CDs – on offer.

Back Beat Records Egelantiersstraat 19, Jordaan ☎020 627 1657, ⓦbackbeat.nl; map p.75. Small specialist in soul, blues, jazz and funk, with a helpful and enthusiastic owner. Tues–Sat 11am–6pm.

Broekmans & Van Poppel Badhoevelaan 78 ☎020 679 6575, ⓦbroekmans.com; map p.122. Set on the outskirts, but still the city's best selection of classical and opera CDs and sheet music. Mon–Fri 9am–6pm, Sat 10am–5pm.

Concerto Utrechtsestraat 52–60, Grachtengordel south ☎020 261 2610, ⓦconcerto.amsterdam; map p.65. Around since the 1950s, this excellent music store stocks new and used records and CDs in all categories: they're equally good on baroque as on grunge. One of the best all-round selections in Amsterdam, with the great

option to listen before you buy. Mon–Sat 10am–6pm, Sun noon–6pm.

Discostars Haarlemmerdijk 86, western docklands ☎020 626 1777, ⓦdiscostars-recordstore.nl; map p.75. Brilliantly chaotic CD and vinyl store, with a vast collection of music of all genres you won't find anywhere else. Mon & Sun 1–6pm, Tues–Sat 10am–6pm.

Distortion Records Westerstraat 244, Jordaan ☎020 627 0004, ⓦdistortion.nl; map p.75. This secondhand independent shop specializes in vinyl, with new and secondhand records covering a broad range of genres, from jazz and funk to drum'n'bass and house. Tues–Sat 11am–6pm, Thurs 11am–9pm.

Killa Cutz Nieuwe Nieuwstraat 21hs, Old Centre ☎020 428 4040, ⓦkillacutz.nl; map p.34. Relegated upstairs to small corner of a bike rental shop, Killa Cutz specializes in techno, house and electronica, with prices from as low as €1, and have a modest listening corner. Daily 10am–6pm.

South Miami Plaza Albert Cuypstraat 116b/c, De Pijp ☎020 626 1777, ⓦsouthmiamiplaza.nl; map p.107. Large store specializing in Portuguese and Surinamese music, but plenty of other styles too, along with posters and DVDs. Mon–Sat 10am–6pm.

SPORTS AND GAMES

Gamekeeper Hartenstraat 14, Grachtengordel west ☎020 638 1579, ⓦgamekeeper.nl; map p.55. All kinds of fantasy games, mainly for adults, from Games Workshop to role-play games, as well as collectible cards, backgammon and magic bits. Mon & Sat 10am–6pm, Tues, Wed & Fri 10am–6.30pm, Thurs 10am–8.30pm, Sun 11am–6pm.

Joe's Vliegerwinkel Nieuwe Hoogstraat 19, Old Centre ☎020 625 0139, ⓦjoesvliegerwinkel.nl; map p.34. This colourful shop is crowded with kites, frisbees, boomerangs, diablos, yo-yos, juggling balls and clubs. Tues–Fri noon–6pm, Sat noon–5pm.

Kathmandu Haarlemmerstraat 123 ☎020 624 3652, ⓦkathmandu.nl; map p.75. A large sports shop situated only 10 minutes from Centraal Station, selling everything you could need for hiking and camping. Mon noon–6pm, Tues–Fri 10am–6pm, Sat 10am–5pm, Sun noon–5pm.

Rodolfo's Van Woustraat 44, De Pijp ☎020 622 5488, ⓦrodolfos.nl; map p.107. Rodolfo's stocks a huge collection of skates and skateboards, including rental options, plus the latest matching fashions. Tues–Sat 10am–6pm.

13

HEAD SHOPS AND SMART SHOPS

Riding on the coat-tails of Amsterdam's liberal policy towards cannabis are the city's **head shops**, selling all manner of dope-related paraphernalia, including pipes, bongs, vaporizers – and the obligatory weed-leaf T-shirt. **Smart shops**, ostensibly established as outlets for "smart" drugs (memory enhancers, concentration aids and so on), do most of their business selling natural alternatives to hard drugs such as LSD, speed or ecstasy – as well as a variety of natural aphrodisiacs. These substitutes often have many or all of the effects of the real thing, but with greatly reduced health risks – and the added bonus of legality. Though it's now illegal to sell magic mushrooms, smart shops sell "truffles", which supposedly have a similar effect, and mushroom seeds for home-growing.

Azarius Kerkstraat 119, Grachtengordel south ☎020 737 2107, ⓦazarius.net; map p.65. Knowledgeable, multilingual staff can advise you on numerous legal-high products and their array of vaporizers. Mon–Wed 11am–7pm, Thurs–Sat 11am–8pm, Sun noon–6pm.

The Head Shop Kloveniersburgwal 39, Old Centre ☎020 624 9061, ⓦheadshop.nl; map p.34. Every dope-smoking accessory you could possibly need, along with assorted marijuana memorabilia. Daily 10am–10pm.

The Magic Mushroom Gallery Spuistraat 249, Old Centre ☎020 427 5765, ⓦmagicmushroom.com; map p.34. One of the city's oldest smart shops, with the usual array of sexual stimulants, hallucinogens, pipes and basic drug accessories – and truffles, of course. Daily 10am–10pm.

When Nature Calls Keizersgracht 508, Grachtengordel south ☎020 330 0700, ⓦwhen naturecalls.nl; map p.65. Specializes in cannabis products such as hemp chocolate and beer, plus seeds. Daily 9am–10pm.

SPECIALITY SHOPS

3-D Holograms Grimburgwal 2, Old Centre ☎020 624 7225, ⓦ3-dhologrammen.com; map p.34. All kinds of holographic art, big and small. Tues & Sun 3–6pm, Wed–Sat noon–6pm.

Amsterdam Tulip Museum Prinsengracht 116, Jordaan ☎020 421 0095, ⓦamsterdamtulipmuseum. com; map p.75. Charming little shop that belongs to the museum (see page 77) and sells packets of tulip bulbs in season, as well as cards and gifts such as tulip-patterned pillows and pottery. Daily 10am–6pm.

★**Condomerie Het Gulden Vlies** Warmoesstraat 141, Old Centre ☎020 627 4174, ⓦcondomerie.com; map p.34. This shop sells condoms of every shape, size and flavour imaginable (and unimaginable). Mon & Wed–Sat 11am–9pm, Tues 11am–6pm, Sun 1–6pm.

Gerda's Runstraat 16, Grachtengordel west ☎020 624 2912, ⓦbit.ly/GerdaFlorist; map p.55. Amsterdam is full of flower shops, but this one is the most imaginative, with bouquets to melt the hardest of hearts. Mon–Fri 9am–6pm, Sat 9am–5pm.

★**Jacob Hooy** Kloveniersburgwal 10–12, Old Centre ☎020 624 3041, ⓦjacob-hooy.nl; map p.34. This homeopathic chemist has been in business at this address since 1778 – and the shop and its stock seem as if they are the same now as then. They sell no end of herbs and natural

cosmetics, as well as a huge stock of *drop* (Dutch liquorice). Mon 1–6pm, Tues–Fri 10am–6pm, Sat 10am–5pm.

Kramer and Pontifex Reestraat 20, Grachtengordel west ☎020 626 5274, ⓦpontifex-kaarsen.com; map p.55. On one sid, Mr Kramer repairs old and broken dolls and teddies; on the other, Pontifex sells all kinds of candles, oils and incense. Mon–Fri 10am–6pm, Sat 10am–5pm.

P.G.C. Hajenius Rokin 96, Old Centre ☎020 623 7494, ⓦhajenius.com; map p.34. Long-established tobacconist selling its own and other brands of cigars, tobacco and smoking accessories. There's also a room at the back where you can sit and smoke and have a coffee as you view the amazing range of cigars and pipes, and leaf through a magazine or book from its library. Mon noon–6pm, Tues–Sat 9.30am–6pm, Sun noon–5pm.

Tibet Winkel Spuistraat 185a, Old Centre ☎020 420 4538, ⓦtibet.nu/tibetwinkel; map p.34. Books, music, jewellery and more, all made by Tibetan refugees in Nepal and India. Mon–Fri 1–6pm, Sat 11am–6pm, Sun 1–5pm.

Witte Tandenwinkel Runstraat 5, Grachtengordel west ☎020 623 3443, ⓦdewittetandenwinkel.nl; map p.55. The "White Teeth Shop" sells wacky toothbrushes and just about every dental hygiene accoutrement you could ever need. Tues–Sat 1–6pm, Sun 1–5pm.

LGBTQ Amsterdam

Amsterdam is one of the top LGBTQ destinations in Europe. The Netherlands was the first country to legalize same-sex marriage, in 2001, and the Dutch reputation for tolerance has only grown since then. No other city in Europe accepts gay people quite as readily, and locals make no distinction or judgement about a person's sexual preferences whatsoever. This liberalism is displayed publicly at the festivals and events organized throughout the year: Amsterdam Pride is a big occasion on the LGBTQ calendar, as are King's Day and the many memorial events that take place around the Homomonument. These festivals, together with city's excellent and plentiful bars and clubs, are a huge draw for international LGBTQ travellers.

GAY AMSTERDAM: MARRIAGE CONSENT

Homosexuality was decriminalized in the Netherlands way back in 1811; a century later – still sixty years ahead of the UK – the gay **age of consent** was reduced to 21, and in 1971 it was brought into line with that of heterosexuals, at 16. In 2001 the Netherlands was again at the vanguard of gay and lesbian rights, when the country legalized **same-sex marriages** and introduced non-discriminatory adoption rights, with gay couples enjoying equal legal rights with heterosexuals.

14

For all the city's inclusiveness, it's fair to say that gay men in Amsterdam are much better catered for than **lesbians**. Although there is a sizeable lesbian community, the city lacks strictly women-only establishments, and the lesbian scene is largely limited to a few nights held in men-only or mixed clubs.

The city has four recognized **LGBTQ areas: Reguliersdwarsstraat** in Grachtengordel south, with its trendy bars and clubs, is the best known, attracting a young, lively and international crowd, while quieter **Kerkstraat**, a few streets south, is populated as much by locals as visitors, and includes a smattering of straight venues. The streets just north of **Rembrandtplein** and along the Amstel, on the eastern edge of Grachtengordel south, are a camp focus, as well as being home to a number of traditional Dutch pubs and rent-boy bars, while **Warmoesstraat** and **Zeedijk**, in the heart of the Red Light District, are cruisey and mainly leather-oriented options.

CONTACTS

COC Stadhouderskade 89, De Pijp ☎ 020 626 3087, ⓦ cocamsterdam.nl. This organization is actively involved in gaining equal rights for gay men and lesbians, as well as informing society's perceptions of homosexuality. They also run the LGBT+ Switchboard.

Gala Kerkstraat 52, Grachtengordel south ⓦ gala -amsterdam.nl. Co-responsible for Pink Point and the Homomonument festivals (see page 206), King's Day and Amsterdam Pride, as well as themed parties at *Club Church*.

LGBT+ Switchboard ☎ 0300 330 0630, ⓦ switchboard. LGBT. An English-speaking service run by COC (see above), providing help and advice on all manner of LGBTQ-related things, including the best places to go out in Amsterdam. Mon–Fri noon–10pm, Sat & Sun 4–8pm.

Pink Point Near the Homomonument (see page 206), Westermarkt, Jordaan ☎ 020 559 5385. This free advice and information kiosk, situated on the corner of Raadhuisstraat and Keizersgracht, is run by a team of knowledgeable volunteers and offers practical information about where to go and what to do in the city. It's stocked with flyers and brochures, as well as souvenirs and T-shirts. They also publish the excellent *Bent Guide*. Daily 10am–6pm.

Roze in Blauw ☎ 088 169 1234. "Pink in blue" is a new initiative launched by the Amsterdam police force to promote the interests of the LGBTQ community. You can call the number to report incidences of discrimination, insults and assault.

THE MEDIA

BOOKS AND MAGAZINES

The American Book Center and Xantippe Unlimited bookshops both have large LGBTQ sections (see pages 192 and 194).

Bent Guide To Gay & Lesbian Amsterdam A practical and witty guidebook (€9.95) written in English by the volunteers at Pink Point and available from the booth at Westermarkt.

Gay & Night ⓦ gay-night.nl. A free monthly magazine published in English, with news, interviews and film reviews, available in newsagents and online.

Winq ⓦ winq.com. This bi-monthly, glossier than *Gay & Night*, focuses on luxury lifestyle and is published in English.

WEBSITES

Gay Amsterdam ⓦ gayamsterdam.com. A good resource for bar and club listings.

GayLINC ⓦ gaylinc.nl. This website has a plethora of useful information on gay and lesbian life in Amsterdam, covering everything from accommodation to historic gay haunts.

Gay News ⓦ www.gay-news.com. For the latest information about gay parties, pick up this monthly magazine, available from the COC (see above), or from most of the bars listed in this chapter.

Nighttours ⓦ nighttours.com. A guide to events, clubs and bars in English, as well as more general information on Amsterdam's LGBTQ scene.

Stichting Tijgertje ⓦ tijgertje.nl. Provides information on gay and lesbian sports clubs throughout Amsterdam.

Vrolijk Boeken & Films ⓦ vrolijk.nu. Vast stock of new and secondhand books and magazines, as well as music and DVDs.

RADIO

MVS Gaystation ⓦ mvs.nl. Amsterdam's gay and lesbian

radio station has an evening slot on Salto Stads FM 106.8FM (or 103.3 via cable). Mon–Sat 7–8pm.

ACCOMMODATION

Amistad Kerkstraat 42, Grachtengordel south ☎ 020 624 8074, ⓦ amistad.nl; tram #1, #2 or #5 to Koningsplein; map p.65. This is a stylish and cosy LGBTQ hotel, its rooms equipped with soft lighting and snug duvets. Standard rooms come with sink and shared shower; deluxe rooms have a bathtub and stereo. Breakfast is served until noon, in a convivial communal room that later becomes a public internet lounge. **€185**

Anco Oudezijds Voorburgwal 55, Old Centre ☎ 020 624 1126, ⓦ ancohotel.nl; 10min walk from Centraal Station; map p.34. A heavily sex-orientated option in the Red Light District, with a private bar catering exclusively to leather-wearing gay men. There are three- and four-person dorms with shared facilities, as well as singles and doubles, and a studio with private bathroom and kitchenette. Booking advised. Doubles **€129**, studios **€195**

Hotel Casa Eerste Ringdijkstraat 4, Amsterdam Oost ☎ 020 665 1171, ⓦ hotelcasa.nl; Metro Wibautstraat,

then a short walk; map p.122. This slick, modern hotel offers a mix of minimalist singles, doubles and twins, as well as rooms with disabled facilities. Added perks include a wine bar, coffee bar, restaurant and an underground car park. **€104**

Golden Bear Kerkstraat 37, Grachtengordel south ☎ 020 624 4785, ⓦ quentingoldenbear.com; tram #1, #2 or #5 to Prinsengracht; map p.65. Amsterdam's first LGBTQ hotel is a two-star with simple, homely rooms, some en suite. All come with sinks, fridges and DVD players. Booking essential. **€127**

Sir Albert Albert Cuypstraat 2–6, De Pijp ☎ 020 305 3020, ⓦ sirhotels.com/albert; tram #16 or #24 from CS; map p.107. This first-rate boutique hotel is owned by a gay couple. The building used to be a diamond factory and it's lost none of its bling: rooms come with fine Egyptian cotton linens, goose-down duvet and pillows and an Illy espresso machine. **€200**

NIGHTLIFE

While there are plenty of dedicated **gay bars and clubs**, some venues also put on mixed gay/straight nights. Although there are currently no clubs exclusively for **lesbians**, lesbian-only nights are on the increase, and the gay bars and clubs that welcome women are indicated below; it's worth checking with the LGBT+ Switchboard (see page 204) for the latest information. Flyers and brochures for parties and LGBTQ-oriented shops can be found in most gay bars and businesses, and various websites have listings. **Cruising** is generally tolerated in known gay areas, and most bars and clubs have **darkrooms**, which are legally obliged to provide safe sex information and condoms.

BARS

OLD CENTRE

Cuckoo's Nest Nieuwezijds Kolk 6 ☎ 020 627 1752, ⓦ cuckoosnest.nl; map p.34. An ever-popular cruisey leather bar, with an infamous darkroom. Mon–Thurs & Sun 1pm–1am, Fri & Sat 1pm–2am.

Dirty Dicks Warmoesstraat 86 ☎ 020 808 5283, ⓦ dirtydicksamsterdam.com; map p.34. One of the city's oldest fetish bars, *Dirty Dicks* has been spiced up with a new "leather, latex or shirtless" dress code. Mon–Thurs & Sun 8pm–3am, Fri & Sat 8pm–4am.

The Eagle Warmoesstraat 90 ☎ 06 4787 7614, ⓦ eagle amsterdam.com; map p.34. Under the same ownership as *Dirty Dicks*, this is the city's oldest denim and leather bar, with three floors. The basement is reserved for communal sex. Men only. Expect queues at weekends. Mon–Thurs & Sun 11pm–4am, Fri & Sat 11pm–5am.

Prik Spuistraat 109 ☎ 020 320 0002, ⓦ prikamsterdam. nl; map p.34. An award-winning gay bar, with tasty cocktails, smoothies and snacks, plus DJs at weekends. Mon–Thurs 4pm–1am, Fri & Sat 4pm–3am, Sun 3pm–1am.

The Web St Jacobsstraat 6 ☎ 020 623 6758, ⓦ theweb amsterdam.com; map p.34. This friendly bear bar-club attracts an older crowd, and has a pool table, dancefloor and darkrooms. Mon–Thurs & Sun 1pm–1am, Fri & Sat 1pm–2am.

GRACHTENGORDEL SOUTH

Café Dubbel D Amstel 60 ☎ 020 354 2695; map p.65. New owners have given this welcoming bar, popular with both tourists and locals, a fresh new look, and regular drag shows are organized. Mon, Thurs & Sun 5pm–1am, Fri & Sat 5pm–3am.

Entre Nous Halvemaansteeg 14 ☎ 020 623 1700; map p.65. Camp brown café that's packed out with a merry crowd during peak times, when everyone joins in the raucous sing-alongs to cheesy Eighties music. Women welcome. Mon–Thurs & Sun 8pm–3am, Fri & Sat 8pm–4am.

La Cage Regulierdwarsstraat 44 ☎ 020 320 9108, ⓦ lacageamsterdam.nl; map p.65. This glamorous LGBTQ-friendly bar-restaurant has mood lighting, fancy snacks and first-rate drinks. They host a "Happy Oyster Hour" on Fri from 5pm. Mon–Thurs & Sun 4pm–1am, Fri & Sat 4pm–3am; temporarily closed at the time of writing.

14

14

FESTIVALS AND EVENTS

The festival year kicks off with the Amsterdam LGBTQ Film Festival (ⓦrozefilmdagen.nl), usually held in mid-March. Inaugurated in 1996, the event features films, documentaries and shorts traditionally shown in Het Ketelhuis cinema and other locations around the Westergasfabriek. Next up is **King's Day**, held on April 27, when the whole city has a big knees-up, with LGBTQ parties and drag acts hosted throughout the city. A few days later, the two leading events in Amsterdam's LGBTQ calendar are **Remembrance Day** (May 4) and **Liberation Day** (May 5), both of which prompt ceremonies and events around the Homomonument, the symbolic focus of the city's gay community (see page 59). As summer hits full swing, (July 30), the party moves to Amsterdam Beach (at Zandvoort aan Zee), where Pride at the Beach celebrations include a mix of events, performances and firework displays.

The highlight of the summer is **Amsterdam Pride** (ⓦamsterdamgaypride.nl), taking place on the first weekend in August, with street parties and performances along the Amstel, Warmoesstraat and Reguliersdwarsstraat. "Canal Pride" takes place on the Saturday, with a flotilla of up to eighty boats cruising along the Prinsengracht, watched by over 350,000 people.

Other events include **Leather Pride** (ⓦleatherpride.nl) in October, film festivals in the spring and summer (see page 207), and the infamous organized fetish party **Wasteland** (ⓦwasteland.nl), held regularly throughout the year, although this is not strictly aimed at the LGBTQ community.

For more information on the above events, or other special parties held throughout the year, see ⓦnighttours.com.

Lellebel Utrechtsestraat 4 ☎020 233 6533, ⓦlellebel.nl; map p.65. Small and popular drag-show bar, with a lively and cheerful atmosphere. Mon–Thurs 9pm–3am, Fri & Sat 8pm–4am, Sun 3pm–3am.

Lunchroom Downtown Reguliersdwarsstraat 31 ☎020 789 0554, ⓦlunchroomdowntown.nl; map p.65. Popular café in the heart of the main LGBTQ district that's a favourite meeting place for visitors and locals. Relaxed and friendly, with inexpensive meals, but no alcohol. Mon–Wed & Sun 10am–7pm, Thurs–Sat 10am–9pm.

Mankind Weteringstraat 60 ☎020 638 4755, ⓦmankind.nl; map p.65. Quiet, non-scene, traditional Dutch bar away from the usual LGBTQ hangouts, with its own terrace beside the canal attracting locals and visitors alike. It serves inexpensive meals and is lovely in summer. Mon–Sat noon–midnight.

Montmartre de Paris Halvemaansteeg 17 ☎020 625 5565, ⓦcafemontmartre.nl; map p.65. A convivial brown café that's usually packed, with an emphasis on music and entertainment (courtesy of Whitney and Madonna). Happy hour 6–8pm. Mon–Thurs & Sun 5pm–3am, Fri & Sat 5pm–4am.

De Spijker Kerkstraat 4 ☎020 233 8665, ⓦspijkerbar.nl; map p.65. Relaxed cruising bar with a pool table and Bingo every Sat afternoon. Women welcome. Happy hour daily 5–7pm. Mon–Thurs & Sun 4pm–1am, Fri & Sat 4pm–3am.

JORDAAN

Saarein Elandsstraat 119 ☎020 623 4901, ⓦsaarein2.nl; map p.75. Amsterdam's first women-only bar, *Saarein*

now welcomes all 'queer minded people'. Some of the former glory of this split-level café may be gone, but it's still a warm, relaxing place, with a cheerful atmosphere, and is also a useful source of contacts and information. Tues–Thurs 4pm–1am, Fri 4pm–2am, Sat 1pm–2am, Sun 4pm–1am.

CLUBS

OLD CENTRE

Getto Warmoesstraat 51 ☎020 421 5151, ⓦgetto.nl; map p.34. Relaxed, local bar-club in the heart of the Red Light District, serving home-cooked comfort food (from 5.30pm) and cocktails. Cocktail party with DJs every Sun 5pm–midnight. Tues–Thurs 4.30pm–1am, Fri & Sat 4.30pm–2am, Sun 4.30pm–midnight.

GRACHTENGORDEL SOUTH

Club Church Kerkstraat 52 ☎020 421 0392, ⓦclubchurch.nl; map p.65. Full-on cruising scene with "onderbroek" (underpants) nights every Fri and first Sat of the month. Tues–Wed 8pm–1am, Thurs–Sat 10pm–5am, Sun 4–8pm.

Club NYX Reguliersdwarsstraat 42 ☎020 625 8788, ⓦclubnyx.nl; map p.65. This is one of the city's largest dance clubs, with three floors each offering a different style of music, from r'n'b to house and dance. Predominantly male, though women and straights are admitted. Thurs 11pm–4am, Fri & Sat 11pm–5am.

AMSTERDAM WEST

De Trut Bilderdijkstraat 165 ☎020 612 3524, ⓦtrutfonds.nl; map p.75. In the sweltering basement of a former factory building, this popular squat venue holds a lesbian dance party on Sun nights (gay men welcome), with a large dancefloor, cheap drinks and a varied mix of music. Very popular– the doors close at midnight and if you arrive after 11pm you may not get in. Sun 11pm–4am.

CINEMAS AND SAUNAS

Call the LGBT+ Switchboard (see page 204) for details of gay film showings around town, or take a look at the Uitkrant (see page 181). The Rialto (see page 188) screens new gay and lesbian films every Sunday evening throughout June, July and August in the **Gay and Lesbian Summer Festival**. See ⓦgaylinc.nl for comprehensive sauna listings.

Cavia Van Hallstraat 52, western docklands ☎020 681 1419, ⓦfilmhuiscavia.nl. The only cinema showing gay films regularly. In conjunction with De Balie (see page 187), it hosts an annual event in March called De Roze Filmdagen (Pink Film Days; ⓦrozefilmdagen.nl), a festival of gay and lesbian movies.

Nieuwezijds Gay Sauna Nieuwezijds Armsteeg 95, Old Centre ☎020 331 8327, ⓦsaunanz.nl. A new opening from the owners of Club Church, this stylish sauna has a proper bar, and massages are also available. Entrance €19.50. Mon–Fri noon–6am, Sat & Sun noon–10am.

14

ARTIS ROYAL ZOO

Kids' Amsterdam

With its canals, narrow cobbled alleys and trams, the novelty value of Amsterdam can prove entertaining enough for many kids. There's also a whole host of attractions specifically aimed at young children, ranging from circuses and puppet theatres to urban farms and one of the best zoos in Europe. There are also plenty of opportunities for play – practically all of the city's parks and most patches of greenery have some form of playground, and the recreation area in the Vondelpark is heaven for kids and parents alike. You'll find most places pretty child-friendly; the majority of restaurants have highchairs and kids' menus, and bars don't seem to mind accompanied kids, as long as they're well behaved. Indeed, having a small child in your care is unlikely to close many doors to you in Amsterdam.

BABYSITTING

Oppascentrale Kriterion ☎020 624 5848, ⊛oppas centralekriterion.nl. Most, though not all, hotels welcome young children, and many now offer child-minding services, but if you get stuck try Oppascentrale Kriterion, a long-established babysitting agency with a good reputation. Mon–Sat 4.30–8pm.

PARKS, FARMS AND PLAYGROUNDS

There are plenty of **petting farms** dotted around the city – two of the most central are listed below but check ⊛iamsterdam.com for a full list. The **Artis Zoo** is also well worth a visit (see page 210), which can be visited alongside Micropia – a unique museum dedicated to microbes.

Amsterdamse Bos Nieuwe Meerlaan 3 ☎020 545 6100, ⊛amsterdamsebos.nl. This area of woodland (see page 123) offers playgrounds, outdoor theatre, lakes and cycle paths. You can also rent canoes and pedalos to explore the Bosbaan canal, and visit the Ridammerhoeve goat farm (Mon & Wed–Sun 10am–5pm; free; ☎020 645 5034, ⊛geitenboerderij.nl), which makes its own ice cream.

Amstelpark Petting Zoo Amstelpark 22 ☎020 644 1744, ⊛speeltuin-amstelpark.nl; bus #62 to Weerdestein. Situated next to a playground, this petting zoo has chickens, rabbits, goats and donkeys and is free to enter. Tues–Sun 10am–6pm.

De Pijp Petting Zoo Lizzy Ansinghstraat 82, De Pijp ☎020 644 8303, ⊛kinderboerderijdepijp.nl; tram #16 to Museumplein, then #12 to Cornelis Troostplein. A variety of farm animals such as sheep, goats, ponies, pigs and chickens, as well as guinea pigs, rabbits and salamanders. Free. Mon–Fri 11am–5pm, Sat & Sun 1–5pm.

Rembrandtpark Oreliuskade 57, Amsterdam West ⊛rembrandtpark.org. Situated to the southwest of the city, the Rembrandtpark has several walking and biking paths, as well as De Uylenberg – Amsterdam's oldest petting zoo.

't Brinkie Meerkerdreef 27, Amsterdam Zuidoost, ☎020 696 5346, ⊛www.kinderboerderijbrinkie.nl; Metro 50 or 54, Bus 47. Children will love this petting zoo full of turkeys, sheep, donkeys, peacocks and goats. The knowledgeable staff will gladly offer chats about animals and nature. Wed–Mon 10am–5pm.

Vondelpark Main entrance on Stadhouderskade ⊛hetvondelpark.net. The city's most central park, the leafy and lawned Vondelpark (see page 116) has an excellent playground, as well as sandpits, paddling pools and a couple of cafés where you can take a break and order drinks and light bites. *De Vondeltuin* (Vondelpark 7; ☎0627 565 576, ⊛devondeltuin.nl), a café on the Amstelveen side of the park, rents out skates in the summer and is perfectly situated opposite the playground. Also in summertime, the open-air theatre, Openluchttheater, usually puts on some free entertainment for kids – mime, puppets, acrobats and the like.

THEATRES AND PUPPET SHOWS

A number of **theatres** put on inexpensive kids' entertainment (around €3–4) most afternoons, and a fair proportion offer **mime**- or **puppet**-based shows – including the Openluchttheater (see page 219) – that are suitable for English-speakers. Check the children's section ("Jeugdagenda") of the monthly *Uitkrant* (see page 181), and look for the words *mimegroep* and *poppentheater*. Public holidays and the summer season bring touring **circuses** and the occasional travelling **funfair** (*kermis*) to the city, usually setting up on the Dam or in one of the city's many parks. Lastly, check out the **festivals** listings in Chapter 17; many of them, such as the King's Day celebrations, are enjoyable for kids too.

Amsterdam Marionette Theatre Nieuwe Jonkerstraat 8, Old Centre ☎020 620 8027, ⊛marionettentheater. nl. This intimate theatre housed in a former blacksmith's puts on traditional marionette performances. Because plays are set to classical music there's no language confusion, and the costumes are fabulous. It's best to reserve tickets in advance (adults €16, 9- to 14-year-olds €7.50, under-14s free). Check the website for details.

Koos Kneus Puppet Theatre Iepenplein 40, Amsterdam Oost ☎020 692 8532, ⊛kooskneus.nl. Puts on puppet shows for 2- to 8-year-olds at 10.30am, noon and 2pm on Sun (the first two are best for 2–4-year-olds) and at 2pm on Wed. Afterwards kids can play dress-up and get their face painted. €8/child.

De Krakeling Nieuwe Passeerdersstraat 1, Jordaan ☎020 624 5123, ⊛krakeling.nl. Permanent children's theatre, with theatre, puppet and dance shows for youngsters up to the age of 17, often with an emphasis on full-scale audience participation. Performances are mostly in Dutch, though the theatre also puts on a number of dance events that non-Dutch speakers will appreciate – look for "LNP" (Language No Problem) on the programme list.

THE ZOO AND MUSEUMS

The Amsterdam Dungeon Rokin 78, Old Centre ☎020 530 8500, ⊛thedungeons.com. This popular sight is housed in a former church. Tours last for around an hour, during which you're handed from one ham actor to another, making believe you've been sentenced by the Inquisition, press-ganged onto the high seas, chased by witches and surrounded by plague victims – until you're finally swept around the interior of the church on a short roller-coaster

15

AMSTERDAM'S BEST ACTIVITIES FOR KIDS

For older children, a good introduction to Amsterdam might be one of the **canal trips** that start from Centraal Station or Damrak, or for 5- to 12-year-olds try the Blue Boat Company's pirate-themed audio guide: while their parents are enjoying a standard cruise, the audio guide helps kids to spot animals using binoculars and to listen out for water sounds; at the end of the journey they get a certificate proving their qualification as a freshwater pirate. Cruises leave regularly from Stadhouderskade, near the Vondelpark (daily: Mar–Oct every 30min; Nov–Feb 1hr 15min; adults €18, or €16 if you book online, children €8.50, or €7.50 online; ☎020 679 1370, ⊕ blueboat.nl).

Another fun water-based activity is a ride on a pedalo-style **canal bike** (see page 23). This can get tiring, but jetties where the bikes can be picked up and dropped off are numerous, and it's quite safe. You could also take the kids on a free **ferry ride** to Amsterdam Noord (only 5min from Centraal Station), or the up-and-coming NDSM district (a 10min ride away) aboard a small, tug-like passenger ferry, which leaves every few minutes from behind Centraal Station (see page 23). Alternatively, see Amsterdam on two wheels by **renting a bike** – either with a child seat attached, or a tandem. MacBike (see page 193) rents out both types and gives friendly advice too.

In summer you can climb the **tower** of the Westerkerk (see page 58) for panoramic views of the city. In winter, there's **ice-skating** at the Jaap Eden IJsbanen (see page 214), as well as, outdoor rinks. If the canals are frozen over and you don't have any skates, just teeter along on the ice with everybody else. Good rainy-day options include bowling or laser gaming at the new Lovers Power Zone (see page 213) or browsing the books at the Bibliotheek (see page 98): the city's library has a whole floor dedicated to kids' activities, with plenty of reading material in English.

The best **swimming pool** for kids is the indoor, tropical-style Mirandabad, De Mirandalaan 9 (see page 216), which has all sorts of gimmicks such as wave machines, slides and a beach with palm trees; there's also a separate toddlers' pool. In summer, the most popular outdoor pools are the Flevoparkbad (see page 215) and Brediusbad (see page 215).

---

ride. Adults €23 (€20 online), children 5–15 €18; joint tickets with Madame Tussaud's are available too. Daily 11am–6pm.

Artis Royal Zoo Plantage Kerklaan 38–40, Plantage ☎020 523 3670, ⊕ artis.nl. Artis Royal Zoo (see page 91) is a fun day out for kids, all the more so if you time your visit to coincide with feeding times. Adults €23, 3- to 9-year-olds €19.50, under-2s free; there are also joint tickets available with Artis' other attraction, Micropia. Daily: March–Oct 9am–6pm (June–Aug Sat til sunset); Nov–Feb 9am–5pm.

Dutch Resistance Museum Junior Plantage Kerklaan 61, Plantage ☎020 620 2535, ⊕ verzetsmuseum.org. A free audio guide (in English) leads children around this add-on to the main Dutch Resistance Museum (see page 92), explaining World War II from a child's perspective using true stories and authentic items. Adults €11, children 7–16 €6. Mon–Fri 10am–5pm, Sat & Sun 11am–5pm.

JHM Children's Museum Nieuwe Amstelstraat 1, old Jewish quarter ☎020 531 0380, ⊕ bit.ly/JHMuseum. Children aged 6–12 can learn about the Jewish faith and traditions on a tour that leads them through the house of the Jewish Hollander family, learning about kosher food in the kitchen, and Jewish music from around the world, among other topics. Adults €15, children 6–12 €3.75, 13–

17 & students €7.50, under-6s free. The ticket also allows you to visit other sites of the Jewish quarter: the Joods Historisch Museum, Portuguese Synagogue, Hollandse Schouwburg and the National Holocaust Museum. Daily 11am–5pm.

Madame Tussaud's Dam 20, Old Centre ☎020 522 1010, ⊕ madametussauds.nl. A large waxworks collection with the usual smattering of famous people and rock stars, as well as Dutch celebrities and the royal family, plus a few Amsterdam peasants and merchants thrown in for local colour. Family and joint tickets with Amsterdam Dungeon are available. Adults €29 (if bought online, price includes combined ticket with the Amsterdam Dungeon), 5- to 15-year-olds €24, under-5s free. Daily 10am–8pm (last admission 6pm), school summer holidays 9.30am–9.30pm.

Micropia Artisplein, Plantage Kerklaan 36–38, Plantage ⊕ micropia.nl. If you have a budding biologist in the family, this new museum, part of Artis, is bound to appeal. Dedicated to the secretive and silent world of microorganisms, it's best suited to older kids, with exhibits on the bacteria that live in elephant dung and a kiss-o-meter that measures how many critters a couple swaps when they French kiss. Children aged 3–9 €13, over-10s €15, students €7.50. Joint tickets with Artis Royal Zoo:

adults €29.50, 3- to 9-year-olds €25.50, under-2s free. Mon–Wed & Sun 9am–6pm, Thurs–Sat 9am–8pm.
NEMO Oosterdok 2, eastern docklands ☎ 020 531 3233, ⓦ nemosciencemuseum.nl. The whopping great green building that marks the entrance to the IJ tunnel is home to NEMO, a six-floor science and technology centre, with labelling in Dutch and English, whose interactive exhibits are geared towards pre-teenage kids. Interaction is encouraged and the whole experience is very hands-on. Come summer, kids can also frolic in their rooftop water feature – a cascade of thirty shallow pools ideal for splashing through. €16.50, under-4s free. Tues–Sun 10am–5pm; also open Mon mid-March to early-Sept.

Tropenmuseum Junior Tropenmuseum, Linnaeusstraat 2, Amsterdam Oost ☎ 088 004 2800, ⓦ tropenmuseum. nl; tram #9 to Van Swindenstraat or #14 or #7 to Alexanderplein. Designed especially for children between the ages of 6 and 13, the museum's aim is to promote international understanding through exhibitions, tours and performances on other cultures. It's nowhere near as dry as it sounds, and although the shows are in Dutch only, this is more than compensated for by the lively exhibits, which are expertly presented and supported by music and dance performances. Workshops take place on Sat, Sun and school holidays at 1pm and 3pm, plus Wed 3pm; call to reserve. Adults €15, 4- to 18-year-olds €8, under-3s free. Tues–Sun 10am–5pm, also open Mon on public and school holidays.

Van Gogh Museum Paulus Potterstraat 7, Museum Quarter ☎ 020 570 5200, ⓦ vangoghmuseum.nl. The Van Gogh Museum (see page 113) runs family guided tours every half hour from 9.30am, as well as English workshops on request (email ⓔ educatie@vangoghmuseum.nl). Adults €18, under-18s free; tours €95.

CAFÉS AND PANCAKE HOUSES

KinderKookKafé Vondelpark 6b ☎ 020 625 3257, ⓦ kinderkookkafe.nl. This "kids' kitchen" has a self-service bar where kids under-13s can prepare food, along the likes of pizzas, sandwiches and cakes (€2.50–7.50), for their "guests", aka parents. The café is open to all, unless booked for a party. Booking is essential at weekends. Daily 10am–5pm.

The Pancake Bakery Prinsengracht 191, Grachten-gordel west ☎ 020 625 1333, ⓦ pancake.nl. This busy pancake and omelette house caters especially well for children. The pancakes are delicious, and kids are kept entertained at the table with pens, paper and novelty toys. Children's pancakes start at €5.25; adults' pancakes start at €6.50. Daily 9am–9.30pm.

SHOPS

Azzurro Kids Van Baerlestraat 6, Museum Quarter ☎ 020 673 0457, ⓦ azzurrokids.nl. The city's chicest kids' clothes store, stocking labels such as Diesel, Replay, Armani and Baby Dior. Mon & Sun noon–6pm, Tues– Sat 10am–6pm, Thurs 10am–8pm.

De Bijenkorf Dam 1, Old Centre ⓦ debijenkorf.nl. This department store has one of the best (and most reasonably priced) toy sections in town. Mon & Sun 11am–9pm, Tues–Sat 10am–9pm.

Broer & Zus Stadhouderskade 92, Museum Quarter ☎ 020 221 0501, ⓦ broerenzus.nl. Cool clothes and gifts with a funky twist for babies and children up to age 8, from logo T-shirts to wooden toys and cute bags. The range includes the store's own clothing label plus a few mid-range Dutch children's designers. Mon 1–6pm, Tues–Fri 10am–6pm, Sat 10am–5pm.

Goochem Toys 1e Constantijn Huygensstraat 80, Vondelpark ☎ 020 612 4704, ⓦ goochem.amsterdam. Sells a wonderful collection of durable wooden children's toys, furniture, books and games. Mon 1–6pm, Tues–Fri 9.30am–6pm, Sat 9.30am–5.30pm.

Intertoys Damrak 28–30, Old Centre ☎ 020 638 3356, ⓦ intertoys.nl. Amsterdam's largest toy shop, selling everything from puzzles to scooters. Mon 11am–8pm, Tues, Wed & Sat 9.30am–8pm, Thurs & Fri 9.30am–9pm, Sun 10am–8pm.

Nijntje Scheldestraat 61, Nieuw Zuid ☎ 020 664 8054, ⓦ dewinkelvannijntje.nl. "Nijntje" – the white rabbit known as Miffy in the English translation – is the Netherlands' most beloved children's storybook character. This store is dedicated to her and stocks books, clothes, bedspreads and other souvenirs. Mon 1–6pm, Tues–Fri 10am–6pm, Sat 10am–5pm, Sun noon–5pm.

Poppendokter Reestraat 18-20, Grachtengordel west ☎ 020 626 5274, ⓦ www.poppendokter.fiberworld. nl. Don't be deterred by the lacklustre window front – this quaint shop is a little slice of city history: Poppendockter has been repairing the teddy bears and dolls of Amsterdammer children since the 70s. Mon–Fri 10am–6pm, Sat 10am–5pm.

Teuntje Haarlemmerdijk 132, western docklands ☎ 020 625 3432, ⓦ teuntje.nl. Large shop stocking a wide range of prams and strollers, as well as carriers and highchairs. The store also sells toys and a good range of clothes and shoes for babies to 8-year-olds. Mon 1–6pm, Tues–Fri 10am–6pm, Sat 10am–5pm.

Tinkerbell Spiegelgracht 10, Grachtengordel south ☎ 020 625 8830, ⓦ tinkerbelltoys.nl. A wonderful shop full of old-fashioned toys, mobiles, models and books suitable for children up to 9, with all purchases beautifully gift-wrapped. Mon 1–6pm, Tues–Sat 10am–6pm, Sun noon–5pm.

15

ICE-SKATING THE CANALS

Sports and activities

Most visitors to Amsterdam tend to confine their exercise to walking around the major sights, but if you do get the urge to stretch your muscles, there's a wide range of sports to enjoy. In summer, Amsterdammers hit the pool or the (urban) beach. In winter – if it's cold enough – skating on the frozen waterways is the most popular and enjoyable activity; other winter sports are mostly played in private health or sports clubs, to which you can usually get a day pass. The chief spectator sport is football, and Amsterdam is home to the legendary Ajax (pronounced "eye-axe") who play in the impressive Johan Cruijff Arena in the eastern suburbs. Less mainstream offerings include Holland's own *korfbal* and *carambole*.

For information on **cycling** in Amsterdam – arguably the locals' favourite pastime – see the Basics section of this guide. For up-to-the-minute details on all sporting activities in the city, visit ⊛iamsterdam.com or ⊛amsterdam.nl/sport.

BASEBALL (HONKBAL)

Amsterdam Pirates Herman Bonpad 5 ☎020 616 2151, ⊛amsterdampirates.nl; tram #1 then bus #69 or #61. The local team are in the top baseball division, and based to the west of the centre. Matches take place in the afternoons (around 2pm or 7.30 pm) in the summer, and most games are free.

BOWLING

Knijn Bowling Centre Scheldeplein 3, opposite the RAI complex, Nieuw Zuid ☎020 664 2211, ⊛knijnbowling. nl; tram #4 to RAI or #25 to Scheldtstraat. This bowling alley has eighteen lanes and a café; on Friday and Saturday evenings there's "twilight bowling" (€12/ person), accompanied by a DJ. Lanes cost between €24 and €29.50/hr, with a maximum of six people/ lane. Reservations recommended. Mon–Thurs 10am– midnight, Fri 10am–12.30am, Sat noon–12.30am, Sun noon–11pm.

Lovers Power Zone De Ruyterkade 153, eastern docklands ☎020 760 7600, ⊛powerzone.amsterdam. This bowling alley is the closest to the city centre, with six glow-in-the-dark alleys, and laser gaming too. Mon–Wed & Sun noon–10pm, Thurs noon–midnight, Fri & Sat noon–1am.

FOOTBALL

The football season runs from August to May, and matches are generally on Sundays, with occasional games at 8pm on Wednesdays. As a last resort, you can always catch a game on screen in a bar.

Ajax Amsterdam Johan Cruijff Arena, Arena Boulevard 1–3 ☎020 311 1336, ⊛ajax.nl; either take the metro to Strandvliet and walk around the stadium to the main entrance on the far side, or go a stop further on to Bijlmer station, from which the Arena Boulevard leads to the main entrance. Ticket "packages" (with prices starting from around €25 and increasing in value depending on the importance of the match) usually include an Ajax scarf and can be bought online, but for some matches visitors need a club card. These only cost €6 for five years, but you must apply in advance (☎0900 232 2529) and wait up to five weeks for your application to be processed. Having done all that, you can then buy your ticket.

Feyenoord Rotterdam Olympiaweg 50, Rotterdam ☎061 907 1908, ⊛feyenoord.com; trains from Amsterdam (30min) stop near the ground.

PSV Eindhoven Frederiklaan 10a, Eindhoven ☎040 250 5505, ⊛psv.nl; trains from Amsterdam (1hr 20min) stop a 10min walk from the stadium.

16

HIT THE BEACH

The Netherlands has some great sandy **beaches**, although it has to be said that the weather is notoriously unreliable and temperatures can be bracing. What's more, the North Sea is pretty murky and often teeming with jellyfish. For swimming and sunbathing, the nearest resort is **Zandvoort**, a couple of short train rides from Amsterdam (via Haarlem), but there are nicer, quieter stretches of coast nearby, most notably amid the wild expanse of dune and beach that makes up the **National Park Zuid-Kennemerland**. The park is easily reached from Amsterdam by train; get off at Overveen or Santpoort-Noord and then walk 10 minutes.

Amsterdam's own city beach is **Blijburg**, a small stretch of sand on the IJsselmeer, and a popular spot on warm summer days. The improvised beach bar *Blijburg aan Zee* (see page 178) has frequent live music and cheap food. To reach Blijburg, take tram #26 from Centraal Station and get off at the last stop.

Failing all that, try one of Amsterdam's urban beaches. **NEMO** – Amsterdam's science and technology museum (see page 211) – converts its rooftop into a panoramic "beach" terrace (daily May–Aug, closed in bad weather). Entry is free and it comes complete with deckchairs, sandpits, a series of thirty shallow cascading pools of water you can splash in, and gigantic chess sets. In addition, **Pllek** (see page 169) in the NDSM district, creates its own beach for lounging with summer drinks; and for six weeks from mid-July the waterfront area opposite Centraal Station along Prins Hendrikkade is converted into a **city beach** (⊛playgroundcs.nl), with 350 cubic metres of sand, family activities and food trucks on hand for refreshments.

DUTCH FOOTBALL

It's a mark of the dominance of Amsterdam's **Ajax**, Eindhoven's **PSV** and Rotterdam's **Feyenoord** that most foreigners would be hard pushed to name any other Dutch football team. More generally familiar, perhaps, is the Dutch style of play – based on secure passing with sudden, decisive breaks – which has made Dutch players highly sought-after all over Europe. Ticket packages to see Ajax can be bought online, but you'll need to be quick for major matches. Buying tickets for Feyenoord and PSV, whose grounds are both within easy striking distance of Amsterdam by public transport, is a little more awkward: some games require a club card, and limited numbers of tickets are available for visitors from abroad, purchasable only by prior application.

GYMS AND YOGA

Health Club Jordaan 1e Rozendwarsstraat 10, Jordaan ☎020 489 7676, ⓦ healthclubjordaan.nl. Excellent club offering yoga, pilates, bodypump, kickboxing and spinning classes. In addition to a one-off €29 admin fee, a four-week pass costs from €57 (basic fitness) through to €89 (all-inclusive), with discounts for year-long memberships; ID required. Mon–Fri 7am–10pm, Sat 9am–6pm, Sun 9am–5pm.

Iyengar Nieuwe Achtergracht 138h, Plantage ☎020 627 6523, ⓦ iyengaryogaamsterdam.com. All classes at this yoga institute are walk-in, range from 1hr 30min to 2hr. Beginner's lessons are held daily; see the website for class times and fees.

Splash Lijnbaansgracht 241, Grachtengordel south ☎020 422 0280, ⓦ splashamsterdam.nl. Very popular hi-tech fitness centre with sauna, tanning salon, Turkish bath and a range of daily aerobic classes delivered in both Dutch and English. Student monthly passes cost around €62, while an all-inclusive year-long package is €840; ID required. Mon–Fri 7am–midnight, Sat & Sun 8am–9pm.

HORSERIDING

Amsterdamse Manege Nieuwe Kalfjeslaan 25, Amstelveen ☎020 643 1342, ⓦ deamsterdamsemanege. nl; bus #347 from Centraal Station to Kalfjeslaan, then a 1.5km walk. Superbly located in the Amsterdamse Bos, although unfortunately it's not possible to go for a ride unless you are a regular customer. However, you can book a lesson: an hour costs €25 for adults and €21 for under-16s. Mon–Fri 8.30am–11pm, Sat & Sun 8am–6pm.

Hollandsche Manege Vondelstraat 140, Vondelpark ☎020 618 0942, ⓦ dehollandschemanege.nl. Stables built in 1882 in neo-Renaissance style located on the edge of the Vondelpark. You'll need your own riding boots, though hats can be rented. A private one-hour lesson costs €62. Discounts offered with the I amsterdam card (see page 30). Mon–Fri 10am–11pm, Sat & Sun 10am–6pm.

ICE-SKATING

One of the great events in Holland's sporting calendar, when it happens, is the **Elfstedentocht** (ⓦ elfstedentocht.frl), a race across eleven towns and 200km of frozen waterways in Friesland, in the north of the Netherlands. If you're around in January and the ice is good, you'll hear talk of little else, but it's been over twenty years since the last big freeze allowed it to go ahead, so you'll have to be very lucky to catch the race. However, if you're not a pro skater, the easiest and safest option is probably skating on one of the rinks below.

ICE*Amsterdam Muntplein, Grachtengordel south ⓦ iceamsterdam.nl. An outdoor skating rink with a difference – you can pirouette on skates with the Rijksmuseum as a backdrop. There's also a restaurant on site, serving up winter warmers, and a twinkly "Christmas Village" in Dec. Entry €6, skate rental €10 (two hours). Mid-Nov to Feb Mon–Thurs & Sun 10am–9pm, Fri & Sat 10am–10pm.

Jaap Eden IJsbanen Radioweg 64, Amsterdam Oost ☎0900 724 2287, ⓦ jaapeden.nl; tram #9 to Kruislaan. This large ice-skating complex to the east of the city centre has an indoor and an outdoor rink. You can rent skates for €6 from Waterman Sport next door (☎020 694 9884, ⓦ watermansport.nl); they have to be used at Jaap Eden IJsbanen and you have to leave your passport or driving licence as a deposit. "Disco skating" is organized on Sat nights. Adults €7.20, under-16s €4.30. Oct to mid-March Mon 8am–4.30pm, 5–7pm & 8.30–11.10pm, Tues 9am–4.30pm, 9–11.10pm, Wed 8am–5.30pm, Thurs 9am–4.30pm, 5–7pm & 8.30–11.10pm, Fri 8am–4.30pm, & 9–11.10pm, Sat noon–4.30pm, Sun 10.30am–5.30pm.

Leidseplein ice rink Leidseplein, Grachtengordel south ⓦ kermisplaza.nl. Every winter, an ice-skating rink is set up on Leidseplein. There's skate rental and a small Christmas market too. Mid-Nov to early Jan.

16

KORFBAL

A home-grown sport, **Korfbal** is cobbled together from netball, basketball and volleyball, and played with mixed teams, a high basket and two teams of eight players. Each match lasts an hour with a ten-minute break in the middle, and the aim is to shoot the ball through a bottomless basket mounted on a high pole without a player leaving their "zone".

Blauw Wit Sportcomplex Joos Banckersweg 18a Amsterdam West w akcblauw-wit.nl; tram #12 to Karel Doormantstraat/De Rijpstraatwhich from Amsterdam Sloterdijk train station. Local team AKC Blauw-Wit usually play matches on Saturday and Sunday from Sept to June.

POOL AND CARAMBOLE

A number of bars and cafés have **pool** tables, although you may have to go to a hall to play snooker. A popular local variation on billiards (*biljart*) is **carambole**, played on a table without pockets. You score by *caroming* (rebounding) off the cue ball and the opponent's ball; the skill of some of the locals can be mind-boggling.

Final Touch Prinsengracht 735, Grachtengordel south ☎ 020 620 9252, w scfinaltouch.nl. This club has five snooker tables and five pool tables all lined up in a row, so there's no knocking of elbows. Mon–Thurs & Sun 2pm–1am, Fri & Sat 2pm–2am.

Poolcafé de Keu Eerste Helmersstraat 5–7, Vondelpark ☎ 020 230 0551, w dekeu.nl. A cosy, welcoming billiards café where there'll be locals on hand to guide you through the rules of the game. Mon–Fri 4pm–1am, Sat & Sun 4pm–3am.

SAUNAS AND SPAS

As well as the options below, there are also **spas** at a number of the city's swanky hotels, including the *Grand* (see page 146), the *Park Plaza Victoria* (see page 147), the *InterContinental Amstel* (see page 150) and the *Okura* (see page 151), and some gyms (see page 214) offer spa-style treatments. For gay saunas, see Chapter 14.

Koan Float Herengracht 321, Grachtengordel west ☎ 020 555 0333, w koanfloat.nl. The place to come in Amsterdam to float in a large bath of warm water, with magnesium and sodium salt added for muscular relaxation and buoyancy. There are three individual soundproof floating cabins, each with its own shower; once you're inside, lights, music and clothing are optional. Advance reservations are essential. Prices start from €32.50 for 45min. The centre also offers massages, from €52.50 for 45min. Daily 9.30am–11pm.

Sauna Deco Herengracht 115, Grachtengordel west ☎ 020 623 8215, w saunadeco.nl. Built in 1920, this is possibly Amsterdam's most stylish sauna and steam bath, with a magnificent Art Deco interior. A range of massages is available (from €37.50 for 25min). Entry costs €23.50 (€19 Mon & Wed–Fri noon–3pm); towels (€2.50) and bathrobes (€3.50) cost extra. There's also a menu of light meals and healthy juices. Mon & Wed–Sat noon–11pm, Tues 3–11pm, Sun 1–7pm.

SWIMMING POOLS

It's a good idea to call before setting out for any of the **pools** (*zwembaden*) listed below, since certain times are set aside for small children, family groups or classes. Some hotel spas also have indoor pools.

Brediusbad Spaarndammerdijk 306, western docklands ☎ 020 684 6984. A large outdoor pool, plus a separate shallow pool for children, and a toddlers' pool with spray fountain. There's also a kiosk selling food and drink, and picnic tables on the grass. Adults €4.05, 5- to 15-year-olds €1.80, under-5s free. Late April to early Sept Mon–Fri 7am–5.30pm, Sat & Sun 10am–5.30pm.

Flevoparkbad Insulindeweg 1002, Amsterdam Oost ☎ 020 692 5030, w flevoparkbad.com; tram #7 or #14 to Flevopark, bus #37 to Insulindeweg. The best outdoor swimming pool in the city; it gets very busy on sunny days. Adults €3.35, 3- to 15-year-olds €3.25, under-3s free. End April to early Sept daily 10am–5.30pm, until 7pm on warm days.

16

ICY AMSTERDAM

Whenever the city's canals and waterways freeze over (which does not happen every winter by any means), local **skaters** are spoiled for choice, with almost every stretch of water utilized, providing an exhilarating way to whizz round the city – much more fun than a rink. Surprisingly, canal cruises continue even when the waterways are frozen over, with the boats crunching their way up and down the Prinsengracht, but they leave the **Keizersgracht** well alone, to be occupied by bundled-up Amsterdammers who take to the ice in droves. Most locals have their own skates, so unless you feel like shelling out over €100 for a pair from a department store, skating on the canals is best enjoyed as a spectator sport.

IN-LINE SKATING

If you're equipped with **skates or a skateboard**, head for the free public **ramp** at the northeastern edge of the Museumplein (see page 115). For the more experienced skater there's also the free **Friday Night Skate** (ⓦfridaynightskate.com), a 20km tour around Amsterdam, which takes place – weather permitting – every week at 8.30pm, departing from outside the former Filmmuseum in the Vondelpark. If you're skating around town, take care not to get stuck in the tram tracks.

Mirandabad De Mirandalaan 9, Nieuw Zuid ⓣ020 252 4444; tram #4 to Europaplein. Superbly equipped swimming centre (outdoor and indoor pools), with wave machine, whirlpools and slides. Admission €4.25. Opening times vary, but usually daily 10am–8pm.

Zuiderbad Hobbemastraat 26, Museum Quarter ⓣ020 252 1390. Lovely old pool dating from the nineteenth century and refreshingly gimmick-free, though they do have a naturist hour on Sun afternoons (4.30–5.30pm). Admission €3.75.

TENNIS AND SQUASH

Most outdoor **tennis** courts are for members only, and those that aren't generally need to be reserved well in advance. Your best chance of getting a game at short notice is either at the open-air tennis courts in the Vondelpark (see page 116) or at one of the following.

Frans Otten Stadion IJsbaanpad 43, Nieuw Zuid ⓣ020 662 8767, ⓦfransottenstadion.nl; tram #16 or #24 to IJsbaanpad. A sports complex with eight indoor and fifteen outdoor tennis courts, as well as 21 squash courts. Tennis courts cost €20–25/hr; squash courts are €16–23/hr. Racket

rental costs €4. Call ahead to reserve a court in the evening. Mon–Fri 9am–11pm, Sat & Sun 9am–8pm.

Squash City Ketelmakerstraat 6, western docklands ⓣ020 626 7883, ⓦsquashcity.com. This gym has thirteen squash courts. They'll push for membership, but you can pay per visit at €12–14/person for 45min, in addition to racquet rental (€20.50). Be sure to call ahead to reserve courts. Mon–Thurs 7am–midnight (last entry 10.30pm), Fri 7am–10.30pm, Sat & Sun 8.30am–7.30pm.

AMSTERDAM ROOTS FESTIVAL

Festivals and events

Most of Amsterdam's festivals are music and arts events, supplemented by a sprinkling of religious celebrations, some of which are public holidays (see page 29). The King's Birthday (usually referred to as King's Day), at the end of April, is the city's most touted and exciting annual event, which sees the city brimming over with street parties and fairs. On a more cultural note, the Holland Festival arts extravaganza, held throughout June, attracts a handful of big names. Check with the VVV (see page 30) for dates and details, and remember that many other interesting events, such as the Easter performance of Bach's St Matthew Passion in the Grote Kerk at Naarden (ⓦbachvereniging.nl) and the North Sea Jazz Festival in Rotterdam (see page 183), are only a short train ride away.

JANUARY

Chinese New Year Late Jan/early Feb depending on lunar calendar. Dragon dance and fireworks display to celebrate the Chinese New Year, held at Nieuwmarkt and along the Zeedijk.

National Tulip Day Late Jan ⓦ facebook.com/tulpen. nl. To kick off the Dutch tulip season, locals and tourists are invited to come and pick one of these colourful flowers for free from a huge temporary garden on Dam square.

FEBRUARY

Wonderland Festival Second or third weekend ⓦ verknipt.org. This nonstop sixteen-hour rave of house and techno beats played by international DJs is held at the Warehouse Elementenstraat.

Februaristaking Feb 25 ⓦ februaristaking.nl. A combination of moving speeches and wreath-laying at the foot of the *Dokwerker* statue, located on J.D. Meijerplein,

marks the commemoration of the February Strike (see page 87).

Sonic Acts Festival Late Feb ⓦ sonicacts.com/portal. This eclectic mix of concerts, exhibitions and debates aims to bridge the gap between music, art and science, with events held at locations throughout the city, including Paradiso, the Stedelijk Museum and Brakke Grond.

MARCH

Roze Filmdagen (Pink Film Days) Early to mid-March ⓦ rozefilmdagen.nl. This long-running LGBTQ film festival, held every March since 1996, screens a mix of feature films, documentaries and shorts at Het Ketelhuis cinema and other spots around the Westergasfabriek.

Stille Omgang Sun closest to March 15 ⓦ stille-omgang.nl. This "silent procession" of local Catholics commemorates the Miracle of Amsterdam (see page 46),

starting and finishing at the Spui and passing through the Red Light District.

Head of the River Amstel Mid-March ⓦ headoftheriver. nl. Amsterdam's answer to the Oxford–Cambridge Boat Race, this rowing regatta sees some four thousand rowers tackle the 8km course from Rozenoordbrug to Ouderkerk. Flocks of people watch from the riverbanks, while others follow participants by bike.

APRIL

Imagine Film Festival Throughout April ⓦ imagine filmfestival.nl. Hosted inside the Eye (see page 188), this festival of film offers a mix of features and short films, ranging from science fiction to horror, produced by both local and international directors.

Tulp Festival Throughout April ⓦ tulpfestival.com. In celebration of the most enduring symbol of Amsterdam, over 500,000 beautiful tulips can be admired among the colourful gardens of museums, private homes and dozens of other locations all across the city. Popular with locals and visitors.

KunstRAI First week, Mid-April ⓦ kunstrai.nl. Amsterdam's annual contemporary arts fair showcases works from over 120 galleries; entry costs €15. A less commercial alternative is the Kunstvlaai (ⓦ kunstvlaai.nl) in the Amstelpark, usually held the week before KunstRAI.

National Museum Week Mid- to end April ⓦ nationale museumweek.nl. Free or discounted entrance to most of the museums in the Netherlands. Contact the VVV (see page 30) for more information.

King's Day/King's Birthday (Koningsdag) April 27. See box.

MAY

Herdenkingsdag (Remembrance Day) May 4 ⓦ 4en5mei.nl. There's a wreath-laying ceremony and a two-minute silence at the National Monument on the Dam, commemorating the Dutch dead of World War II, as well as a smaller event at the Homomonument in Westermarkt, in honour of the country's gay soldiers who died in the conflict.

Bevrijdingsdag (Liberation Day) May 5 ⓦ 4en5mei. nl. The country celebrates the 1945 liberation from Nazi occupation with bands, speeches and impromptu markets.

Rolling Kitchens First half of May ⓦ rollendekeukens. amsterdam. An open-air culinary feast for all the food-truck fans out there, with excellent smorgasbord, pizzas, seafood and Dutch specialities, held annually at Westergasfabriek.

National Mills Day Second Sat & Sun ☎ 020 623 8703, ⓦ molens.nl. On this day over half the country's remaining windmills and watermills, indicated by blue flags, are opened to the public free of charge.

JUNE

Taste of Amsterdam Early June ⓦ tasteofamsterdam. com. Four-day food and drink event in Amstelpark bringing together the city's top chefs – expect excellent food, wine tastings, cook-off competitions, demos and a farmers' market.

Holland Festival Throughout June ⓦ hollandfestival. nl. The largest music, dance and drama event in the Netherlands draws in a huge crowd of music fans from across the country (see page 186).

KING'S DAY

Held to celebrate the birthday of Dutch queens since 1885, this annual knees-up was changed to **King's Day** (Koningsdag) in 2014, in honour of King Willem-Alexander after his mother's abdication. Taking place on April 27, it's one of the most popular dates in the Dutch diary, celebrated with a street event *par excellence*, which seems to grow each year and is almost worth planning a visit around. Celebrations take place throughout the Netherlands, though festivities in Amsterdam tend to be somewhat wilder and larger in scale.

Special **club nights and parties** are held both the night before and the night after King's Day; however, to gain entry you'll need to book in advance, either at the club or at music shops (see page 201). King's Day itself sees the city's streets and canals lined with people, most of whom are dressed in ridiculous **costumes**. Anything goes, especially if it's **orange** – the Dutch national colour. A fair is held on the Dam, and music blasts continuously from huge sound systems set up across most of the major squares. This is also the one day of the year when goods can be bought and sold **tax-free** to anyone on the streets; a large portion of the city is given over to an impromptu flea market with hundreds of stalls set up in front of people's houses.

Vondelpark Open-Air Theatre (Openluchttheater) Mid-June to mid-Aug Fri–Sun w openluchttheater.nl. Theatre, dance and music performances take place on summer weekends in the Vondelpark, covering everything from jazz and classical concerts to stand-up comedy. Free, but donations appreciated.

Nomads Festival Late June w nomadsfestival.nl. Hugely popular house music festival with its own organic market and Arabian-style chill-out lounge. Tickets sell out fast.

Open Garden Days Third weekend w opentuinendagen.nl. Three-day event which sees some thirty private gardens – usually designed around a particular theme – open their gates to the public. Gardens are open Fri & Sun 10am–5pm

and there's a canal boat to take you around. Tickets cost €18.

International Theatre School Festival Third or last week w itsfestival.com. Six-day programme of events showcasing aspiring actors, dancers, musicians and opera singers in theatres on Nes (see box, page 186).

Awakenings Festival Late June to late July w awakeningsfestival.nl. Held in Spaarnwoude, very close to Amsterdam, this huge open-air techno festival attracts around 80,000 fans from all over the world every year.

Summer Breeze Latin Night June to Aug w mysummerbreeze.nl. A night of live DJs playing a mix of *bachata* and West Coast swing-style Latino music and events spread over four areas on the Westergasterras, by the Westergasfabriek.

JULY

Pitch Festival A weekend in early July w pitchfestival.nl. Kooky electronic music by the likes of James Blake and Jungle are played at this two-day festival held at the Westergasfabriek.

Amsterdam Fashion Week First and second week w fashionweek.nl. The summer version of this bi-annual fashion extravaganza hosts dozens of shows, and they're all open to the public. (The autumn/winter edition takes place in January.)

Amsterdam Roots Festival First week w amsterdamroots.nl. A week-long world music and film festival, with over sixty acts performing in the Melkweg, Paradiso and Bimhuis, culminating on the Sun with a free open-air concert – the Roots Open Air Festival – in Park Frankendael.

Julidans First half of July w julidans.nl. Held in theatres in the Leidseplein area every July, this is the leading dance event in the city (see page 187).

Over Het IJ Festival 13–22 July w overhetij.nl. This young and vibrant summer theatre festival takes over the NDSM shipyard for nine days (see page 186).

Cannabis Cup Mid-Jul w cannabiscup.com. Organized by *High Times* magazine since 1987, this three-day event celebrates and judges new strains of cannabis, accompanied by a mix of seminars and music performances, usually held at the Melkweg and coffeeshops around town.

Kwaku Summer Festival Weekends from mid-July to early Aug w kwakufestival.nl. A Surinamese and Antillian festival held in Nelson Mandelapark (Metro Bijlmer), featuring music, workshops, dance acts and stand-up comedy. In the middle of the festival there's a football competition between several teams. Caribbean delicacies such as *roti* and Surinamese *bakabana* – baked banana with peanut sauce – can be sampled at stalls around the festival site.

Amsterdam Pride End July to early Aug w amsterdamgaypride.nl. The city's LGBTQ community holds street parties and performances, and there's a "Canal Pride" flotilla of boats down Prinsengracht to musical accompaniment (see page 206).

17

AUGUST

Parade Second two weeks ⓦ deparade.nl. An excellent sixteen-day travelling theatrical fair, which puts on a host of short, independent performances, ranging from cabaret to theatre, given in or in front of artists' tents. Held in the Martin Luther King park (tram #25), next to the River Amstel, with special kid-friendly performances in the afternoon.

Grachtenfestival Ten days in mid-Aug ⓦ grachten festival.nl. For ten days international musicians perform at over ninety classical music events at historic locations around the main canals (see page 186).

Hartjesdag Third weekend in Aug ⓦ stichting hartjesdagen.nl. The "Day of Hearts" sees cross-dressing events and a drag parade (see page 206).

Encore Festival Last weekend ⓦ encorefestival.nl. This festival of hip-hop, r'n'b and soul has outgrown its former *Melkweg* home and is now hosted outside, at the NDSM shipyard across the river.

Uitmarkt Last weekend ⓦ uitmarkt.nl. Every cultural organization in the city, from opera to dance, advertises its forthcoming programme of events during this weekend, with free preview performances held over three days at Oosterdok.

Pluk de Nacht (Seize the Night) Mid-Aug ⓦ plukde nacht.nl. Ten-day open-air film festival on the banks of River IJ with free screenings of international features that have not yet been released in the Netherlands, accompanied by art, music and culinary events.

Jordaan Festival Last weekend ⓦ jordaanfestival.nl. This Jordaan street festival packs a lot into three days: a fair on Palmgracht, talent contests on Elandsgracht, a handful of street parties, and a food fair at the Noordermarkt.

SEPTEMBER

Amsterdam City Swim Early Sept ⓦ amsterdam cityswim.nl. Every year, over 2,500 participants take part in this 2km charity swim along the River IJ and through the city canals to raise money for motor neurone disease research.

Amsterdam Fringe Festival Usually first week ⓦ amsterdamfringefestival.nl. Held at more than 30 venues across town, this eleven-day dance and theatre festival brings together talented young artists from different backgrounds (around half the performances are suitable for non-Dutch speakers).

Open Monument Day Second weekend ⓦ open monumentendag.nl. For two days monuments throughout the Netherlands that are normally closed or have restricted opening times open their doors to the public for free.

OCTOBER

TCS Amsterdam Marathon Usually third Sun ⓦ tcsamsterdammarathon.nl. The 42km course around Amsterdam starts and finishes inside the Olympic Stadium south of the city, passing through the Old Centre along the way.

Read My World Second week ⓦ readmyworld.nl. Every year, international authors, poets, journalists and literature-lovers descend on Tolhuistuin to attend literary lectures, workshops and debates.

Amsterdam Dance Event Late Oct ⓦ amsterdam-dance-event.nl. A four-day clubbing festival, hosting hundreds of national and international DJs taking over every club in the city. Tickets for all events have to be purchased in advance and tend to sell out quickly.

NOVEMBER

Museum Night First Sat ⓦ museumnacht.amsterdam. Over fifty museums open their doors to the public from 7pm to 2am, with various events put on, accompanied by DJs and live music. Tickets cost €19.95 and sell out quickly.

Parade of Sint Nicolaas Second or third Sun ⓦ sintin amsterdam.nl. Traditional parade of Sinterklaas (Santa Claus) through the city on his white horse. He arrives by steamboat around 11.30am, mooring at the Scheepvaartmuseum, then proceeds down Prins Hendrikkade to Centraal Station, then down Damrak towards the Dam, finishing up in Leidseplein around 3pm, all the while accompanied by his helpers the Zwarte Pieten (Black Peters) – so called because of their blackened faces – who hand out sweets and little presents.

International Documentary Film Festival Mid- to late Nov ⓦ idfa.nl. The world's largest documentary festival is held over ten days in Nov (see page 188).

Amsterdam Art Weekend Third weekend ⓦ weekend. amsterdamart.com. A four-day cultural affair for art enthusiasts who get an opportunity to explore Amsterdam's vibrant contemporary art scene and meet up-and-coming young artists.

Amsterdam Light Festival Late Nov to late Jan ⓦ amsterdamlightfestival.com. For two months, light sculptures, projections and illuminations transform Amsterdam's wintry nights. Be sure to follow the "Illuminade" – a lit-up walkway through the city centre taking you past staggering light artworks.

DECEMBER

Christmas markets Throughout December. Amsterdammers flock to Christmas markets in every part of town to stock up on food delicacies, handmade art and accessories, while keeping warm with *glühwein* (mulled wine) and *oliebollen* (Dutch doughnuts). Some of the most popular can be found at Westergasfabriek (Funky Xmas Market) and Kromhouthal (Amsterdamsche Kerstmarkt).

Pakjesavond Dec 5. Pakjesavond (Present Evening), rather than Christmas Day, is when Dutch kids receive their Christmas presents. Though it tends to be a private affair, if you're in the city on that day and have Dutch friends, it's worth knowing that it's traditional to give a present, together with an amusing poem you've written caricaturing the recipient.

New Year's Eve Dec 31. New Year's Eve is big in Amsterdam, with fireworks and celebrations everywhere. Most bars and clubs stay open until morning – make sure you get tickets in advance. This might just qualify as the wildest and most reckless street partying in Europe, but a word of warning: Amsterdammers seem to love the idea of throwing lit fireworks around, and don't hesitate to send them careering into the crowd.

REMBRANDT STATUE, REMBRANDTPLEIN

Contexts

History

To a large extent, a history of Amsterdam is also a history of the whole of the Netherlands, a country that was an integral part of the so-called Low Countries, including Belgium and Luxembourg, for many centuries. The first version of the Netherlands emerged in the late sixteenth century. It was then that the Dutch broke with their Spanish Habsburg masters and, ever since, Amsterdam has been at the centre of Dutch events. The city was the country's most glorious cultural and trading centre throughout its seventeenth-century heyday, the so-called Golden Age, and, after a long downturn in the eighteenth century, picked itself up to emerge as a major metropolis in the nineteenth. In the 1960s, Amsterdam was galvanized by its youth, who took to hippy culture with gusto; their legacy is a social progressiveness – most conspicuously over soft drugs and prostitution – that still underpins the city's international reputation, good and bad, today.

Medieval foundations

Amsterdam's earliest history is as murky as the marshes from which it arose. Archeological finds have revealed signs of human habitation dating to around 2600 BC – the **Neolithic era** – much earlier than was previously thought, but almost nothing is known of these early settlers. Legend, on the other hand, asserts that two Frisian fishermen were the first inhabitants, and it is indeed likely that the city began as a fishing village at the mouth of the **River Amstel**, probably at some point in the twelfth century. Previously, this area had been a stretch of peat bog and marsh, but a modest fall in the sea level seems to have permitted settlement on the high ground along the riverside. The village was first given some significance when the local lord built a castle here around 1204, and shortly afterwards its position was further enhanced when the Amstel was dammed – hence the name **Amselredam**, later shortened to Amsterdam. In 1275, a new feudal overlord, Count Floris V, granted the settlement a municipal **charter**, which ceded certain trading rights, and in 1323 one of his successors designated the village a toll port for beer imported from Hamburg. Later still, Amsterdam also became an important transit port for Baltic grain destined for the burgeoning cities of the Low Countries.

Early commercial success

As Amsterdam prospered, so its **trade** diversified. In particular, it made a handsome profit from English **wool**, which was imported into the city and barged onto Leiden and Haarlem, where it was turned into cloth – with the finished products returned to Amsterdam for export. The cloth trade drew workers into the town to work along

12th century	c.1204
Two Frisian fishermen who set up camp by the banks of the River Amstel to escape a storm are believed to have been Amsterdam's first settlers	The local lord builds a castle (or at least fortified house) by the River Amstel – and Amsterdam is on its commercial way

THE DUTCH – ACCORDING TO PLINY

Never overly sympathetic to their unruly "barbarian" neighbours, the Romans were particularly dismissive of the Dutch. As **Pliny** observed of what is now the Netherlands in 50 AD: "Here a wretched race is found, inhabiting either the more elevated spots or artificial mounds… When the waves cover the surrounding area they are like so many mariners on board a ship, and when again the tide recedes their condition is that of so many shipwrecked men."

Warmoesstraat, and ships were able to sail right up the River Amstel to the Dam to pick up the finished work and drop off imported wood, grain, fish, salt and spices. By the late fourteenth century, Amsterdam had become a small but flourishing trading centre, its **population** growing steadily, if not spectacularly, from around 5000 in 1400 to 13,500 in 1500 – the slow rate of growth at least partly explained by the difficulty of building on Amsterdam's waterlogged soil, requiring timber piles to be driven into the firmer sand below.

Nevertheless, in the mid-sixteenth century Amsterdam underwent its first major **expansion** as the burgeoning trade with the **Hanseatic towns** of the Baltic made the city second only to Antwerp as a marketplace and warehouse for Northern and Western Europe. The trade in cloth, grain and wine brought craftsmen to the city, and its merchant fleet grew; by the 1550s three-quarters of all grain cargo brought out of the Baltic was carried in Amsterdam vessels. The foundations were being laid for the wealth of the Golden Age.

The Reformation

An **alliance of Church and state** had dominated the medieval world: pope and bishops, kings and counts were supposedly the representatives of God on earth, and they combined to crush any religious dissent. Much of their authority relied on the ignorance of the population, who were dependent on priests for the interpretation of the scriptures, the general population's view of the world carefully controlled. The **development of typography**, therefore, was a key factor in the **Reformation**, the stirring of religious revolt that stood sixteenth-century Europe on its head. For the first time, printers were able to produce relatively cheap bibles in quantity, and religious texts were no longer the exclusive property of the Church.

Consequently, as the populace snaffled up the bibles, so a welter of debate spread across much of Western Europe. First, Erasmus of Rotterdam promoted ideas of reformation, and then, in 1517, **Martin Luther** (1483–1546) went one step – or rather, leap – further, producing his 95 theses against the Church practice of indulgences, a prelude to his more comprehensive assault on the entire institution. There was no way back, and when Luther's works were disseminated his ideas gained a European following among reforming groups that were soon branded **Lutheran** by the Catholic Church.

Religious turmoil

Luther asserted that the Church's political power was subservient to that of the state, whereas the supporters of another great reforming thinker, **John Calvin** (1509–64), emphasized the importance of individual conscience and the need for redemption

1432	1452	1480
Philip the Good, the Duke of Burgundy, incorporates the Netherlands within his territories	Wooden Amsterdam goes up in flames – and the city council insists future buildings be made of brick and stone	Amsterdam's Old Centre assumes its present shape, enclosed by the Singel canal, which acts as a defensive moat

through the grace of Christ rather than the confessional. In Amsterdam, the doctrines of Calvin proved more popular than those of Luther, setting the seal on – and tone for – the city's religious transformation. Calvin was insistent on the separation of Church and state, but the lines were easily fudged in Amsterdam by the Church's ruling council of ministers and annually elected elders, who soon came to exercise considerable political clout. The Calvinists also had little time for other (more egalitarian) Protestant sects, and matters came to a head when, in 1535, one of the radical splinter groups, the **Anabaptists**, occupied Amsterdam's town hall, calling on passers-by to repent. Previously the town council had tolerated the Anabaptists, but, prompted by the Calvinists, it acted swiftly when civic rule was challenged; the town hall was besieged and, after its capture, the leaders of the Anabaptists were executed on the Dam.

The revolt of the Netherlands

In 1555, the fanatically Catholic **Philip II** succeeded to the Spanish throne. Through a series of marriages the Spanish monarchy – and **Habsburg** family – had come to rule over the Low Countries, and Philip was determined to rid his empire of its heretics, regardless of whether they were Lutherans, Calvinists or Anabaptists. Philip promptly garrisoned the towns of the Low Countries with Spanish mercenaries, imported the **Inquisition** and passed a series of anti-Protestant edicts. However, other pressures on the Habsburg Empire forced him into a tactical withdrawal and he transferred control of the Low Countries to his sister, **Margaret of Parma**, in 1559. Based in Brussels, the equally resolute Margaret implemented the policies of her brother with gusto. In 1561 she reorganized the Church and created fourteen new bishoprics, a move that was construed as a wresting of power from civil authority and an attempt to destroy the local aristocracy's powers of religious patronage. Right across the Low Countries, **Protestantism** – and Protestant sympathies – spread to the nobility, who now formed the "League of the Nobility" to counter Habsburg policy. The League petitioned Margaret for moderation but were dismissed out of hand by one of her (French-speaking) advisers, who called them "*ces geux*" (those beggars), an epithet that was to be enthusiastically adopted by the rebels.

The Iconoclastic Fury

In 1565 a harvest failure caused a winter famine among the urban workers of the region and, after years of repression, they struck back. In 1566 a Protestant sermon in the tiny Flemish textile town of Steenvoorde incited the congregation to purge the local church of its "papist" idolatry. The crowd smashed up the church's reliquaries and shrines, broke the stained-glass windows and terrorized the priests, thereby igniting what is commonly called the **Iconoclastic Fury** – the Beeldenstorm (statue storm). The rioting spread like wildfire and within ten days churches had been ransacked from one end of the Low Countries to the other, nowhere more so than in Amsterdam – hence the plain, whitewashed interiors of many of the city's churches today. The ferocity of this outbreak shocked the upper classes into renewed support for Spain, and Margaret regained the allegiance of most of her nobles – with the principal exception of the country's greatest landowner, Prince William of Orange-Nassau, known as **William the Silent**, who prudently slipped away to his estates in Germany.

1482	1517	1555
Mary of Burgundy is killed in a riding accident; the Netherlands is absorbed into the Habsburg Empire	Luther nails up his 95 theses against the sale of indulgences by the Catholic Church; Protestants anxious	The resolutely Catholic Philip II of Spain prepares to weed out his Protestant subjects in the Low Countries; Protestants very anxious

The Duke of Alva and the Waterguezen

Philip II was encouraged by the increase in support for Margaret and so, in 1567, he sent the **Duke of Alva**, with an army of ten thousand men, to the Low Countries to suppress his religious opponents absolutely. One of Alva's first acts was to set up the Commission of Civil Unrest, which was soon nicknamed the "**Council of Blood**", after its habit of executing those it examined. No fewer than twelve thousand citizens were polished off, mostly for taking part in the Fury. Initially the repression worked; in 1568, when **William the Silent** attempted an invasion from Germany, the towns, including Amsterdam, offered no support. William withdrew and conceived other means of defeating Alva, sponsoring a band of Protestant privateers, the so-called **Waterguezen** or sea-beggars, who took their name from the epithet provided by Margaret's advisor. At first, the Waterguezen were obliged to operate from England, but it was soon possible for them to secure bases in the Netherlands, whose citizens had grown to loathe the autocratic Alva and his Spanish army.

The spreading of the revolt

The revolt spread rapidly. By June the rebels controlled all of the province of Holland except for Amsterdam, which steadfastly refused to come off the fence. Alva and his son Frederick fought back, but William's superior naval power frustrated him and a mightily irritated Philip replaced Alva with **Luis de Resquesens**. Initially, Resquesens had some success in the south (today's Belgium), where the Catholic majority were more willing to compromise with Spanish rule than their northern neighbours, but the tide of war was against him – most pointedly in William's triumphant relief of Leiden in 1574.

The Spanish Fury and its aftermath

When Resquesens died in 1576, the (unpaid) Habsburg garrison in Antwerp mutinied and assaulted the town, slaughtering some eight thousand of its people in what was known as the **Spanish Fury**. The massacre alienated the south and pushed its peoples into the arms of William, whose troops now swept into Brussels, the heart of imperial power. Momentarily, it seemed possible for the whole region to unite behind William, and all signed the **Union of Brussels**, which demanded the departure of foreign troops as a condition for accepting a diluted Habsburg sovereignty. This was followed, in 1576, by the **Pacification of Ghent**, a regional agreement that guaranteed freedom of religious belief, a necessary precondition for any union between the largely Protestant north (the Netherlands) and Catholic south (Belgium and Luxembourg).

The end of the revolt

Philip was, however, not inclined to compromise, especially when he realized that William's Calvinist sympathies were giving his newly found Walloon and Flemish allies the jitters. The king bided his time until 1578, when, with his enemies arguing among themselves, he sent another army from Spain to the Low Countries under the command of Alessandro Farnese, the **Duke of Parma**. Events played into Parma's hands. In 1579, tired of all the wrangling, seven northern provinces (including Holland) broke with their southerly neighbours to sign the **Union of Utrecht**, an alliance against Spain that was to be the first unification of the Netherlands as an identifiable country – the

1566	1578
Rebellious Protestants smash up hundreds of Catholic churches in the Iconoclastic Fury	Amsterdam finally breaks with the Habsburgs, declaring for the rebels and switching from Catholicism to Calvinism in the "Alteratie" (Alteration)

self-styled **United Provinces**. In the same year, representatives of the southern provinces signed the **Union of Arras**, a Catholic-led agreement that declared loyalty to Philip II in counterbalance to the Union of Utrecht in the north. Parma used this area as a base to recapture all of Flanders and Antwerp, but was unable to advance any further north and the Low Countries were, de facto, divided into two – the Spanish Netherlands and the **United Provinces** – beginning a separation that would lead, after many changes, to the creation of **three modern countries** – Belgium, Luxembourg and the Netherlands.

The Alteratie
Despite its Protestant sympathies, Amsterdam had proved reluctant to join the revolt, but in 1578 the city finally declared for the rebels and switched from Catholicism to Calvinism in what became known as the "**Alteratie**". The rebels had conceded freedom of religious belief under the terms of the Union of Utrecht (see page 226), but in Amsterdam, as elsewhere, this did not extend to freedom of worship. Nonetheless, a pragmatic compromise was reached in which a blind eye was turned to the celebration of the Mass if it was done privately and inconspicuously; it was this ad hoc arrangement that gave rise to the country's "hidden churches" (*schuilkerken*), like Amsterdam's Ons' Lieve Heer op Solder, on Oudezijds Voorburgwal (see page 47).

The formation of the United Provinces
The assembly of the newly formed **United Provinces** was known as the **States General**, and it met at Den Haag (The Hague); it had no domestic legislative authority, and could only carry out foreign policy by unanimous decision, a formula designed to reassure the independent-minded merchants of every Dutch city. The role of **Stadholder** was the most important in each province, roughly equivalent to that of governor, though the same person could occupy this position in any number of provinces – and mostly did, with the Orange-Nassaus characteristically picking up five or six provinces at any one time. Pieter Geyl in his seminal *Revolt of the Netherlands* (see page 254) defined the end result as the establishment of a republic which was "oligarchic, erastian [and] decentralized".

The Twelve Year Truce
Meanwhile, the war with Spain rumbled on, but its main instigator, Philip II of Spain, the scourge of the Low Countries, died in 1598, a necessary preamble to the **Twelve Year Truce** (1609–21) signed between the Habsburgs and the United Provinces, which grudgingly accepted the independence of the new republic. With the signing of the peace treaty, Amsterdam was free to carry on with what it did best – trading and making money.

The Thirty Years' War
With the end of the Twelve Year Truce in 1621, fighting with Spain broke out once again, this time as part of the more general **Thirty Years' War** (1618–48), a largely religion-based conflict between Catholic and Protestant countries that involved most of Western Europe. In the Low Countries, the Spanish were initially successful, but

1579	**1613**
The seven provinces of the Netherlands break with Habsburg Spain, establishing the United Provinces; Protestants relieved	Work begins on the Grachtengordel canals, which will encircle the city within three decades

> ## THE FLYING DUTCHMAN
>
> The speed of the vessels of the VOC (see page 95) amazed the company's competitors, giving rise to the legend of the **Flying Dutchman**, a kind of ghost ship doomed never to arrive in port. One story has it that the fastest VOC captain of them all, a certain Bernard Fokke, only achieved the sailing times he did with the help of the **devil** – and his reward was and is to sail the seven seas forever; another has the VOC's Captain Hendrik van der Decken sailing round the Cape of Good Hope for eternity after blaspheming against the wind and the waves. Whatever the truth, it was certainly a myth born of commercial envy.

from 1625 they suffered a series of defeats on land and sea that forced them out of what is today the southern part of the Netherlands. Finally, in 1648, they were compelled to accept the humiliating **Peace of Westphalia**, the general treaty that ended the Thirty Years' War along with its subsidiary agreement, the **Treaty of Münster**, which produced a batch of celebratory paintings that now hang in their own room in the Rijksmuseum (see page 106). Under the terms of the Peace, the independence of the United Provinces was formally recognized and the Dutch were even able to insist that the Scheldt estuary be closed to shipping, an action designed to destroy the trade and prosperity of Antwerp, which – along with the rest of modern-day Belgium – remained part of the Habsburg Empire. By this act, the commercial expansion and pre-eminence of Amsterdam was assured, and the Golden Age began.

The Golden Age

The brilliance of Amsterdam's explosion onto the European scene is as difficult to underestimate as it is to detail. The size of the city's **merchant fleet** carrying Baltic grain into Europe had long been considerable, and even during the long war with Spain it had continued to expand. Indeed, not only were the Spaniards unable to undermine it, but they were, on occasion, even obliged to use Dutch ships to supply their own troops – part of a burgeoning **cargo trade** that was a key ingredient of Amsterdam's economic success. It was, however, the emasculation of Antwerp by the Treaty of Westphalia that really launched the so-called **Golden Age**, a period of extraordinarily dynamic growth, with Amsterdam becoming the emporium for the products of north and south Europe and the new colonies in the East and West Indies. Dutch banking and investment brought further prosperity, and by the mid-seventeenth century Amsterdam's wealth was spectacular.

The Dutch East and West India companies

The **Dutch East India Company**, or Vereenigde Oost-Indische Compagnie – VOC (see page 95) – controlled the immensely profitable trade with the East, thereby keeping the country's coffers brimming throughout the Golden Age and becoming a colonial power in its own right, governing, at one time or another, parts of Malaysia, Sri Lanka and Indonesia. Almost inevitably, the success of the VOC led, in 1621, to the creation of the **West India Company**, or Geoctroyeerde Westindische Compagnie (GWIC), which was designed to protect Dutch interests in the Americas and Africa. In the event, it proved a failure, expending most of its energies in waging war on Spanish and

1642	1648	1688
Rembrandt paints the *De Nachtwacht* ("The Night Watch"), which now has pride of place in Amsterdam's Rijksmuseum	The Peace of Westphalia heralds Amsterdam's Golden Age	William III of Orange successfully invades England – and adds "King of England" to his several titles

Portuguese colonies from its base in Suriname, but it did make handsome profits until the 1660s. The company was dismantled in 1674, ten years after its nascent colony of New Amsterdam had been ceded to the British – and renamed **New York**.

Civic pride and religious toleration

Taking their new-found riches as a sign of God's pleasure, Amsterdam's Calvinist bourgeoisie indulged in fine canal houses and commissioned images of themselves in group portraits. Civic pride knew no bounds, as great monuments to self-aggrandizement – principally the new **town hall**, the Koninklijk Paleis (see page 37) – were hastily erected, and, if some went hungry, few starved, as the poor were cared for in municipal almshouses. The arts flourished and **religious tolerance** extended even to the traditional scapegoats, the **Jews**, and in particular the Sephardic Jews, who had been hounded from Spain by the Inquisition, but were guaranteed freedom from religious persecution under the terms of the Union of Utrecht of 1579. By the end of the eighteenth century, Jews accounted for ten percent of the city's inhabitants.

Population explosion

Guilds and craft associations thrived and the relatively high wages paid by the city's industries attracted agricultural workers from every part of the country, while Protestant refugees arrived from every corner of Catholic Europe. No wonder, then, that Amsterdam's **population** quadrupled in the first half of the seventeenth century. Although Amsterdam was the centre of this boom, economic ripples spread across much of the United Provinces. Dutch farmers were, for instance, able to sell all they could produce to the expanding city, and a string of Zuider Zee ports cashed in on the flourishing Baltic trade.

Expansion

To accommodate its growing populace, Amsterdam **expanded** several times during the seventeenth century. The grandest and most elaborate plan to enlarge the city was begun in 1613, with the digging of the western stretches of the Herengracht,

---

TULIPOMANIA

Nothing exemplifies the economic bubble of seventeenth-century Amsterdam more than the arrival of the **tulip**. As a relatively exotic flower, a native of Turkey, it had already captured the imagination of other parts of Europe, and its arrival in the United Provinces – coinciding as it did with an abrupt rise in personal domestic wealth – led to it becoming the bloom of choice for the discerning collector and horticulturalist. New varieties were developed voraciously and the trade in **tulip bulbs** boomed in the 1630s, with prices spiralling out of control and culminating in three rare bulbs changing hands for the price of a house. By this time it was less about flowers and more about speculation, with tulips being seen as a way of getting rich quick. However, such speculation couldn't be sustained, and the bottom fell out of the tulip market in 1637 when, in the space of three months, prices collapsed to around ten percent of their previous value, and thousands lost everything they possessed. Today tulips and other blooms still define some of the Dutch landscape, but seeing them up close is easiest at the Keukenhof Gardens (see page 135), if you're here in springtime, or at Amsterdam's Bloemenmarkt (see page 200).

1713	1750	1795
Treaty of Utrecht: Spain finally abandons the Spanish Netherlands (Belgium), which is passed to the Austrians	Handel visits Amsterdam to gee-up its musical scene	Napoleon's revolutionary army occupies the United Provinces; Amsterdam's merchants are stripped of most of their privileges

Keizersgracht and Prinsengracht, the three great canals of the **Grachtengordel** (literally "girdle of canals") that epitomized the wealth and self-confidence of the Golden Age. In 1663 this sweeping crescent was extended beyond the River Amstel, but by this time the population had begun to stabilize, and the stretch that would have completed the ring of canals around the city was left only partially developed – an area that would in time become the Jewish quarter (see Chapter 4).

Political squabbling

Although the economics of the Golden Age were dazzling, the **politics** were dismal. The United Provinces was dogged by interminable wrangling between those who hankered for a central, unified government under the pre-eminent **House of Orange-Nassau** and those who championed provincial autonomy. Frederick Henry, the powerful head of the House of Orange-Nassau who had kept a firm centralizing grip, died in 1647 and his successor, William II, lasted just three years before his death from smallpox. A week after William's death, his wife bore the son who would become William III of England, but in the meantime the leaders of the province of Holland, with the full support of Amsterdam, seized their opportunity. They forced measures through the States General abolishing the position of Stadholder, thereby reducing the powers of the Orangists and increasing those of the provinces, chiefly Holland itself, whose foremost figure in these years was Johan de Witt, Council Pensionary (chief minister) to the States General.

Johan de Witt

In control, **Johan de Witt** guided the country through wars with England and Sweden, concluding a triple alliance between the two countries and the United Provinces in 1668. This was a striking reversal of policy: the economic rivalry between the United Provinces and England had already precipitated two **Anglo-Dutch wars** (in 1652–54 and 1665–67) and there was much bitterness in Anglo-Dutch relations – a popular English pamphlet of the time was titled *A Relation Shewing How They* [the Dutch] *Were First Bred and Descended from a Horse-Turd Which Was Enclosed in a Butter-Box*. England's Charles II, who certainly knew how to bear a grudge, was particularly irritated by an embarrassing defeat in the second Anglo-Dutch war, when **Admiral Michiel de Ruyter** had sailed up the Thames and caught the English fleet napping.

William III of Orange as national saviour

Charles II had his revenge in 1672, when, breaking with his new-found allies, he joined a French attack on the United Provinces. The republic was now in deep trouble – previous victories had been at sea, and the army, weak and disorganized, could not withstand the onslaught. In panic, as the so-called **Rampjaar (Year of Disaster)** unfurled, the country turned to **William III of Orange** for leadership and Johan de Witt was brutally murdered by a mob of Orangist sympathizers in Den Haag. By 1678 William had defeated the French and made peace with the English – and was rewarded (along with his wife Mary, the daughter of Charles I of England) with the English crown ten years later.

1814	1815	1830
Amsterdam recognized as the capital of the United Provinces	Belgium and the Netherlands (forcibly) united as the "United Kingdom of the Netherlands"	Belgium revolts – and the Netherlands goes it alone

French designs on the Low Countries

Though William III had defeated the French, **Louis XIV** retained designs on the United Provinces, and the military pot was kept boiling in a long series of dynastic wars that ranged across Northern Europe. In 1700, Charles II of Spain, the last of the Spanish Habsburgs, died childless, bequeathing the Spanish throne and control of the Spanish Netherlands (now Belgium) to Philip of Anjou, Louis' grandson. Louis promptly forced Philip to cede the latter to France, which was, with every justification, construed as a threat to the balance of power by France's neighbours. The **War of the Spanish Succession** ensued, with the United Provinces, England and Austria forming the **Triple Alliance** to thwart the French king. The war itself was a haphazard, long-winded affair that dragged on until the **Treaty of Utrecht** of 1713, in which France finally abandoned its claim to both the United Provinces and the Spanish Netherlands, which reverted to the Austrian Habsburgs (as the Austrian Netherlands).

Dutch stagnation

All this warfare had drained the United Provinces' reserves, and from 1713 onwards a slow **economic decline** began, accelerated by a trend towards conservatism. This in turn reflected the development of an increasingly socially static society, with power and wealth concentrated within a small, self-regarding elite. Furthermore, with the threat of foreign conquest effectively removed, the Dutch ruling class divided into two main camps – the **Orangists** and the pro-French "**Patriots**" – whose endless squabbling soon brought political life to a virtual standstill. The situation deteriorated even further in the latter half of the eighteenth century, and the last few years of the United Provinces present a sorry state of affairs.

French occupation

In 1795 the **French** invaded and swiftly swept their opponents aside. They were welcomed by the Patriots, who helped them dismantle the entrenched privileges of the merchant oligarchy, dissolving the United Provinces and establishing the **Batavian Republic** in its stead – named after the warlike Germanic Batavia tribe who inhabited the area around Nijmegen in Classical times. Now part of the Napoleonic Empire, the Dutch were obliged to wage unenthusiastic war with England, and in 1806 Napoleon appointed his brother **Louis** as their king in an attempt to unite the rival Dutch groups under one (notionally independent) ruler. Louis was installed in Amsterdam's town hall – hence today's Koninklijk Paleis, or Royal Palace (see page 37) – but in the event he wasn't willing to allow the Netherlands to become a simple satellite of France; Louis ignored Napoleon's directives and after just four years of rule his brother forced him to abdicate. The country was then formally incorporated into the French Empire, and for three gloomy years suffered occupation and heavy taxation to finance French military adventures.

The United Kingdom of the Netherlands

Following Napoleon's disastrous retreat from Moscow, the **Orangist faction** surfaced to exploit weakening French control. In 1813, Frederick William (1772–1843), son

1889	1914	1932
Centraal Station opens, putting Amsterdam back on Europe's main transport routes	The Netherlands stays neutral in World War I	Afsluitdijk completed, thereby separating the old Zuider Zee (now the IJsselmeer) from the North Sea

of the exiled William V, returned to the country and eight months later, under the terms of the **Congress of Vienna**, he was crowned **King William I of the United Kingdom of the Netherlands**, incorporating both the old United Provinces and the Austrian Netherlands. A strong-willed man, the new king spent much of his time trying to control his disparate kingdom but failed, primarily because of the Protestant north's attempt – or perceived attempt – to dominate the Catholic south. The southern provinces rose against his rule and in 1830 the separate kingdom of **Belgium** was proclaimed. During the years of the United Kingdom, **Amsterdam**'s status was dramatically reduced. Previously, the self-governing city, made bold by its wealth, could (and frequently did) act in its own self-interest, at the expense of the nation. From 1815, however, it was integrated within the country, with no more rights than any other city despite becoming the **capital** of the country – a fairly meaningless sop offered by the new king to placate his opponents. The seat of government (and the centre for all decision-making) was Den Haag (The Hague), and so it remained after the southern provinces broke away.

Amsterdam's economic reorganization

In the first decades of the nineteenth century, the profitable colonial trade with the East Indies (Indonesia) camouflaged the erosion of Amsterdam's pre-eminent position among Dutch cities. This trade was however hampered by the character of the **Zuider Zee**, whose shallows and sandbanks presented all sorts of navigational problems given the increasing size of merchant ships. The **Noordhollandskanaal** (North Holland Canal), completed in 1824 and running north from Amsterdam to bypass the Zuider Zee, made little difference, and it was Rotterdam, strategically placed on the Rhine inlets between the industries of the Ruhr and Britain, that prospered at Amsterdam's expense. Even the 1876 opening of the **Nordzeekanaal** (North Sea Canal), which provided a direct link west from Amsterdam to the North Sea, failed to push Amsterdam's trade ahead of rival Rotterdam's, though the city did hold on to much of the country's **shipbuilding industry** until the 1960s. The city council was also slow to catch on to the possibilities of rail, but finally, in 1889, the opening of **Centraal Station** put the city back on the main transport routes.

Slum clearance

Amsterdam may have been slow out of its nineteenth-century starting block, but the city was far from being a backwater: in the second half of the nineteenth century its **industries boomed**, attracting a new wave of migrants who were settled outside of the centre in the vast tenements of De Pijp and the Oud Zuid (Old South). These same workers were soon to radicalize the city, supporting a veritable raft of Socialist and Communist politicians. One marker was a reforming **Housing Act** of 1901 that pushed the city council into a concerted effort to clear the city's slums. Even better, the new municipal housing was frequently designed to the highest specifications, no more so than under the guidance of the two leading architects of the (broadly Expressionist) **Amsterdam School**, Michael de Klerk (1884–1923) and Piet Kramer (1881–1961). The duo was responsible for the layout of much of the Nieuw Zuid, or New South (see page 122), as well as the Oud Zuid's De Dageraad housing project (see page 120).

1940	1944	1944–45
The Germans occupy the Netherlands in World War II	Betrayal and capture of Anne Frank in Amsterdam	Allied forces liberate the Netherlands, but not fast enough: hundreds of Amsterdammers starve to death in the "Hunger Winter" (*Hongerwinter*)

The reconfiguration of the Netherlands

Nationally, **Johan Rudolph Thorbecke** (1798–1872), the outstanding political figure of the times, formed three ruling cabinets (in 1849–53, 1862–66 and 1872) and steered the Netherlands through a profound attitudinal change. The political parties of the late eighteenth century had wanted to resurrect the power and prestige of the seventeenth-century Netherlands; Thorbecke and his liberal allies resigned themselves to the country's reduced status as a small power and eulogized its advantages. For the first time, from about 1850, liberty was seen as a luxury made possible by the country's very lack of power, and the malaise that had long disturbed public life gave way to a positive appreciation of the very narrowness of its national existence. One of the results of Thorbecke's liberalism was a gradual extension of the franchise, culminating in the **Act of Universal Suffrage** in 1917.

The war years

The Netherlands remained neutral in **World War I** and although it suffered privations from the Allied blockade of German war materials, this was offset by the profits many Dutch merchants accrued by trading with both sides. Similar attempts to remain neutral in **World War II** failed: the **Germans invaded** on May 10, 1940, and the Netherlands was quickly overrun. Queen Wilhelmina fled to London to set up a government-in-exile, and members of the **NSB**, the Dutch fascist party, which had welcomed the invaders, were rewarded with positions of authority. Nevertheless, in the early months of the occupation, life for the average Amsterdammer went on pretty much as usual, which is just what the Germans wanted – they were determined to transform the Netherlands by degrees. Even when the first roundups of the **Jews** began in late 1940, many managed to turn a blind eye, though in February 1941 Amsterdam's newly outlawed Communist Party did organize a widely supported strike, spearheaded by the city's transport and refuse workers, shipbuilders and dockers, who rallied in support of the Jews. It was a gesture rather than a move to undermine German control, but an important one all the same. Interviewed after the war, one of the leaders summarized it thus: "If just one of Amsterdam's Jews did not feel forgotten and abandoned as he was packed off in a train, then the strike was well worth it."

As the war progressed, so the German grip got tighter – especially for the Jews (see page 84) – and the **Dutch Resistance** stronger, its activities focused on destroying German supplies and munitions as well as the forgery of identity papers, a real Dutch speciality. The Resistance also trumpeted its efforts in a battery of underground newspapers, most notably *Het Parool* (The Password), which still survives in good form today. Inevitably, the Resistance paid a heavy price, with some 23,000 of its fighters and sympathizers losing their lives, but Amsterdam's Jews took the worst punishment: in 1940, the city's Jewish population, swollen by refugees from Hitler's Germany, was around 140,000, but by the end of the war there were only a few thousand left. The old Jewish quarter – the Jodenhoek – was rendered, deserted and derelict, a rare crumb of comfort being the survival of the diary of a young Jewish girl, **Anne Frank** (see page 255).

Liberation

The **Liberation** of the Netherlands from German occupation began from the south in the autumn of 1944. To speed the process, the Allies determined on **Operation**

1947	**1963**	**1975**
Johan Cruyff, arguably the greatest European footballer of all time, is born in Amsterdam	Jasper Grootveld kick-starts the Provos, a playful anarchist movement that magnetizes the city's youth	Soft drugs (partly) decriminalized

Market Garden, an ambitious plan to finish the war quickly by creating an Allied corridor stretching from Eindhoven to Arnhem, but the military thrust failed and the Allies were obliged to resort to more orthodox military tactics. They slowly cleared the east and south of the country in the winter and spring of 1944–45, leaving the coastal provinces – including Amsterdam – pretty much untouched, though here lack of food and fuel created the **Hongerwinter** (Hunger Winter), in which hundreds died of hunger and/or hypothermia, their black cardboard coffins being trundled to mass graves. The remains of the German army in the Netherlands surrendered on **May 5, 1945.**

Postwar reconstruction

Across the Netherlands, the **postwar years** were spent patching up the damage of occupation and liberation, though at first progress was hindered by a desperate shortage of food, fuel and building materials. Neither did it help that the retreating Germans had blown up all the dykes and sluices on the North Sea coast at IJmuiden, at the mouth of the Nordzeekanaal. Nevertheless, Amsterdam had not received an aerial pounding like the ones dished out to Rotterdam and Arnhem, and the reconstruction soon built up a head of steam. One feature was the creation of giant suburbs like **Bijlmermeer**, to the southeast of the city, the last word in early 1960s large-scale residential planning, with low-cost modern housing, play areas and foot- and cycle paths.

Colonial misadventure

In the late 1940s, the Dutch became embroiled in a disgraceful **colonial war**. The former Dutch colonies of **Java and Sumatra** had been occupied by the Japanese in 1942, but – with the Japanese defeated – they were now ruled by a nationalist republican government that refused to recognize Dutch sovereignty. Following the failure of talks between Den Haag and the nationalists, the Dutch sent the troops in – a military enterprise that soon became a bloody debacle. International opposition was intense and, after much condemnation, the Dutch reluctantly surrendered their most important Asian colonies, which were ultimately incorporated as **Indonesia** in 1950.

The North Sea flood and the Delta Project

Tragedy struck the Netherlands on February 1, 1953, when an unusually high tide was pushed over Zeeland's sea defences by a westerly wind, **flooding** around 150 square kilometres of land and drowning over 1800 people. The response to the flood – the **Watersnoodramp** – was the **Delta Project**, which closed off the western part of the Scheldt and Maas estuaries with massive sea dykes, thereby ensuring Zeeland's future safety. Amsterdam itself had already been secured by the completion of the **Afsluitdijk** between Noord-Holland and Friesland in 1932. This dyke separated the North Sea from the former Zuider Zee, which now became the freshwater **IJsselmeer**, and in 1976 a second dyke was added, carving the Markermeer from the IJsselmeer.

1976	1980	1984
Another decade, another dyke: the Houtribdijk dyke carves the Markermeer from the IJsselmeer	The coronation of Queen Beatrix is marked by mass protests across the city against the lavishness of the proceedings	The last mass squat in Amsterdam meets a troublesome end

THE PROVOS

In 1963, one-time window cleaner and magician extraordinaire **Jasper Grootveld** won celebrity status by painting "K" – for *kanker* (cancer) – on cigarette billboards throughout Amsterdam. His actions inspired others, most notably **Roel van Duyn**, a philosophy student at Amsterdam University, who set up a left-wing-cum-anarchist movement known as the **Provos** – short for *provocatie* (provocation) – and organized street "**happenings**" that proved fantastically popular among young Amsterdammers. The number of Provos never exceeded about thirty and the group had no coherent structure, but they did have one clear aim – to bring points of political or social conflict to public attention. More than anything they were masters of publicity, and pursued their "games" with a spirit of fun rather than grim political fanaticism. The reaction of the police, however, was aggressive; the first two issues of the Provos' magazine were confiscated and, in July 1965, they intervened at a Saturday-night "happening", setting a pattern for future confrontations. The magazine itself contained the Provos' manifesto, a set of policies that later appeared under the title "**The White Plans**". These included the famously popular **white bicycle plan**, which proposed that the council ban all cars in the city centre and supply twenty thousand bicycles (painted white) for public use instead.

Yet it was the **wedding of Princess Beatrix** to Claus von Amsberg, on March 10, 1966, that provoked the most serious unrest. Amsberg had served in the German army during World War II and many Netherlanders were offended by the marriage. Consequently, when hundreds took to the streets to protest, pelting the wedding procession with smoke bombs, a huge swathe of Dutch opinion supported them. Amsberg himself was jeered with the refrain "Give us back the bicycles", a reference to the commandeering of hundreds of bikes by the retreating German army in 1945.

The wedding over, the next crisis came in June 1966, when it appeared that students, workers and Provos were about to combine. In panic, the Dutch government ordered the dismissal of Amsterdam's police chief, who was deemed to be losing control, but in the event the Provos had peaked and the workers proved far from revolutionary, settling for arbitration on their various complaints instead.

Counterculture

The radical and youthful mass movements that swept through the West in the 1960s transformed Amsterdam from a middling, rather conservative city into a turbo-charged hotbed of **hippy action**. Initially, it was the **Provos** (see page 235) who led the countercultural charge, but in 1967 they formally dissolved their movement at a happening in the Vondelpark and many of their supporters moved on to **neighbourhood committees**, set up to oppose the more outlandish development plans of the city council. The most hated scheme by a long chalk was the plan to build a **metro line** through the Nieuwmarkt to the new suburb of Bijlmermeer, as this involved both wholesale demolitions and compulsory relocations. For six months there were regular confrontations between the police and the protestors and, although the council eventually had its way, the scene was set for more trouble. In particular, to many the council seemed unwilling to tackle Amsterdam's acute **housing shortage**, neglecting the needs of its poorer citizens in favour of business interests. It was this perception that fuelled the **squatter movement**, which coalesced around a handful of symbolic squats.

1990	**2001**
The World Cup: Amsterdam's Frank Rijkaard, one of the Netherlands' finest footballers, hits the German Rudi Völler with a long-range spit that soon passes into Dutch folklore	The Netherlands is the first country in the world to legalize same-sex marriage

The squatter movement

The first major police-squatter confrontation came in March 1980 when several hundred police evicted squatters from premises on **Vondelstraat**. Afterwards there was widespread rioting, but this was small beer in comparison with the protests of April 30, 1980 – the **coronation day of Queen Beatrix** – when a mixed bag of squatters and leftists vigorously protested both the lavishness of the proceedings and the expense of refurbishing Beatrix's palace in Den Haag. Once again there was widespread rioting in Amsterdam and this time it spread to other Dutch cities, though the unrest was short-lived.

Now at its peak, Amsterdam's squatter movement boasted around ten thousand activists, many of whom were involved in two more major confrontations with the police. The first was at the Lucky Luyk squat, on Jan Luykenstraat, and the second at the Wyers building, on Nieuwezijds Voorburgwal, where the squatters were forcibly cleared to make way for a hotel. The final showdown – the **Stopera** campaign of the early 1980s – arrived with the construction of the Muziektheater and Stadhuis complex on Waterlooplein (see page 86), but once again the squatters were defeated. Thereafter, the movement faded away, at least partly because of its failure to stop the developers, who could now claim, with limited justification, to be more sensitive to community needs.

Into the twenty-first century

In the 1990s, Amsterdam's street protests and squats became an increasingly distant memory, though some of the old ideas – and ideals – were carried forward by the **Greens**, who attracted, and continue to attract, a small but significant following in every municipal and national election. One of the recurring political problems was that the city's finely balanced system of **proportional representation** brought little rapid change – and sometimes no change at all. The same was true **nationally**, where politics resembled a bland if necessary business conducted between the three main parties, the **Protestant-Catholic CDA** coalition, the **Liberal VVD** and the **Socialist PvdA**. The jolt came in April 2002, when the country's political class was deeply embarrassed by the publication of a damning report on the failure of the Dutch army to protect the **Bosnian Muslims** ensconced in the UN safe haven of **Srebrenica** in 1995. The report told a tale of woeful incompetence: the UN's Dutch soldiers were inadequately armed but refused American assistance, and watched as Serb troops separated Muslim men and women in preparation for the mass executions, which the Dutch soldiers did nothing to stop (though they were never involved). In a country that prides itself on its internationalism, the report was an especially hard blow, and the Socialist PvdA-led government, under **Wim Kok**, promptly resigned.

The rise and fall of Pim Fortuyn

In the national elections of May 2002, the three main parties suffered a further shock when a new rightist grouping – **Lijst Pim Fortuyn (LPF)** – swept to second place, securing seventeen percent of the national vote. The LPF was named after its founder and leader, Rotterdam's **Pim Fortuyn**, who was stylish and witty, openly gay and a former Marxist. Fortuyn managed to cover several popular bases at the same time, from the need for law and order through to tighter immigration controls, but most crucially he also attacked the liberal establishment's espousal of **multiculturalism**, pointing out

2002	2004
Controversial politician Pim Fortuyn is assassinated in Hilversum; the guilder is replaced by the euro	Filmmaker Theo van Gogh is murdered on an Amsterdam street

AYAAN HIRSI ALI

Shown on Dutch TV in 2004, Theo van Gogh's film *Submission* (see below) was scripted by **Ayaan Hirsi Ali**, a one-time Somali refugee who had successfully sought asylum in the Netherlands in 1992. Hirsi Ali progressed through Dutch society, obtaining a degree at Leiden University, working as a translator and becoming an MP for the VVD in 2003. She renounced Islam in 2002 and thereafter received death threats, obliging her to seek police protection and even forcing her into hiding. Hirsi Ali refused to be cowed and her pronouncements on Islam were hard-hitting and headline-grabbing. In an interview with the UK's *Daily Telegraph* in December 2004, she said: "But tell me why any Muslim man would want Islamic women to be educated and emancipated? Would a Roman voluntarily have given up his slaves?"

Unfortunately for Hirsi Ali, she was engulfed by controversy of a different kind in 2006, when it turned out that her **application for asylum** had not been entirely truthful. Some supported Hirsi Ali, others argued that she should be stripped of her parliamentary seat, and the furore brought the governing coalition down amid an avalanche of mud-slinging. In the meantime, Hirsi Ali decided to parachute out of the whole mess and now lives in the USA. Her autobiography, *Infidel: My Life* (see page 254) was published in September 2006, followed by her second autobiographical book, Nomad, in 2010.

that many representatives of minority ethnic groups were deeply reactionary, anti-gay and sexist. Politically, it worked a treat, but a few days before the election Fortuyn was murdered by Volkert van der Graaf, an animal rights activist who claimed to have killed Fortuyn to stop him exploiting Muslims as scapegoats. Without its leader, the LPF rapidly unravelled, breaking up the governing coalition that took office after May 2002 and then losing most of its seats in the general election of January 2003.

The murder of Theo van Gogh
With a coalition of established parties running the government after the national election of 2003, it seemed that normal political service had been resumed. Yet, in truth, there was an uneasy undertow as Fortuyn's popularity had pushed certain social issues, particularly **immigration**, to the right. The situation got much worse – and race relations much more tense – when, in late 2004, filmmaker **Theo van Gogh** was shot dead on an Amsterdam street by a Moroccan man who objected to a film he had made – *Submission* – about Islamic violence against women. Sensing the danger, Amsterdam city council in general – and the mayor, **Job Cohen**, in particular – handled the situation with great aplomb, coining the slogan "keeping things together" (*de boel bij elkaar houden*) and organizing several candlelit vigils.

The changing city
Back in the 1970s, many Amsterdammers may have had their misgivings, but the vast majority came to accept that their country's liberal attitude to **soft drugs and prostitution** was sane and pragmatic. They couldn't have foreseen that almost nobody else in Europe would follow in their slipstream and that, as a result, Amsterdam would become a target for thousands of tourists seeking the city's twin indulgences. By the early 2000s, a solid bloc of Amsterdammers was appalled by this state of affairs and this played into the hands of a new breed of city politician, who wanted to cast Amsterdam

2007	2008
Amsterdam city council moves to restrict and reduce its Red Light District	Work is halted on Amsterdam's subterranean Noord-Zuidlijn when buildings start to collapse on the Vijzelgracht

as a **dynamic metropolis**. To this new breed, the Red Light District was unpleasant, if not downright offensive, and as a consequence there have been intermittent political rumblings about closing down the "window brothels" ever since, though the main result to date has been a reduction in the number of licences. Similarly, the city's coffeeshops have come under pressure, and although only a few have lost their licences, all have been – and still are – subject to some legislative tinkering (see page 171).

Despite the focus on these issues, these new politicians were far more interested in **redevelopment**, which they conceived as the key to the city's future success. Initial efforts to resuscitate the former **docklands** bordering the River IJ had started in the 1990s, but it wasn't until a few years later that this colossal project picked up a real head of steam, and Amsterdammers did indeed begin to think that their city could become an ultramodern metropolis – until the **Noord-Zuidlijn** battered their confidence.

The rise of Geert Wilders

After the 2003 national election, the established political parties kept power by means of a series of unstable coalitions, though their seat-swapping was temporarily interrupted following the **national election of 2010** when a new right-wing party, the **Partij voor de Vrijheid** (Party For Freedom; PVV), secured fifteen percent of the popular vote. Much to the dismay of many Amsterdammers, the new prime minister, **Mark Rutte** of the VVD, sought – and secured – the tacit support for his coalition from the PVV leader, **Geert Wilders**, a controversial figure (to put it mildly), who is, among much else, an outspoken Eurosceptic and a man whose views on Islam are regarded by many as being inflammatory. The coalition didn't last long, however: in April 2012, Wilders stormed out of a meeting, refusing to support the government's plan to slice €16 billion off the national budget.

In the run-up to the **national election of September 2012**, the established parties were notably apprehensive, but in the event the PVV was unable to hold onto a large slice of its vote, and the threat of Wilders was contained, certainly for now and maybe for good. By contrast, both the VVD and the PvdA did well and afterwards Mark Rutte formed a new governing coalition. At the 2017 election, the VVD managed to grip onto its position as the country's largest party (despite losing several seats) and, after torturous negotiations, went on to form another ruling coalition (with Christian Democratic Appeal, Democrats 66 and Christian Union), led yet again by Mark Rutte.

In Amsterdam, Wilders and the PVV never had much traction, but there was a political shock in the **municipal elections of 2014** when the PvdA, who had been in power in the city either alone or in coalition since World War II, were eased out by a platoon of smaller parties, mostly of the left. After local elections in March 2018, a total of 12 smaller parties now make up the city council, with the greens from GroenLinks party holding the largest number of seats.

The present day

Unfurling slowly, the prolonged fiasco of the **Noord-Zuidlijn** undermined faith in the municipal council and contributed to Amsterdammers' general sense of angst. This

2010	2013
The Netherlands reaches the final of the World Cup – but loses to Spain	Queen Beatrix abdicates after 33 years on the throne and is succeeded by her eldest son, Willem-Alexander

angst would seem to derive from the gap between how the Dutch conceive themselves and how things seem to be turning out. The vast majority want their country to be liberal and tolerant, and yet there are undoubtedly racial tensions; nearly everyone wants the Netherlands to be prosperous, and yet they have been stung by the worldwide recession; and while most of the Dutch are still proud of the progressive social policies they introduced in the 1960s and 1970s, these very policies are not wearing well. It's true that the Netherlands is always reckoned to be in the top ten of desirable places to live in any "happiness poll", but many Netherlanders are clearly not convinced. Most still hope for better times, but others have simply given up and are voting with their feet: in 2017, 150,000 mostly middle-class Dutch citizens emigrated, one of the largest numbers ever.

2014

A Malaysia Airlines plane (MH17) flying from Amsterdam to Kuala Lumpur is shot down by pro-Russian separatists over eastern Ukraine, killing all 298 people on board, the vast majority of them Dutch

2018

After many delays, the beleaguered Noord-Zuidlijn (North-South) metro line is finally completed and in action

Dutch art and architecture

The following is the very briefest of introductions to a subject that has rightly filled volumes. Inevitably, it covers artists that lived and worked in both the Netherlands and Belgium, as these two countries have – along with Luxembourg – been bound together as the "Low Countries" for most of their history. For a run-down of the architectural styles you'll come across in Amsterdam, see page 250.

Beginnings: the Flemish Primitives

Throughout the medieval period, **Flanders**, in modern-day Belgium, was one of the most artistically productive parts of Europe, and it was here that the realist base of later Dutch painting developed. Today, the works of these early Flemish painters, the **Flemish Primitives**, are highly prized, and although examples are fairly sparse in the Netherlands, all the leading museums – especially Amsterdam's Rijksmuseum and Den Haag's Mauritshuis – have a healthy sample.

Jan van Eyck (1385–1441) is generally regarded as the first of the Flemish Primitives, and has even been credited with the invention of oil painting – though it seems more likely that he simply perfected a new technique by thinning his paint with turpentine (at the time a new discovery), thus making it more flexible. The most famous of his works still in the Low Countries is the altarpiece in Belgium's Ghent Cathedral, which was revolutionary in its realism, for the first time using elements of native landscape in depicting biblical themes. Van Eyck's style and technique were to influence several generations of the region's artists.

The Master of Flemalle and Rogier van der Weyden

Firmly in the Eyckian tradition were the **Master of Flemalle** (1387–1444) and **Rogier van der Weyden** (1400–64), one-time official painter to the city of Brussels. The Flemalle master is a shadowy figure; some believe he was the teacher of van der Weyden, others that the two artists were in fact the same person. There are differences between the two, however: the Flemalle master's paintings are close to Van Eyck's, whereas van der Weyden shows a greater degree of emotional intensity in his religious works. Van der Weyden also produced serene portraits of the bigwigs of his day and these were much admired across a large swathe of Western Europe.

Bouts and Goes

Van der Weyden's style, never mind his success, influenced many painters, one of the most talented of these being **Dieric Bouts** (1415–75). Born in Haarlem but active in (Belgium's) Leuven, Bouts is recognizable by his stiff, rather elongated figures and penchant for horrific subject matter – the tortures of damnation for example – all set against carefully drawn landscapes. **Hugo van der Goes** (d.1482) was the next Ghent master after van Eyck, most famous for the Portinari altarpiece in Florence's Uffizi gallery. Van der Goes died insane and his later works have strong hints of his impending madness in their subversive use of space and implicit acceptance of the viewer's presence.

Memling, David and Bosch

Few doubt that **Hans Memling** (1440–94) was a pupil of van der Weyden. Active in Bruges throughout his life, he is best remembered for the pastoral charm of his landscapes and the quality of his portraiture, much of which survives on the rescued

---

AMSTERDAM GALLERIES: A HIT LIST

Of the galleries in Amsterdam, the **Rijksmuseum** (see page 106) owns a fabulous and wonderfully comprehensive collection of Dutch/Low Countries art, featuring the major artists of the Golden Age, most memorably Rembrandt. The **Van Gogh Museum** (see page 113) is best for the Impressionists and, of course, van Gogh, while for contemporary Dutch art there's the compendious **Stedelijk Museum** (see page 115) and the avant-garde **De Appel** gallery (see page 98). Contemporary photographers, on the other hand, are featured at the **Museum voor Fotografie** (see page 63) and **FOAM** (see page 68). In the city's southern suburbs, the **Cobra Museum** (see page 124) is dedicated to the Cobra art movement of the 1950s and 1960s, and the neighbouring town of **Haarlem** possesses the excellent **Frans Hals Museum** (see page 131), which holds some of the best work of Hals, his predecessors and his successors.

---

side panels of triptychs. **Gerard David** (1460–1523) was a native of Oudewater, near Gouda, but he moved to Bruges in 1484, becoming the last of the great painters to work in that city, producing formal religious works of traditional bent. Strikingly different, but broadly contemporaneous, was **Hieronymus Bosch** (1450–1516), who lived for most of his life in the Netherlands, though his style is linked to that of his Flemish contemporaries. His frequently reprinted religious allegories are filled with macabre visions of tortured people and grotesque beasts, and appear at first faintly unhinged, though it's now thought that these are visual representations of contemporary sayings, idioms and parables. While their interpretation is far from resolved, Bosch's paintings draw strongly on subconscious fears and archetypes, giving them a lasting, haunting fascination.

The sixteenth century

At the end of the fifteenth century, Flanders was in economic and political decline and the leading artists of the day were drawn instead to the booming port of **Antwerp**, also in present-day Belgium. The artists who worked here soon began to integrate the finely observed detail that characterized the Flemish tradition with the style of the Italian painters of the Renaissance. **Quentin Matsys** (1464–1530) introduced florid Classical architectural details and intricate landscapes to his works, influenced perhaps by the work of Leonardo da Vinci. As well as religious works, he painted portraits and genre scenes, all of which have recognizably Italian facets – and in the process he paved the way for the Dutch genre painters of later years. **Jan Gossaert** (1478–1532) made the pilgrimage to Italy too, and his dynamic works are packed with detail, especially finely drawn Classical architectural backdrops. He was the first Low Countries artist to introduce the subjects of Classical mythology into his paintings, part of a steady trend towards secular subject matter, which can also be seen in the work of **Joachim Patenier** (d.1524), who painted small landscapes of fantastical scenery.

The Bruegels, Aertsen and Pourbus

The middle of the sixteenth century was dominated by the work of **Pieter Bruegel the Elder** (c.1525–69), whose gruesome allegories and innovative interpretations of religious subjects are firmly placed in Low Countries settings. Pieter also painted exquisitely observed peasant scenes, though he himself was well connected in court circles in Antwerp and, later, in Brussels. **Pieter Aertsen** (1508–75) also worked in the peasant genre, adding aspects of still life; his paintings often show a detailed kitchen scene in the foreground, with a religious episode going on behind. Bruegel's two sons, **Pieter Bruegel the Younger** (1564–1638) and **Jan Bruegel** (1568–1625), were lesser painters; the former produced fairly insipid copies of his father's work, while Jan developed a style of his own – delicately rendered flower paintings and genre pieces that earned him the nickname "Velvet". Towards the latter half of the sixteenth century highly stylized Italianate portraits became the dominant fashion, with **Frans Pourbus the Younger** (1569–1622) the leading practitioner. Frans hobnobbed across Europe, working for the likes of the Habsburgs and the Medicis.

Dutch beginnings

Meanwhile, there were artistic rumblings in the province of Holland. Leading the painterly charge was **Geertgen tot Sint Jans** (Little Gerard of the Brotherhood of St John; d.1490), who worked in Haarlem, initiating – in a strangely naive style – an artistic vision that would come to dominate Dutch painting in the seventeenth century. There was a tender melancholy in his work, which was very different from the stylized paintings produced in Flanders, and, most importantly, a new sensitivity to light. **Jan Mostaert** (1475–1555) took over after Geertgen's death, developing similar themes, but the first painter to effect real changes in northern painting was Leiden's **Lucas van Leyden** (1489–1533). Leyden's bright colours and narrative technique were refreshingly novel, and he introduced a new dynamism into what had become a rigidly formal treatment of devotional subjects. There was rivalry, of course. Eager to publicize Haarlem as the artistic capital of the northern Netherlands, **Karel van Mander** claimed **Jan van Scorel** (1495–1562) as the better painter, complaining, too, of van Leyden's dandyish ways.

Scorel and Heemskerck

Jan van Scorel's influence should not be underestimated. Like many of his contemporaries, van Scorel hotfooted it to Italy to view the works of the Renaissance, but in Rome his career went into overdrive when he found favour with Pope Hadrian VI, one-time bishop of Utrecht, who installed him as court painter in 1520. Van Scorel stayed in Rome for four years and when he returned to Utrecht, armed with all that papal prestige, he combined the ideas he had picked up in Italy with those underpinning Haarlem realism, thereby modifying what had previously been an independent artistic tradition once and for all. Among his several students, probably the most talented was **Maerten van Heemskerck** (1498–1574), who duly went off to Italy himself in 1532, staying there for five years before doubling back to Haarlem.

The Golden Age

The seventeenth century begins with **Karel van Mander** (1548–1606), Haarlem painter, art impresario and one of the few contemporary chroniclers of the art of the Low Countries. His *Schilderboek* of 1604 put Flemish and Dutch traditions into context for the first time, and in addition specified the rules of fine painting. Examples of his own work are rare – though Haarlem's Frans Hals Museum (see page 131) weighs in with several – but his followers were many. Among them was **Cornelius Cornelisz van Haarlem** (1562–1638), who produced elegant renditions of biblical and mythical themes; and **Hendrik Goltzius** (1558–1616), who was a skilled engraver and an integral member of van Mander's Haarlem academy. The enthusiasm these painters had for Italian art, combined with the influence of a late revival of Gothicism, resulted in works that combined **Mannerist** and **Classical** elements. An interest in realism was also felt, but, for them, the subject became less important than the way in which it was depicted: biblical stories became merely a vehicle whereby artists could apply their skills in painting the human body, landscapes or copious displays of food. All of this served to break the religious stranglehold on art, and make legitimate a whole range of everyday subjects for the painter.

North and south diverge

The break with tradition that started in Haarlem and spread across the Netherlands was compounded by the **Reformation** – and this was where the north and the south finally diverged: the austere Calvinism that had replaced the Catholic faith in the United Provinces had no use for images or symbols of devotion in its churches. Instead, painters catered to the burgeoning middle class, and no longer visited (Catholic) Italy to learn their craft. Indeed, the real giants of the seventeenth century – Hals, Rembrandt, Vermeer – stayed in the Netherlands all their lives. Another innovation was that painting split into more distinct categories – genre, portrait, landscape – and artists tended (with notable exceptions) to confine themselves to one field throughout their careers. So began the **Golden Age** of Dutch art.

Historical and religious painting

The artistic influence of Renaissance Italy may have been in decline, but Italian painters still had clout with the Dutch, most notably **Caravaggio** (1571–1610), who was much admired for his new realism. Taking Caravaggio's cue, many artists – Rembrandt for one – continued to portray Classical subjects, but in a way that was totally at odds with the Mannerists' stylish flights of imagination. The Utrecht artist **Abraham Bloemaert** (1564–1651), though a solid Mannerist throughout his career, encouraged these new ideas, and his students – **Gerard van Honthorst** (1590–1656), **Hendrik Terbrugghen** (1588–1629) and **Dirck van Baburen** (1590–1624) – formed the nucleus of the influential **Utrecht School**, which followed Caravaggio almost to the point of slavishness. Honthorst was perhaps the leading figure, learning his craft from Bloemaert and travelling to Rome, where he was nicknamed "Gerardo delle Notti" for his ingenious handling of light and shade. In his later paintings, however, this was to become more routine technique than inspired invention, and though a supremely competent artist, Honthorst is somewhat discredited among critics today. Terbrugghen's reputation seems to have aged rather better; he soon developed a more individual style, with his later, lighter work having a great influence on the young Vermeer. After a jaunt to Rome, Baburen shared a studio with Terbrugghen and produced some relatively original work – work which also had some influence on Vermeer – but today he is the least studied member of the group and few of his paintings survive.

Rembrandt as an historical and religious painter

Without doubt **Rembrandt** (see page 109) was the most original historical artist of the seventeenth century, also painting religious paintings throughout his career. In the 1630s, the poet and statesman Constantijn Huygens procured for him his greatest commission – a series of five paintings of the Passion, beautifully composed and uncompromisingly realistic. Later, however, Rembrandt drifted away from the mainstream, ignoring the smooth brushwork of his contemporaries and choosing instead a rougher, darker and more disjointed style for his biblical and historical subjects. This may well have contributed to a decline in his artistic fortunes, and it is significant that while the more conventional Honthorst was busy decorating the Huis ten Bosch near Den Haag for the Stadholder Frederick Henry, Rembrandt was having his monumental *Conspiracy of Julius Civilis* – painted for the Amsterdam's brand-new Town Hall – thrown out. The reasons for this rejection have been hotly debated, but it seems likely that Rembrandt's rendition was thought too suggestive of cabalistic conspiracy – the commissioners wanted to see a romantic hero and certainly not a plot in the making. Julius had organized a revolt against the Romans, an important event in early Dutch history, which had obvious resonance in a country just freed from the Habsburgs. Even worse, perhaps, Rembrandt had shown Julius to be blind in one eye, which was historically accurate but not at all what the city's burghers had in mind.

Genre painting

Often misunderstood, the term **genre painting** initially applied to everything from animal paintings and still lifes through to historical works and landscapes, but later

– from around the middle of the seventeenth century – referred only to **scenes of everyday life**. Its target market was the region's burgeoning middle class, who had a penchant for non-idealized portrayals of common scenes, both with and without symbols – or subtly disguised details – making one moral point or another. One of its early practitioners was Antwerp's **Frans Snijders** (1579–1657), who took up still-life painting where Aertsen (see page 241) left off, amplifying his subject – food and drink – to even larger, more sumptuous canvases. Snijders also doubled up as a member of the Rubens art machine (see page 247), painting animals and still-life sections for the master's works. In Utrecht, Hendrik Terbrugghen and Gerard van Honthorst adapted the realism and strong chiaroscuro learned from Caravaggio to a number of tableaux of everyday life, though they were more concerned with religious works (see opposite), while Haarlem's Frans Hals dabbled in genre too, but is better known as a portraitist.

Brouwer, Teniers and Ostade

One of Frans Hals' pupils, **Adriaen Brouwer** (1605–38), chose to concentrate on genre painting, and his riotous tavern scenes were well received in their day and collected by, among others, Rubens and Rembrandt. Brouwer spent only a couple of years in Haarlem under Hals before returning to his native Flanders, where he influenced the inventive **David Teniers the Younger** (1610–90), who worked in Antwerp and later in Brussels. Teniers' early paintings are Brouwer-like peasant scenes, although his later work is more delicate and diverse, including *kortegaardje* – guardroom scenes that show soldiers carousing. **Adriaen van Ostade** (1610–85), on the other hand, stayed in Haarlem most of his life, skilfully painting groups of peasants and tavern brawls – though his later acceptance by the establishment led him to water down the realism he had learnt from Brouwer. He was teacher to his brother **Isaak** (1621–49), who produced a large number of open-air peasant scenes, subtle combinations of genre and landscape work.

Jan Steen

The English critic E.V. Lucas dubbed Teniers, Brouwer and Ostade "coarse and boorish" compared with **Jan Steen** (1625–79) who, along with Vermeer, is probably the most admired Dutch genre painter. Steen's paintings offer the same Rabelaisian peasantry in full fling, but they go their debauched ways in broad daylight, and nowhere do you see the filthy rogues in the shadowy hovels favoured by Brouwer and Ostade. Steen offers more humour, too, as well as more moralizing, identifying with the hedonistic mob and reproaching them at the same time. Indeed, many of his pictures are illustrations of well-known contemporary proverbs – popular epithets on the evils of drink or the transience of human existence that were supposed to teach as well as entertain.

Gerard Dou, his pupils and Nicholas Maes

Leiden's **Gerard Dou** (1613–75) was one of Rembrandt's first pupils – and surprisingly enough nineteenth-century connoisseurs actually preferred his work to that of his master. That said, it's difficult to detect any trace of Rembrandt's influence in his paintings as Dou initiated a (genre) style of his own: tiny, minutely realized and beautifully finished views of a kind of ordinary life that was decidedly more genteel than Brouwer's – or even Steen's for that matter. He was admired, above all, for his painstaking attention to detail and he would, it's said, sit in his studio for hours waiting for the dust to settle before starting work. Among Dou's students, **Frans van Mieris** (1635–81) continued the highly finished portrayals of the Dutch bourgeoisie, as did **Gabriel Metsu** (1629–67) – perhaps Dou's most talented pupil – whose pictures often convey an overtly moral message. Another pupil of Rembrandt's, though a much later one, was **Nicholas Maes** (1629–93), whose early works were almost entirely genre paintings, sensitively executed and with an obvious didacticism. His later paintings show the influence of a more refined style of portraiture, which he had picked up in France.

Gerard ter Borch and Pieter de Hooch

As a native of Zwolle, well to the east of Amsterdam, **Gerard ter Borch** (1619–81) remained very much a provincial painter, despite trips to most of Europe's artistic capitals. He depicted the country's merchant class at play and became renowned for his curious doll-like figures and his ability to capture the textures of different cloths. His domestic scenes were not unlike those of **Pieter de Hooch** (1629–84), whose simple depictions of everyday life are deliberately unsentimental and have little or no moral commentary. De Hooch's favourite trick was to paint darkened rooms with an open door leading through to a sunlit courtyard, a practice that, along with his trademark rusty-red colour, makes his work easy to identify and, at its best, exquisite. Nevertheless, his later pictures lose their spartan quality, reflecting the increasing opulence of the Dutch Republic; the rooms are more richly decorated, the arrangements more contrived and the subjects less homely.

Johannes Vermeer

It was **Johannes Vermeer** (1632–75) who brought the most sophisticated methods to painting interiors, depicting the play of natural light on indoor surfaces with superlative skill – as well as creating the tranquil intimacy for which he is now internationally famous. Like de Hooch (see above), Vermeer was an observer of the well-heeled Dutch household without a moral tone and today he is regarded (with Hals and Rembrandt) as one of the big three Dutch painters – though it seems he was a slow worker: only about forty paintings can be attributed to him with any certainty. Living all his life in Delft, Vermeer is perhaps the epitome of the seventeenth-century Dutch painter – rejecting the pomp and ostentation of the High Renaissance to record quietly his contemporaries at home, painting for a public that demanded no more than that: bourgeois art at its most complete.

Portraiture

Predictably enough, the ruling bourgeoisie of the United Provinces was keen to record and celebrate its success, and consequently portraiture became a reliable way for a painter to make a living. **Michiel Jansz Miereveld** (1567–1641), court painter to Frederick Henry of Orange-Nassau in Den Haag, was the first real portraitist of the Dutch Republic, but it wasn't long before his stiff and somewhat formal figures were superseded by the more spontaneous renderings of **Frans Hals** (1585–1666). Hals is perhaps best known for his "corporation pictures" – **group portraits** of the Dutch Civil Guard regiments that had been formed in most of the larger towns during the war with Spain, but subsequently became social clubs. These large group pieces demanded superlative technique, since the painter had to create a collection of individual portraits while retaining a sense of the group, and accord prominence based on the relative importance of the sitters and the size of the payment each had made. Hals was particularly good at this, using innovative lighting effects, arranging his sitters subtly, and putting all the elements together in a fluid and dynamic composition. Hals also painted many individual portraits, making fleeting and telling expressions his trademark; his pictures of children are particularly sensitive. Later in life, however, his work became darker and more akin to Rembrandt's, spurred – it's conjectured – by his penury.

Verspronck and van der Helst

Jan Cornelisz Verspronck (1597–1662) and **Bartholomeus van der Helst** (1613–70) were the other great Haarlem portraitists after Frans Hals – Verspronck recognizable by the smooth, shiny glow he always gave to his sitters' faces, van der Helst by his willingness to flatter his subjects in a notably unadventurous style. Of the two, van der Helst was the more popular, influencing a number of later painters and leaving Haarlem as a young man to begin a solidly successful career as portrait painter to Amsterdam's upper crust.

Rembrandt as a portraitist

Rembrandt's early portraits and self-portraits show the confident face of security, when he was on top and sure of his direction – the exquisite detail and half-smile in the *Portrait of Maria Trip* being a case in point. Rembrandt would not always be the darling of the Amsterdam merchants, but his fall from grace was still some way off when he completed his most famous painting, *The Night Watch* (see page 109), a group portrait whose fluent arrangement of its subjects was almost entirely original. The painting was once associated with the artist's decline in popularity, but this is incorrect and there's no evidence that the military company who commissioned it was anything but pleased with the result.

Rembrandt's pupils

The early work of **Ferdinand Bol** (1616–80) was heavily influenced by Rembrandt, so much so that for centuries art historians couldn't tell the two apart, though Bol's later paintings are readily distinguishable, blandly elegant portraits which proved very popular with the wealthy. At the age of 53, Bol married a rich widow and promptly hung up his easel – perhaps he knew just how emotionally tacky his work had become. Another pupil was **Govert Flinck** (1615–60), formerly an apprentice silk mercer and perhaps Rembrandt's most faithful follower. In 1659, as a sign of Rembrandt's fading fortunes, Flinck was given the job of decorating Amsterdam's new Stadhuis (Town Hall) in preference to his master, but died before he could execute his designs; the commission passed to Rembrandt, whose *Conspiracy of Julius Civilis* was installed in 1662, but discarded a year later. Like Bol, Flinck married into money and his best paintings date from the 1630s. Most of the pitifully scarce extant work of **Carel Fabritius** (1622–54) is portraiture, but he also died young, before he could properly realize his promise as perhaps the most gifted of all Rembrandt's students. Generally regarded as the teacher of Vermeer, he forms a link between the two masters, combining Rembrandt's technique with his own practice of painting figures against a dark background, prefiguring the lighting and colouring of Vermeer.

Landscapes

Aside from Pieter Bruegel the Elder (see page 241), whose depictions of his native surroundings make him the first true Low Countries landscape painter, **Gillis van Coninxloo** (1544–1607) stands out as the earliest Dutch landscapist. He imbued his native scenery with elements of fantasy, painting the richly wooded views he had seen on his travels around Europe as backdrops to biblical scenes. Coninxloo's apprentice, **Hercules Seghers** (1590–1638), carried on his mentor's style of depicting forested and mountainous landscapes, some real, others not; his work is scarce but is believed to have had considerable influence on the landscape work of Rembrandt himself. **Esaias van der Velde**'s (1591–1632) quaint and unpretentious scenes show the first real affinity with the Dutch countryside, but while his influence was considerable, his pupil, Jan van Goyen, soon overshadowed him.

Van Goyen and the van Ruysdaels

A remarkable painter, **Jan van Goyen** (1596–1656) belongs to the so-called "**tonal phase**" of Dutch landscape painting. His early pictures were highly coloured and close to those of his teacher, Esaias van der Velde, but it didn't take him long for him to develop a marked touch of his own, using tones of green, brown and grey to lend everything a characteristic translucent haze. A long-neglected artist, van Goyen only

---

THE GOLDEN AGE: THE DUTCH ARTIST AS SPECIALIST

Most of the leading Dutch painters of the seventeenth century could, if push came to shove, try their brush at pretty much anything, but some preferred to specialize. Among them, **Paulus Potter** (1625–54) came up trumps with his animals, producing a string of lovingly executed paintings of cows and horses. **Pieter Saenredam** (1597–1665), on the other hand, zoned in on architecture, becoming famous for his finely realized paintings of Dutch church interiors, as did **Emanuel de Witte** (1616–92), though his churches lack the austere crispness of the former. Haarlem's **Gerrit Berckheyde**'s (1638–98) interest was architecture too, but he limited his views to the outside of buildings, painting glossy townscapes with a precise eye and cool detachment. Nautical scenes in praise of the Dutch navy were the speciality of **Willem van der Velde II** (1633–1707), whose melodramatic canvases, complete with churning seas and chasing skies, are a delight. Two Haarlem painters dominated the field of still life – **Pieter Claesz** (1598–1660) and **Willem Heda** (1594–1680) – in which objects were gathered together to remind the viewer of the transience of human life and the meaninglessness of worldly pursuits. Thus, a skull would often be shown alongside a book, pipe or goblet and some half-eaten food.

---

received recognition with the arrival of the Impressionists, when his fluid and rapid brushwork was at last fully appreciated.

Another "tonal" painter, Haarlem's **Salomon van Ruysdael** (1600–70) was also directly affected by Esaias van der Velde, and his simple and atmospheric, though not terribly adventurous, landscapes were for a long time consistently confused with those of van Goyen. More esteemed is his nephew, **Jacob van Ruysdael** (1628–82), generally considered the greatest of all Dutch landscapists, whose fastidiously observed views of quiet flatlands dominated by stormy skies were to influence European landscapists right up to the nineteenth century; John Constable certainly acknowledged a debt to him.

Rubens and his followers

Down in the south, in Antwerp, **Pieter Paul Rubens** (1577–1640) was easily the most important exponent of the Baroque in Northern Europe. Born in Siegen, Westphalia, he was raised in Antwerp, where he entered the painters' guild in 1598. Thereafter, he travelled extensively in Italy, absorbing the art of the High Renaissance, and by the time of his return to Antwerp in 1608 he had acquired an enormous artistic vocabulary, with the paintings of Caravaggio especially influential. His first major success came shortly after his return and this prompted a string of commissions that enabled him to set up his own studio.

The division of labour in **Rubens' studio** – and the talent of the artists working there (who included Anthony van Dyck and Jacob Jordaens) – ensured an extraordinary output of excellent work. From the early 1620s onwards he turned his hand to a plethora of themes and subjects – religious works, portraits, tapestry designs, landscapes, mythological scenes, ceiling paintings – each exhibiting an acute **sense of light**, in association with colour and form. The drama in his works comes from the vigorous animation of his characters: his large-scale allegorical works, especially, are packed with heaving, writhing figures that appear to tumble out from the canvas.

Meanwhile, Rubens also undertook diplomatic missions to Spain and England, and used these opportunities to study the works of other artists and – as in the case of Velázquez – to meet them personally. In the 1630s, **gout** began to hamper his activities, and his painting became more domestic and meditative. **Hélène Fourment**, his second wife, was the subject of many of these later portraits and she also served as a model for characters in his allegorical paintings, her figure epitomizing the buxom, well-rounded women found throughout his work.

Anthony van Dyck and Jacob Jordaens

Rubens' influence on the artists of the period was enormous. The huge output of his studio meant that his works were universally seen and also widely disseminated by the engravers he employed to copy his work. Chief among his followers was the portraitist **Anthony van Dyck** (1599–1641), who worked in Rubens' studio from 1618, often taking on the depiction of religious figures in his master's works, or at least those that required particular sensitivity and pathos. Eventually, van Dyck developed his own distinct style and technique, establishing himself as court painter to Charles I of England, and creating portraits of a nervous elegance that would influence the genre there for the next 150 years. **Jacob Jordaens** (1593–1678) was also an Antwerp native who studied under Rubens. Although he was commissioned to complete several works left unfinished by Rubens at the time of his death, his robustly naturalistic works have an earthy – and sensuous – realism that is quite different and distinct in style and technique.

The eighteenth century

In the eighteenth century, the Netherlands' economic decline was mirrored by a gradual deterioration in the quality and originality of Dutch painting. The subtle delicacies of the great paintings of the Golden Age were replaced by finicky still lifes and minute studies of flowers, or overly finessed portraiture and religious scenes: the work of **Adrian van der Werff** (1659–1722) is typical. Of the era's other big names, **Gerard de Lairesse** (1640–1711) spent most of his time decorating a rash of brand-new civic halls and mansions, but, like the buildings he worked on, his style and influences were French. **Jacob de Wit** (1695–1754) continued where Lairesse left off, painting burgher ceiling after ceiling in flashy style. He also benefited from a relaxation in the laws against Catholics, decorating several of their (newly legal) churches. The eighteenth century's only painter of any real talent was **Cornelis Troost** (1697–1750) who, although he didn't produce anything stunningly original, painted competent portraits and some neat, faintly satirical pieces that have since earned him the title of the "Dutch Hogarth". Cosy interiors also continued to prove popular, and the Haarlem painter **Wybrand Hendriks** (1744–1831) satisfied demand with numerous proficient examples.

The nineteenth century

Born in Overijssel, **Johann Barthold Jongkind** (1819–91) was the first important Dutch artist to emerge in the nineteenth century, painting landscapes and seascapes that were to influence Monet and the early Impressionists. He spent most of his life in France and his work was exhibited in Paris with the Barbizon painters, though he owed less to them than to van Goyen and the seventeenth-century "tonal" artists of the United Provinces. Jongkind's work was a logical precursor to the art of the **Hague School**. Based in and around Den Haag between 1870 and 1900, this prolific group of painters tried to re-establish a characteristically Dutch school of painting. They produced atmospheric studies of the dunes and polders around Den Haag, nature pictures that are characterized by grey, rain-filled skies, windswept seas and silvery, flat beaches. **J.H. Weissenbruch** (1824–1903) was a founding member, a specialist in low, flat beach scenes dotted with stranded boats. The banker-turned-artist **H.W. Mesdag** (1831–1915) did the same but with more skill than imagination, while **Jacob Maris** (1837–99), one of three artist brothers, was perhaps the most typical, with his rural and sea scenes heavily covered by grey, chasing skies. His brother **Matthijs** (1839–1917) was less predictable, ultimately tiring of his colleagues' interest in straight observation and going to London to design windows, while the youngest brother **Willem** (1844–1910) is best known for his small, unpretentious studies of nature.

Mauve, Israëls and Bosboom

More talented than many of his contemporaries, **Anton Mauve** (1838–88) was an exponent of soft, pastel landscapes and an early teacher of van Gogh. Profoundly influenced by the French Barbizon painters – Corot, Millet et al – he went to Hilversum near Amsterdam in 1885 to set up his own group, which became known as the "Dutch Barbizon". **Jozef Israëls** (1826–1911) has often been likened to Millet, though it's generally agreed that he had more in common with the Impressionists, and his best pictures are his melancholy portraits and interiors. Lastly, **Johan Bosboom**'s (1817–91) church interiors may be said to sum up the romanticized nostalgia of the Hague School; shadowy and populated by figures in seventeenth-century dress, they seem to yearn for the country's Golden Age.

Toorop and Breitner

Very different, and slightly later, **Jan Toorop** (1858–1928) went through multiple artistic changes, radically adapting his technique from a fairly conventional pointillism through a tired Expressionism to Symbolism with an Art Nouveau feel. Roughly contemporary, **George Hendrik Breitner** (1857–1923) was a better painter, and one who refined his style rather than changed it. His snapshot-like impressions of his beloved Amsterdam figure among his best work.

Vincent van Gogh

Vincent van Gogh (1853–90) was one of the least "Dutch" of Dutch artists, and he spent most of his relatively short painting career in France. After countless studies of Dutch peasant life – studies which culminated in his sombre *Potato Eaters* – he went to live in Paris with his art-dealer brother Theo. There, under the influence of the Impressionists, he lightened his palette, following the pointillist work of Seurat and "trying to render intense colour and not a grey harmony". Two years later he went south to Arles, the "land of blue tones and gay colours", and, struck by the brilliance of the Mediterranean light, began to develop his characteristic style. A disastrous attempt to live with Gauguin, and the much-publicized episode in which he cut off part of his ear and presented it to a local prostitute, led to his committal in an asylum at St-Rémy. Here he produced some of his most famous, and most Expressionistic, canvases – strongly coloured and with the paint thickly, almost frantically, applied. Van Gogh is now one of the world's most popular – and popularized – painters, and Amsterdam's **Van Gogh Museum** has the world's finest collection of his work (see page 113).

The twentieth century and contemporary art

Each of the major modern art movements has had – or has – its followers in the Netherlands and each has been diluted or altered according to local taste. Of many lesser names, **Jan Sluyters** (1881–1957) stands out as the Dutch pioneer of Cubism, but this is small beer when compared with the one specifically Dutch movement – **De Stijl** (The Style). **Piet Mondriaan** (1872–1944) was De Stijl's leading figure, developing the realism he had learned from the Hague School painters – via Cubism, which he criticized for being too cowardly to depart totally from representation – into a complete abstraction of form which he called **Neo-Plasticism**. Mondriaan was something of a mystic, and this was to some extent responsible for the direction that De Stijl – and his paintings – took: canvases painted with grids of lines and blocks made up of the three primary colours plus white, black and grey. Mondriaan believed this freed his art from the vagaries of personal perception, making it possible to obtain what he called "a true vision of reality". Mondriaan split with De Stijl in 1925, going on to attain new artistic extremes before moving to New York in the 1940s and producing atypically exuberant works such as *Victory Boogie Woogie* – named for the artist's love of jazz and now owned by Den Haag's Gemeentemuseum.

Van Doesburg and van der Leck

Theo van Doesburg (1883–1931) was a De Stijl cofounder and major theorist. His work is similar to Mondriaan's except for the noticeable absence of thick, black borders and the diagonals that he introduced into his work, calling his paintings "contra-compositions" – which, he said, were both more dynamic and more in touch with the twentieth century. **Bart van der Leck** (1876–1958) was the third member of the circle, identifiable by white canvases covered by seemingly randomly placed interlocking coloured triangles. De Stijl took other forms too; there was a magazine of the same name, and the movement introduced new concepts into every aspect of design, from painting to interior design and architecture. Yet in all these media, lines were kept simple, colours bold and clear.

The Bergen School, De Ploeg and Magic Realism

During and after De Stijl, a number of other movements flourished in the Netherlands, though their impact was not so great and their influence was largely local. The Expressionist **Bergen School** was probably the most localized, its best-known exponent, **Charley Toorop** (1891–1955), daughter of Jan, developing a distinctively glaring but strangely sensitive realism. **De Ploeg** (The Plough), centred in Groningen, was headed by **Jan Wiegers** (1893–1959) and influenced by Ernst Ludwig Kirchner and the

---

ARCHITECTURE IN AMSTERDAM

Amsterdam has one of the best-preserved city centres in the world, largely free of the high-rises and cluttered modern development that characterize so many other European capitals. Despite that, it is not a monumental city – there are no triumphal thoroughfares and few memorable palaces and churches. This was not a royal or an aristocratic city but a merchant one, with a tolerant attitude to religion, and the character of the architecture reflects this; it is Amsterdam's private, mercantile dwellings, rather than its grand monuments, that give the city its distinctive charm.

BEGINNINGS

Amsterdam was a great site for a trading city, bang on the confluence of two rivers. But in other respects it was a terrible choice – like many Dutch towns, a flat and waterlogged plain in which buildings needed to be supported by thousands of wooden piles bashed into the sandy soil. Just across from Centraal Station, the wooden house at **Zeedijk 1** – now home to the In 't Aepjen bar – is one of very few timber buildings still left, dating back to around 1550, while not far from here, one of Amsterdam's oldest surviving buildings is the **Oude Kerk**, dating from the 1300s. Deeper into the city centre, the **Houten Huys** in the **Begijnhof** dates from 1477, and still boasts its original (albeit much restored) Gothic timber frontage.

THE GOLDEN AGE

Brick became the building material of choice from the late sixteenth century onwards, and buildings began to acquire the distinctive **gables** that adorn houses all over the city. The earliest type was the step-gable; the house at **Oudezijds Voorburgwal 14** is a good example of this early Renaissance style, with its stone embellishments on red brick. The gable soon developed – most notably under the greatest Dutch architect of the period, **Hendrick de Keyser** (1565–1621) – into a more distinctively "Amsterdam" form, in which the previously plain step-gables were decorated with stonework and sculpture. One of the most lavish examples is the double-step-gabled residence at **Singel 140–142** – where Captain Banning Cocq (the principal figure in Rembrandt's The Night Watch) lived – built in 1600 by de Keyser.

The seventeenth century saw a surge in the city's population, and a major **expansion** was required to successfully absorb its newcomers. This exercise in city planning was way ahead of its time, using the expansion to create the graceful sweep of canals you see today. It was also the heyday of Dutch architecture, and Hendrick de Keyser, and others, left their mark with a series of trailblazing works, such as the **Huis Bartolotti** at Herengracht 170–172, with its ornate step-gables, as well as two of the city's most characteristic seventeenth-century churches: the **Westerkerk** and the **Zuiderkerk**.

German Expressionists; the group's artists set out to capture the remote landscapes around their native town, and produced violently coloured canvases that hark back to van Gogh. Another group, known as the **Magic Realists**, surfaced in the 1930s, painting quasi-surrealistic scenes that, according to their leading light, **Carel Willink** (1900–83), revealed "a world stranger and more dreadful in its haughty impenetrability than the most terrifying nightmare".

Cobra and Karel Appel

Postwar Dutch art began with **Cobra** – a loose grouping of like-minded painters from Denmark, Belgium and the Netherlands, whose name derives from the initial letters of their respective capital cities. Their first exhibition at Amsterdam's Stedelijk Museum in 1949 provoked a furore, at the centre of which was **Karel Appel** (1921–2006), whose brutal Abstract Expressionist pieces, plastered with paint inches thick, were, he maintained, necessary for the era – indeed, inevitable reflections of it. "I paint like a barbarian in a barbarous age", he claimed. In the graphic arts, the most famous twentieth-century Dutch figure was **Maurits Cornelis Escher** (1898–1972), whose Surrealistic illusions and allusions were underpinned by his fascination with mathematics. Many remain unconvinced by Escher, but the Dutch took a liking to his work and he now has his own museum in Den Haag.

De Keyser's distinctive Westerkerk tower was finished by his successor as the leading city architect, **Jacob van Campen** (1595–1657), who brought overseas influences to his work. He is best known for building Amsterdam's new town hall in 1665, now the **Koninklijk Paleis**, or Royal Palace – a more restrained building than its predecessors, exhibiting the Palladian proportions that the architect had absorbed in Italy. Van Campen's contemporary, **Philip Vingboons** (1607–78), was responsible for a number of the private houses on the by now burgeoning city extension, many of them sporting the fashionable neck-gable – a slimmed-down version of the step-gable; some appealing examples can be seen at **Herengracht 168** and the Cromhouthuizen at **Herengracht 364–370**.

THE NINETEENTH CENTURY

The eighteenth century was relatively uneventful, but in the nineteenth century the city developed a distinctive new style, partially spearheaded by **Petrus J.H. Cuypers** (1827–1921), famed for his Neogothic creations. Cuypers not only built the monumental **Centraal Station**, but also contributed a series of buildings in the outskirts – not least the **Rijksmuseum**, which was purpose-built as the country's national museum, and shouts from its gabled rooftops the importance of tradition and the legacy of Dutch art.

The turn of the century ushered in further changes with the international, modern style of **Hendrik Petrus Berlage** (1856–1934), exemplified in his **Beurs** on Damrak, exhibiting the attributes of a restrained yet highly decorative vision. Berlage's work inspired the **Amsterdam School**, a group of architects working in the city in the early twentieth century, led by **Piet Kramer** (1881–1961) and **Michael de Klerk** (1884–1923). The movement's keynote building was de Klerk's **Het Schip** housing complex of 1920, on the western edge of the centre.

CONTEMPORARY AMSTERDAM

Modern Amsterdam is changing fast, with new developments constantly adding to the city's architectural variety. The largest, perhaps most influential of these are the **docklands** schemes to the west and east of the city centre, where some of the city's long-neglected waterways are being transformed into a modern-day version of the seventeenth-century master plan. The docklands to the east, and **Zeeburg** in particular, are home to some of the city's most exciting new architecture – a mixture of renovated warehouses and assertive new structures, the most notable being the avant-garde **Muziekgebouw**. There are also some clever contemporary takes on the traditional Dutch waterfront on **Java Island**, whose modern terraces and curvy bridges evoke the canal houses of the city centre – while the startlingly modern **EYE**, across the river from Centraal Station, heralds the city's willingness to embrace the new.

Contemporary art

The Netherlands boasts a vibrant art scene, with all the major cities possessing at least a couple of art galleries that showcase regular exhibitions of **contemporary art**, but it's Amsterdam that leads the artistic way with its three prestigious museums supplemented by several smaller, avant-garde galleries. Among modern Dutch artists, look out for the abstract work of **Edgar Fernhout** (1912–74) and **Ad Dekkers** (1938–74); the reliefs of **Jan Schoonhoven** (1914–94); the multimedia productions of **Jan Dibbets** (b.1941); the imprecisely coloured geometric designs of **Rob van Koningsbruggen** (b.1948); the smeary Expressionism of **Toon Verhoef** (b.1946); the exuberant figures of **Rene Daniels** (b.1950); the exquisite realism of **Karel Buskes** (b.1962); the unsettling photographic portraits of **Rineke Dijkstra** (b.1959); the blending of art and engineering in the work of **Theo Jansen** (b.1948); and the witty, hip furniture designs of **Piet Hein Eek** (b.1967) – to name just a few of the more important figures.

Books

Most of the books listed below are in print and in paperback, and those that are out of print (o/p) should be easy to track down either in secondhand bookshops or online. Books marked with ★ are particularly recommended.

AMSTERDAM

Fred Feddes *A Millennium of Amsterdam.* Inventive, well-illustrated book comprising forty studies of the Amsterdam landscape – its reclamation, building and rebuilding. Starts at the Dam and ends at the beach in IJburg.

★ **Geert Mak** *Amsterdam: A Brief Life of the City.* First published in 1995, this infinitely readable trawl through the city's past is a wonderful book – amusing and perceptive, alternately tart and indulgent. It's more a social history than anything else, so – for example – you'll find out quite why Rembrandt lived in the Jewish quarter and why the city's merchant elite ossified in the eighteenth century. It's light and accessible enough to read from cover to cover, but its index of places makes it easy to dip into as well. If you like this, try also Mak's *An Island in Time*, an evocative (but never sentimental) native-son return to the flailing Frisian village of Jowert.

Heather Reyes (ed.) *City-Pick Amsterdam.* Enjoyable anthology of writing about Amsterdam, including big names – Alain de Botton, Cees Nooteboom – and small. Divided into themes – "Water, water everywhere", "Amsterdam the tolerant" and so forth.

★ **Manfred Wolf (ed.)** *Amsterdam: A Traveler's Literary Companion* (o/p). One of a series published by Whereabouts Press (ⓦ whereaboutspress.com), this anthology tries to get to the heart of Amsterdam. Contains a well-chosen mix of travel pieces, fiction and reportage, uncovering a low-life aspect to the city that exists beyond the tourist spots. A high-quality and evocative selection, and often the only chance to read some of this material in translation.

ART

Svetlana Alpers *Rembrandt's Enterprise.* Intriguing 1988 study of Rembrandt, positing the theory – in line with findings of the Leiden-based Rembrandt Research Project – that many previously accepted Rembrandt paintings are not his at all, but merely the products of his studio.

Anthony Bailey *A View of Delft.* Concise, startlingly well-researched book on Vermeer, with an accurate and well-considered exploration of his milieu. Hard to beat.

Walter Bosing *Bosch: The Complete Paintings.* Attractive little book in the Taschen art series that covers its subject in just the right amount of detail (it's 96 pages long). Well conceived and well illustrated.

Wayne Franits *Dutch Seventeenth-Century Genre Painting: Its Stylistic and Thematic Evolution.* Well-argued, immaculately researched and attractively illustrated book – the best on its subject. Hardly deckchair reading, perhaps, but fascinating all the same. Also *Vermeer*, a thoroughgoing examination of the artist's milieu and technique alongside an attempt to unravel the meanings behind the paintings.

★ **R.H. Fuchs** *Dutch Painting* (o/p). As complete an introduction to the subject – from Flemish origins to the postwar period – as you could wish for, in just a couple of hundred pages. Published in the 1970s and sadly out of print, there's still nothing better.

Walter S. Gibson *Hieronymus Bosch* and *Bruegel* (o/p). Two wonderfully illustrated Thames & Hudson titles on these two exquisite allegorical painters, both published in the 1970s. The former contains everything you wanted to know about Hieronymus Bosch, his paintings and his late fifteenth-century milieu, while the latter takes a detailed look at Pieter Bruegel the Elder's art, with nine well-argued chapters investigating its various components.

Melissa McQuillan *Van Gogh.* A small army of books examine van Gogh's paintings, life and hard times, but this superbly researched and illustrated version is hard to beat – and comes in at a very manageable 216 pages.

Steven Naifeh & Gregory White Smith *Van Gogh: The Life.* This serious tome received mixed reviews, but it is a thunderous volume, whose 992 pages explore the man's life, times and art in exhaustive detail.

Susie Nash *Northern Renaissance Art.* An erudite book that examines how art was made, valued and viewed in Northern Europe from the late fourteenth to the early sixteenth century. All the leading Netherlandish figures are examined – van Eyck, Memling, van der Weyden and so forth – and by these means Nash argues that it was these painters who set the artistic tone of the Europe of their day, rather than the Italians.

Simon Schama *Rembrandt's Eyes.* This scholarly work received good reviews, but it's very, very long – and often very long-winded.

★ **Gary Schwartz** *Rembrandt's Universe: His Art, His Life, His World.* Beautifully illustrated and well-considered account of the artist's life and work.

★ **Mariet Westerman** *The Art of the Dutch Republic 1585–1718* (o/p). This excellently written, immaculately illustrated and enthralling book tackles its subject thematically, from the marketing of works of art to an exploration of Dutch ideologies. Highly recommended, but sadly out of print, so see if you can get your hands on a secondhand copy. Also by Westerman is an all-you-could-ever-want-to-know book about Rembrandt.

Christopher White *Rembrandt*. Now well into his 80s, Christopher White has long been something of a Rembrandt specialist, responsible for a series of well-regarded books on the man and his times. Most of these books are expensive and aimed at the specialist art market, but this particular title is perfect for the general reader. It's well illustrated with a wonderfully incisive and extremely detailed commentary, though the index is disappointingly poor. Published in 1984, but still very much on song – though there is tough competition from Gary Schwartz.

Frank Wynne *I was Vermeer: The Forger who Swindled the Nazis*. The art forger Han van Meegeren fooled everyone, including Herman Goering, with his "lost" Vermeers, when in fact he painted them himself. This story of bluff, bluster and fine art is an intriguing tale, but Wynne's book, though extremely well informed, is overwritten.

BIOGRAPHY

Ayaan Hirsi Ali *Infidel: My Life*. This powerful and moving autobiography, written by one of the Netherlands' most controversial figures, begins with Ali's harsh and sometimes brutal childhood in Somalia and then Saudi Arabia, where – among other tribulations – she was subjected to genital mutilation when she was 5. Later, in 1992, Ali wound up in the Netherlands at least partly to evade an arranged marriage. Thereafter, she made a remarkable transition from factory cleaner to MP, becoming a leading light of the rightist VVD political party and remaining outspoken in her denunciations of militant Islam (see page 237), a theme she returned to recently in her *Heretic: Why Islam needs a Reformation now*. Hirsi Ali now lives in the USA.

A.C. Grayling *Descartes: The Life and Times of a Genius*. One of the greatest philosophers of all time, René Descartes (1596–1650) was a key figure in the transition from medieval to early modern Europe. He also made key contributions to optics and geometry and, among his miscellaneous travels, spent time living in Amsterdam (see page 60). This crisply written, erudite biography deals skilfully with the philosophy – Grayling is himself a philosophy professor – and argues that Descartes was almost certainly a Jesuit spy acting on behalf of the Habsburg interest during his time in Amsterdam.

Carol Ann Lee *Roses from the Earth: the Biography of Anne Frank*. Among the many publications trawling through the life of the young Jewish diarist, this is probably the best, written in a straightforward and insightful manner without sentimentality. Lee's *The Hidden Life of Otto Frank* is equally clear, lucid and interesting.

HISTORY

Leo Akveld et al *The Colourful World of the VOC*. Beautifully illustrated, coffee-table book on the VOC – the East India Company. The subject is dealt with in a series of intriguing essays on the likes of the uses of Eastern spices, Indonesian fashion and furniture, rituals and beliefs.

★ **Paul Arblaster** *A History of the Low Countries*. Welcome addition to the limited range of English-language books on this wide-ranging subject. Arblaster covers the ground methodically, with impeccable research, and has added lots of fascinating detail – and all in just 322 pages. An excellent survey.

J.C.H. Blom (ed.) *History of the Low Countries*. Books on the totality of Dutch history are thin on the ground, so this heavyweight volume fills a few gaps, though it's hardly sun-lounger reading. A series of historians weigh in with their specialities, from Roman times onwards, and its forte is in picking out those cultural, political and economic themes that give the region its distinctive character. Blom has also edited a second, top-notch anthology, *The History of the Jews in the Netherlands*.

Mike Dash *Tulipomania*. Dash examines the introduction of the tulip into the Low Countries at the height of the Golden Age – and the mind-boggling speculative boom that ensued (see page 229). There's a lot of padding and scene-setting, but it's an engaging read, with nice detail on seventeenth-century Amsterdam, Leiden and Haarlem. Also by Dash is *Batavia's Graveyard*, a tale of mutiny and cannibalism among the shipwrecked crew of the East India Company's *Batavia*.

Pieter Geyl *The Revolt of The Netherlands 1555–1609* and *The Netherlands in the Seventeenth Century 1609–1648*. These detailed accounts of the Netherlands during its formative years chronicle the uprising against the Spanish and the formation of the United Provinces. First published in 1932, they have long been regarded as classic texts on the subject, though they are a hard and somewhat ponderous read.

Lisa Jardine *The Awful End of Prince William the Silent*. Great title for an intriguing book on the premature demise of one of the country's most acclaimed heroes, who was assassinated in Delft in 1584. At just 160 pages, the tale is told succinctly, but – unless you have a particular interest in early firearms – there is a bit too much information on guns and more guns.

Henk van Nierop *Treason in the Northern Quarter*. Thoughtful, studious account of the reasons for – and ideologies behind – the Revolt of the Netherlands. The chapter on "Treason" – who to did what to whom and why – is especially illuminating.

★ **Geoffrey Parker** *The Dutch Revolt* and *The Army of Flanders and the Spanish Road 1567–1659* (o/p). The first of these two titles provides a compelling account of the struggle between the Netherlands and Spain and is quite the best thing you can read on the period. The second may sound academic, but it gives a fascinating insight into the Habsburg army that occupied the Low Countries for well over a hundred years – how it functioned, was fed and moved from Spain to the Low Countries along the so-called Spanish Road.

Simon Schama *The Embarrassment of Riches: An Interpretation of Dutch Culture in the Golden Age.* Long before his reinvention on British TV, Schama specialized in Dutch history, and this chunky volume draws on a huge variety of archive sources. Also by Schama, *Patriots and Liberators: Revolution in the Netherlands 1780–1813* focuses on a less familiar period of Dutch history and is particularly good on the Batavian Republic set up in the Netherlands under French auspices. Both are heavyweight tomes, and leftists might well find Schama a tad reactionary. See also Schama's *Rembrandt's Eyes* (see page 253).

Russell Shorto *Amsterdam: A History of the World's Most Liberal City.* A must-read for history buffs, this highly enjoyable book offers an insight into the city's history through the lens of liberal attitudes and an extraordinary spirit of solidarity – both of which went some way in helping Amsterdammers to survive numerous wars and natural disasters.

Andrew Wheatcroft *The Habsburgs.* Excellent and well-researched trawl through the family's history, from eleventh-century beginnings to its eclipse at the end of World War I. Enjoyable background reading.

LITERATURE

A.C. Baantjer *De Kok and the Mask of Death.* An ex-Amsterdam policeman, who racked up nearly forty years' service, Baantjer is one of the most widely read authors in the Netherlands. This rattling good yarn, perhaps the best in the Inspector De Kok series, has all the typical ingredients – crisp plotting, some gruesomeness and a batch of nice characterizations on the way. More? Try *De Kok and the Somber Nude* or *De Kok and the Dead Harlequin.* Baantjer himself died in 2010.

Jessie Burton *The Miniaturist.* This award-winning novel set in seventeenth-century Amsterdam has garnered plenty of hype since its publication in 2014. The story revolves around 18-year-old Nella Oortman, recently married to a wealthy merchant, and the wedding present she receives from her new husband: a cabinet-sized replica of their house. With evocative depictions of everyday life and supernatural touches, this is an intriguing debut.

Tracey Chevalier *Girl with a Pearl Earring.* Chevalier's novel is a fanciful piece of fiction, building a story around the subject of one of Vermeer's most enigmatic paintings. It's an absorbing read, if a little too detailed and slow-moving for some tastes, and it paints a convincing picture of seventeenth-century Delft, exploring its social structures and values.

★ **Anne Frank** *The Diary of a Young Girl.* Lucid and moving, this is the most revealing book you can read on the plight of Amsterdam's Jews during the German occupation. An international bestseller since its original publication in 1947.

★ **Willem Frederik Hermans** *The Dark Room of Damocles.* Along with Wolkers (see page 256), Mulisch (see page 256) and Gerard Reve, Hermans is considered one of the four major literary figures of the Dutch postwar generation. This title, first published in 1958, is about the German occupation and its concomitants – betrayal, paranoia and treason. Indeed, the reader is rarely certain what is truth and what is false. If this whets your appetite for Hermans, try *Beyond Sleep*, a psychological drama set in northern Norway. Hermans died in 1995.

Etty Hillesum *An Interrupted Life: the Diaries and Letters of Etty Hillesum, 1941–43.* The Germans transported Hillesum, a young Jewish woman, from her home in Amsterdam to Auschwitz, where she died. As with Anne Frank's more famous journal, it's penetratingly written – though on the whole less readable.

★ **Arthur Japin** *The Two Hearts of Kwasi Boachi.* Inventive re-creation by Haarlem-born Japin of a true story in which the eponymous Ashanti prince was dispatched to the court of King William of the Netherlands in 1837. Kwasi and his companion Kwame were ostensibly sent to Den Haag to further their education, but there was a strong colonial subtext. Superb literary descriptions of Ashanti-land in its pre-colonial pomp. Also Japin's *Lucia's Eyes*, an imaginative extrapolation of a casual anecdote found in Casanova's memoirs and set for the most part in eighteenth-century Amsterdam.

★ **Otto de Kat** *Julia.* From one of the country's most praised contemporary novelists, this is perhaps de Kat's best novel so far, an engaging exploration of love and regret in which a suicide leads back to the events of World War II. Also the comparable *Man on the Move*, set in the Dutch East Indies as the Dutch face the Japanese, and *News from Berlin*, also with a World War II setting and exploring guilt, memory and collaboration. De Kat is the pseudonym of Rotterdam-born Jan Geurt Gaarlandt.

Herman Koch *The Dinner.* A modern Dutch classic, *The Dinner* tells the story of two couples who meet in a fancy Amsterdam restaurant to discuss how they can protect their sons who have committed a hideous crime. Over aperitifs and hors d'oeuvre, they desperately conspire against the course of justice with a growing sense of discomfort and restlessness.

Sylvie Matton *Rembrandt's Whore*. Taking its cue from Chevalier's *Girl with a Pearl Earring* (see above), this slim novel tries hard to conjure Rembrandt's life and times, with some success. Matton certainly knows her Rembrandt – she worked for two years on a film of his life.

Sarah Emily Miano *Van Rijn*. Carefully composed re-creation of Rembrandt's milieu, based on the (documented) visit of Cosimo de Medici to the artist's house. As an attempt to venture into Rembrandt's soul it does well – but not brilliantly.

Deborah Moggach *Tulip Fever*. At first Deborah Moggach's novel seems no more than an attempt to build a story out of her favourite domestic Dutch interiors, genre scenes and still-life paintings. But ultimately the story is a basic one – of lust, greed, mistaken identity and tragedy. The Golden Age Amsterdam backdrop is well realized, but almost incidental.

Marcel Moring *In Babylon*. Popular Dutch author with an intense style spliced with thought-provoking, philosophical content. *In Babylon* has an older Jewish man and his niece trapped in a cabin in the eastern Netherlands and here they ruminate on their family's history. Moring's *Dream Room* is also gracefully nostalgic in its concentration on the family of Boris and his son, David, while the author's *In a Dark Wood* is set in the town of Assen, again in the east of the country, during the annual Dutch TT motorbike races.

Harry Mulisch *The Assault*. Set part in Haarlem, part in Amsterdam, this novel traces the story of a young boy who loses his family in a reprisal-raid by the Nazis. A powerful tale, made into an excellent and effective film. Also, *The Discovery of Heaven*, a gripping yarn of adventure and happenstance; *The Procedure*, featuring a modern-day Dutch scientist investigating strange goings-on in sixteenth-century Prague; and *Siegfried: a Black Idyll*, whose central question is whether a work of imagination can help to understand the nature of evil in general and Hitler in particular. Mulisch died in Amsterdam in 2010.

Multatuli *Max Havelaar: Or, The Coffee Auctions of the Dutch Trading Company*. Classic nineteenth-century Dutch satire of colonial life in the East Indies by Dutch writer Multatuli (see page 57). Eloquent and intermittently amusing. If you have Dutch friends, they should be impressed (dumbstruck) if you have actually read it, not least since it's 352 pages long.

Saskia Noort *Back to the Coast*. One of the most popular/populist contemporary novelists in the Netherlands, Noort sets this thriller on the Dutch coast where all sorts of fear and loathing ensue. There are more thrills and spills, murder and adultery in *The Dinner Club*.

Cees Nooteboom *Rituals*. Nooteboom (b.1933) published his first novel in 1955, but only hit the literary headlines with this, his third novel, in 1980. The central theme of all his work is the phenomenon of time; *Rituals* in particular is about the passing of time and the different ways of controlling the process. Inni Wintrop, the main character, is an outsider, a well-heeled, antique-dabbling "dilettante" as he describes himself. The book is almost entirely set in Amsterdam, and although it describes the inner life of Inni himself, it also paints a strong picture of the city.

Jeroen Thijssen *Solitude*. Two brothers living in a squat discover their family's less than wholesome history as plantation owners in the Dutch East Indies (Indonesia). Thijssen interweaves the colonial past and the brothers' impoverished present with considerable skill.

Esther Verhoef *Rendezvous*. Verhoef is one of the Netherlands' most popular thriller writers, and this tale of unfaithfulness and abandon in a French setting is an emotional roller coaster. If you fancy more emotional carnage, there's also Verhoef's *Close-Up*.

Janwillem van de Wetering *Tumbleweed; Hard Rain; Corpse on the Dyke; Outsider in Amsterdam*. Offbeat detective tales set in Amsterdam and the provinces. Humane, quirky and humorous, Wetering's novels have inventive plots and feature unusual characters in interesting locations, though the prose itself can be a bit indigestible. Wetering himself died in 2008.

Jan Wolkers *Turkish Delight* (o/p). Wolkers, who died in 2007, was one of the Netherlands' best-known artists and writers, and this is an early novel, a close examination of the relationship between a bitter working-class sculptor and his young middle-class wife. If you like it, try Wolkers' *Horrible Tango* (o/p).

Dutch

It's unlikely that you'll need to speak anything other than English while you are in Amsterdam: the Dutch have a seemingly innate talent for languages, and your attempts at speaking theirs may be met with some bewilderment – though this can have as much to do with your pronunciation (Dutch is very difficult to get right) as their surprise that you're making an effort. That said, the Dutch words and phrases below are useful, especially in the small towns outside of Amsterdam, and we have also included a basic food and drink glossary, though menus are nearly always multilingual – where they aren't, ask and one will almost invariably appear. As for phrasebooks, the *Rough Guide Dutch Phrasebook* is pocket-sized, with a good dictionary section (English–Dutch and Dutch–English) as well as a menu reader; it also provides a useful introduction to grammar and pronunciation.

Pronunciation

Dutch is **pronounced** much the same as English. However, there are a few Dutch sounds that don't exist in English, which can be difficult to get right without practice.

Consonants

Double-consonant combinations generally keep their separate sounds in Dutch: kn, for example, is never like the English "knight". Note also the following consonants and consonant combinations:

j is an English y

ch and **g** indicate a throaty sound, as at the end of the Scottish word loch

ng as in bring

nj as in onion

y is not a consonant, but another way of writing ij

Vowels and diphthongs

A good rule of thumb is that doubling the letter lengthens the vowel sound.

a is like the English apple

aa like cart

e like let

ee like late

o as in pop

oo in pope

u is like the French tu if preceded by a consonant; it's like wood if followed by a consonant

uu is the French tu

au and **ou** like how

DOUBLE DUTCH?

Dutch is a Germanic language – the word itself is a corruption of "Deutsche", a label inaccurately given by English sailors in the seventeenth century – and indeed, although the Dutch are at pains to stress the differences between the two languages, if you know any German you'll spot many similarities. Spoken Dutch, however, is far from consistent, with a hatful of regional dialects: the inhabitants of Amsterdam have a very different accent and slang to someone, say, from Den Haag, while in Limburg the dialect is closer to German and Flemish than to Dutch. The Netherlands has a second official language too, **Fries**, the pride and joy of the people of Friesland – and incomprehensible to everyone else.

SIGNS AND ABBREVIATIONS

AUB Alstublieft: please (also shown as SVP, from French)
BG Begane grond: ground floor
BTW Belasting Toegevoegde Waarde: VAT
geen toegang no entry
gesloten closed
ingang entrance
K kelder: basement
let op! attention!
heren/dames men's/women's toilets
open open
T/M Tot en met: up to and including
toegang entrance
uitgang exit
VA vanaf: from
VS Verenigde Staten: United States
VVV Tourist office – once universal, but now a brand name
ZOZ please turn over (page, leaflet, etc)

BASICS

yes ja
no nee
please alstublieft
thank you dank u or bedankt
hello hallo or dag
good morning goedemorgen
good afternoon goedemiddag
good evening goedenavond
goodbye tot ziens
see you later tot straks
Do you speak English? Spreekt u Engels?
I don't understand Ik begrijp het niet
women/men vrouwen/mannen
children kinderen
men's/women's toilets heren/dames
I want... Ik wil...
I don't want to... Ik wil niet...(+verb)
I don't want any... Ik wil geen... (+noun)
How much is...? Wat kost...?
here/there hier/daar
good/bad goed/slecht
big/small groot/klein
open/closed open/gesloten
push/pull duwen/trekken
new/old nieuw/oud
cheap/expensive goedkoop/duur
hot/cold heet or warm/koud
with/without met/zonder

TRAVEL, DIRECTIONS AND SHOPPING

How do I get to...? Hoe kom ik in...?

ei and **ij** as in fine, though this varies strongly from region to region; sometimes it can sound more like lane
oe as in soon
eu is like the diphthong in the French leur
ui is the hardest Dutch diphthong of all, pronounced like "how" but much further forward in the mouth, with lips pursed (as if to say "oo").

WORDS AND PHRASES

Where is...? Waar is...?
How far is it to...? Hoe ver is het naar...?
When? Wanneer?
far/near ver/dichtbij
left/right links/rechts
straight ahead rechtdoor
airport luchthaven
post office postkantoor
post box postbus
stamp(s) postzegel(s)
money exchange geldwisselkantoor
cash desk kassa
railway platform spoor or perron
ticket office loket
North noord
South zuid
East oost
West west

USEFUL CYCLING TERMS

brake rem
broken kapot
chain ketting
cycle path fietspad
handlebars stuur
pedal trapper
pump pomp
puncture lek
tyre band
wheel wiel

MONTHS, DAYS AND TIMES

January januari
February februari
March maart
April april
May mei
June juni
July juli
August augustus
September september
October oktober
November november

December december	**NUMBERS**
Monday maandag	0 nul
Tuesday dinsdag	1 een
Wednesday woensdag	2 twee
Thursday donderdag	3 drie
Friday vrijdag	4 vier
Saturday zaterdag	5 vijf
Sunday zondag	6 zes
yesterday gisteren	7 zeven
today vandaag	8 acht
tomorrow morgen	9 negen
tomorrow morning morgenochtend	10 tien
year jaar	11 elf
month maand	12 twaalf
week week	13 dertien
day dag	14 veertien
hour uur	15 vijftien
minute minuut	16 zestien
What time is it? Hoe laat is het?	17 zeventien
It's… Het is…	18 achttien
3.00 drie uur	19 negentien
3.05 vijf over drie	20 twintig
3.10 tien over drie	21 teen en twintig
3.15 kwart over drie	22 twee en twintig
3.20 tien voor half vier	30 dertig
3.25 vijf voor half vier	40 veertig
3.30 half vier	50 vijftig
3.35 vijf over half vier	60 zestig
3.40 tien over half vier	70 zeventig
3.45 kwart voor vier	80 tachtig
3.50 tien voor vier	90 negentig
3.55 vijf voor vier	100 honderd
8am acht uur 's ochtends	101 honderd een
1pm een uur 's middags	200 twee honderd
8pm acht uur 's avonds	201 twee honderd een
1am een uur 's nachts	500 vijf honderd
	525 vijf honderd vijf en twintig
	1000 duizend

MENU READER

BASICS

boter butter	**patat/friet** chips/french fries
boterham/broodje sandwich/roll	**peper** pepper
brood bread	**pindakaas** peanut butter
dranken drinks	**sla/salade** salad
eieren eggs	**slagroom** whipped cream
groenten vegetables	**soep** soup
honing honey	**stokbrood** french bread
hoofdgerechten main courses	**suiker** sugar
huzarensalade potato salad with pickles	**uitsmijter** ham or cheese with eggs on bread
kaas cheese	**vegetarisch** vegetarian
koud cold	**vis** fish
nagerechten desserts	**vlees** eat
	voorgerechten starters/hors d'oeuvres

vruchten fruit
warm hot
zout salt

MEAT AND POULTRY

biefstuk (duitse) hamburger
biefstuk (hollandse) steak
eend duck
fricandeau roast pork
fricandel frankfurter-like sausage
gehakt minced meat
kalfsvlees veal
kalkoen turkey
karbonade a chop
kip chicken
kroket spiced veal or beef hash, coated in breadcrumbs
lamsvlees lamb
lever liver
ossenhaas beef tenderloin
rookvlees smoked beef
spek bacon
worst sausages

FISH

forel trout
garnalen prawns
haring herring
kabeljauw cod
makreel mackerel
mosselen mussels
oesters oysters
paling eel
schelvis haddock
schol plaice
tong sole
zalm salmon

VEGETABLES

aardappelen potatoes
bloemkool cauliflower
bonen beans
champignons mushrooms
erwten peas
hutspot mashed potatoes and carrots
knoflook garlic
komkommer cucumber
prei leek
rijst rice
sla salad, lettuce
stampot andijvie mashed potato and endive
stampot boerenkool mashed potato and cabbage
uien onions
wortelen carrots
zuurkool sauerkraut

COOKING TERMS

belegd filled or topped
doorbakken well-done
gebakken fried or baked
gebraden roast
gegrild grilled
gekookt boiled
geraspt grated
gerookt smoked
gestoofd stewed
half doorbakken medium-done
rood rare

INDONESIAN DISHES AND TERMS

ajam chicken
bami noodles with meat and vegetables
daging beef
gado gado vegetables in peanut sauce
goreng fried
ikan fish
katjang peanut
kroepoek prawn crackers
loempia spring rolls
nasi rice
nasi goreng fried rice with meat/chicken and
  vegetables
nasi rames a *rijsttafel* on a single plate
pedis hot and spicy
pisang banana
rijsttafel assortment of spicy dishes served with plain
  rice
sambal hot chilli-based sauce
sate meat on a skewer
satesaus peanut sauce to accompany meat grilled on
  skewers
seroendeng spicy, shredded and fried coconut
tauge bean sprouts

SWEETS AND DESSERTS

appelgebak apple tart or cake
drop Dutch liquorice, available in *zoet* (sweet) or *zout*
  (salted) varieties
gebak pastry
ijs ice cream
koekjes biscuits
oliebollen traditional sweet sold at New Year – a little
  like a doughnut
pannenkoeken pancakes
pepernoten Dutch ginger nuts
poffertjes small pancakes, fritters
(slag)room (whipped) cream
speculaas spice and cinnamon-flavoured biscuit
stroopwafels waffles
taai-taai spicy Dutch cake

vla custard

FRUITS AND NUTS
aardbei strawberry
amandel almond
appel apple
appelmoes apple purée
citroen lemon
druiven grape
framboos raspberry
hazelnoot hazelnut
kers cherry
kokosno0ot coconut
peer pear
perzik peach
pinda peanut
pruim plum/prune

DRINKS
anijsmelk aniseed-flavoured warm milk
appelsap apple juice
bessenjenever blackcurrant gin

chocomel chocolate milk
citroenjenever lemon gin
droog dry
frisdranken soft drinks
jenever Dutch gin
karnemelk buttermilk
koffie coffee
koffie verkeerd coffee with warm milk
kopstoot beer with a *jenever* chaser
melk milk
met ijs with ice
met slagroom with whipped cream
pils Dutch beer
proost! cheers!
sinaasappelsap orange juice
thee tea
tomatensap tomato juice
vruchtensap fruit juice
wijn wine
(wit/rood/rosé) (white/red/rosé)
vieux Dutch brandy
zoet sweet

DUTCH GLOSSARY

Abdij Abbey.

Amsterdammertje Phallic-shaped bollard placed in rows alongside many Amsterdam streets to keep drivers off pavements and out of the canals.

Begijnhof Similar to a *hofje* but occupied by Catholic women (*begijns*) who led semireligious lives without taking full vows.

Belfort Belfry.

Beurs Stock exchange.

Botermarkt Butter market.

Brug Bridge.

Burgher Member of the upper or mercantile classes of a town, usually with certain civic powers.

Gasthuis Hospice for the sick or infirm.

Gemeente Municipal, as in *Gemeentehuis* (town hall).

Gerechtshof Law Courts.

Gezellig A hard term to translate – something like "cosy", "comfortable" and "inviting" all in one – which is said to lie at the heart of the Dutch psyche. A long, relaxed meal in a favourite restaurant with friends is *gezellig*; grabbing a quick snack is not. The best brown cafés ooze *gezelligheid*; Kalverstraat on a Saturday afternoon definitely doesn't.

Gilde Guild.

Gracht Canal.

Groentenmarkt Vegetable market.

Grote Kerk Literally "big church" – the main church of a town or village.

Hal Hall.

Hijsbalk Pulley beam, often decorated, fixed to the top of a gable to lift goods and furniture. Essential in canal houses whose staircases were – and mostly still are – narrow and steep, *hijsbalken* are still very much in use today.

Hof Courtyard.

Hofje Almshouse, usually for elderly women who could look after themselves but needed small charities such as food and fuel; usually a number of buildings centred around a small, enclosed courtyard.

Huis House.

Jeugdherberg Youth hostel.

Kasteel Castle.

Kerk Church.

Koning King.

Koningin Queen.

Koninklijk Royal.

Kunst Art.

Lakenhal Cloth hall: the building in medieval weaving towns where cloth would be weighed, graded and sold.

Markt Central town square and the heart of most Dutch communities, normally still the site of weekly markets.

Molen Windmill.

Nederland The Netherlands.

Nederlands Dutch.

Omgang Procession.

Paleis Palace.

Plein A square or open space.

Polder An area of land reclaimed from the sea.
Poort Gate.
Raadhuis Town hall.
Randstad Literally "rim-town", this refers to the urban conurbation that makes up much of Noord- and Zuid-Holland, stretching from Amsterdam in the north to Rotterdam and Dordrecht in the south.
Rijk State.
Schepezaal Alderman's hall.
Schone Kunsten Fine arts.
Schouwburg Theatre.
Sierkunst Decorative arts.
Spionnetje Small mirror on a canal house enabling the occupant to see who is at the door without descending the stairs.

Stadhuis The most common word for a town hall.
Stedelijk Civic, municipal.
Steeg Alley.
Steen Stone.
Stichting Institute or foundation.
Straat Street.
Toren Tower.
Tuin Garden.
Vleeshuis Meat market.
Volkskunde Folklore.
VVV Tourist information office
Waag Old public weigh house, a common feature of most Dutch towns.
Weg Way.
Wijk District (of a city).

ART AND ARCHITECTURE GLOSSARY

Ambulatory Covered passage around the outer edge of the choir of a church.
Apse Semicircular protrusion, usually at the east end of a church.
Art Deco Geometrical style of art and architecture popular in the 1930s.
Art Nouveau Style of art, architecture and design based on highly stylized vegetal forms, especially popular in the early part of the twentieth century.
Balustrade An ornamental rail, running, almost invariably, along the top of a building.
Baroque The art and architecture of the Counter-Reformation, dating from around 1600 onwards. Distinguished by extreme ornateness and by the complex but harmonious spatial arrangement of interiors.
Carillon A set of tuned church bells, either operated by an automatic mechanism or played on a keyboard.
Carolingian Dynasty founded by Charlemagne; mid-eighth to early tenth century. Also refers to art of the period.
Caryatid A sculptured female figure used as a column.
Chancel The eastern part of a church, often separated from the nave by a screen (see "rood screen"). Contains the choir and ambulatory.
Classical Architectural style incorporating Greek and Roman elements – pillars, domes, colonnades, etc – at its height in the seventeenth century and revived, as Neoclassical, in the nineteenth.
Clerestory Upper storey of a church with windows.
Diptych Carved or painted work on two panels. Often used as an altarpiece – both static and, more occasionally, portable.
Expressionism Artistic style popular at the beginning of the twentieth century, characterized by the exaggeration of shape or colour; often accompanied by the extensive use of symbolism.

Flamboyant Florid form of Gothic.
Fresco Wall painting – durable through application to wet plaster.
Gable The triangular upper portion of a wall – decorative or supporting a roof – which is a feature of many Amsterdam canal houses. Initially fairly simple, they became more ostentatious in the late seventeenth century, before turning to a more restrained if imposing classicism in the eighteenth and nineteenth centuries.
Genre painting In the seventeenth century the term "genre painting" applied to everything from animal paintings and still lifes through to historical works and landscapes. In the eighteenth century, the term came to be applied only to scenes of everyday life.
Gothic Architectural style of the thirteenth to sixteenth centuries, characterized by pointed arches, rib vaulting, flying buttresses and a general emphasis on verticality.
Grisaille A technique of monochrome painting in shades of grey.
Misericord Ledge on a choir stall on which the occupant can be supported while standing; often carved with secular subjects (bottoms were not thought worthy of religious subject matter).
Nave Main body of a church.
Neoclassical A style of classical architecture revived in the nineteenth century, popular in the Low Countries during and after the Napoleonic occupation.
Neogothic Revived Gothic style of architecture popular between the late eighteenth and nineteenth centuries.
Pediment Feature of a gable, usually triangular and often sporting a relief.
Pilaster A shallow rectangular column projecting, but only slightly, from a wall.
Renaissance The period of European history marking the end of the medieval period and the rise of the

modern world. Defined, among many criteria, by an increase in classical scholarship, geographical discovery, the rise of secular values and the growth of individualism. Began in Italy in the fourteenth century. Also refers to the art and architecture of the period.

Retable Altarpiece.

Rococo Highly florid, light and intricate eighteenth-century style of architecture, painting and interior design, forming the last phase of Baroque.

Romanesque Early medieval architecture distinguished by squat, heavy forms, rounded arches and naive sculpture.

Rood screen Decorative screen separating the nave from the chancel. A rood loft is the gallery (or space) on top of it.

Stucco Marble-based plaster used to embellish ceilings, etc.

Transept Arms of a cross-shaped church, placed at ninety degrees to nave and chancel.

Triptych Carved or painted work on three panels. Often used as an altarpiece.

Tympanum Sculpted, usually recessed, panel above a door.

Vault Arched ceiling or roof.

Small print and index

A ROUGH GUIDE TO ROUGH GUIDES

Published in 1982, the first Rough Guide – to Greece – was a student scheme that became a publishing phenomenon. Mark Ellingham, a recent graduate in English from Bristol University, had been travelling in Greece the previous summer and couldn't find the right guidebook. With a small group of friends he wrote his own guide, combining a contemporary, journalistic style with a thoroughly practical approach to travellers' needs.

The immediate success of the book spawned a series that rapidly covered dozens of destinations. And, in addition to impecunious backpackers, Rough Guides soon acquired a much broader readership that relished the guides' wit and inquisitiveness as much as their enthusiastic, critical approach and value-for-money ethos. These days, Rough Guides include recommendations from budget to luxury and cover more than 120 destinations around the globe, from Amsterdam to Zanzibar, all regularly updated by our team of roaming writers.

Browse all our latest guides, read inspirational features and book your trip at **roughguides.com**.

Rough Guide credits

Updater: Maciej Zglinicki
Editor: Joanna Reeves
Cartography: Carte
Managing editor: Rachel Lawrence

Picture editor: Aude Vauconsant
Cover photo research: Aude Vauconsant
Senior DTP coordinator: Dan May
Head of DTP and Pre-Press: Rebeka Davies

Publishing information

Twelfth Edition 2019

Distribution

UK, Ireland and Europe
Apa Publications (UK) Ltd; sales@roughguides.com
United States and Canada
Ingram Publisher Services; ips@ingramcontent.com
Australia and New Zealand
Woodslane; info@woodslane.com.au
Southeast Asia
Apa Publications (SN) Pte; sales@roughguides.com
Worldwide
Apa Publications (UK) Ltd; sales@roughguides.com
Special Sales, Content Licensing and CoPublishing
Rough Guides can be purchased in bulk quantities
at discounted prices. We can create special editions,
personalised jackets and corporate imprints tailored to
your needs. sales@roughguides.com.

roughguides.com
Printed in China by CTPS
All rights reserved
© 2019 Apa Digital (CH) AG
License edition © Apa Publications Ltd UK

Help us update

We've gone to a lot of effort to ensure that the twelfth
edition of **The Rough Guide to Amsterdam** is accurate
and up-to-date. However, things change – places get
"discovered", opening hours are notoriously fickle,
restaurants and rooms raise prices or lower standards. If
you feel we've got it wrong or left something out, we'd like
to know, and if you can remember the address, the price,
the hours, the phone number, so much the better.

Please send your comments with the subject line
"**Rough Guide to Amsterdam Update**" to mail@
uk.roughguides.com. We'll credit all contributions and
send a copy of the next edition (or any other Rough Guide
if you prefer) for the very best emails.

Photo credits
(Key: T-top; C-centre; B-bottom; L-left; R-right)

Index

Map symbols

The symbols below are used on maps throughout the book

– – –	Chapter division boundary	Ⓜ	Metro	⚠	Camping
▬▬▬	Motorway	✉	Post office	▦	Building
———	Major road	ⓘ	Tourist office	⬌	Church/cathedral
········	Minor road	⊞	Hospital	⬭	Stadium
▭▭▭	Pedestrian road	🕯	Windmill		Christian cemetery
▬▬	Railway	⬱	Gardens		Jewish cemetery
——	Ferry route	⊙	Statue		Park
– – – –	Footpath	✡	Synagogue		Beach
✈	Airport	⊠	Entrance/gate		

Listings key

- ■ Accommodation
- ● Eating
- ■ Drinking/nightlife
- ● Shopping

City plan

The **city plan** on the pages that follow is divided as shown:

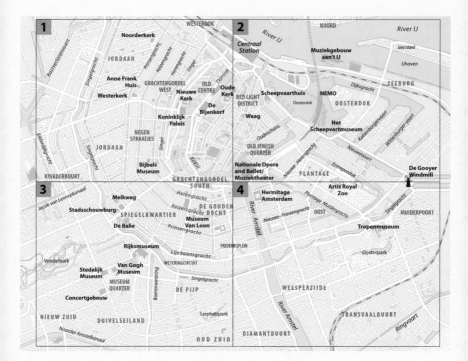

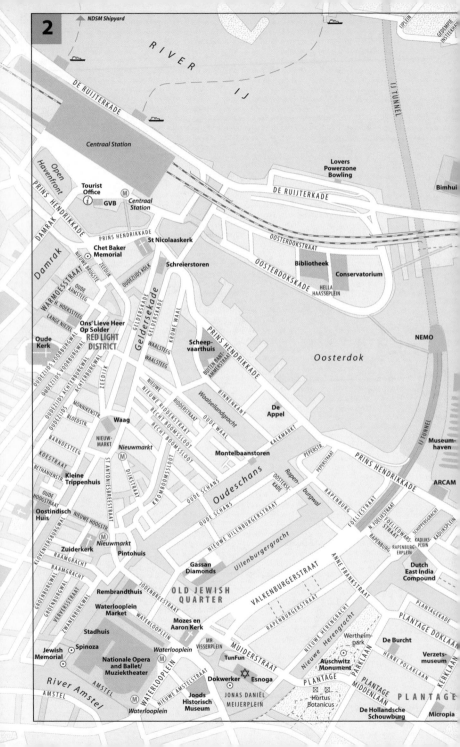

NOORDWAL

RIVER IJ

N

0   200
metres

Java Island

SUMATRAKADE

JAVAKADE

Muziekgebouw
aan't IJ

IJhaven

VEEMKADE

Amsterdam
Passenger
Terminal

JAN SCHEEPBRUG

PIET HEINKADE

ZEEBURG

VEEMKADE

Dijksgracht

PIET HEINKADE

OOSTERDOK

Oosterdok

KATTENBURGERSTRAAT

Oostenburgervaart

De
Amsterdam

Het
Scheepvartmuseum

KATTENBURGERKADE

KATTENBURGERVAART

WITTENBURGERKADE

GROTE WITTENBURGERSTRAAT

KLEINE WITTENBURGERSTRAAT

Wittenburgervaart

OOSTENBURGVOOR-STRAAT

KATTENBURGER-
PLEIN

KATTENBURGERGRACHT

WAAIGAT

Oostenburgervaart

NIEUWEVAART

OOSTENBURGVOOR-STRAAT

CONRAD-STRAAT

HOOGTE KADIJK

OVERHAALSGANG

CZAAR PETER STRAAT

LAAGTE   KADIJK

Nieuwevaart

WITTENBURGERGRACHT

ENTREPOTDOK

ENTREPOTDOK

Entrepotdok

KRUITHUIS-
STRAAT

CRUQUIUS-KADE

Nieuwevaart

HOOGTE KADIJK

ZEEBURGER-
STRAAT

De Gooyer
Windmill

ZEEBERGERPAD

Artis Royal Zoo

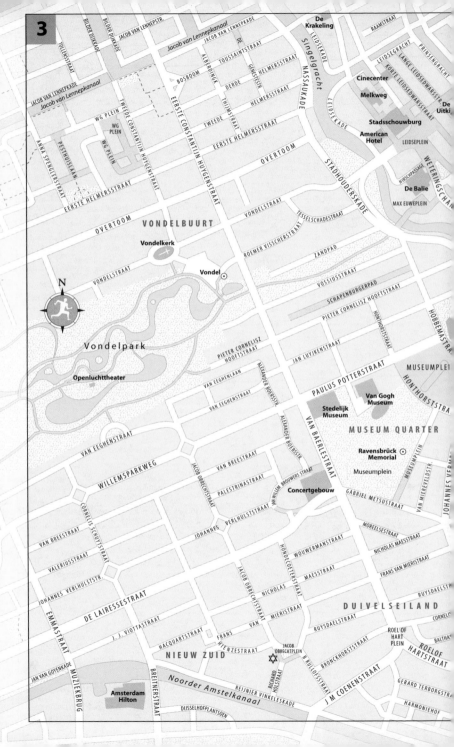

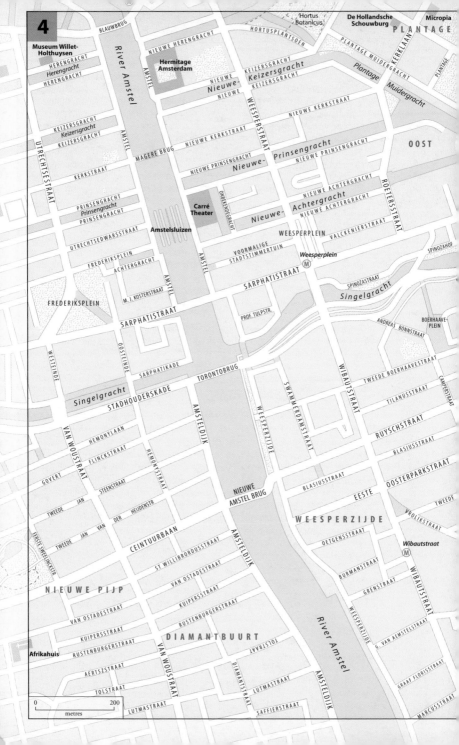

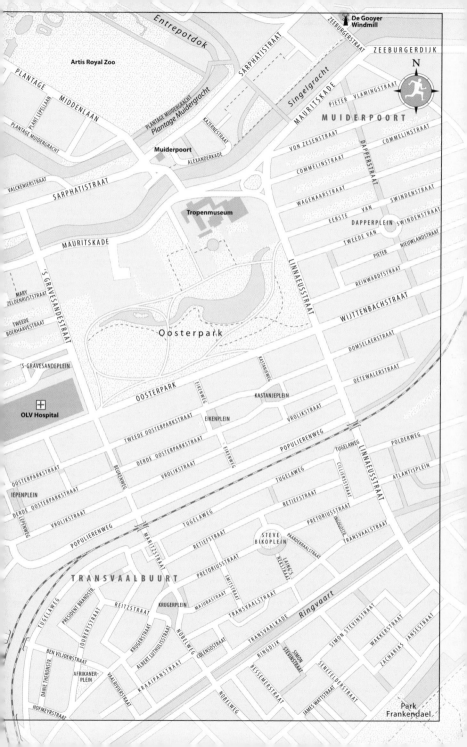